Jeremiah O'Donovan Rossa

Jeremiah O'Donovan Rossa

Unrepentant Fenian

SHANE KENNA

MERRION
PRESS

First published in 2015 by Merrion Press
8 Chapel Lane
Sallins
Co. Kildare

© 2015 Shane Kenna

British Library Cataloguing in Publication Data
An entry can be found on request

978-1-78537-013-7 (Paper)
978-1-78537-014-4 (Cloth)
978-1-78537-015-1 (PDF)
978-1-78537-017-5 (Epub)
978-1-78537-016-8 (Kindle)

Library of Congress Cataloging in Publication Data
An entry can be found on request

Printed in Ireland by Sprint-Print Ltd.

CONTENTS

ACKNOWLEDGEMENTS

This book is the culmination of several years of research into the life and times of Jeremiah O'Donovan Rossa. In the course of over a decade of studying Irish history I have always found him to be one of the most remarkable and defining characters in nineteenth-century Ireland. His funeral at Glasnevin Cemetery in the twentieth century is rightly seen as one of the most important political funerals in modern Ireland, setting the scene, as it did, for the Easter Rising of 1916. Indeed it was at this funeral that Pearse delivered his famous panegyric commenting on how revolution was inevitable and defining O'Donovan Rossa as an 'unrepentant Fenian'. In this decade of commemorations, upon the 100th anniversary of his death, I feared that the life of O'Donovan Rossa could be lost as the centenary of his death focused more on the relevance of his funeral at the expense of the man. With this in mind I chose to write this biography of a figure who can only be described as an iconic revolutionary within the great pantheon of Irish Republicanism.

In the course of this biography I was incredibly fortunate to meet a number of people who were instrumental to this publication. Special thanks to my friends in Cork for their support of this initiative and without them it would have been impossible. One of these has been inspirational and is a remarkable individual. His love for O'Donovan Rossa and commitment to maintaining Irish history is truly exceptional and when time passes the work he has done will be remembered by those whom he touched. I am indebted to the family of O'Donovan Rossa, in particular Williams and Rossa Cole, their Cousin Eileen and the National Graves Association for introductions and support. I would like to pay special tribute to Robert Ballagh. Robert is an inspirational man who I am proud to know. His art is internationally acclaimed and he has kindly agreed to allow his new print, the Funeral of O'Donovan Rossa, to be reproduced in this book. For this I am greatly humbled. I would like to thank the staff of the National Library of Ireland, the New York Public Library, The Catholic University of America and the Irish-American Historical Association. I am exceedingly grateful to Irish Academic Press and Conor Graham for their support in this project and would also like to thank George McCullough, CEO of Glasnevin Cemetery, Paddy Gleeson, Head Guide Glasnevin Museum, Gabriel Doherty of UCC and Dan Breen of the Cork City Museum and Archive. As always I am greatly indebted to my family and sincerely thank my mother Olive, fiancée Edel, John, Lisa, Darcy and Lily.

LIST OF PLATES

1. Jeremiah O'Donovan Rossa, photograph taken in America in 1864. (Image courtesy of the National Library of Ireland)
2. Mary Jane O'Donovan Rossa who married Jeremiah in 1864. (Image courtesy of the Cole/O'Donovan Rossa family)
3. The wedding certificate of Jeremiah and Mary Jane O'Donovan Rossa, dated 22 October 1864. (Image courtesy of the Cole/O'Donovan Rossa family)
4. The Fenian executive were the most senior staff of the *Irish Republican* Brotherhood. All men photographed belonged to the Irish People newspaper. O'Donovan Rossa is in the photograph in the bottom right of the image. (Image from author's collection)
5. Dublin Metropolitan Police raid the offices of the *Irish People* newspaper on 14 September 1865. Following this raid widespread arrests were made including the arrest of O'Donovan Rossa. (Image courtesy of Aidan Lambert)
6. Mugshot of Jeremiah O'Donovan Rossa taken at Mountjoy Gaol following his arrest. (Image courtesy of the Cole/O'Donovan Rossa family)
7. James Maxwell O'Donovan Rossa, who was born on 30 April 1866 during O'Donovan Rossa's imprisonment. This photograph had been suppressed from O'Donovan Rossa on account of prison regulations. (Image courtesy of the Cole/O'Donovan Rossa family.)
8. John Devoy, Charles Underwood O'Connell, Henry Mulleda, Jeremiah O'Donovan Rossa and John McClure. Released from prison on 7 January 1871 the five men became known as the Cuba Five. Their arrival in America was a scene of pandemonium as various political parties and Irish–American organisations sought their favour. (Image from author's collection)
9. Dynamite O'Donovan Rossa had spearheaded a bombing campaign against Britain seeking Irish independence. Establishing a new organisation called The United Irishmen of America, their militant wing, known as the skirmishers, had undertaken a number of small-scale bombings in London. (Image courtesy of the Cole/O'Donovan Rossa family.)
10. Red Jim McDermott was Agent Provocateur who had used O'Donovan Rossa to infiltrate a skirmishing conspiracy. He had been responsible

for the arrest of several Fenian conspirators between March to April 1883 and had planned simultaneous bombings in Britain and Ireland, clandestinely funded by British intelligence. He was one of the most notorious exposed British Agents of the late nineteenth century. (Image from author's collection)

11. Captain Thomas Phelan was stabbed in O'Donovan Rossa's office. A British Agent, he had been exposed by fellow British Agent John Francis Kearney, who deemed his exposure necessary for his personal protection within O'Donovan Rossa's company. (Image from author's collection)

12. Yseult Dudley, who attempted to assassinate O'Donovan Rossa at Broadway on 2 February 1885. (Image from author's collection)

13. Jeremiah O'Donovan Rossa delivering the oration at the unveiling of the Manchester Martyrs Memorial, Birr, Co. Offaly in July 1894. (Image courtesy of the National Library of Ireland)

14. Jeremiah and Mary Jane O'Donovan Rossa with their daughters at the family home in Staten Island. Note that O'Donovan Rossa looks frail and emaciated by the time of this photograph as he had developed chronic neuritis as a result of his earlier prison treatment, which affected his motor skills. (Image courtesy of the Cole/O'Donovan Rossa family)

15. Jeremiah O'Donovan Rossa died in St Vincent's Hospital, Staten Island on 29 July 1915. In this photograph, taken prior to his death, the once unconquerable O'Donovan Rossa is prostrate in his hospital bed. Suffering from dementia, in addition to chronic neuritis, he increasingly regressed and believed himself to be in prison once more. (Image courtesy of the Cole/O'Donovan Rossa family)

16. Mary Jane O'Donovan Rossa, Fr Michael Flangan, Eileen O'Donovan Rossa and Thomas James Clarke. Clarke, a former Dynamitard, believed the funeral of O'Donovan Rossa could awaken a national spirit amongst the Irish people. (Image from author's collection)

17. Patrick Pearse delivering the oration over the grave of O'Donovan Rossa on 1 August 1915. Note Major General John MacBride, who is standing behind Pearse and Thomas J. Clarke in the far right of the photo. All three would be shot for their part in the Easter Rising the following year. (Image courtesy of Glasnevin Museum)

A colour foldout of a new work by Robert Ballagh of the O'Donovan Rossa funeral.

INTRODUCTION

On 29 June 1915 Jeremiah O'Donovan Rossa died in St Vincent's Hospital, Staten Island. The following day the pro-British *Irish Times* newspaper announced his death, stating that 'there was a time in Ireland when his death would have created a sensation, but it is no exaggeration to say that today there are many who had almost forgotten his existence'.[1] Dying aged 84, throughout his long life, O'Donovan Rossa was perhaps one of the most famous Fenians of his generation. John Devoy described O'Donovan Rossa's life as 'an epitome of the history of Fenianism'.[2] Devoy was also confident that historians of future generations examining the history of Fenianism would come to regard O'Donovan Rossa as 'the very incarnation of its spirit'.[3] James Connolly, perhaps one of the most famous figures in the the great pantheon of Irish Revolutionaries, similarly agreed, believing O'Donovan Rossa to be 'an unconquerable fighter'.[4] Arthur Griffith, the founder of Sinn Féin and a future signatory to the Anglo-Irish Treaty of 1921, eulogised O'Donovan Rossa as a man 'whose spirit was the free spirit of the Irish Nation'.[5] His daughter, Eileen, regarded her father as 'unconquerable'.[6] Finally, Patrick Pearse, a name forever associated with the Easter Rising of 1916, regarded O'Donovan Rossa as a revolutionary chieftain, as 'a man that to the masses of his countrymen then and since stood most starkly and plainly for the Fenian ideal'.[7] Pearse also celebrated O'Donovan Rossa as an 'unrepentant Fenian'.[8] While his entire life was the very personification of the Fenian struggle, paradoxically, his death was similarly so. The death of O'Donovan Rossa in June 1915, despite what *The Irish Times* had suggested, had transformed his life of unyielding resistance to British rule in Ireland into a symbol of resistance for Irish nationalism. His death was almost prophetic and symbolised the beginnings of great change in Ireland. Thomas MacDonagh, himself a future leader of the Easter Rising, eulogised him with a poetic prophesy:

> Grieve not for him: speak not a word of sorrow;
> Although his eyes saw not his country's glory,
> The service of his day shall make our morrow:
> His name shall be a watchword in our story.

Him England for his love of Ireland hates:
This flesh we bury England's chains have bitten:
That is enough; for our deed he waits;
With Emmet's let his epitaph be written.[9]

It is clear from this that O'Donovan Rossa's life and death play an important part in the understanding of the Easter 1916 Rising. In many respects his death can be seen as the precursor to the great Revolutionary Epoch in Irish history. O'Donovan Rossa's final wish was to be buried in Ireland; he was desirous to be taken home to his home in Roscarbery, West Cork, where he would be buried in a humble Famine graveyard alongside his father and other victims of the Great Hunger. With the permission of his family, however, Clan na Gael and the IRB, through John Devoy and Thomas James Clarke, buried O'Donovan Rossa in Ireland's national graveyard: Glasnevin Cemetery, Dublin. Both men had realised that the return of O'Donovan Rossa to Ireland, and his burial in Dublin, could act as a precursor to rebellion and a show of strength for advanced Irish nationalism. They predicted that the funeral of Jeremiah O'Donovan Rossa could re-awaken a national spirit in the Irish people, whom they feared were becoming more British than the British themselves. It was at this funeral that Thomas James Clarke instructed Patrick Pearse to deliver the graveside oration over O'Donovan Rossa's remains. In a reference to the assembled crowd and the British authorities, Clarke instructed Pearse to make it 'as hot as hell'. Staying true to Clarke's instructions at the funeral, Pearse famously declared:

Life Springs from death; and from the graves of patriot men and women spring living nations. The defenders of this realm have worked well in secret and the open. They think that they have pacified Ireland. They think they have purchased half of us and intimidated the other half. They think that they have foreseen everything, think that they have provided against everything; but the fools, the fools, the fools! – they have left us our Fenian dead, and while Ireland holds these graves, Ireland unfree shall never be at peace.

O'Donovan Rossa had lived a full and varied life. He had witnessed the Irish Famine at first hand. He had been a founding figure in Fenianism in both Ireland and America and had overseen the emergence of the Fenian newspaper, *The Irish People*. He had been arrested and imprisoned, thus experiencing the harsh realities of the Victorian prison system. After being amnestied, he had been forced into a conditional exile in America for the duration of his prison sentence. Embracing life within America, O'Donovan Rossa initiated the first modern bombing campaign in Britain and remained an active Fenian until his death. He had doggedly stood by the Fenian principle of an Irish Republic, never veering from his principles and his great desire to break the political connection between Britain and Ireland. O'Donovan Rossa was also much more than a political man; he was also a family man and was regarded as warm, intimate, big hearted and jolly by his family and friends. His daughter, Eileen, described him as 'a gentleman in every sense of the word',[10] who possessed 'a great love for Ireland, his religion and his family… In the opinion of all his many sons and daughters he was just perfect and we adored him.'[11] This persona of O'Donovan Rossa, as a kind-hearted and warm individual, is often lost in the study of his character, with most historians focusing strictly on the revolutionary rather than the man.

This book marks the 100th anniversary of the death of Jeremiah O'Donovan Rossa and is the first biography of the Irish rebel to be written in the English language. The intention of this book is to commemorate O'Donovan Rossa as the man he was – a greatly complicated individual who was both a family and political man. This book will tell his story from his earliest years to his death and funeral, bringing to life a man whose entire life's work was dedicated to the establishment of an Irish Republic.

1

THE O'DONOVANS OF WEST CORK

Jeremiah O'Donovan Rossa was born Jeremiah O'Donovan, in Reenascreena, in the idyllic setting of West Cork on 10 September 1831. As will be seen, he adopted the appellation of 'Rossa' later in life.[1] He was the second of four children. His parents, Denis O'Donovan and Nellie O'Driscoll, were reasonably well to do, and they owned a Linen bleaching business, a linen shop, which included four working looms and employed a team of weavers, and they also rented a sizable plot of land for £18 a year. From the age of 3 the young Jeremiah was sent to live with his maternal grandparents, Cornelius and Anna O'Driscoll (nee O'Leary), near the village of Reenascreena. His mother had given him over to her parents as she was pregnant with her third child and it was decided that they could provide better for him until he was prepared for his First Holy Communion at the age of 7. Here he lived with his four aunts: Nance, Johanna, Bridget and Anna, and his three maternal uncles: Denis, Conn and Michael. Life at his grandparents' home was tranquil, sublime, and at times, utopian. Their home was one of music, song, poetry and history and the young O'Donovan Rossa was enchanted by ghost stories and tales of the fairies roaming mischievously throughout the rural countryside; indeed, for much of his life he believed in fairies and superstition. The nostalgic fireside talks about rebellions and his families' revolutionary antecedents also served to inspire him and shape his beliefs. The family were well-off tenant farmers and Jeremiah O'Donovan Rossa recalled that there were always servants about the house. They had a large proportion of livestock consisting of over twenty cows, as well as a number of horses, goats, pigs and sheep. The family was brought up entirely in the Irish language, and despite learning English at school, it was understood that Irish was the family tongue and 'the language of the table, the language of the milking [woman], the language of the sowing and the reaping'.[2]

It was from these fond experiences that O'Donovan Rossa developed a life-long love of the Irish language and an image of an idealised Ireland that was rural and Gaelic. As a boy he adored the wild and verdant surroundings of the farm and was regarded as a wanderer. He was a gentle and polite boy who was slow to anger. He was inspired by the ideas of Gaelic mythology and the existence of fairies roaming throughout the land, the nostalgic fireside talks about rebellions and his families' revolutionary antecedents. At 7- years-of-age O'Donovan Rossa left his grandparents' home and returned to his father and mother in Roscarbery. He had returned to his parents to prepare for the sacrament of Communion in their home, which was constantly visited by neighbours, he was embraced by a culture that enjoyed a Gaelic tradition called *scoruíocht,* where friends would sit by the fireside and tell stories of fairies, history, gossip and familial news, similar to the fireside stories he so enjoyed in his grandparents' homestead. Surrounded by a strong circle of friends in school, he excelled as a pupil and despite being nurtured in the Irish language; he was commended in his use of English. The initial adoption of English was not easy for O'Donovan Rossa; he had grown up using the Irish language and recalling a youthful struggle to learn English, found that all he could say was A, B, C. He was a quick learner, however, and was recognised as a great pupil by his teachers, to such an extent that he ran ahead of his class.[3] In his recollections Rossa recalled joyful schooldays where he would memorise all his lessons, and thoroughly read his schoolbooks, many of which enflamed his burgeoning nationalism in future years. Of these, he recalled textbooks which nursed 'the Irish youth into a love of country, or a love of freedom'.[4] At the time of his childhood, however, rebellions and revolutionary antecedents were confined to the fringe of nationalist politics, where advanced nationalist thought was dominated by the charismatic and eloquent Daniel O'Connell.

O'Connell was one of the most revered and respected politicians of his generation. He had become known as 'the Liberator' for his role in securing Catholic Emancipation in 1829, following his election as the first Roman Catholic to the British Parliament the previous year. He also represented a rising Irish-catholic middle-class that was not prepared to be treated with condescension within politics. O'Connell had instilled Irish catholics with a real sense of purpose and made them feel part of an important movement for social change. Inspired by his victory for Catholic Emancipation, O'Connell next sought to achieve a peaceful repeal of the Act of Union, which had abolished the Irish Parliament and united the Kingdom of Ireland with Great Britain. Establishing the Repeal Association to build a viable campaign to rescind the Act of Union, the O'Connell name continued to command respect amongst nationalist families. The O'Donovans were equally inspired by O'Connell and actively supported the Liberator; the young Jeremiah's uncle, Patrick O'Donovan, become a campaigning activist within the Repeal Association. Through his uncle, he had been introduced to a world of political demonstration, oration and activism. He recalled seeing his Uncle Patrick out canvassing for O'Connell and pinning badges onto supporters who eagerly approached him to show their support for the Liberator. He was mesmerised by the great spectacle of monster meetings as thousands of O'Connell's supporters descended en-masse to hear about the Repeal Campaign and learn of how Ireland could function with its own parliament. Each monster meeting represented a great spectacle for the young Jeremiah; he gazed at the green banners and flags proudly unfurled by the nationalist supporters, enjoyed the almost military processions of O'Connell's uniformed police and were enthralled by atmospheres that resembled carnivals rather than political rallies. As a child he had even met the great man and recalled that on a visit from Skibbereen, O'Connell had passed through Roscarbery in 1843, and the young Rossa was picked up over a crowd of people to glance at the arrival of the Liberator in the town. Making his way through the crowd, 'between the legs of some of them, I made my way up to the carriage that the Liberator was in. I was raised up, and had a hearty handshake with him'.[5] He was also introduced to repeal songs and ballads by an apprentice weaver, Peter Crowley, who was employed by his father. The young Rossa was by now introduced to a political culture that disapproved of the Union and saw the great potential of an independent Ireland. The name of O'Connell seemed to magically promise a bright, new future.

While O'Connell enjoyed popular adulation amongst the ordinary people of Ireland, and while his Repeal Association was in the ascendency within Irish politics, privately, he was challenged by younger members of the association who became known as 'Young Ireland'. This grouping was an intellectual gathering, the progenitor of which was the radical newspaper, *The Nation*. Amongst its luminaries were Charles Gavin Duffy, Thomas Francis Meagher, John Mitchel and Thomas Davis. Young Ireland rejected what they saw as O'Connell's increasing sectarianism, his pandering toward the hierarchy of the Catholic Church, his willingness to advance his children within the movement through patronage and his use of the Repeal Association as his personal fiefdom. The Young Irelanders sought to re-define Ireland on a principle of nationality and unity of people, irrespective of religious and cultural difference. *The Nation* newspaper would become one of the most important and influential nationalist newspapers of the 1840s, and O'Donovan Rossa, already being reared within a political family, was increasingly exposed to its ideas, soon becoming a regular reader, often visiting the workshop of Mick Hurley in Pound Square to listen to a reading of *The Nation*. O'Donovan Rossa had developed a marked respect for Thomas Davis. He enjoyed his poetry and poetic style and found a great resonance in his political thought, for Davis had reaffirmed the inclusive republicanism of the United Ireland and their concept of an all-inclusive nation. Exposed to the ideas of *The Nation*, O'Donovan Rossa recalled how the newspaper had given him an understanding of Irish politics and the nature of Ireland's relationship to Great Britain. He recalled in *Recollections* a growing awareness of the reality that Ireland was subservient to Britain, and its people were intrinsically different to the British, not only in religion and culture, but language and heritage too. He recalled some years later that, through *The Nation*, he had had a baptism in Irish nationalism and began to question why Ireland was governed by her nearest neighbour. Within a short time of his introduction to *The Nation*, however, Ireland was faced by a profound political crisis that would harden O'Donovan Rossa's opinions; the country would experience famine.

The Great Famine of 1845-52 had resulted from *phytophthora infestans*, or potato blight, combined with a poor government response and a strict *laissez faire* interpretation of economics. Of the tenant farmers identified by the 1841 census, the great majority of these were entirely reliant on the potato crop, the cheapest and most easily produced food source. Many of these tenant farmers were dependent on Lumpers, a form of potato that was highly susceptible to disease. By 1845, the first reports of potato blight had been recorded, and the following year the harvest failed again. This triggered a tragedy of unprecedented proportions and while the people starved, other Irish produce was often shipped out to Britain and the imperial markets under armed guard.

While towns and villages throughout Ireland were damaged by the Famine, West Cork, where the O'Donovan's lived, was particularly affected. James Mahony, a young artist who was touring West Cork for the *Illustrated London News*, was horrified by what he had seen. Mahony provided a vivid description for the readers of the newspaper, which drew on poverty, hunger and death, reporting that:

> I started from Cork, by the mail, for Skibbereen and saw little until we came to Clonakilty, where the coach stopped for breakfast; and here, for the first time, the horrors of the poverty became visible, in the vast number of famished poor, who flocked around the coach to beg alms: amongst them was a woman carrying in her arms the

corpse of a fine child, and making the most distressing appeal to the passengers for aid to enable her to purchase a coffin and bury her dear little baby. This horrible spectacle induced me to make some inquiry about her, when I learned from the people of the hotel that each day brings dozens of such applicants into the town.[6]

Similar to Mahony, a sailor from the HMS *Tartarus*, delivering food to Ballydehob, West Cork, claimed that: 'The deaths here average forty to fifty daily; twenty were buried this morning and they were fortunate in getting buried at all.'[7] Similar to many families in West Cork, the O'Donovans were horribly affected by the Famine. O'Donovan Rossa had experienced the horrific realities of famine life first hand and was inevitably affected by what the *Illustrated London News* reported as 'the horrors of poverty'[8] in West Cork. In 1845, at the onset of the Famine, Jeremiah O'Donovan Rossa was 14-years-of-age. In his recollections, he recalled the almost apocalyptic scene of when his father had opened the family's potato pit. With tension palpable and a growing sense of unease spreading throughout the country, he remembered the fear and horror his parents experienced:

> The leaves had been blighted, and from being green, parts of them were turned black and brown, and when these parts were felt between the fingers they'd crumble into ashes. The air was laden with a sickly odour of decay, as if the hand of death had stricken the potato field, and that everything growing in it was rotting... The stalks withered away day by day. Yet the potatoes had grown to a fairly large size. But the seed of decay and death had been planted into them... By and by an alarming rumour ran through the country that the potatoes were rotting in the pits. Our pit was opened, and there, sure enough, were some of the biggest of the potatoes, half rotten.[9]

Representing the unfolding crisis as experienced throughout Ireland, each day Denis O'Donovan attended the family potato plot in the hope of seeing the crop flourish rather than diminish. On each occasion he was left disappointed as the potato stalks turned black and crumbled to dust as the crop rotted within the ground. Separating his rotten potatoes from good Lumpers, Denis O'Donovan carted them to a specially built chamber house on his land which he had padded with straw to keep the potatoes dry and maintain a proper temperature. To his great horror, the good potatoes were rotting here too.

Specially constructing room for them above the family kitchen, in their loft, the family once again toiled to separate the good potatoes from the bad and stored them in the cool, dry loft. Again, every potato that was stored in the loft rotted.

To meet the crisis in Ireland, Sir Robert Peel, the British Prime Minister, initially acted promptly by clandestinely securing maize from America known as Indian corn to avert the hunger in Ireland and allowed the coast guard to open up seventy-six food depots along the west coast of Ireland, the worst area affected by the Famine. Peel was replaced by Sir John Russell of the Whigs, whose government adopted a more *laissez faire* attitude to famine relief in Ireland. Leaving much of the governmental response to the Famine in the hands of Charles Trevelyan, the Chancellor of the Exchequer, the government moved to transfer the burden of famine relief from the central exchequer to the local tax rates. Peel had previously established a Board of Works to provide work for the starving poor and give them money to purchase food. In this view the government was of the opinion that the people did not require handouts; they required work to survive. This scheme was continued under the Russell administration. However, under Trevelyan, it was decided that while money for the Board of Works would be provided by the Central Government Fund, the money advanced by the British government was to be repaid from local rates over a ten-year period.

By 1847 some 700,000 people were employed by the board. These people were, however, grossly underpaid, receiving between 8d to one shilling per day. This money was not in keeping with the rising cost of living during Famine-stricken Ireland and was insufficient for survival considering the cost of food and the increasing problem of shopkeepers and food providers taking advantage of the peoples' hunger. By 1847, the British government introduced a temporary Soup Kitchen Scheme, with three million people using the service by the summer. Relying on the Irish Poor Law System, the government also turned to workhouses as a means of Famine relief. The cost of the Poor Law System, however, fell upon landlords who, rather than aid the starving, set about a process of evicting tenants from their land so as to reduce their liability to Poor Law funding. Amending Irish Poor Law, an infamous clause was introduced into the British Parliament known both as the Gregory or Quarter Acre Clause, which ruled that tenant farmers would be denied Famine relief either inside or outside a workhouse if they were farming more than a quarter an acre of land. As thousands were evicted from their homes, they had little choices of life within workhouses, as a result, many wandered aimlessly throughout Ireland, turning to criminality or emigrating in search of a better life. The exact human cost of the Famine in Ireland can never be adequately examined, but most estimates suggest that the population went into free fall, with more than one million people choosing to leave Ireland in search of a better life, and some two million people dying. The 1841 census noted there were over eight million people living in Ireland that year. Every census since 1841 has been substantially lower.

The Famine placed an immense strain on the O'Donovans, and all resources were dried up to provide for the family. O'Donovan Rossa recalled that early on in the Famine all their money was lost to pay the rent for their tenant farm. He noted that the wheat from his parents' farm came to £18.5s, but had been seized by the landlord who, fearing it would be used by the family rather than as a means of generating money for rent, employed men to watch over it so that it was threshed, bagged and taken to the mill by the family rather than be used for any other purpose. The problem for the O'Donovans was that their rent was also £18 and this money was promptly handed over to the landlord's agent, Garrett Barry. Lamenting the horror of the Famine in his later years, he recalled how, as a boy, he did not know 'how my father felt. I don't know how my mother felt. I don't know how I felt. There were four children of us there. The potato crop was gone; the wheat crop was gone.'[10] By 1846, the second year of the Famine, there was further distress throughout the country as the blight struck again, but on this occasion the potato did not grow at all, and as fields became increasingly untended, the rural landscape was dotted with yellow ragwort – a worthless weed. Standing on a hill overlooking Roscarbery, O'Donovan Rossa saw over a mile of land covered in the weed; he recalled that despite the horror unfolding, it was a beautiful sight to see as it glistened in the sun. He realised that the beautiful scene, which he watched from upon high, was the baleful beauty of decay and death.

Financially, the family could no longer survive after their rent had been paid to the landlord, and Denis O'Donovan, increasingly desperate, had plunged the family into debt. Their resources, already stretched, were further exasperated when a family friend, Donal O'Donovan Buidhe, arrived at their home looking for shelter. Unable to pay his rent, he had been evicted and arrived with his family of six children and distressed wife. Unable to turn their friends away, Denis O'Donovan helped to clear an outhouse on his land for them to live in. The O'Donovan Buidhe's had a donkey, which the young

O'Donovan Rossa was taken by, but looking for it one day he could not locate it; the family, in their desperation, had eaten it. Seeking to relieve their distress, Denis and Nellie agreed that they needed to seek assistance. Denis O'Donovan's sister was quite wealthy and he sent Nellie to her to ask for help. While his sister was favourable to helping her brother, her son-in-law, whom she asked for advice, prevented her from giving them money as the family were so sunk in debt that they would never be able to pay it back and the money would be lost.

Like so many fathers in Famine Ireland, to relieve his family's distress, Denis O'Donovan turned to the Board of Works for support and was employed as labourer supervisor. He had worked on a road through Rory Glen, West Cork and had employed the young Rossa as one of his workers. Struggling for preservation, the O'Donovans were working extraordinarily hard. While working on the local roads surrounded by farms and fields, O'Donovan Rossa could not help but notice that despite the increasing hunger and deprivation in Ireland, there was still an abundance of food in the country, and recalling his personal experience of the Famine, he explained:

> During those three years in Ireland, '45, '46, and '47 the potato crops failed, but the other crops grew well, and as in the case of my people in '45, the landlords came in on the people everywhere and seized the grain crops for the rent – not caring much what became of those whose labour and sweat produced those crops. The people died of starvation, by the thousands.[11]

One of those who died was O'Donovan Rossa's father on 25 March 1847. Denis O'Donovan had contracted fever and O'Donovan Rossa replaced his father as labourer–supervisor at 16–years-of-age. He realised that his father's death had left a family of five fatherless and effectively penniless. Denis was waked the day after his death and a great crowd descended on the family home to pay their respects to him. The following day he was buried in the family plot at Ross Abbey. This was not the only Famine tragedy to befall the 16–year-old Rossa. The following year, a woman whom he had been friendly with, Jillen Andy, died of Famine fever, leaving four sons orphaned. He had been particularly friendly with Jillen's fourth son, Tade. O'Donovan Rossa was kind to Tade, who was mentally disabled, and he recollected how he would regularly take Tade on his back to school and tell him stories to make him laugh. One evening in 1848, while playing on the street, Tade came to him with the news that his mother had died, and he asked the young Rossa to help him bury her. With no money for a coffin and no mourners, they buried the woman in a shallow grave and tied a pillow to her head. Laying an apron over her head, so the dirt could not touch her face, Tade and Rossa filled the shallow grave. Within one month his friend was buried with his mother, his life another casualty of the Famine.

Like his father, O'Donovan Rossa, shortly after the burial of Tade, was struck by fever. Lying in bed for a little over a week, his family thought he was dying. While he was in great pain and his life was challenged, he survived the bout of fever but recovering from his illness he complained about his eyes, which became infected. The pain in his eyes was attributed to fairies and his mother wondered what the fairy world had against them and why they were being punished so much. By now the family were heavily in debt and debt collectors increasingly ploughed pressure on Nellie O'Donovan, keenly aware that she was at her lowest ebb. The family had no money and could not oblige the collectors; as a result everything inside the house was seized and sold, much to the family's indignity. Rossa recalled how the family were left hungry and dependent on relatives and neighbours for assistance. On one particular occasion, he remembered how, coming home from playing with his friends, he found his mother in tears – there was no food in the house and she was unable to provide for her children. Searching through his pockets he found a single penny piece. He was so hungry. Leaving the house the young O'Donovan Rossa made his way to a nearby shop and bought a penny bun, recalling how 'I stole to the back of the house and thievishly ate that penny bun without sharing it with my mother, my sister and my brothers.'[12]

Soon after this an eviction notice was given to Nellie O'Donovan. The family moved into a house formally owned by a neighbour Darby Holland, who had died. They secured the house through a family relative who lived there rent free during her life. As part of the agreement Nellie O'Donovan would be paid £12 for a wheat crop growing in Darby Holland's former hill field. This money was not used to provide for the family; the £12 was needed to pay back debts incurred since Denis O'Donovan died.

The year of 1848 was a tough one for the O'Donovan family, but it was also a year of great social change throughout Europe. In January 1848 there was a rebellion in Sicily; by February the winds of change had reached France where there was a republican revolution and the French monarchy was overthrown.

In March, Germany was the scene of a failed wave of protest seeking German national unity and freedom of assembly, while in nearby Denmark later that month there was popular opposition levelled against a system of monarchical absolutism. The revolutions sweeping throughout Europe certainly influenced nationalist Ireland. While the Repeal movement looked on many within its offshoot, Young Ireland became convinced that the time had come for Ireland to proclaim its right to independence. William Smith O'Brien, perhaps one of the most famous of the Young Irelanders, inspired by the success of the French Revolution, aimed to establish an Irish National Guard and a council of 300 members to function as the embryo of an independent Irish parliament. In deference to the French Republic, Smith O'Brien, with Thomas Francis Meagher travelled to Paris to seek recognition of their aims. The French were, however, unwilling to support the Young Irelanders, as the recognition of their aims would antagonise the British. O'Brien and his followers in the Young Irelanders regarded the republic as a necessary evil, not in the context that they supported its establishment, but as a means to threaten the government to terms. In this regard the Young Irelanders' strategy had initially held out for an Irish parliament by peace, or a republic by force. By May 1848 the Young Irelanders led an abortive and disastrous uprising, the largest skirmish of which was at a widow's cottage in Ballingarry, County Tipperary, where a number of police officers had barricaded themselves into a house and were surrounded by rebels. Poorly equipped and lacking popular support, the rebellion easily shot its bolt and in the aftermath the leaders of the Young Irelanders were either rounded up and deported to Australia and Van Diemen's Land or escaped to Europe and America.

The Young Irelanders heavily influenced the young Jeremiah O'Donovan Rossa. The Irishman recalled that in the period of 1848–58, with the transference from Young Irelanderism to Fenianism, he was effectively carried from 'boyhood to manhood'.[13] The fireside stories of his youth and his eager absorption of the ideas disseminated in *The Nation,* coupled with his experiences of the Famine, certainly played a crucial role in the radicalisation and politicisation of the young O'Donovan Rossa. The rigours of the Famine had forced the family to scatter throughout the globe. Following the 1848 Rebellion, the O'Donovans emigrated to America, yet for one reason or another, including a perception that O'Donovan Rossa could look after himself, Nellie O'Donovan had chosen to leave Jeremiah in Ireland. O'Donovan Rossa now lived with his father's niece, Ellen Dowling, who had previously secured him work in her husband Mortimer Dowling's hardware shop in Skibbereen. Remembering the passage of his family to America, O'Donovan Rossa lamented the event:

> The day they were leaving Ireland, I went from Skibbereen to Renascrenna to see them off. At Renascrenna Cross we parted... Five or six other families were going away, and there were five or six cars to carry them and all they could carry with them, to the Cove of Cork. The cry of the weeping and wailing of that day rings in my ears still. That time it was a cry heard every day at every cross roads in Ireland. I stood at that Renascrenna Cross till this cry of the emigrant party went beyond my hearing. Then, I kept walking backward toward Skibbereen, looking at them till they sank from my view.[14]

Life without his family was tough for O'Donovan Rossa, and despite working for his cousin's husband, he had no paid salary from Mortimer Dowling. His job was secured on the understanding that the Dowlings would feed, shelter and clothe him in return for his labour. In 1849, however, business began to improve for Mortimer Dowling, and he changed premises, enlarging his business from general hardware and including cutlery, agricultural seeds and farm and ironmongery tools. Later on, Dowling expanded into the wool, cotton and flax industry, and as a Poor Law Guardian, won contracts to supply them to the Poor Law Unions in Skibbereen, Bantry and Kenmare. With the expansion of his business, O'Donovan Rossa now could draw a salary and earned the tidy sum of £2 per year. He was also offered to work for Dowling for five years, but he was reluctant to sign such a long and binding contract. Mortimer Dowling had been a Young Irelander and had volumes of *The Nation* and Repeal pamphlets stored in his home, which the young Rossa eagerly read. Of particular interest to O'Donovan Rossa was the Young Irelander John Mitchel. Mitchel had been the most vocal advocate of violent revolution amongst the ranks of the Young Irelanders and had broken from the organisation in his desire to see a violent uprising. Explaining the Famine of 1852, Mitchel, who would eventually be deported to Van Diemen's Land, found that the disaster was not manmade but was the result of a British policy to starve Ireland into submission. O'Donovan Rossa agreed with this analysis of the Famine as a man-made catastrophe, stating in retrospect:

Coroners' Juries would hold inquests on Irish people who were found dead in the ditches, and would return verdicts of 'murder' against the English government, but England cared nothing for that; her work was going on splendidly; she wanted the Irish race cleared out of Ireland – cleared out entirely, and now something was doing for her what her guns and bayonets had failed to do. She gave thanks to God that it was so; that the Irish were gone – 'gone with a vengeance.'[15]

2

THE RISE OF THE PHOENIX

In 1853 O'Donovan Rossa married Nora Eager, from Milltown, County Kerry, and coming into some money, he rented a shop and house from Mortimer Dowling in Skibbereen.[1] Continuing Dowling's trade of agricultural seeds and hardware, his new business was a commercial success and was supported by local farmers. Settling into married life, Jeremiah and Nora had four children: Denis, John, Cornelius and Jeremiah. For all means and purposes, O'Donovan Rossa was by now following the path of a well-to-do businessman who was providing for his family. He had also established a good reputation in Skibbereen as a local bard, writing what was termed *skellig lists,* a popular tradition of writing scurrilous and satirical verses. Within three years of opening his shop and getting married, O'Donovan Rossa began correspondence with John O'Donovan, a professor of the Irish language, editor of the famed *Annals of the Four Masters*, and a noted antiquarian living at No. 36 Northumberland Street, Dublin. O'Donovan Rossa was familiar with the stories of his family's Celtic roots, with his father often using the nickname 'Rossa' in reference to the family's perceived Celtic roots in the Rossmore area of Cork. O'Donovan had suggested that Jeremiah O'Donovan's family were direct descendants of the MacAinee branch of the O'Donovan dynasty, and from this he adopted the name 'Rossa' to signify his family's Celtic lineage.[2]

In 1856, O'Donovan Rossa became a founding member of the Phoenix National and Literary Society. This would chart the beginning of a revolutionary career that would span over fifty years. The society represented the culmination of several individuals with the common aim of the liberation of Ireland by force of arms. It had been founded in the home of Jeremiah Crowley, a chemist, at North Street, Skibbereen. Initially, it closely resembled a debating society and social outlet for Irish nationalists to discuss revolutionary ideas and Irish history and culture. It was not originally a revolutionary body. The preamble of the Phoenix Society read:

For years past, since 1848 particularly, the people of Ireland have been looked upon as having silently acquiesced in their position as a conquered province, and having given up all idea of a national existence, apart from that of England, the desire for independence and self-government is thought to have been completely trodden out, or to be restricted to a few 'mere enthusiasts'.

To show, as far as in us lies, the fallacy of this opinion; to advocate and assert our right to a distinct national existence; to make the peasantry in our own locality, at least, understand that for them exists but one country which they are bound to love, and cherish, and defend; to make them understand their rights as men; to combat against the widely spread and corrupt leprosy of Imperialism; and to foster and rouse into action the latent spirit of nationality, are the first and most immediate objects of this society.

Impressed with the conviction that, to be free, a nation must be enlightened, it shall be with us an object to which every energy will be devoted; to place within the reach of the members of this Society a national literature of the purest and best description; to afford them every useful information connected with the past, and a knowledge of what they are justly entitled to for the future – so that they may ponder on their present degraded position, contrast it with that of various other nations inferior to Ireland in extent, population, and resources; and make it their constant aim and labour to regain those rights which have been, and are, forcibly and unjustly withheld. By this Society an effort will be made for the establishment of the same or similar Societies throughout the country; and, as far as its own immediate influence extends, to found branch Societies, which, if not taking the same name and title, shall, at least, keep in view objects similar to those here stated.[3]

Those who had joined the Phoenix Society were frightened by the state of Ireland in the aftermath of the Famine and the disastrous failure of the 1848 Rebellion. According to O'Donovan Rossa, representative of this feeling of malaise, he had suggested the name of the society so as to represent a mythical bird, the Phoenix, famed for its ability to rise from the ashes. In proposing the name for the society he recalled how 'Ireland was dead, but from the ashes of her martyred nationality she should phoenix-like, arise again.'[4] It was evident that within his political thinking the name was chosen as a metaphorical symbol

17

for Ireland and the potential for rebellion in the aftermath of famine. The society grew throughout West Cork and into Kerry, its members consisting of those who were nationally minded and disaffected with the nature of British rule in Ireland. The organisation was not secretive and regular meetings were held in Morty Dowling's pub. Dowling was a prominent member of the society, and the pub was only three doors down from the Constabulary barracks. Dowling had even written to the local Constabulary asking them whether he was 'acting illegally in renting a room to the literary society who sit after hours'.[5] Marking the anniversary of the foundation of the Phoenix Society in 1858 O'Donovan Rossa even made a public speech, which was printed by the *Dundalk Democrat* newspaper. In it he commended the concept of Irish independence and the threat of force, and announced in a provocative manner that:

> We Irishmen are slaves and outcasts in the land of our birth. What a shame! What a disgrace! Yes; disgraceful alike to peer and peasant – Protestant, Catholic and Presbyterian. Thus may foreign nations believe this country is not ours, and I am sure you will not be surprised that England is particularly positive on this point. She has made all possible efforts to convince us of it. She has broken the heads of many Irishmen trying to hammer this opinion into them. For seven long and dreary centuries has she been trying to force it on us; and against her during all this time the majority of Irishmen protested. Yet has she disregarded every protestation, every claim, and every petition, and instead of treating us as human beings or subjects, she has made every effort that pen, fire and sword could make to extirpate our race.[6]

At the same time that the Phoenix Society was developing in the south, a new constitutional initiative was beginning to emerge in London. This new initiative sought to address the Irish Question within Parliament and seize the potential of establishing an independent Irish party at Westminster to use the power of moral persuasion to force British politicians to consider Irish political issues. Known as the Tenants' Rights League, and founded by Charles Gavin Duffy, this organisation had actively fought a campaign both within and outside the British Parliament to achieve better rights on the land for tenant farmers and oppose the introduction of an Ecclesiastical Titles Bill, making it a criminal offence for Roman Catholics to use episcopal titles within the United Kingdom outside of the Anglican Church. Two of the strongest opponents of this bill were William Keogh and John Sadlier, who had pledged never to take any office in the British government until the Ecclesiastical Titles Bill was revoked and the British government made laws favourable to Ireland. Both Keogh and Sadlier reneged on these pledges and soon took office within the government as Solicitor General and Lord of the Treasury respectively. With their defection, the Tenants' Rights League was greatly weakened and as others followed, the potential to establish an independent Irish party in the British Parliament floundered. Many advanced nationalists, including O'Donovan Rossa, looked at the failure of the Tenants' Rights League and were convinced that no political concessions for Ireland could be won from the British Parliament. They also shared a common perception, as represented by Keogh and Sadlier that the election of Irishmen to Westminster would only serve to corrupt Irish interests and political representatives rather than advance the cause of Irish nationalism. There arose from this perception a belief that nothing but force or the threat of force could make the British government consider Irish political grievances. This perception was widely shared within the ranks of the Phoenix Society and became a foundation stone in their growing commitment to advanced Irish nationalism, and their desire to co-operate with others of a similar opinion.[7]

Parallel to the rise of the Phoenix Society in West Cork, in 1858 several former Young Irelanders had met in Lombard Street, Dublin, including James Stephens, Thomas Clarke Luby, Joseph Denieffe and Peter Langan. Here they founded a secret, oath-bound revolutionary movement called the Brotherhood. James Stephens became the autocratic leader of the Brotherhood, earning the official title of Chief Organiser of the Irish Republic. James Stephens was the sole director of Fenian policy and strategy; the entire direction of the movement was left to his sole arbitration. In this regard, Stephens jealously held the reins of power within the burgeoning movement and no one, not even those within his inner council, was allowed to share power and authority. In effect everyone, even those with whom he was closely associated, represented a perceived threat to his leadership and strategy. Later becoming known as the Irish Revolutionary Brotherhood, and then Irish Republican Brotherhood (IRB), this organisation was to function as a secret, clandestine, oath-bound society dedicated to the organisation of a rebellion in Ireland.

In this endeavour the IRB was to be supported by an American Auxiliary known as the Fenian Brotherhood. While both of these organisations were organised independently of each other, they would become popularly known as the Fenians. This new organisation was conceived in New York by a circle of 1848 Rebellion veterans organised in the Emmet Monument Association centred around John O'Mahony, Michael Doheny and Joseph Denieffe. It was Denieffe who had originally made contact in Ireland with existing veterans of the 1848 Rebellion and started a process of revolutionary reorganisation. As part of a process of organising the movement, Stephens, with Thomas Clarke Luby, made a tour of every principle town and village in Ireland to meet like-minded individuals and establish the revolutionary society on a secure footing. Visiting West Cork, Stephens was determined to make the acquaintance of the Phoenix National and Literary Society. He considered the body to be a well-established organisation and could be amiable to a merger with the IRB. Arriving in Skibbereen in May 1858, one of Stephens' first recruits to the IRB was O'Donovan Rossa, who actively worked on recruiting for the organisation and establishing an oath-bound network in West Cork amongst men of trusted opinions. Explaining his routine, O'Donovan Rossa recalled how he would drive to a chapel every Sunday morning with other IRB men and attend Mass and afterwards 'get into conversation with the trustworthy men of the place, and we generally planted the seed of our mission there'.[8] In his recollections he noted how he loved the thrill of recruiting in West Cork and knowing many of the people in the district, he was well trusted by those who he swore into the conspiracy. According to a fellow Fenian, John Devoy, O'Donovan Rossa was one of the most gifted of the Fenian organisers and during this time 'began to sacrifice himself, his family and his interests at the very inception of the movement, and he continued to do it to his last conscious hour'.[9] Such was the growth of the IRB within West Cork that Rossa recollected: 'We were not long working when a great change was noticeable in the temper of the people. In the cellars, in the woods, and on the hillsides, we had our men drilling in the night time, and wars and rumours of wars were on the wings of the wind.'[10]

As part of the merging of the Phoenix Society with the IRB it was understood that the American Auxiliary, the Fenian Brotherhood, would provide arms and military instructors to the men in West Cork. True to the agreement between the IRB and the Phoenix Society, by October 1858 an Irish-American officer, Colonel P. J. Dowling, had arrived in Skibbereen to train the Phoenix men in styles of warfare and combat. Each evening under the moonlight, and protected by sentries, O'Donovan Rossa and his colleagues would climb mountains or make for forests and woods to drill and practice military formation under Dowling's tuition. Here they would drill with pikes, guns and other weapons in preparation for the IRB ambition of revolution.

Each member was trained in the use of a rifle, and part of their drilling would involve rifle practice, while those who could not afford to pay arms would pay one shilling per week to eventually get an advance on arms from a senior officer.[11] As the training progressed O'Donovan Rossa was more confident of the imminence of insurrection – he was increasingly self-assured by being a member of the IRB, a figure in a movement that would inevitably strike a blow for rebellion. The West Cork Fenians had also come to believe that the rebellion would be a clean fight between the entire country and the British Army; they had James Stephens' personal assurances that within the Irish Republic, 'landlordism would be abolished and every man would be his own landlord'.[12]

Despite the security precautions taken, the West Cork drillings had come to the notice of the Irish Constabulary, who increasingly began to monitor the individuals taking part. Internal police correspondence indicates that the local constabulary were growing anxious as to the activities of the Phoenix men. Sub-Inspector Mason of the local Skibbereen police, making internal investigations of their activities, believed the society to be 'strongly disaffected', and 'a revival of the Young Ireland party of 1848'.[13] One of Mason's senior officials recommended that the best way of dealing with the Phoenix Society was 'to be vigilant in watching their movements and proceedings of the society and ascertain if possible the nature of the oath and find some person who will dispose to it and the individuals concerned in administering it'.[14] They received confirmation from a former member, Robert Cusack, that the Phoenix Society was oath-bound. Police believed the oath to be:

> I [NAME] to sincerely swear in the presence of God that I renounce all allegiance to the Queen of England and that I will yield implicit obedience to the commands of my superiors and that I will keep secret regarding this brotherhood. That I will take up arms and fight at a moment's warning and finally that I take this oath without any mental reservation. So help me God.[15]

Examining the validity of this oath, police discovered that there was no set oath as such, but confirming that Cusack's recollection of an oath was correct, police discovered the following verse, which Cusack had omitted: 'That I will do my upmost at any risk to make Ireland an independent Democratic Republic.'[16]

Sub Inspector Mason, rather ominously, warned Dublin Castle that 'the society is spreading. Not long ago they did not number over a dozen in the town and are now over 100, it is also spreading in the country.'[17] F. J. Davies, a Royal Magistrate at Bantry, wrote to Dublin Castle of a system of intimidation with a base in Skibbereen 'endeavouring to coerce persons to join the Phoenix Society'.[18] Consolidating this report, at Bantry, Sub-Inspector Caulfield, on the basis of an informant's information, warned of a conspiracy with access to widespread rifles and pikes. His information had warned that the Phoenix Society was committed to an uprising and when the time would come, 'police barracks would be first attacked and if the men gave up their arms they would not be injured, but if not they would be severely dealt with'.[19] The weapons he spoke of were supposedly purchased by 'a considerable sum of money' collected in America.[20] In this regard the local police were convinced that:

> The object of the Phoenix Society is to keep alive a spirit of hatred to the British Crown and government. [It] was formed under the direct of and is in close communication with a similar one in America which supplies funds. [They] are making every exertion to procure arms and are having pikes made.[21]

According to the police network, Jeremiah O'Donovan Rossa was the ringleader of the Phoenix Society and needed close observation.[22] He was officially regarded as 'one of the strictest members at Skibbereen'.[23] Relying on the statement of Robert Cusack, police could establish O'Donovan Rossa's recruiting role in the society, with Cusack recalling that:

> About the middle of April Jeremiah O'Donovan (Rossa) and McCarty or Carte called in a covered car for Cusack and took him to Clonakilty, where they collected a number of tradesmen, had drink and swore them in. It was supposed this was the beginning of society in Clonakilty.[24]

These constabulary reports were forwarded to the government, and new Resident Magistrate, George Fitzmaurice, was purposely sent down from the North to monitor their activities, taking residence in Skibbereen in December. Having interviewed the local constabulary and magistrates, Fitzmaurice expressed his desire to put down secret societies in Cork. Upon arrival it had been recommended to him that he should enforce crime and outrage acts against the Phoenix Society or introduce a proclamation offering a large reward for information. Fitzmaurice was against both and insisted that if he could get someone within the movement to act as a spy, to give him regular information and break the movement from within, 'he would take care of him'.[25]

One of these informers that Fitzmaurice began to 'take care of' was Dan O'Sullivan Goula, a process server originally from Kenmare, who had been sworn into the movement in August 1858. O'Sullivan Goula had moved from County Kerry to Skibbereen where he took rooms in Morty Dowling's pub. Befriending Dowling, O'Sullivan Goula quickly joined the Skibbereen Phoenix men. He was placed within the movement at the behest of George Fitzmaurice to gather intelligence as to who the society consisted of, what it was doing and where they would meet. Parallel to the work of Fitzmaurice and O'Sullivan Goula, the new Resident Magistrate also moved in extra police to the locality in preparation for moving against the Phoenix Society.[26] Rossa recollected how he regularly met with Goula and saw him playing with Dowling's children, and in hindsight recalled how this endearing man entertaining his friends' children was actually engaged in swearing Dowling and his comrades into jail. Parallel to official concern as to the activities of the Phoenix Society, there was growing recognition within the local Catholic clergy that something was afoot in the community. The Catholic Church had steadfastly opposed all secret societies and forms of oath taking, particularly in Skibbereen where the Eucharist had been politicised and men known to the clergy of being active in the Phoenix Society were in some cases refused the sacrament of Eucharist and absolution from confession unless they renounced their oath.

At Caheragh, County Cork, the parish priest, Fr David Dore, threatened his congregation with excommunication from the Catholic Church if they took an oath to the Phoenix Society. A police constable in attendance at the sermon noted how Dore was an energetic opponent of secret conspiracy, exclaiming how it was 'folly to try and separate Ireland from England'.[27] In nearby Kerry, at Listowel, the Rev. McCormick 'told his flock to hand over to Police anyone who might ask them to be sworn'.[28] At Kenmare, Fr John O'Sullivan was of a similar opinion and regularly denounced the Phoenix Society and any ambition to lead a rising against Britain. In one powerful sermon, O'Sullivan denounced the ambition of revolution and conspiracy, holding that 'the laws of England are better than those of France'.[29] So powerful were his sermons against secret conspiracy that a Phoenix man came to him to confess that he had taken an oath. Learning from the communicant in the confessional that the Phoenix Society was now being organised as a secret, oath-bound society, O'Sullivan informed Dublin Castle of what he understood to be an extensive conspiracy, telling them that he had the names of men involved and the oaths they had taken. These oaths were forwarded on to Dublin Castle, with the names of what he termed 'misguided young men'.[30] On 3 December 1858 Dublin Castle issued a proclamation acknowledging the danger posed by secret societies. Such was the extent of the government's determination to undermine secret societies, that the state offered a reward of £100 for information leading to the conviction of individuals who had administered oaths. The substantial reward was consolidated by an offer of £50 for the arrest of anyone who was proven to be a member of a secret society.[31]

Aside from his political activity, O'Donovan Rossa had applied to become the Skibbereen postmaster in November 1858. His interest in the job had been spurred by the former postmaster, Owen Leonard, who, after an administrative error, was forced to resign his position. Writing an application to the British government, it was evident that he did not take the job seriously and wrote a poem to Lord Colchester, the Post Master General. In his application to Colchester, he stated in verse:

> I trust I'll meet with no disaster,
> Till you address me as postmaster,
> Excuse my Lord, the wish most fervent,
> I have to be your lordships servant![32]

O'Donovan Rossa received a curt response stating that the position was not yet open for recruitment. By 6 December 1858, George Fitzmaurice had made up his mind to move against the Phoenix Society and arrest all of those suspected of active membership in the organisation. Fitzmaurice and F.J. Davies, the Resident Magistrate at Bantry, agreed that the arrests of the Phoenix men were to take place simultaneously, and in a major blow to the morale of the organisation, were to take place in Kerry, Bantry and Skibbereen.[33] The arrests were spurred by a police report from a Sub-Inspector Curling, stationed at Kenmare, who claimed that 300 pikes had been smuggled into Skibbereen and were passed to leading figures within the Phoenix Society. According to the Sub-Inspector, the pikes were to be followed by arms and were going to be distributed throughout neighbouring Bantry, Glengarrif and Kenmare. The following morning at 4 a.m., police stormed O'Donovan Rossa's home, and from memory he wrote that:

> I went to bed and was soon aroused from sleep by a thundering knocking at the hall door. When it was opened a dozen policemen

rushed in and took charge of me and everyone in the house. Then every room was ransacked for papers, and for everything contraband of war – contraband of peace, I may say. I stood in the drawing room under arrest. The sergeant-in-command was smashing the drawers of the chiffonier in search of documents. My wife rushed toward him, crying out not to break the drawers, as she would get the keys. He rudely shoved her away.[34]

A family friend, Tom O'Shea, had been staying in the house that evening and with O'Donovan Rossa was arrested on suspicion of being involved with the Phoenix Society. O'Shea had no involvement with the Phoenix Society, but was incredibly superstitious and held a great fear of fairies; he had been too afraid to go home that evening, for fear of a fairy puck at nearby Steam Mill Cross and so O'Donovan Rossa had allowed him to stay at his house for the night. O'Shea and Rossa were taken to the local police barracks where they were greeted by several Phoenix men including, John Stack, P. J. Dowling, Timothy Duggan, Morty Dowling, William O'Shea and Dan McCartie. McCartie had been due to leave Skibbereen the following day to start a new job in a brewery in Galway.[35] Held in Skibbereen Barracks until mid-morning, they were then escorted by individual policemen through Roscarbery and Clonakilty to Bandon, County Cork. *The Freeman's Journal* reported that on leaving Skibbereen by three train coaches, and under heavy police escort, the prisoners were cheered and applauded by spectators, with the prisoners themselves joining in the cheering and calling upon the crowd to be louder.[36] Arriving in Bandon at 7 p.m., O'Donovan Rossa met Jerrie and Pat Cullinane, William O'Shea and Denis O'Sullivan, who had all been arrested at Bantry as part of the investigations into the Phoenix Society.[37] O'Donovan Rossa despondently recalled how the conditions at Bantry, prior to their removal to Cork, were horrendous, and 'arriving at nine in the evening we were huddled into cells flooded with water. Having travelled all day under rain, and having received neither food nor drink, we now would get neither bread nor a bed. Next morning we found ourselves in Cork Jail, awaiting prosecution on charges of conspiracy'.[38] Following on from the Cork arrests, police raided the homes of several advanced nationalists in Killarney, arresting Denis O'Shea, Patrick Hennessy, Jeremiah Sullivan, Patrick Sullivan, Valentine Browne, Thomas Neary, Timothy Leary, Thomas Leahy and Thomas Sullivan. Two additional men in Killarney, Daniel O'Sullivan, a schoolteacher in possession of an incriminating letter, and Florence O'Sullivan, later consolidated these arrests. In Belfast a great stir was occasioned as a final batch of arrests was made against several Ribbonmen, whom the media wrongly believed were implicated in the Phoenix society.

In Cork Jail each of the Phoenix men were separated and treated as ordinary prisoners by being given menial tasks common to Victorian prison life. This included oakum picking, the rather laborious chore of unravelling old tarred rope in fibre. What made this work more odious to the Phoenix men was that they were not convicted prisoners. O'Donovan Rossa and his co-conspirators had been detained without trial and were yet to receive one. For two weeks of their imprisonment there had been no charges against any of the men and protesting to the prison authorities, their pronouncements were ignored – they were bluntly told that unless they could pay for their own maintenance within the prison, they would have to work. O'Donovan Rossa resolved to work and endure the rigours of life in Cork jail. Increasingly, however, as the mundane and lethargic hours of jail life crept by, he was growing evermore despondent and his resolution to 'suffer and be strong'[39] was weakening:

> Some of the detained arranged to get their own food, but the rest of us thought that we would inure ourselves to hardship. But we could not eat the fare we got; and this, with the solitary confinement imposed, starved us out of our resolution 'to suffer and be strong.' The bread was made with rye/wheat flour; it had the appearance of brown turf and you could squeeze the water out of it. The porridge, about the same colour, was flavoured with leeks, which made it disgusting, for when you drew your spoon out of the bowl you would draw up one of those foot-long leeks, and unless you had gone through a course of starvation your stomach would refuse to receive the product as food.[40]

With the Phoenix men imprisoned at Cork Jail, George Fitzmaurice instructed police to co-operate with local post offices to intercept the mail of the imprisoned men. This order was compounded by a further dictate that the correspondence of their solicitor, Timothy McCarthy Dowling, was also to be secretly opened and copied by police. Fitzmaurice had evidently sought to establish a clandestine means of cumulative evidence to prove that the Phoenix prisoners were guilty of revolutionary conspiracy. All of this was inadmissible in court, however. To strengthen the case against the Phoenix prisoners, Fitzmaurice now extracted Dan O'Sullivan Goula from the conspiracy, and the informant emerged within a fortnight of the arrests in Cork Jail, accompanied by Sir

Matthew Barrington, Crown Solicitor. O'Sullivan Goula identified all of the prisoners as members of a secret society and claimed that they had been intent on leading a rebellion in Ireland against Britain. Recalling a visit to Skibbereen on the 5 December 1858, O'Sullivan Goula placed O'Donovan Rossa, Morty Dowling, Tim Duggan, Denis Downing, Morty Moynahan, Pat Dowling, Daniel McCarthy and William O'Shea at a Phoenix Society meeting in a back room in Morty Dowling's pub. Furthering this accusation, O'Sullivan Goula told Barrington that he had personally witnessed the prisoners drilling in military formation with swords and canes, led by McCarthy and O'Donovan Rossa.[41] Morty Moynahan was a regular driller of men, and with almost forensic precision, O'Sullivan Goula recalled how Moynahan would order the men to 'fall in line',[42] and march like regular soldiers. O'Donovan Rossa was more of a strict drill master, and in O'Sullivan Goula's narrative O'Donovan Rossa had, in his presence, drilled some 300 men in Skibbereen. Once again O'Sullivan Goula identified the Phoenix men as actively drilling in West Cork, and claimed to have taken and administered two oaths to several individuals, swearing them into the revolutionary movement. While not producing any written oath as evidence, he verbally cited the oath as:

> I_____ do solemnly swear that I will, to the utmost of my power, endeavour to subvert and overthrow the British government; that I will join and assist any foreign army who may arrive in this country with that object, and that I will obey and carry out the orders of my superiors to the best of my ability.[43]

Each of the Phoenix prisoners denied this oath and continued to argue that O'Sullivan Goula was lying on behalf of the state to secure convictions. O'Sullivan Goula next swore of a meeting which took place on the rural border between Cork and Kerry, where he had heard talk of American and French intervention designed to make Ireland 'an Independent Republic'.[44] The prisoners, particularly O'Donovan Rossa, strenuously denied his claims to Barrington, insisting that the informer was lying. Recalling Sullivan Goula's performance in his later years, O'Donovan Rossa angrily remembered:

> O'Sullivan Goula was brought among us, and there he stood shivering, side by side with the man who had been honoured with England's knighthood [Sir Matthew Barrington]. Tim Duggan was moving up close to the informer, the informer complained to Sir Matthew that

the prisoner was looking threateningly at him and asked to be taken into another room till his evidence was required. Sir Matthew sent for extra police; they came and stood between Goula and the prisoners. No matter how bad and wicked a character I may be considered now, the adoration I received in youth was a moral and religious one. I had not till then realized the possibility that any man would go on a witness table, kiss the Book, invent a pack of lies and deliberately swear they were the truth, and do all this to put into jail and keep them there, men who never did him, or anyone belonging to him, hurt or harm. But there was that Goula before me, deliberately swearing that he saw me drilling three hundred men one night, and swearing to other things against me which he never saw and which I never did. All pure invention of his own; all false swearing. But no; it was not invention of his; the invention was Fitzmaurice's and Sir Matthew Barrington's. They had made up their minds to fasten their irons well on me, and they had made up the informer for the work.[45]

Under British law, however, despite what O'Donovan Rossa suggested, the word of an informer was not, strictly speaking, admissible in any future trials. Considering the informer was paid by the state and had offered to give information leading to the conviction of the Phoenix prisoners, witnesses were required to corroborate his narrative. Fitzmaurice now eagerly sought to elucidate a confession from the Phoenix prisoners; none could be found, however, to give evidence. O'Donovan Rossa remembered, for the benefit of an American newspaper, how:

The usual English tactics were resorted to for the purpose of weakening some of us and getting us to become informers on others to save ourselves. A warder would see me, pretend to be a secret sympathiser with me, tell me something very confidential, caution me for my life not to breathe a word of it to anyone unless I wanted to effect his ruin; thou he'd come next day and repeat confidence again, and by and by he'd whisper something very suspicious of the prisoner in the next corridor: 'Did I know him well?' 'Was I sure of him?' 'Could there be anything wrong about him?' or 'Was he in a position to do much harm if it could turn out that he was bad?' Then it would very confidentially transpire that that prisoner in the next corridor was day after day being taken to the Governor's private room and having interviews with detective[s] and other agents of the English Government.[46]

A search was also made for impeccable witnesses, including policemen, to testify that the Phoenix men were engaged in active conspiracy and military drilling. The state had great difficulty in securing witnesses amongst the ordinary people of Skibbereen as the community remained remarkably tight-lipped as to the activities of the Phoenix men. This meant that the prosecution of the Phoenix men was more reliant on the evidence of informers supported by police statements. One of these policemen testified in the Magistrates Court that he had seen one of the men, Denis Dowling, out marching in military formation in Skibbereen. Pressed by McCarthy Dowling as to who was seen marching with Denis Dowling, the policeman was forced to admit that Dowling was in fact on his own, and therefore could not have been marching in military formation. The Phoenix men arrested and examined in Cork Jail were released on bail following their inquisition. Only O'Donovan Rossa, William O'Shea and Morty Moynahan were to remain in prison on remand. While the trials were taking place, George Fitzmaurice was actively working behind the scenes to secure a conviction of the Phoenix prisoners. He had grounded this in a perception that the government needed to act firmly with the society, considering they had the potential to work up further conspiracy in Skibbereen.[47] Explaining to Dublin Castle the reality of the situation on the ground, he anxiously wrote:

There is, however, the greatest possible feeling of sympathy evidenced here for the parties in custody which daily impresses upon my mind more fully the great necessity there was for the measures resorted to by the government for the suppression of the society... If such had not been so timely done this county as well as many others in Ireland would be by this time in a bad state.[48]

The first of the Phoenix men to be tried was Daniel O'Sullivan, one of the arrested Kerry men. Tried at the Kerry Assizes on Thursday 10 March 1859 for conspiracy, he was sentenced to ten years of imprisonment and moved to Mountjoy Jail, Dublin. Florence O'Sullivan, who had been arrested with him, had earlier confessed to the police that he had been recruited into the society by Daniel O'Sullivan and was aware of 'an organisation in course of formation throughout the length and breadth of our island, having for its object the restoration of Ireland to freedom under the form of a Republican government or a repeal of the Union by force of arms'.[49] Within a week, on 17 March 1859, O'Donovan Rossa, Morty Moynahan, Daniel McCarthy, William O'Shea, Denis O'Sullivan and Patrick Dowling were due to attend the Cork Assizes. In preparation for the case against the Phoenix men, the state had made an offer to McCarthy Dowling suggesting that if the prisoners pleaded guilty to conspiracy at the Assizes they would be released on assurances of good behaviour with no further charges pressed against them. The Phoenix men refused on account of the imprisonment of Dan Sullivan in Tralee and remained insistent that the informer, O'Sullivan Goula, was lying; any guilty plea would only consolidate O'Sullivan Goula's series of events and be detrimental for Dan Sullivan and the men whom he had been arrested with in Kerry. O'Donovan Rossa recounted the events:

> Goula had sworn against a number of men in Kerry, too, and several of them were indicted for trial at the Kerry Assizes in Tralee. The Tralee Assizes were to come on before the Cork Assizes, and the Kerry men were to be tried before our trial would come on. Propositions were made to us that if we formally pleaded 'guilty,' we would be released on our own recognizances, but this we refused to do. Our prosecutors know that all Goula swore against us was false; they knew we could break down his evidence in public court; our pleading guilty would be admitting a guilt we did not feel, would be putting a kind of brand of truth on the informer's lies and would be periling the safety of the Kerry men. Our attorney approved of our action; he submitted the proposal as made to him, without any advice of his own, and now that we had decided, he was glad we viewed the matter correctly and came to the decision he desired. On his way to the Kerry Assizes he visited us in jail and told us to be in good cheer, that he had evidence secured, which would be produced at Tralee, showing that Goula was swearing falsely in matters connected with the Kerry men, too; that Father John O'Sullivan, of Kenmare, was to come on the witness table in Tralee and swear Goula was a perjurer. Goula swore that before he became informer he had been at confession with Father O'Sullivan, and Father O'Sullivan was coming forward to swear he had never been at confession with him.[50]

Despite the assurances of Timothy McCarthy Dowling, their solicitor, Fr John O'Sullivan, who had earlier been instrumental in the arrest of the Phoenix men, would stand as a witness against O'Sullivan Goula, Fr O'Sullivan did not act as a witness. On learning that Daniel O'Sullivan was sentenced to ten years in Mountjoy Jail, O'Donovan Rossa was infuriated with McCarthy Dowling. He demanded to know why Fr John O'Sullivan had not been called forward as a witness to denounce O'Sullivan Goula. While initially coy as to why he did not bring Fr Sullivan forward, McCarthy Dowling later revealed Fr Sullivan's part in the arrests and his correspondence with Dublin Castle. McCarthy Dowling then told O'Donovan Rossa that Sir Matthew Barrington and George Fitzmaurice had threatened Sullivan with fears of exposure of his correspondence should he take the witness stand against O'Sullivan Goula. Furious, O'Donovan Rossa castigated of Fr. Sullivan, and the Catholic Church:

> A pleasant thing it would be for peoples if they could get their rights from those who lord a mastery over them by the force of prayer and petition; if I could enjoy that pleasure of believing Ireland could gain her rights by each force, I would keep praying till doomsday before I would hurt the hair of a head of English man or woman. Yes, let the expression stand, 'till doomsday,' because till doomsday the praying should last before Ireland could be free.[51]

At the Assizes trial on 17 March 1859, O'Donovan Rossa was greeted by the face of Judge William Keogh, the former nationalist who crossed the floor to support the British government.

> The 17th of March St. Patrick's day, 1859, came on and Cork Assizes opened. We were ready for trial. William O'Shea, Mortimer Moynahan and I were brought from the prison to the Court House and escorted to the underground waiting room, convenient to the dock. Here we were visited by our attorney and counsel and counsel for the Crown, and propositions were made to us that if we pleaded guilty we would be let free, a mere formal recognizance of our own personal security for twenty pounds to appear when called would be taken, and that would be the last heard of the prosecution. We would not plead guilty and by and by we were led into the dock. On the bench before us sat the famous, or the infamous, Judge Keogh. Into the dock also came Patrick J. Downing, Morty Downing and Denis O'Sullivan, who had been out on bail. They brought some shamrocks

into the dock with them and gave us some sprigs of the national emblem and we put them in the buttonholes of our coats. We were ready for trial, ready for fight, but no fight came. England's Attorney General stood up and asked for a postponement of those cases till the next assizes, as the Crown was not fully prepared at the present. Our counsel opposed the motion of postponement, but Judge Keogh did not seem to care much for the opposition; he granted the motion of the Attorney General and ordered the prisoners to be put back till the next assizes in August. Our counsel applied that we be let out on bail. No, Judge Keogh decided that we be kept in without bail; and off, back to prison, we were taken. It was vexatious, but what were we to do? The stone walls were there around us, but it was no use to us knocking our heads against them. There was no case on which to prosecute us, no informers to swear against us – even the unfortunate fallen women of the streets would not come forward to swear they saw us out at night, and so corroborate the swearing of Goula regarding the nightly drillings. We were offered our liberty, and would not take it. Some of our people had no pity for us; they never considered what we considered, that one of our men, Daniel O'Sullivan Agreem, had been convicted and sentenced to ten years' transportation on Sullivan Goula's swearing and that our pleading 'Guilty' to get out free would confirm his sentence and put the brand of truth on what Goula swore.[52]

Once again, all the prisoners earlier released on bail were free to leave the court, while O'Donovan Rossa, Morty Moynahan and William O'Shea, despite application for bail were returned to Cork Jail to resume their imprisonment.

O'Donovan Rossa relieved himself of the mundane life of the Victorian prison system by increasingly turning to satire. In one of his lesser known satirical writings he sought permission from the prison authorities to write to the Lord Lieutenant, the Earl of Eglington, to demand his right to vote during the 1859 general election. While this letter was seen as appropriate, its contents were entirely tongue-in-cheek. O'Donovan Rossa wrote that it was his civic duty to be temporarily released so he could be returned to Skibbereen and vote for Lord Derby's Conservative Party. His justification for this demand was that if he did not vote he feared his absence could be the catalyst for a European war, considering Lord Derby's support for the concert of Europe and the peaceful balance of power within the continent. O'Donovan Rossa sardonically suggested that if allowed to vote, his candidate could keep Lord Derby in office and thus prevent conflict:

> Need I remind your lordship how unconstitutional it would be to deprive an innocent man of his voice in this important crisis; and, such a deprivation of right may entail the most disastrous results. For instance, my lord, my support may be instrumental in returning an honourable and independent man to the Imperial Parliament; the support of this honourable and independent man may be instrumental in maintaining Lord Derby in office, and the retention of Lord Derby in office may be the means for preventing the shedding of oceans of blood, by affording him the time and opportunity for bringing the troublous affairs of Europe to a speedy and pacific conclusion; whereas, opposite and most disastrous results may follow from my inability to attend the poles… In counting up the Liberal and Derbyite gains and losses, we must admit at least that Lord Derby, through adverse circumstances, lost one ardent supporter, and if war follows his lordships resignation, we shall remember this new prophet Jeremiah…[53]

The Lord Lieutenant did not reply and O'Donovan Rossa remained in Cork Jail. As predicted by O'Donovan Rossa, Lord Derby lost the general election. The boredom of life in Cork Jail was finally relieved when McCarthy Dowling returned to the prisoners to inform them that their trial had been moved to the Cork Summer Assizes, taking place on 26 July 1858. McCarthy Dowling was increasingly worried, however, that the prisoners would be kept in jail without charge until 1860, and making applications on behalf of his clients, the state once again offered terms. Under the states' proposal, if the prisoners pleaded guilty to the charges levelled against them they would at once be released on their own assurances of good behaviour. Having approached the prisoners with this deal for their consideration, soon after, their solicitor informed them that the state pledged that if they changed their plea to guilty, Dan O'Sullivan would be released from jail on a similar bond of assurance of good behaviour.

The Phoenix prisoners remained stubbornly opposed to pleading guilty at the Summer Assizes; McCarthy Dowling stressed to them that if they failed to change their plea they would not get bail and would remain lodged at Cork Jail. O'Donovan Rossa, Dowling and William O'Shea were allowed to discuss the terms proposed by the state. They remained opposed to pleading guilty, yet they had other interests outside. O'Donovan Rossa in particular was hit hard by his imprisonment and his family were unable to pay debts to creditors. There was also a dispute between his landlord and another man as to who actually owned the home O'Donovan Rossa's family lived in, forcing his wife and their four children to move into another house. Leaving the decision to O'Donovan Rossa as to how the prisoners were to respond to the state's offer, Dowling and O'Shea deferred to him. O'Donovan Rossa reluctantly recommended they change their plea. It had been hard for him to come to this decision and he recalled that the Phoenix men outside of the prison had suggested that the IRB was dead, and James Stephens had fled to France in the wake of the Phoenix arrests. Arriving at the Cork Summer Assizes in July 1859, as recommended by O'Donovan Rossa, the Phoenix prisoners agreed to the state's terms and were released without charge with an understanding that if they continued in conspiracy they would be arrested and imprisoned. To their vexation, despite the state's offer, Dan O'Sullivan remained imprisoned. O'Donovan Rossa furiously wrote to McCarthy Dowling, accusing the state of reneging on their agreement and threatened to go to the newspapers unless something was immediately done for his imprisoned comrade. It was not until October 1859 that Daniel O'Sullivan was released.

Freed from Cork Jail, O'Donovan Rossa returned home to Skibbereen to a lost family home and a temporary residence. Considering how his name had been heavily publicised in the local newspapers in relation to the Phoenix arrests, and his plea of guilty to charges of conspiracy, the O'Donovan Rossa's were increasingly ostracised within the local community from all but a loyal gathering of friends and those of similar nationalist opinions. Equally, the landlords, the clergy and the local magistrates used all of their influence to undermine his business within the community and discourage trade. Many of his more wealthy customers who formerly patronised his shop now abandoned his business; he became increasingly reliant on poorer and less well-to-do customers, which affected his income. To carry on his business, in terms of practicalities, his customers would often have to visit his family home when making orders or addressing commercial matters. Following his arrest, however, many of his customers were unwilling to come to his home considering police interest in his activities and a fear of being drawn to the attention of the police. There was also a further practical concern for O'Donovan Rossa: his business traded alcohol, and on each occasion when he sought a licence to trade, the police obstructed it. True to character, O'Donovan Rossa always challenged the police opposition to a renewal of his licence, and putting him to much expense and trouble, he would appeal the decision to not renew his licence to a superior court. On each occasion he won, considering that 'no charge of keeping an irregular house could be sustained'.[54] This continued opposition to the renewal of his alcohol licence represented for O'Donovan Rossa part of what he perceived to be an official 'system of terrorism,' designed to subvert his business arising from his political beliefs.[55] Symbolically, within his shop, O'Donovan Rossa also chose to display a gun and a pike ostensibly this was to warn off potential thieves or burglars, but in reality was to prove to those interested in advanced nationalism that there was no problem with the owning of a weapon. Considering whom he was, however, and that he had pleaded guilty of conspiracy, he was approached on several occasions by Charles O'Connell, the new Resident Magistrate appointed to replace George Fitzmaurice. O'Connell, despite his position, was representative of the constitutional nationalist persuasion and was married to Kathleen O'Connell, Daniel O'Connell's daughter. O'Connell had warned O'Donovan Rossa that the gun and pike had to be removed from his shop at once as he was 'disturbing the community'.[56] O'Donovan Rossa protested that their display was not illegal and he would be keeping them above his counter. Pressing O'Connell as to who in the community was protesting against his display, O'Connell explained it caused great alarm to the respectable people in Skibbereen, and that if they were not removed, he would have O'Donovan Rossa brought up for sentence in Court on his plea of guilty the previous year. Displaying his rebellious streak, before ejecting O'Connell from his shop, O'Donovan Rossa angrily exclaimed that: 'Respectable people are honest people and are in no way afraid of having a rifle or pike in my shop; that it was robbers, and thieves who were afraid of such things and I would not give up my rights for such things.'[57]

Within days, McCarthy Dowling, O'Donovan Rossa's solicitor, followed up O'Connell's visit to the Skibbereen shop. It was apparent to O'Donovan Rossa that O'Connell had been talking with McCarthy Dowling about the rifle and pike display. McCarthy Dowling pleaded with O'Donovan Rossa to take down the offending display and give it to him, where he would keep it in safe possession. O'Donovan Rossa still refused to oblige the request. In fact, in direct contravention to what O'Connell had demanded and what McCarthy Dowling had asked, O'Donovan Rossa and his friend, Tim Duggan, would publicly polish the rifle and pike every Sunday morning outside his shop in a marked display of resistance. O'Connell then dispatched the police to see O'Donovan Rossa and complained that Duggan was not polishing the weapons but showing people how to use them. Warned by the police that a report was being sent to Dublin Castle, and reminding O'Donovan Rossa that he was only released from jail on assurances of good behaviour, the police demanded the rifle and pike to be surrendered at once. Once again, O'Donovan Rossa protested that he was doing no wrong and was legally entitled to carry arms. McCarthy Dowling again pleaded with O'Donovan Rossa to allow him take the rifle and pike and hold it in trust. With increasing pressure from McCarthy Dowling and Resident Magistrate O'Connell, O'Donovan Rossa finally conceded that he would have to surrender his arms. True to form, however, in surrendering these arms, with a friend, William McCarthy, both men marched in military formation through the town to McCarthy Dowling's home, carrying the weapons. McCarthy had the rifle tied across his shoulder, and O'Donovan Rossa carried the pike. What made the spectacle more surreal was that it was market day in Skibbereen, and the town was thronged with people. Making their appearance in the town centre, the pair was surrounded by bemused and astonished onlookers, O'Donovan Rossa remembered the occasion with pride:

> It was market day, and both of us walked through the town, showing the people we could carry arms, making our act of surrender as prideful as possible to our cause, and as disagreeable as it could be to English stipendiaries.[58]

One of O'Donovan Rossa's greatest critics was a Dr Michael O'Hea, the Catholic Bishop of Ross. Ironically, O'Hea, while a parish priest, had given O'Donovan Rossa a character reference in his youth, describing him as a 'smart intelligent young lad', who was 'honest and trustworthy'.[59] O'Hea became quite vocal in his denunciations of O'Donovan Rossa and the Phoenix Society to the extent that he encouraged his parishioners to boycott the businesses of those involved. According to O'Donovan Rossa, the Bishop of Ross also 'challenged a man and his wife in the confessional for frequenting' the O'Donovan Rossa family home.[60] The Bishop firmly believed that the O'Donovan Rossas needed to be ostracised within the community less their radicalism spread. Recalling the Bishop of Ross as he tried to rebuild his business, O'Donovan Rossa ironically noted: 'I am sure he never recognized in the "young lad" to whom he gave that character when he was parish priest the young man who troubled him so much when he was Bishop.'[61] The Bishop of Ross need not have concerned himself with the politics of the O'Donovan

Rossa family, however, as soon after this, Nora O'Donovan Rossa fell ill and died in 1859. She was not a supporter of her husband's politics and had serious disagreement with his political activism; and it was speculated that her illness, which remains unknown, was brought on by the stress of her husband's imprisonment. Her death left O'Donovan Rossa widowed, financially broken and in charge of four young children. Writing to his friend, John O'Donovan, to explain his loss, he received a sympathetic note in return:

> You are young and vigorous; and time, the *dulce molimen* − the soft soother − will finally reduce your grief to a softer sadness. Your imprisonment must have weighed heavily on her spirits. [62]

O'Donovan Rossa wrote sparsely about Nora; within his memoirs there is only one paragraph about her death. This is an indication of the grief he experienced following her death and how deeply he was affected. It also indicated that perhaps this unconquerable Fenian felt a degree of responsibility coupled with anger for the circumstances of her death.

3

THE IRISH REPUBLICAN BROTHERHOOD

When O'Donovan Rossa was released from Cork Jail in July 1859, the work of organising the Irish Republican Brotherhood had been momentarily suspended. James Stephens, the enigmatic leader of the Fenians, had[1] disappeared and for all means and purposes was on the run from the British state. As O'Donovan Rossa was settling into normality after his wife's death, it seemed that the political side of his life, apart from his personal beliefs and desire to annoy and harass the local authorities, was coming to an end. Being a single father in Victorian Ireland was incredibly difficult, and O'Donovan Rossa now began a relationship with Eileen Buckley, aged 17. Eileen was a native of Gortbrack, Castlehaven, County Cork and was the only daughter of Cornelius Buckley, a butter merchant and wealthy farmer. Eileen was well travelled and had been educated in Europe; she was regarded as a warm, jovial and attractive woman who was much sought after by the bachelors of Castlehaven. Irish was her first language and she regularly embraced the rural Gaelic tradition of dancing at the crossroads and could be seen on Sundays dancing at Crois na Cora Boige (Curraghbeg Cross, Castlehaven). It was here that she met O'Donovan Rossa, and the two developed a relationship. Their relationship, however, got off to a difficult start as the Buckleys wanted nothing to do with O'Donovan Rossa considering his politics, his age and his four children from a previous marriage.

When the couple became engaged, Cornelius Buckley forbade the marriage – he perceived that O'Donovan Rossa was more trouble than he was worth and was only after Eileen's sizable dowry. Eileen and O'Donovan Rossa realised that they were going to have to elope, which they did in 1861. The couple would have one child to add to O'Donovan Rossa's already sizable family, whom they named Florence Stephens in honour of the Fenian chief, James Stephens. Having married Eileen, O'Donovan Rossa now looked for a new job – he was determined to do right by Eileen and his family and prove Cornelius wrong. Eventually he secured a position as a temporary relieving officer, through McCarthy Dowling, his solicitor, who sat on the Board of Guardians of the Skibbereen Poor Law Union.

Off the south-west coast of Cork are two islands named Sherkin and Cape Clear. In 1862, just as O'Donovan Rossa had been made a temporary relief officer, the islands had been affected by a near famine, and there was a growing crisis as the people starved due to a shortage of food. The situation was far worse for those living on Cape Clear than Sherkin, considering its distance from the mainland. The Skibbereen Board of Guardians pressed for immediate relief, and O'Donovan Rossa, with his friend and neighbour, Michael O'Driscoll, and the permission of the Board of Guardians, undertook a mission to deliver a ton of meal to the islands to alleviate the hunger of the inhabitants. Seeing the poverty and destitution of the Cape horrified O'Donovan Rossa and brought back memories of the Great Famine. Arriving at Sherkin, O'Donovan Rossa saw a man lying on the grass, almost as if he were basking in the sunshine. Asking for his help unloading sacks, the man looked up but did not make any move to help. O'Donovan Rossa chose to confront him and ask why he would not help the relief effort. As he approached the man lying in the grass, he saw he was starving and in tremendous pain:

> I leaped ashore and found the man was unable to stand on his own legs; he was dying of hunger – a man named O'Driscoll, over six feet, and about twenty-six years of age. My wife had thought I would be out on the islands for a few days, and she had sandwiched up as much food for me as would feed me for a week; Michael O'Driscoll's wife had done the same for him; we took our lunch baskets from the boat, laid them before the hungry man, and left him to help himself while we were landing the meal.[2]

Arriving back the following day at Sherkin, O'Donovan Rossa found the once hungry man dead. The food that they had left him prior to their departure had been too much.

At Cape Clear, the relief party were met by a local Catholic priest, Fr Collins. The relief team stored the meal at the priest's home and distributed food to the starving masses. By order of the Board of Guardians, the distribution of the food was under a strict ration of no more than three and a half pounds of meal per person. Distributing the food and having stayed loyal to the Board of Guardians' ration instruction, the relief effort was left with 100 lbs of meal. This was again stored in Fr Collins' house, for the next event of food distribution. The priest was determined to show the relief team the horror and destitution of Cape Island. Taking them on a tour of the locality, they were evidently moved by what they saw. Collins took O'Donovan Rossa to one of his parishioners, a young woman who lived inside the cleft of a large rock. To his horror, O'Donovan Rossa, after following Collins inside on his hands and knees, found the woman lying on flagstones and covered in light heather, making a makeshift blanket to keep her warm. This woman was too cold and hungry to move. An equally poor 'neighbour' of hers had collected meal for her from the relief team, but she was unable to cook it. Fr Collins pleaded with O'Donovan Rossa to give her some more food, and he was inclined to agree with the priest, issuing her with an unauthorised stock of meal. Leaving the island he recalled:

> Father Collins accompanied us to the other end of the island to take the boat for Sherkin. The walk was about three miles. We entered many houses on the way. Some of them had flags for doors – the wooden doors having been burnt for firing. In one house were five or six children; one of them was dead – evidently died from starvation. I reported that case of death to the first coroner I could communicate with when I reached the mainland; and inquest was held and the coroner's jury brought in a verdict of: 'Death from starvation.'[3]

Returning to Skibbereen, O'Donovan Rossa found himself in trouble with the Board of Guardians. The largest owner of land on Cape Clear, John Wrixon Beecher, had complained that in giving extra meal to the starving, O'Donovan Rossa had exceeded his brief, had violated the trust of the Poor Law System and had been in breach of its rules and regulations. Beecher insisted that O'Donovan Rossa was not fit to be a temporary relief officer, that he should be discharged from his position and should not be paid for the weeks of service he provided. Beecher also proposed that O'Donovan Rossa should pay for the extra meal, which he had distributed beyond the ration set, from his own pocket. Without O'Donovan Rossa's consent or knowledge, he was relieved of his duties and replaced. Furious with his treatment, he defended his actions to the Board of Guardians and the Poor Law Commissioners in Dublin, citing how he was not prepared to allow the people to starve. He further suggested that the real reason why he lost his job was not because he distributed greater levels of food than he was allowed to do, but because he reported the death of a child due to starvation rather than keeping it a secret.

At the end of 1860, John O'Mahony, the founder of the Fenian Brotherhood, arrived in Ireland. O'Mahony's visit was organised clandestinely for fear of arrest. O'Mahony was born near Mitchelstown, County Cork and was eager to revisit the province of his birth. It was decided by what remained of the local organisation of the Phoenix Society/IRB in Skibbereen that O'Mahony would be welcomed to the community. It had been arranged that the Fenian leader would be picked up at Roscarbery and then taken to Skibbereen where he would meet the local IRB and discuss the state of West Cork and Fenianism in the aftermath of the crushing Phoenix arrests. Before arriving in Ireland in 1860, O'Mahony had called upon Stephens in Paris, where the IRB chief was hiding since the Phoenix arrests in 1858, and it was on his initiative that Stephens returned home to Dublin to begin to reorganise the revolutionary movement in the spring of 1861. There was an understanding between Stephens and O'Mahony that the Fenians would supply the IRB with 5,000 soldiers and 50,000 rifles and muskets. Stephens agreed to this on an understanding that no insurrection would be attempted against the British Administration without this Irish-American support. Touring the country and visiting his sister in County Tipperary, O'Mahony eventually arrived in Rosscarbery. The Fenian leader entered the town on an early form of public transport, known as Bianconi's Long Car. Greeted by O'Donovan Rossa, Dan McCarthy and Morty Moynahan, he was then taken to Skibbereen where he was received as a returning hero by the local IRB. Listening to O'Mahony speak of the idea of a republican government, O'Donovan Rossa was greatly impressed by his style, virtue and principles. He regarded O'Mahony as one of the finest Irishmen that he had the pleasure of meeting, and describing the Fenian leader he claimed that: 'He made the impression on me that he was a man proud of his name and of his race. And I liked him for that.'[4]

While O'Mahony was in Ireland, back in America, Terence Bellew MacManus a veteran of the 1848 Rebellion, originally from County Fermanagh, had died in San Francisco. Buried in Calvary Cemetery, San Francisco, it was decided by the Fenian Brotherhood that he should be exhumed and buried in Ireland. This decision was based on a calculation that the MacManus funeral could galvanise the Fenian base in Ireland and prove a means to radicalise and educate the people as to the concept of republicanism as an alternative to British administration of Ireland. It also provided an opportunity to establish a cult of the Dead Rebel, which in turn would provide an opportunity to recruit thousands of Irishmen to the cause of Fenianism, thus revitalising the movement. Arriving in New York City, prior to his departure to Ireland, Bellew

MacManus' remains were greeted by huge crowds of Irish-Americans, and his was one of the largest funeral cortege's seen in that city's history. As part of the planning of the Bellew MacManus funeral it had been decided that his remains were to be buried in Glasnevin Cemetery, Dublin. James Stephens, in his capacity as Chief Organiser of the Irish Republic, had personally written to O'Donovan Rossa, asking him to meet the body at Cork. Stephens also wanted O'Donovan Rossa to accompany MacManus's remains to Dublin, and the Cork Fenian eagerly accepted. O'Donovan Rossa took his place in the delegation accompanying MacManus' remains, and when the body arrived in Cork there were crowds of onlookers to witness the arrival. As the body came in quite a stir was caused when a little boy had been seen climbing up a nearby ships flagpole to remove an overlooking British Union flag. Briefly staying in Cork O'Donovan Rossa helped to put the MacManus' coffin on a train for Dublin and like the other delegates accompanying the remains, he was armed with a pistol. Each delegate had been given a pistol due to a rumour that some people within the IRB organisation would attempt to commandeer the body and use the seizure as a means to rally the people to a premature insurrection.

With the train moving apace from Cork en route to Dublin, there was a stop of seven minutes at Limerick Junction. Here, the anxiety was palpable for O'Donovan Rossa and the delegates accompanying the body. Knowing that the train was carrying Bellew MacManus, hundreds of onlookers had arrived on the platform and thronged fields surrounding the train station. In anticipation of this stop at Limerick Junction, Stephens had ordered local IRB men to be at the station to protect the body and the delegates in the event of an IRB mutiny. With anxiety growing, and the train due to depart Limerick Junction, Stephens shouted out of the window, calling on those assembled to kneel and pray out of respect to Bellew MacManus. The assembled crowd began to recite the Catholic *pater* and *ave* for the dead enmasse. As it was in Cork and Limerick Junction, in Dublin, hundreds of onlookers had turned out to see the remains of Bellew MacManus. O'Donovan Rossa was amazed by a city 'ablaze with torchlights', in the Young Irelander's honour.[5]

> A numerous body of persons, admirers of the deceased were present at the Knightsbridge [sic – Kingsbridge] terminus, and when the train moved toward the platform, the entire assemblage, with uncovered heads, awaited the opening of the van containing the deceased... The van containing the body was then opened, and the coffin, which

was encased in a heavy square wooden box, was removed on the shoulders of a number of men to the hearse prepared for it.[6]

All of this was in defiance to the Roman Catholic Hierarchy, who, led by Archbishop of Dublin Paul Cullen, had condemned the funeral and forbid Catholic clergy from taking part in any funeral service for the Young Irelander. Archbishop Cullen even went so far as to deny the use of Dublin's main Catholic church, the Pro-Cathedral, and was immovable in his opposition. Archbishop Cullen's opposition to the funeral was no surprise: he had earlier been a vehement opponent of the ecumenical Young Irelanders and as a member of the Roman Catholic Hierarchy, he was bound to oppose secret societies such as the Fenians. Considering that the archbishop would not allow MacManus' remains into any Catholic church in Dublin, the funeral committee had secured the lecture theatre of the Mechanics Institute on Lower Abbey Street, the present site of the Abbey Theatre, to house the body before burial. With the remains of Bellew MacManus now in Dublin City, O'Donovan Rossa took his place as one of the Cork delegates accompanying the body to Abbey Street:

> The hearse, preceded by six torch bearers, was immediately followed by Captain M.C. Smith and other members of the Cork and American committees. Then followed about 300 persons, on either side of whom torch bearers walked. The melancholy cortege proceeded along the Quays with a slow and solemn pace. The appearance of torches and the orderly bearing of those who followed the hearse was very impressive and imposing.[7]

In contravention to the Roman Catholic Hierarchy, the Fenians had arranged for people to come and pay their respects to MacManus while he lay in rest in the Mechanics Institute, and despite religious opposition, thousands of people visited the coffin.[8] Inside the Mechanics Institute, the room had been decked in black and the coffin had been placed on a table in the centre of the room, surrounded by a guard of honour, a standing crucifix at the top of the casket and two candles, providing a 'sombre and peculiar effect'.[9] At one o'clock on the 11 November, MacManus was brought from the Mechanics Institute on Abbey Street in a slow procession to Glasnevin Cemetery. Taking a meandering route, the procession passed by several sites associated with Irish republicans, including St Catherine's Church, Thomas Street, opposite where Robert Emmet had been executed in 1803. Taking over four hours, the funeral procession, followed by thousands of people, eventually arrived at Glasnevin Cemetery. Defying Archbishop Cullen's dictate that no Catholic priest was to preside over the funeral of Bellew MacManus, Fr Patrick Lavelle, a radical nationalist and respected priest from County Mayo, known as the Patriot Priest of Partry, delivered the funeral service. Fr Lavelle eulogised all who had attended the procession and had been involved with its organisation. He commented how the procession and the show of support for Bellew MacManus had 'told more forcibly on our hereditary foes and oppressors than any language which that any Irish Priest or patriot could pronounce'. Lavelle went further, and in a remarkable outburst from a Catholic priest, exclaimed: 'Yesterday, that sarcophagus was the symbol of Erin's grave. Tomorrow it will be her resurrection.'[10] Attending the funeral in Glasnevin, and listening attentively to Lavelle, O'Donovan Rossa could only agree, and left knowing that the funeral was laying the ground for the emergence of a serious challenge to British rule in Ireland: 'The MacManus funeral tended very much to increase the strength of the Fenian movement. Men from Leinster, Ulster, Munster, and Connaught met in Dublin who never met each other before. They talked of the old cause, and of the national spirit in their respective provinces, and each went back to his home, strengthened for more vigorous work.'[11]

In January 1863 there had been a rebellion in Poland against the Russian monarchy, and by March of that year, O'Donovan Rossa, with Morty Moynahan and Jerry Crowley, had set his mind to organising a sympathy rally with Polish insurgents in Skibbereen. Once again, O'Donovan Rossa was at odds with the local police, and alongside comrades within the IRB, he actively prepared republican banners and torchlights.[12] Becoming a key organiser of this rally through Skibbereen town centre that would involve marching bands and public speaking, O'Donovan Rossa believed that if a large number of people came out it could be perceived as 'a meeting of organised hostility against England', bringing the community together in a display of strength.[13] In preparation for the rally it had been decided that the marchers were to be properly stewarded, and handbills were produced calling on the people to show no grievance to any police officer observing the parade on the basis that they were Irishmen in uniform who were forced by circumstance to serve the Crown. While O'Donovan Rossa did not agree with this sentiment, the local IRB had produced the flyers for police dissemination so as to avoid potential problems. Learning of the plan to have a rally through the town, police numbers were consolidated and the marchers were confronted by a large body of police led by Charles O'Connell.

O'Connell immediately instructed the marchers to disperse and met with O'Donovan Rossa and the organising committee, demanding that they call upon their followers to disperse as they were disturbing the peace. Explaining to O'Connell that they were peaceful citizens in support of the Polish struggle against tyranny and had a right to peaceful protest, O'Connell read the Riot Act and declared their gathering to be illegal. O'Connell forced the marchers to remove their flags and torchlights but the gathering refused to leave, pointing out that they were now simply walking through the town centre. Allowing a boys band to play 'Garryowen' and march on, the police moved aside and allowed the marchers to hear an address by O'Donovan Rossa. Alongside Morty Moynahan, O'Donovan Rossa was later approached by O'Connell, who warned both men that they needed to readdress their conduct in Skibbereen and that on account of their earlier guilty plea, if they continued to act as they were doing they would be returned to jail. O'Donovan Rossa, as ever, remained unmoved, and noted to O'Connell that if he were arrested again on this occasion: 'They should first prove me guilty of the practices of drilling and of other things sworn against me at my trial; and that while in their eyes I was acting unlawfully, I did not care about their threats.'[14] Returning to his home, with the assistance of his friends, O'Donovan Rossa unfurled several republican flags from his chimney and windows.

Soon afterwards, O'Donovan Rossa made his way to Union Hall, a small fishing village in Cork. At Union Hall, O'Donovan Rossa continued to be a vocal republican, and engaging in republican songs and speeches, he came to the attention of the Local Resident Magistrate, John Limerick, who had let it be known that if he or anyone associated with radical politics returned to Union Hall they would be arrested. Never one to back down from danger, O'Donovan Rossa responded to Limerick's threat by gathering some twenty colleagues and inviting them to Union Hall the following Sunday:

The rumour spread through the country that we would go to Union Hall next Sunday again, and that rumour was met by another one from the English side of the house that if we went we would never come back alive; that we would be shot down like dogs. It would never do for us to be intimidated; our cause would lose prestige. Sunday morning came, and after mass and breakfast some twenty or thirty of us from Skibbereen were on the road toward Union Hall. Limerick, the magistrate, had sent out requisitions to all the surrounding police barracks, calling the police to Union Hall that day, and on Sunday morning the police were marching in from Ross, Drinagh, Leap, Drimoleage, Ceharagh, Skibbereen, Glendore and Castletownsend. War and rumours of war were in the air, and the people the country around, seeing the armed police marching on the several roads toward Union Hall, followed them into the little city. The Men from Ross brought a band of music with them. They crossed the bay from Glendore in boats, and as the boats approached the quay at Union Hall Limerick, the magistrate, stood there and forbade them to land. I stood alongside of Limerick and told the men not to be driven back by such petty tyranny as this. That this was Irish soil and they had as good a right to tread it as Limerick had. Patrick and James Donovan, who are now in New York, steered their boat into shallow water and leaped ashore; the other men in the boat leaped after them. The bandsmen went to the house of Father Kingston and remained there for a short time.[15]

Limerick ordered that all the pubs in Union Hall were to be immediately shut by police. This was undertaken with a marked perception that Fenians in the locality would have made for local pubs. One local pub they went to was owned by O'Donovan Rossa's aunt, Mrs Collins. Learning that the Fenian gathering was in her pub, Limerick directed police to meet with Mrs Collins. She refused to remove her nephew, however, but fearing Limerick would withhold her licence to sell alcohol, and thus ruin her business, O'Donovan Rossa and his gathering left the pub. Limerick read the Riot Act and the police, with fixed bayonets, engaged in a scuffle with the Fenians. While there were no arrests, some of O'Donovan Rossa's friends were fined or lost their jobs when news of the Union Hall scuffle became known.

Life was getting increasingly hot for O'Donovan Rossa in Skibbereen and even if he were arrested the government did not need to prove any accusations against him because of his earlier guilty plea. With his business destroyed because of his politics as the more affluent customers stopped shopping with him, while landlords put pressure on their tenants not to do any business with him, O'Donovan Rossa decided to make for America, and in 1863, left with friends Dan Hallahan, William McCarthy, Simon Donovan, John O'Gorman and Jerrie O'Meara aboard the trans-Atlantic steamer *The City of Edinburgh*.

Leaving on Fenian business, he left Eileen in Ireland to take care of their son, Stephens; he had intended for his family to join him later.

Arriving in America on 13 May, O'Donovan Rossa appreciated America. He had arrived at New York Harbour and taking in a view of the bustling metropolis, he contrasted its urbanity with its rural hinterland. Looking at the Staten Island Hills, which at this point could still be seen, he commented how they reminded him of his beloved Cork.[16] Despite the beauty of America, however, he had entered a society in the midst of a brutal civil war. Within a month of his arrival, New York City had erupted into violent race riots as white immigrants, a good many of whom were Irish, attacked African-Americans as part of a movement which sought to protest President Lincoln's Draft Bill, conscripting men between the ages of 20 to 45 into the Union Army. Many poorer Irish resented conscription and increasingly turned their anger on Lincoln's Republican Party and African-Americans, both of whom they blamed for the Civil War. Beginning on 13 July 1863, many Irish looted the New York homes of wealthy republicans, burned down a home for African-American orphan children and killed a number of African-Americans, a good many of whom were found lynched from lampposts. Lasting for four days, the draft riots resulted in the death of 1,000 people and left New York economically weakened. An eyewitness to the fighting on the streets, O'Donovan Rossa was appalled by the rioting and was horrified by the behaviour of the Irish community. O'Donovan Rossa witnessed looting and unbridled violence, recalling: An old man remonstrated with one of the wreckers, and was struck and thrown down. I went to take up the fallen man, and the man who struck him pulled a pistol out of his pocket and put it to my face. 'Oh' said I. 'I'm only doing what you yourself would do if you saw a poor man struck down by a young, hearty man such as you are.' My comrades came around me, and the fellow did not pull the trigger of his pistol.[17]

Settling in Brooklyn, at No. 226 Schermerhorn Street, he lived with a relative, Timothy Donovan, who had emigrated to America in 1836. He now witnessed the spectacle of the Union soldiers parading and drilling or relaxing in tents. Meeting with John O'Mahony, he found the majority of the Fenian Brotherhood had enlisted as soldiers in the Union Army and took solace in a perspective that as the Irish in America were training as soldiers, 'they might be better able to fight the battles of Ireland against England'.[18] With

O'Mahony, he visited armouries, drill rooms and meeting places of the Fenian Brotherhood. Aside from his political duties, O'Donovan Rossa also went into business with his cousin, Denis Donovan, and ran a saloon selling imported Irish whiskey and stout to the thriving Irish-American community in New York. Establishing their business at the corner of Madison Street, it was noted that his name was proudly displayed over the door. Around the same time he had also applied for naturalised American citizenship, and coming before the Court of Common Pleas in New York, he declared his intention for American citizenship.

O'Donovan Rossa also used the opportunity of his move to America to visit his mother Nellie, who he had not seen since she had emigrated to America in the late 1840s. Nellie had been living in Philadelphia with O'Donovan Rossa's brother and when he had visited her, arriving at ten o'clock in the evening, she did not know who he was. Identifying himself, she still disbelieved her son. Rossa then directed her to a scar on his head, which he received in his youth, and feeling the scar, Nellie broke down crying and embraced her child. Reminiscing about the past and learning of the present, Nellie and Rossa stayed up all night talking and crying; he recalled that in the years since he had last seen his mother she had become a tragically changed woman who looked as old as his grandmother: 'She was nothing more than a sorry caricature of the tall, straight, handsome woman with the hooded cloak, that was photographed, and is still photographed, in my mind as my mother.'[19]

O'Donovan Rossa moved back to Brooklyn after staying with his mother for a week and resumed his duties with the Fenian Brotherhood. He also had the occasion of meeting with Thomas Francis Meagher at New Jersey in the company of O'Mahony, who he claimed had introduced Meagher into the Fenian Brotherhood. Meagher left a favourable impression upon O'Donovan Rossa, and the young Irishman found him to hold a deep interest in Irish affairs. That evening he had travelled with O'Mahony to New York City where he was introduced to Colonel Michael Corcoran, a Sligo-born commander of the 69th New York Regiment, who was hosting a gathering for senior officers within the Fenian Brotherhood. O'Donovan Rossa recalled how all gathered had toasted Ireland and the Irish Republic.[20] Later on, O'Donovan Rossa made the company of William O'Shea, a friend of his from Bantry who had been charged during the Phoenix Trials in 1859. O'Donovan Rossa lamented that he did not have enough time with O'Shea, who was killed shortly afterwards in the American Civil War. Another friend that he had met in America was Michael O'Brien. Originally from Cork, they had been friends while living in Ireland and met again in America. O'Brien told O'Donovan Rossa that he intended to join the Union Army, and O'Donovan Rossa tried to dissuade him, O'Brien argued that he needed military training, and fighting for the United States was the best way to achieve this. Unable to dissuade O'Brien from joining the Union Army, Rossa accompanied him to enlist and watched as he was measured, recorded and sworn in. While waiting on his friend, Rossa was continually asked whether he would consider enlistment within the army, on each occasion, he refused. Waving O'Brien off after his initial enlistment, O'Donovan Rossa would never see his friend again: while surviving the Civil War, Michael O'Brien would be executed in 1867 as a Manchester Martyr with William Allen and Michael Larkin, in the first political executions since Robert Emmet. He took his place within the great pantheon of Irish Nationalist Heroes. Michael O'Brien was not the only friend O'Donovan Rossa lost while in America. In the course of his visit he had learned that Eileen, his wife, had died in Ireland on 9 July 1863. The fact that she had died while he was in America left O'Donovan Rossa distraught. His grievance was compounded by the fact that he could not be with his son Stephens, who had been given to the temporary care of the Buckley's. Returning to Ireland immediately he gave up all plans of settling in America. Throughout the remainder of his life, O'Donovan Rossa did not like to talk about Eileen. Her death, like that of Nora, continued to greatly affect him. Eileen was buried at Castlehaven; Stephens was taken into the care of his maternal grandmother. For a second time he was a widower.

4

THE IRISH PEOPLE AND THE TRIAL OF O'DONOVAN ROSSA

In 1863, the IRB began to publish its own newspaper called *The Irish People*. In quite an audacious move, the IRB had established the newspaper at No. 12 Parliament Street, within walking distance of Dublin Castle, the British Headquarters. The establishment of the newspaper was enthusiastically supported by James Stephens as a propaganda medium and to disseminate Fenian ambitions. The establishment of the newspaper was a calculated risk, however, considering it would bring attention to the IRB.[1] At the time, O'Donovan Rossa recalled that there was much consultation over the newspaper's establishment, with many leading figures fearing it could be 'injurious rather than serviceable to the society'.[2] He remembered how those who had supported the newspaper argued it was a practical necessity and apart from the desire to spread the Fenian ideal, the establishment of the newspaper was also grounded in an urgent need to raise funds so that the IRB would not be entirely reliant on the Fenian Brotherhood. He also recalled how others had suggested that a Fenian newspaper could become a means of offering an alternative perspective to the moderate nationalism of the dominant nationalist paper, *The Nation*, owned by A. M. O'Sullivan. O'Donovan Rossa agreed with the establishment of a newspaper, and while in America he received an invitation from Stephens to come to Dublin and act as the newspaper's business manager. Eagerly accepting the invitation to return to Ireland, he left America in July and moved permanently to Dublin. His role as business manager meant that he was responsible for the circulation and dispatching of the newspaper at home and abroad, paying the staff and ensuring that the paper arrived at newsagents promptly. Later he would write articles under the pseudonym 'Anthony the Jobbler' and produce poetry, such as his famous 'The Soldier of Fortune'. He wrote several leading articles for the newspaper including 'Do-nothings', 'As good as any when the time comes', 'The first man to handle a pike' and 'The martyr nation'. The latter article, 'The martyr nation', gives a good example of O'Donovan Rossa's beliefs at the time of writing:

> The fact that the Irish people are being today destroyed – some of them in soul and body stares us in the face ... instead of flying, we believe it to be our duty to remain in the old land, face the evil, and meet the destroyer with his own weapons ... we do not contemplate Ireland Catholic or Protestant – we contemplate her free and independent; and we extend the love and fellowship, to everyman, of every class and creed who would endeavour to make it so.[3]

O'Donovan Rossa was joined at the newspaper by Thomas Clarke Luby, who functioned as the newspaper's proprietor; John O'Leary and Charles Kickham who were editors; and James O'Connor as book-keeper. These men effectively formed a secret, central committee within the Fenian executive.[4] Other members of the IRB working for the newspaper included Denis Dowling Mulcahy and John Haltigan.

Registering the newspaper on 31 May 1863, its first issue was published on 28 November of that year and consisted of sixteen pages and cost three pence stamped or two pence unstamped. In America, one reader was so enthralled by *The Irish People* that he sought to congratulate Irishmen for producing such a medium, and writing a letter to the newspaper, he commended its staff. Saluting the team behind *The Irish People*, but only O'Donovan Rossa was signalled out by its author, the American felt that by placing the management of the newspaper in O'Donovan Rossa's hands, 'we may judge that the tone of the paper will be one of uncompromising loyalty of the only kind that should pass current among true Irishmen'.[5] As suggested by the American correspondent, the tone of the newspaper was uncompromisingly republican and mirrored Fenian political ambition and ideology, setting itself the task of becoming the organ of the IRB. It examined the American Civil War and detailed the activities of the Fenian Brotherhood in America. It was never reticent in its nationalist views, even declaring in one article the wish for 'the liberation of Ireland from the yoke of England'.[6] The newspaper was decidedly in favour of a democratic republic and advocated the principle of Irish independence. As to how this was to be achieved, in common with Fenian ideology, the newspaper rejected constitutionalism and carried an article noting 'true national independence never was and never will be anywhere achieved save by the sword'.[7] Representing British rule within Ireland as the alien, the newspaper claimed that 'enslaved' people had the right to achieve their national independence.[8] In the same vain, the following year a further edition used more aggressive language, commenting how 'another Patrick's day has passed and Ireland is still in chains'.[9]

The newspaper was equally anti-clerical and decidedly secular; this was particularly noticeable with the writing of Charles Kickham. The newspaper argued that many within the Roman Catholic priesthood, and particularly amongst the hierarchy, were 'West Britons', contented with the established order.[10] In April 1864, the newspaper had condemned the Catholic Church in the most vocal terms and had signalled out the influential Archbishop of Dublin, Dr Paul Cullen, who had earlier denounced Fenianism, describing the Archbishop as 'an individual enemy of Irish liberty'.[11] Later that year, *The Irish People* published a letter which commented on 'the propensity of the priesthood to tyranny,' and denounced the Catholic Clergy as 'a serious obstacle' to advanced nationalism.[12] This marked anti-clericalism hurt the business strategy of the newspaper as the Clergy strenuously piled pressure on its agents within several of its dioceses, making it the case that retailers were forced to withdraw its sale for fear of clerical denunciation.

Within a year of the newspaper's establishment, O'Donovan Rossa had married Mary Jane Irwin, who he had met at a wake. Mary was originally from Clonakilty in County Cork; her family, similar to the Buckleys, had earlier been opposed to the relationship which forced the couple to get engaged in secret. Her parents, Maxwell and Margaret, had felt that O'Donovan Rossa was too old for their daughter and was burdened by a large family and a continual police interest in his career. Her father, who was a veteran of the 1848 Rebellion, was also horrified to learn that O'Donovan Rossa was scheduled to make for England before his wedding on business of James Stephens and had insisted on bringing the wedding forward. Accompanied by James Hopper, Stephens' brother-in-law, he had sought to get a licence for his marriage from his church in Skibbereen, but on account of his politics, the priest found he could not give him his license. The priest argued with O'Donovan Rossa, citing the fact that he would have to come to confession and as a member of a secret society, he could not give him absolution unless he renounced Fenianism. Eventually unable to secure a formal licence from the church, he announced that he had not been to confession and had not met the Church's requirements for marriage. He then left for Cork City.

Arriving in Cork City he had speculated that he could get confession from a priest who did not know him. The priest, however, had a suspicion about his politics and asked him if he belonged to a secret society, where Rossa accordingly told him he belonged to a movement 'sworn to fight for Ireland's freedom'. His confessor refused to give O'Donovan Rossa absolution on account of his membership, and before leaving the confession box he angrily told the priest: 'I do not want absolution for it…. Tis for my sins I seek absolution, not for my virtues.'[13] Unable to receive confession and a formal licence he made for Clonakilty, where he found that Mary Jane's father had relented in his opposition to the marriage. As at Skibbereen and Cork, however, there were more difficulties with the Church, as the priest, Fr Leader, would not marry the couple, stressing that O'Donovan Rossa needed to see the Bishop before the priest could relent. As he needed to leave for England on Fenian business the following day, he could not consent to a meeting with the Bishop and threatened to marry Mary Jane in Cork City, which Fr Leader felt would set a bad example for local girls, as she was leaving the parish with an unmarried man. Eventually forcing an order for the marriage from the Curate of the parish, the couple were married in the Parish Hall on 22 October 1864 and set off for England on what O'Donovan Rossa termed 'a honeymoon conspiracy tour'.[14]

Spending a month in Britain, O'Donovan Rossa and his new wife travelled through Liverpool, Blackburn, Manchester, Edinburgh and Glasgow. Recalling his travels as 'the honeymoon life of an Irish traveling conspirator',[15] he met with Irish centres throughout Irish hamlets and districts. Returning to Ireland from Scotland, O'Donovan Rossa made a tour of Belfast and then returned to Dublin with Mary Jane. Mary Jane was an active poet and contributed regularly to *The Irish People*, using the pseudonym, *Cliodhna*. Mary Jane was a soul mate for the twice-widowed O'Donovan Rossa and mirrored his love of songs, poetry and politics. Within their family life they had endearing nicknames for each other, with O'Donovan Rossa calling his wife 'Mollis', an Irish language term of endearment, and Mary referring to him by the sobriquets of Dear, Cariss or Rossa.[16] Writing a poem about her husband, Mary Jane recalled how:

When first he called me 'Mollis,' he sighed,
And told me he loved one –
One other who was already his bride,
And I should love her for him – I cried;
Then he told me that other was Erin,

53

Oh! But my love is fair to see!
And, Erin, his fairness is all to thee –
Strong with a lion's strength is he,
And gentle with doveling's gentleness he,
My loved and Thine, Oh! Erin.

She was also a republican and staunchly supported her husband's involvement
in the IRB; she soon became a regular acquaintance of the secret central
committee and of James Stephens. On account of her gender, Mary Jane was
not entitled to membership, but she was active within the movement and
regularly delivered and hid messages. Like many of the women associated with
the IRB in the late nineteenth century, her involvement within republican
politics was brushed aside within historiography and lost in the passage of
time. According to John Devoy, women like Mary Jane were instrumental to
the success of the evolution of the movement in Ireland, asserting:

> They took no pledge, but were trusted by the men without one, were
> the keepers of important secrets, travelled from point to point bearing
> important messages... Not one woman betrayed a secret, proved false
> to the trust reposed in her, or by carelessness or indiscretion was
> responsible for any injury to the cause. It was a fine record for Irish
> womanhood.[17]

In March 1864, Pierce Nagle had been appointed to *The Irish People* as a
part-time paper folder, making parcels for agents and suppliers. He had been
vouched for by Denis Dowling Mulcahy and had worked at St Lawrence's
Chapel, Dublin, and was a teacher of English at the Mechanics Institute. Nagle,
however, was working for Dublin Castle as an informer, handled by Sub-
Inspector Hughes and Daniel Ryan of the Dublin Metropolitan Police and
their intelligence unit, G-Division. Nagle was a walk-in informant and had
approached Ryan as to the potential of working within Fenianism to recover
good and reliable intelligence. He had warned Ryan, he later claimed, 'about
the danger of Fenianism and that the government ought to prevent it'.[18]
Despite having a man within *The Irish People*, Nagle was, initially, of little use.
For all means and purposes he was a low-ranking Fenian activist who did not
enjoy the confidence of the secret central committee at *The Irish People* and
only worked two days a week at the newspaper. While Nagle could inform
the Castle of who was behind the paper, and of conversations he had had

with the newspaper's management, his information was of little value. He had even been dismissed from the newspaper by James O'Connor, but upon the insistence of Thomas Clarke Luby, he was reinstated. Dublin Castle were eager to keep him on their payroll, however, and evidence exists that he was paid £41 by the State for a little over a year's work. While Nagle's information was insignificant, it did provide a means for the Castle to bring a low-intensity counter strategy against *The Irish People,* and learning of who was on its staff, they began a process of detailed surveillance of O'Donovan Rossa and his colleagues. From this they sought to build up an extensive profile of the Fenian movement. While *The Irish People* was operating and Nagle was keeping the Castle abreast of developments within the newspaper, the American Civil War was coming to a bloody conclusion. Irish-Americans, who were now demobilised, returned to their earlier activities within the Fenian Brotherhood and pressed for a rebellion in Ireland. To meet the demand of his members, on 10 August 1865 John O'Mahony had announced The Final Call of the Fenian Brotherhood, and this had dispatched hundreds of Irish-Americans to Ireland in what was increasingly looking like preparations for a rebellion. O'Donovan Rossa remembered that as a result of the Final Call, he met with hundreds of Irish-Americans including Colonel Michael Kirwin, and General Denis Burke. He was later introduced to Colonel Thomas Kelly, a native of Galway who had fought in the Union Army during the Civil War, and would become the future leader of the IRB, and General Frank Millen, a veteran of the Mexican Army, who became a key informant within the British counter-Fenian movement the following year.

In July 1865, Stephens had again sent O'Donovan Rossa to America where he was entrusted with dispatches for O'Mahony, James Stephens, Thomas Kelly and General Frank Millen. He sailed for America aboard the *SS Cuba,* and when he arrived in America he witnessed the continuous demobilisation of soldiers and remembered how he knew many of them through the Fenian Brotherhood. Listening to the accents of the soldiers as he waited for a train from Boston to New York City, he commented how someone unfamiliar with the American Civil War, on hearing the men speak, could be forgiven for thinking it to have been 'an Irish war'.[19] Finally meeting O'Mahony in New York, the Fenian leader questioned O'Donovan Rossa as to Irish politics and the current state of Ireland. Far removed from the realities of Irish life, O'Mahony asked him to stay in America and work as a representative of the Fenian Brotherhood. O'Mahony told O'Donovan Rossa that he was constantly asked about Ireland and the IRB but he could never adequately respond to his inquisitors. Resisting O'Mahony's appeals, O'Donovan Rossa announced that his place was in Ireland, and despite the fact that his life would be significantly better in America, if a rebellion took place in Ireland he could not bear to miss it. Recalling his conversation with the Fenian leader, in 1885, he wrote: 'If I stayed in America and the fight took place in Ireland. All the water between here and Ireland would not wash me from the stain of cowardice.'[20] Before returning to Ireland, O'Mahony asked O'Donovan Rossa to accompany Fenian activists PJ Meehan, P. W. Dunne, and his sister, to Ireland.

Meehan had been given a letter by O'Mahony that requested the return of O'Donovan Rossa to America. Boarding the SS Cuba for a second time, O'Donovan Rossa, under the alias of Mr O'Donnell, recommended that Meehan passed O'Mahony's letter to Dunne's sister. Dunne would rather not include his sister in the conspiracy, however, and had argued that the dispatches would not be found as they were stitched into the sole of one of Meehan's slippers. While Meehan had smuggled the dispatches into Ireland, he had lost them when he went to deliver them to James Stephens. Having lost the letters, there was, as a result, an internal tribunal on Meehan as many within the secret Executive Council believed he had lost the letters intentionally. O'Donovan Rossa provided the defence for Meehan and argued it was an unintentional mistake; Meehan was found innocent of the charges, but unbeknownst to the committee, and to Meehan, the letters had fallen into the hands of the British State.

Growing progressively anxious as to Fenian activity, it was by now inevitable that the British Government was going to move against Fenianism. Turning to Nagle, his handlers stressed upon him the necessity of finding clear and accurate information as to what the IRB planned. On this occasion, Nagle provided value for money: within one month of O'Mahony's Final Call, Nagle produced a letter signed by James Stephens stating 'there is no time to be lost. This year – and let there be no mistake about it – must be the year of action. I speak with a knowledge and authority to which no other man could pretend; and I repeat the flag of Ireland – of the Irish Republic – must this year be raised.'[21] Nagle had received the letter from a Clonmel Fenian who was the worse for alcohol after he had called to the offices of the Irish People. The production of the letter delighted Ryan, considering that Nagle, as an informant, could not be used for evidence against the IRB. Taking the letter to Dublin Castle, Ryan demanded immediate action from his superiors lest they lost the opportunity to move against the Fenians. The letter unnerved the Castle so much that the Irish Privy Council was summoned and agreed to suppress *The Irish People* and arrest leading Fenian activists.

On the evening of Friday 18 September 1865, Dublin Castle authorised the suppression of *The Irish People*. The task was to be carried out by the B Division of the Dublin Metropolitan Police, assisted by Daniel Ryan, Nagle's handler in G-Division. The police had placed a cordon around Parliament Street and quickly cleared the area of all civilians. Having done so, G-Division detectives approached the offices of *The Irish People* and there was a standoff of sorts when the occupiers of the office refused to allow them enter the premises. Eventually forcing in the door, the G-men stormed the building, where they found a number of Fenians, including Pierce Nagle. At the time of the suppression, O'Donovan Rossa had been drinking at No.82 Dame Street, and had learned of the suppression through a colleague, Patrick Kearney. Kearney and Rossa mulled over the possibility of fighting the police, but O'Donovan Rossa urged caution as they had few weapons with which to take on the G-men. O'Donovan Rossa left for the offices of *The Irish People*, and searching his pockets, he removed some letters and a pistol which could incriminate him when he would be eventually searched. Arriving in Parliament Street, he was immediately arrested and taken through Dublin Castle to Chancery Lane Police Station. G-Division detectives then smashed up the printing press, seized the typeset and forensically searched the building, including the pulling of floorboards and chimneys – nothing was to be left for granted. Newspapers, legers and bank books were also seized and taken to the headquarters of the B Division in the nearby lower Castle Yard, within the Dublin Castle complex. Finally, the state issued a freeze on the newspaper's bank account, which was a stifling blow to the Fenian movement. *The Irish People* newspaper had come to an abrupt end.

O'Donovan Rossa had lived at No. 62 Camden Street, within a stone's throw of *The Irish People* offices, and had previously given his wife, Mary Jane, instructions to destroy any materials that connected him to Fenianism if he were arrested. When her husband had been arrested she had been packing his bag, as O'Donovan Rossa was due to leave for America on a Fenian errand ordered by James Stephens. Mary Jane was heavily pregnant and she was due to leave with her husband the following day for Cork as he departed for America. She had learned of his arrest through James O'Callaghan, who had been sent to the O'Donovan Rossa home to clarify that she had no documents which could subvert the IRB and be used against her husband. O'Donovan Rossa had given her a letter from James Stephens for Fenian activists in Carlow. The activists had requested his presence at the Ballybar Races in the first week of September, but Stephens had forbidden Rossa from going and instructed him to go to America instead. On O'Callaghan's suggestion, Mary Jane burned the letter; shortly afterwards her house was raided. Overall, ten individuals including Thomas Clarke Luby, John O'Leary, Pierce Nagle and O'Donovan Rossa were arrested during the suppression of *The Irish People*. It was necessary that the state arrested Nagle with the others for reasons of cover and to protect his. However, O'Donovan Rossa's suspicions had been roused when the prisoners had asked to see their wives. The authorities declined, but O'Donovan Rossa commented that Nagle had been allowed to see his wife. He initially put this down to Nagle being friendly with a police officer, until he realised the real reason and became aware of the deception. The prisoners were charged with Treason Felony and attempting to levy war upon the Queen, but later their sentence was increased to High Treason, an offence punishable by death. On learning this, O'Donovan Rossa became convinced that he was going to be hanged by the state, and preparing himself for death, he recalled how he was ready to die, pledging to 'defy them to the bitter end'.[22] Eventually brought before a Magistrates Court, O'Donovan Rossa and his comrades were taken to Richmond Prison in the outer Dublin suburbs to await trial as prisoners on remand. He was concerned for Mary Jane and wrote her a letter suggesting she should leave for America. Explaining why she should emigrate, he suggested that her life in Ireland, due to his imprisonment, would be frightening: 'I would rather have you live there than die, or (what is much the same to you or me) be dependent upon anyone here.'[23]

Arriving at Richmond Prison, O'Donovan Rossa remembered his time in Cork Prison. He noted, however, that the experience in Dublin was far worse – he recalled that upon entry to the institution, 'they stripped me naked, took my clothes… I was told I would be allowed to pay for my board, but if I did not pay I should work'.[24] Once in prison, he was treated to a system of silence, supervision and separation, where prisoners were not allowed to speak to each other and were held in separate cells. He was allowed one hour of exercise in the prison yards, supervised by prison authorities. He recalled that 'the most rigid precautions were taken lest we should carry on any kind of conversation during this hour'.[25] As previously mentioned, O'Donovan Rossa was worried about Mary Jane's welfare, as well as that of his family. O'Donovan Rossa strongly believed that he was going to be convicted and sentenced to either imprisonment or execution, and in this vein recommended to Mary Jane the importance of taking the family to America. He concluded that while in

Ireland, there would be a vendetta against his family because of their convict father, and they would have a greater chance of survival in America within the Irish-American network. He told Mary Jane to use whatever resources she had to leave Ireland and suggested she come to Richmond Prison and collect his watch and chain for pawning. While Mary Jane resolved to go to America while he was in prison, she was determined to remain in Ireland for the duration of her husband's trial and actively played a leading role in the establishment of a Ladies Committee seeking the release of the arrested Fenian prisoners.

The committee had sought to bring popular attention to their case and argue on the behalf of their husbands and brothers. The committee effectively waged a propaganda campaign, albeit couched in terms of charity rather than politics, on behalf of the imprisoned Fenians through *The Irishman* newspaper. It had also functioned as a means of maintaining communication within the broader IRB organisation following the arrests, aided by the fact that the police were anxious not to question the women, believing such behaviour was 'very ticklish work'.[26] Commending the activities of the Ladies Committee, John Devoy later noted:

> In Ireland there was no regular organisation of Fenian women, but a large number of them worked as well as if they had been organised. They took no pledge, but were trusted by the men, were the keepers of important secrets, travelled from point to point bearing important messages, and were the chief agents in keeping the organisation alive in Ireland.[27]

On 28 October 1865 the committee released a statement entitled 'An Appeal to the Women of Ireland', holding that the prisoners were innocent of any crime 'even in the eye of English law'. The Ladies Committee asked whether Irishwomen could stand by and allow the families of the prisoners to fall into destitution.[28] Mary Jane worked as secretary to the Ladies Committee and developed a strong friendship with Letitia Frazier Luby and Eileen O'Leary, wife and sister of Thomas Clarke Luby and John O'Leary respectively. The Ladies Committee had hoped to establish branches throughout the city to actively campaign for the families of the prisoners and for the release of the imprisoned men. Membership was open to all women and the committee was defined as strictly non-political, although it did not 'seek to conceal our sympathies are wholly with the prisoners'.[29] Defining itself as a charitable organisation, the Ladies Committee boldly announced that: 'their [the Fenian prisoners] principles and aspirations were noble and unselfish. Many of them sacrificed their prospects in work to for Ireland's freedom'.[30] The ladies were successful in establishing an argument favourable to the prisoners and their families within the popular mentality, and *The Irishman* regularly published a list of subscribers to the fund. The subscriptions to the Ladies Committee, however, came from the poorer sections of society and regular donations were quite small. This necessitated several appeals and the organising of bazaars, raffles and rallies. The Ladies had also hoped to hold what they termed a *Grand National Fancy Fair and Concert in aid of the families of the State Prisoners.* The State, however, blocked the event, and refused to give the Ladies Committee permission to go ahead with the fair and concert. While the ladies could have continued with their Fair without the State's permission, considering the experience of police harassment, Mary Jane advised the cancellation of the event fearing 'the emptied Richmond and Kilmainham cells would have had promise of an overflow of habitants'.[31]

The Ladies Committee also faced the powerful influence of the Roman Catholic Hierarchy. As mentioned earlier, the Irish Clergy were staunchly opposed to Fenianism. With the arrests of the Fenian prisoners in 1865, the Catholic Church only hardened its position on the movement, lauding the British Government for its stern action. The Church also continued to regularly assail Fenianism through sermons and encyclicals. Archbishop Cullen, remaining dogged in his opposition to Fenianism, welcomed the arrest of O'Donovan Rossa and his colleagues, and the suppression of *The Irish People.* Producing an encyclical, which was read at Masses and published in the newspapers, he stated:

They are said to have proposed nothing less than to destroy the faith of our people by circulating works like those of the impious Voltaire, to preach up socialism, to seize the property of those who have any, and to exterminate both the gentry of the country and the Catholic Clergy. Whatever is to be said of such fearful accusations – which we hope are only founded on vague report – it is too certain that the managers of the Fenian paper, called the *Irish People,* made it a vehicle for scandal, and circulated in its columns most pernicious and poisonous maxims ... it must be admitted, that for suppressing that paper the public authorities deserve the thanks and gratitude of all those who love Ireland, its peace and its religion.[32]

With the Church resolutely against the Fenian prisoners, the work of the Ladies Committee was incredibly difficult and despite early fundraising success, between January to June 1866, monthly subscription totals decreased from £270 to £30.

As a prisoner at Richmond Prison, O'Donovan Rossa rejected the silent treatment enforced upon the Fenian prisoners, not only were they a different category to ordinary prisoners, as prisoners on remand, he also argued that it undermined their defence. This objection was grounded in a consideration that as the prisoners were implicated with each other, the fact that they could not speak to each other meant that they could not prepare for Court together. O'Donovan Rossa became incredibly frustrated, and as he was processed as a prisoner he was asked his religion – deciding he would be difficult, and in an attempt to vent his frustration, when a prison warder asked him if he was Roman Catholic, he responded stating he 'was Irish not Roman', and refused to sign himself as Roman Catholic.[33] Aggravating his jailers, O'Donovan Rossa demanded that he be registered as an Irish Catholic and continued to refuse to sign a declaration professing that he was a Roman Catholic. After much argument, the authorities decided that he would be prevented from attending Catholic Mass while a prisoner until he relented. Bringing further attention on himself, O'Donovan Rossa then demanded that the authorities provide all the evidence they had to them as to why the prisoners were arrested so that they could prepare their defence. While the prisoners were eventually allowed to speak to one another, albeit in the company of their solicitor, the State remained obstinate in allowing them to see the evidence against them. It also increasingly became known amongst the prisoners that Nagle was an informer and would eventually provide evidence against them in Court.

James Stephens now hurriedly moved to prevent rebellion in 1865. His Executive Council had been obliterated and faced imprisonment – 1865 would not be the year of action. With a bounty of £200 on his head, the Chief Organiser of the Irish Republic ensconced himself in Sandymount, Dublin with Charles Kickham, Edward Duffy and Hugh Brophy. The suppression of *The Irish People* had greatly undermined the IRB and Cardinal Cullen had again denounced the movement with the most vocal of terms, holding that it would be a good thing for Ireland if Fenianism were to be eradicated from the country. *The Irish People* newspaper, he argued, was scandalous, preached socialism and 'circulated in its columns the most pernicious and poisonous maxims',[34] for the false education of the Irish people. Cullen continued to wax lyrical on the Fenian threat and held that the British government 'deserve the thanks of all who love Ireland, its peace and its religion'.[35] Within two months of the suppression of *The Irish People*, James Stephens was discovered and taken to Richmond Prison but with the help of two warders: John Breslin and Daniel Byrne, Stephens escaped from the prison. The Fenian network had supplied the warders with copied keys designed by Dublin Fenian, Michael Lambert, an instrument maker and jeweller. Breslin and Byrne helped Stephens climb over the prison wall, where he was met by John Devoy and his lieutenant, Thomas Kelly. O'Donovan Rossa remembered the night of Stephens' escape. That day, with his solicitor, he had met with John O'Leary, Thomas Clarke Luby and Edward Duffy. Duffy had whispered to O'Donovan Rossa that Stephens was leaving the prison that evening, and seeing Stephens' escape as a victory for the Fenian movement, Rossa had tried to stay awake to hear. Eventually falling asleep he was woken up by a prison guard who was frantically checking his cell to confirm if he were still in custody. At this, O'Donovan Rossa joyfully concluded that 'the bird had flown'.[36]

Following Stephens' escape from Richmond Prison, the government decided to move the Fenian prisoners to Kilmainham Gaol, in the Dublin countryside. To this effect it was decided that the newly built east wing of the Gaol would be used exclusively for Fenian prisoners. Instructing the Gaol Governor, Henry Price, of their plans, Dublin Castle insisted that Kilmainham was to become one of Ireland's most secure gaols in preparation for the arrival of the Fenian prisoners. To secure Kilmainham Gaol it was decided that each cell would be double-locked by means of bolts, hasps and padlocks. There were only two master keys to the locks and these were in the possession of the Gaol management. Twelve gates were placed within the prison corridors parallel to a body of armed sentries and soldiers stationed both at the prison and adjoining courthouse. When O'Donovan Rossa arrived at Kilmainham Gaol he was stripped naked, searched, given a prison uniform and number, and taken to a small cell. He had a number of papers which he intended to use for his defence to provide to his Counsel; these papers were seized by Governor Price upon entry and were not returned until his trial. Writing to Mary Jane, he had commented how he felt about the seizure of his papers, implying that the State was acting improperly against him. He insisted to his wife that he would kick up 'hells delights', in Court about Governor Price's behaviour.[37]

On 27 November 1865 a Special Commission was opened in Dublin to oversee the trial of the arrested Fenians. Further commissions were to take place in Cork and Limerick. In total, forty-six men including O'Donovan Rossa,

John O'Leary, Charles Kickham, George Archdeacon, Patrick Haybourne, George Gillis and William Francis Roantree were tried for their part in a Fenian conspiracy in Dublin. Of the forty-six, eleven were admitted bail. Despite his earlier belief that he would be hanged by the State, O'Donovan Rossa had come to terms with the fact that he would probably receive a life sentence. The judge presiding over the Special Commission was William Keogh, an erstwhile nationalist who had presided over Rossa's trial in 1859, despite previous assurances he would reject any official position offered him. The Fenian prisoners had been tried with Treason Felony by attempting to undermine British Rule in Ireland and were actively seeking foreign intervention in Ireland against the State. Nagle provided Crown evidence against the prisoners and taking his place within the witness box, sitting with his back to them, he explained what the Fenian society was. In his narrative the prisoners were involved in a conspiracy to 'overthrow the Queen's government in Ireland and when that was done the Republic was to be established'.[38] He detailed his connection with *The Irish People* newspaper and connected O'Donovan Rossa, John O'Leary, James O'Connor, Charles Kickham and Dowling Mulcahy with James Stephens. While he claimed not to have taken an oath to the IRB, Nagle admitted that he had personally sworn men into the conspiracy, and on one occasion he had visited Clonmel where he discovered that his comrades had initiated a secret means of arming themselves in preparation for rebellion. Nagle also detailed the secret nature of the Fenian cellular system, describing the alphabetical ranking order within Fenian circles. His narrative would be repeated throughout each of the individual trials.

O'Donovan Rossa's was the third trial to take place with Thomas Clarke Luby and John O'Leary preceding him. He was tried from 9 to 11 December 1865. In the case of O'Leary, it had been put to the court that O'Donovan Rossa had travelled to America in 1863 and this was ostensibly on Fenian business under the alias of Anthony O'Donnell. In O'Leary's trial the Crown Prosecution had argued that when O'Donovan Rossa had returned to Ireland he had arrived with two Americans under the name of Dunne and Meehan. The prosecution had also alluded to the dispatches which Meehan had earlier lost, and the shipping magnate and a police detective confirmed that O'Donovan Rossa had boarded the *SS Cuba* at Queenstown. Nagle, in his evidence against O'Leary, had confirmed the handwriting of O'Donovan Rossa in several letters, and claimed that Rossa had asked him about swearing in other Fenians. Nagle also hinted at the existence of a secret central committee within the Fenian executive, claiming that James Stephens, O'Donovan Rossa,

John O'Leary, Charles Kickham and James O'Connor regularly held meetings in a private room in the offices of *The Irish People* that ordinary members of staff were not allowed to attend.[39]

O'Donovan Rossa had no respect for the Court and believed the Commission to be a 'legal farce', which was intent on securing convictions by means of packed juries.[40] Brought before the Court, he was charged with being engaged in a treasonable conspiracy, which sought foreign intervention into Ireland. As a means of showing his disrespect for the Court, he had determined that he would extend his case for as long as possible, and recognising that he was going to be convicted, he had decided to make his trial, as one contemporary noted, 'a defiance of the British Government, a merciless exposure of its utterly unfair methods in conducting political trials and of the rottenness of his judicial system in Ireland'.[41] On the eve of his trial he had written to Mary Jane where he explained the course he was going to follow. O'Donovan Rossa lamented that he would probably be punished by the Court and this would result in the State taking its frustrations out on Mary Jane by blocking her from attending the Commission. O'Donovan Rossa feared his resolve would crumble without his wife and he would be 'deprived of the happiness of [Mary Jane] sitting beside me during my conviction'.[42] He also feared for the welfare of his children and implored Mary Jane to take care of them in his absence, holding: 'I have only to say to you what I said to you before. You are Father and Mother to them while you are alive and while I am dead to the world and you will do for them what you consider best…'[43]

Opening his trial, the Crown Prosecution argued that O'Donovan Rossa was on intimate terms with Clarke Luby, O'Leary, John O'Mahony, and most notoriously, James Stephens, the leader of Irish conspiracy. He held that articles would be produced indicating that the *Irish People* newspaper was seditious and constituted a distinct act of treason felony. O'Donovan Rossa, as the business manager, he argued, must be held accountable for the newspaper. O'Donovan Rossa commented how there was no criminal act with which he could be charged with. He was also determined to bring up allegations made against him in the case of John O'Leary. While not addressing the fact that he had travelled to America under an alias, he had claimed that his American visit was on business. He next addressed the fact that Governor Price had seized a number of papers relating to his defence and he was fearful that there was a possibility that they could be given to the prosecution. Keogh addressed the prosecution, who told him that they had not seen the papers, and summoning Price to court, the Governor argued that he had seized the papers under the rules of the prison. Ordering Price to hand over the documents to O'Donovan Rossa, the prisoner next asked Keogh if he had the right to speak to his fellow prisoners. This offer was declined, despite the fact that his name had been used in their trials and allegations were made against him. Postponing the case, O'Donovan Rossa was taken back to Kilmainham on remand. Returning back to Green Street Courthouse, he announced he would defend himself and did not require a legal team. He grounded this in the fact that he believed the court remained a charade and the jury had been packed to secure a conviction. Despite continued calls from Keogh that he was out of order, he announced that: 'I believe that this trial is a legal farce and I won't be a party to it by being represented by counsel.'[44]

O'Donovan Rossa, true to his earlier intention of making his trial a political theatre, began cross-examining witnesses, including Pierce Nagle. Throughout the course of the *Irish People* trials, Nagle had kept his back to the defendants – his former comrades. This had angered O'Donovan Rossa, who insisted that Nagle should face him as he questioned the erstwhile Fenian. Nagle and the prosecution had objected to this, and as a compromise, he was placed sitting with only the left side of his face directed at O'Donovan Rossa. From the dock, O'Donovan Rossa incessantly goaded Nagle. He had asked him if he had ever seen him administering oaths to anyone – Nagle could not confirm. He had asked him if he had seen anything in *The Irish People* offices which he believed constituted a threat to British rule in Ireland. Nagle responded as to how he had not seen anything but believed that they were engaged in dangerous conspiracy.[45] The prisoner next questioned Nagle as to handwriting and sought clarification as to entries allegedly sighed by O'Donovan Rossa that he had earlier confirmed. Questioning the character and attitude of Nagle, O'Donovan Rossa next asked the informer if he had any guilt as to his role in the imprisonment of men he had known. Nagle refused to answer. O'Donovan Rossa took this as a sign of guilt and asked him about Dowling Mulcahy, whom had got him the job at *The Irish People*, and Thomas Clarke Luby who fought to have him reinstated in his position when he had been discharged by James O'Connor. Judge Keogh interrupted O'Donovan Rossa and called his line of questioning out of order and asserted he was 'wasting the public's time'.[46] Sparring with Judge Keogh, O'Donovan Rossa retorted how 'twenty years is a long time and I want to use these few days as best I can'.[47] Keogh would increasingly become a figure of odium for O'Donovan Rossa throughout the duration of his trial. Levying accusations at Keogh, O'Donovan Rossa compared him to Lord Norbury, the infamous

Hanging Judge of the early nineteenth century who had sentenced the Irish rebel, Robert Emmet, to death in 1803.

O'Donovan Rossa next demanded to be allowed to look through all documents and publications that had been put against him. Initially, he examined a pamphlet produced by the Chicago Convention of the Fenian Brotherhood. In total the pamphlet consisted of eighty pages of small print, including the constitution of the Fenian Brotherhood. He did so to prove that it was irrelevant to his trial and it did not concern him. Judge Keogh was becoming more irritated with Rossa and accused him of wasting time, and that he would not tolerate much more. The Jury had equally pleaded with O'Donovan Rossa to allow them to deliberate on the pamphlet in private. To much laughter in the Court, one juror, breaking ranks, shouted up 'occupying so much time in reading what does not concern this case is enough to stir up an armed insurrection among the persons in court'.[48]

Having laboriously finished reading the Fenian pamphlet to the Jury, O'Donovan Rossa, as business manager of *The Irish People*, charged with publishing the newspaper, noted he had a right to read the newspaper to the Jury. This involved a file including every edition of *The Irish People* ever published between 1863-65. One contemporary recalled 'horror set upon the faces of the Judges, Jurymen, Sheriffs, Lawyers [and] turnkeys'.[49] As a compromise he agreed that he would not read the advertisements. Shifting through the *Irish People*, O'Donovan Rossa had sought to obstruct the court case. Judge Keogh continuously intervened in his readings of articles, many of which he forbade from being read to the Court as he believed it was a dissemination of treasonable ideals. He also directed any reporters in the Courtroom not to transcribe or paraphrase any of the articles which O'Donovan Rossa had read. With the trial continuing until six o'clock in the evening, O'Donovan Rossa, having spoken for eight hours at length, asked Judge Keogh to postpone the case until the following day. Keogh, knowing that O'Donovan Rossa was growing tired, refused to postpone, and directed that the trial continue throughout the evening. Nearing the end of his appeal to the Jury, O'Donovan Rossa closed the file containing the editions of *The Irish People*, and holding it in his hands; he animatedly made a final appeal to the Jury:

And now, gentlemen, a few words. I say that indictment has been brought against me; and that man [pointing to Judge Keogh] has been placed on that bench to try me; and if there is one among you with a spark of honesty in his breast, he will resent such injustice. The article has been brought against me in the indictment; and do you all believe that man on the bench is the proper man to try me? He has been placed there to convict me.[50]

Dramatically, O'Donovan Rossa flung the file containing *The Irish People* onto a nearby table, and announced: 'there, let the law take its dirty course'.[51]

On Wednesday 13 December 1865, Jeremiah O'Donovan Rossa was found guilty of treason and sentenced to life imprisonment. In summing up his case, Judge Keogh had pointed out that he had been arrested and imprisoned for conspiracy in 1859 and was regularly in contact with James Stephens and John O'Mahony. O'Donovan Rossa interrupted the Judge, announcing: 'I am an Irishman since I was born.'[52] Keogh had evidently had enough of O'Donovan Rossa and breaking from his speech, he addressed the prisoner personally, holding: 'He would not now waste words, by trying to bring your word to any sense of the crime of which you have been found guilty.' O'Donovan Rossa retorted 'You need not! It would be useless for you to try!'[53] Taken from the courtroom and down towards an underground passage, O'Donovan Rossa was recorded to have smiled at his sympathisers 'and walked with a light step from the dock'.[54] Shortly afterwards he wrote to his wife:

On the whole, Mollis, I am satisfied with the course I took. I hope you are too. With a view to public good I considered it a good one to adopt, and I believe that all who would sacrifice anything for the cause of country will approve of it... May God guard and strengthen you till we meet again...[55]

5

A PRISONER OF THE QUEEN

Despite the bravado of his trial, the thought of the sentence of life imprisonment weighed heavily on O'Donovan Rossa's mind. Not only was he separated from his heavily pregnant wife and family, he also understood the severe nature of the British Prison system under which he would have to comply. It was a militaristically disciplined system underlined by silence, supervision and separation. It also operated on a system of discipline devised in the 1840s by the prison reformer, Alexander Maconochie. Known as the Marks System, it had been established to 'uniformly subjugate all brought under its influences',[1] and undermined fixed sentences in favour of the potential for reduced punishment. This could be achieved through the accumulation of marks for good, disciplined behaviour and hard work. When a prisoner had accumulated enough marks, relative to the crime he had been imprisoned for, he could be released. Yet if the prisoner broke prison regulation, his marks were to be taken from him, and his sentence would revert to its original status with extra time. Within Victorian parlance, this was a currency of sorts which the prison authorities could use to penalise offenders and reward those who sought moral reform.

Mountjoy Prison was also organised on a strict system of silence and separation. This was grounded in the Victorian belief in the power of contemplation and repetitive thought about one's previous actions. It was hoped that through silence, the prisoner's resolve could be broken, and he would be forced to think about the crime which he had committed, ultimately facilitating his redemption through silent contemplation. In deference to this rule, prisoners were kept separated at all times; this included religious services where prisoners were placed into compartments within the Prison Chapel, allowing them to see only the Chaplain, rather than each other.

As a political prisoner, O'Donovan Rossa believed that once imprisoned, all the anger and hatred felt towards Fenianism which the state had exhibited would only be heightened. He also believed that the Marks System would not be used favourably against the Fenian prisoners, believing it only took the word of a prison guard to undermine its value. Expressing his fears to Mary Jane before he left Green Street Courthouse, he had the opportunity to write her a brief note in which he claimed to endure 'as much suffering as a man can endure bravely'.[2] As he finished his letter to Mary Jane, a combined force of soldiers, police and prison staff arrived and ushered him into a black van. Fearful of an escape, the state had surrounded the black van with mounted soldiers, while police sat on the outside. Leaving the Courthouse at speed, the van made for Mountjoy Prison on the nearby North Circular Road.

Arriving in the imposing institution, O'Donovan Rossa was led inside the prison and was taken to an administrative room. He was stripped naked and thoroughly searched. Examined by a surgeon, he was then washed and given a prison uniform consisting of flannel underpants, shirt, waistcoat, shoes, grey vest, jacket and trousers, a pair of stockings, and cap. He was then registered as a prisoner where he learned the prison rules and was informed that the right to write letters, which most prisoners had, was rescinded, as he was a political prisoner. O'Donovan Rossa began to vocally complain about the conduct of Judge Keogh at his trial but was silenced and was taken away to another room to be shaved. Here he was greeted by a number of prison staff who sat him in a chair and began gruffly shaving him. Starting with his beard, a jailer began to trim it with a scissors, and then moved to his hair. Soon after, the jailer was joined by a colleague with a razor who shaved off O'Donovan Rossa's beard and hair. Feeling despondent, O'Donovan Rossa sat in silence and obeyed the commands of his jailers. Having been shaved, O'Donovan Rossa was then taken to be photographed. He was placed sitting in a small chair and given a slight blackboard with his name and prison number written on it in chalk. O'Donovan Rossa submitted to these tasks silently – he and his fellow Fenian prisoners had resolved to bear their treatment patiently and with dignity, believing that their behaviour would stand to the merit of their membership of the IRB.

Following his reception, he was then taken to his prison cell and shown into a small whitewashed room with a table, stool, hammock-bed and toilet bucket. His first day as a prisoner in Mountjoy was consumed by a rather mundane chore of oakum picking, which consisted of uncoiling old and tarred lengths of rope. Having to untwist the rope was painful and dreary work, with the chore lasting for hours on end. His evening came to an end at 8 p.m., and when he had settled into bed, his door was opened by a prison guard who insisted that he be stripped of his clothing. O'Donovan Rossa speculated that this treatment was related to Stephens' earlier escape from Richmond, and that the prison authorities were taking no chances. Throughout the night he was regularly checked by prison guards who peeped through the spyhole on his cell door, lighting up the cell with a bull's eye lamp. On another occasion a guard had come into his cell and disturbed his sleep putting the lamp to his face to confirm that O'Donovan Rossa remained a prisoner. He lamented this over-extensive security, and for the duration of his stay in Mountjoy; two soldiers remained outside of his cell at night-time, regularly talking with each other. While he initially remained passive in Mountjoy, his resolve was weakening with the treatment he was experiencing, and he grew ever more militant while a prisoner. Recollecting his time in Mountjoy, he recalled:

> I had determined to bear all things patiently; and to obey in everything, conceiving that the dignity of liberty's cause required that men should suffer calmly and strongly for I; but the more obedient and humble we were, the more our masters showed a disposition to trample on us, and the more they badgered us with humiliating annoyances.[3]

This stoic regard to suffer things patiently was not helped by the fact that O'Donovan Rossa remained in virtual isolation while imprisoned, in concurrence with the Victorian belief in the power of silence and separation. While O'Donovan Rossa knew that Clarke Luby, O'Leary and others were in Mountjoy, he had not seen them for the duration of his stay. Even during exercise he would be taken to the recreation yard on his own and his sole company were the prison guards attending him, with whom he was not allowed to make eye contact or communicate.

Throughout the course of December 1865, the State had decided that the Fenian prisoners would be more secure in British, rather than Irish, Gaols. This was of course related to the escape of James Stephens, and a popular perception that there was a possibility that Irish prison wardens and guards had a degree of sympathy for the imprisoned Fenians. Against this background, on Christmas Eve 1865, the government had allowed for the removal of Fenian prisoners from Ireland to England. In the early hours of the morning, O'Donovan Rossa, Thomas Clarke Luby, John Pagan O'Leary, Michael Moore, John O'Leary and Charles Kickham, amongst others, were taken to a large hallway in Mountjoy Gaol and handcuffed to each other in the form of a chain gang. O'Donovan Rossa, like the other men, had been briskly examined by the Gaol physician and pronounced healthy enough to travel. The chain gang were ushered into the prison yard where a Black Maria police van awaited them, to take them on their journey to Dun Laoghaire Harbour. At no point were the prisoners told of their destination and as the van rumbled at speed over the cobblestoned streets, cavalry and a heavy police and military escort surrounded it.

Arriving at Dun Laoghaire Harbour, the prisoners were received into the custody of the Deputy Governor of Millbank Prison, Captain Wallack, and were ushered onto a steamer. They were to make for Britain via Holyhead and then by train to London, where they were to settle in Pentonville Prison. According to one biographer, the original intention was to take the prisoners to the Rock of Gibraltar, but it was then decided that they would be more secure in London and that their first prison would be Pentonville.[4] Fearing a rescue attempt, Dun Laoghaire Harbour contained a heavy security presence including the Navy and Military, while all unessential seamen were ordered to be confined to their vessels. Since Mountjoy, O'Donovan Rossa had been complaining about his handcuffs being too tight and had asked several prison guards to loosen them, all to no avail. On boarding the steamer he again complained of the tightness of his handcuffs, pointing out that his hands were now swollen and he was in great pain. Again his protests were of no avail. Seeing that his protestations were of little use, he promptly asked to see the most senior officer in charge. Becoming increasingly belligerent, he explained to a prison guard, much to the disdain of his fellow prisoners, that 'as we were bound for a free country, I might be supplied with freer irons'.[5] While some of the Fenian prisoners found his interjection amusing, others pleaded with O'Donovan Rossa to be quiet and not to show any sarcasm or offence to the jailers as they felt that this would impact on them negatively. Shortly afterwards. O'Donovan Rossa developed acute seasickness and started vomiting heavily. He was then visited by Captain Wallack, the Deputy Governor of Millbank Prison. Wallack examined Rossa's handcuffs and instructed guards to loosen his bind. He was given mild relief but remained as part of the chain gang.

Arriving in Britain, their journey had taken them a little over three hours, and at Holyhead a large gathering had assembled to see them disembarking. Being mid winter, there was a heavy snow dusting the harbour town and O'Donovan Rossa recalled how the cold was numbing. Escorted on a train by the military, they were making for Chester. At Chester the prisoners were allowed a small break; a prison guard had given them a small pie to be eaten between themselves. Their journey again commenced and as their train passed though train stations enroute, they could make out people with Christmas parcels and lamented Christmas away from their families and friends. Arriving in London, the train pulled into Euston Station, and the chain gang again emerged, amidst heavy smoke from the bellowing steam train, to be greeted by a further contingent of British soldiers, London police and Pentonville prison guards. They were then escorted into further prison vans and taken at speed from Euston to their new home. The journey to Pentonville was incredibly uncomfortable and the prison van was cramped and laced with a pungent odour. O'Donovan Rossa recollected how: 'So close a place of confinement I was never before in. The compartments were about two feet square; and having been unbound from the others and getting a pair of handcuffs all to myself, I was locked into one.'[6]

Arriving at Pentonville Prison, where they would stay for the first six months of their imprisonment, the prisoners were greeted by Governor Mark Gambier, and the senior warder in the company of the gaol physician and selected staff. Gambier was a man who instantly stood out to O'Donovan Rossa: he was tall, regal and smooth-tonged, with a head of snow-white hair. In contrast to his white hair, his face was flushed and he had a glass eye. O'Donovan Rossa recollected in later life how the governor could prescribe fifty lashes on the bare back without a second thought and in the most pathetic tones of regret claimed that the lashes were necessary in the interests of discipline. Gambier and his senior warder introduced the prisoners to the rules of the prison, including strict silence and observation of religious morality. They were then stripped naked for physical examination. O'Donovan Rossa refused to comply, however, and stood in his flannel under trousers, kicking off his boots, jacket and trousers. Standing in disobedience, he insisted he had been searched at Mountjoy and was not willing to strip any further. This was regarded by the governor as an act of insubordination and O'Donovan Rossa was ordered to comply. Soon after, despite much rancorous discourse, he stood naked on cold granite flagstones. Again examined by the prison physician, in the view of the governor and prison wardens, he recalled how the experience left a memory which could never be forgotten.

Under prison regulations, the uniforms that the Fenian prisoners were given at Mountjoy were taken away and replaced by new uniforms approved by Pentonville Prison. The new uniforms were, however, extraordinarily light, and did not offer protection against the cold. O'Donovan Rossa protested against this and asked for flannel trousers; his request was not acceded to, and he then asked for a return of the flannels he had been given while staying at Mountjoy. Again the prison authorities denied him, and O'Donovan Rossa learned that under prison regulations, his uniform was to be folded and left outside his cell each evening. He also learned that while a prisoner within Pentonville, he would no longer be addressed by his name and had to answer to the appellation of number 26, a reference to his prison cell number. With the cold weather piercing through the institution walls, the Fenian prisoners were escorted in handcuffs to their cells. For security reasons, there were to number no more than two Fenian prisoners per wing and they were to remain isolated while incarcerated in the institution. Like in Ireland, O'Donovan Rossa's prison cell was Spartan and frugal, containing a wooden bed, a small desk, stool and bible. He noticed that his window had been artificially blackened, so as to keep natural light out; mixed with the cold, the darkness of his cell cast a ghastly gloom over his mentality. He recalled at Pentonville how he could not sleep and shivered under the bed clothes from the cold, feeling nothing but physical discomfort while an inmate there. To break the monotony of prison life he was given reading material, but the books which he had been given (generally about nature or religion) were of no interest to his intellect. As he sat isolated in his prison cell, he longed for newspapers, political books and reading which would stimulate his mind. Each morning he faced a regimental regime which began with an awakening at six o'clock in the morning and finishing at half past seven that evening. He recalled, however, that the regimental regime of work was a relief from the physical discomfort of the cell and helped him stay warm. Resultant from his experiences in Pentonville, his body became rough and worn, and he lost twenty pounds in weight.

His day entailed a great degree of laborious work including sewing and regular bouts of oakum picking, floor polishing. He was also subjected to daily body searches by staff. He recalled a maddening hunger while he stayed at Pentonville, and how the food provided was not sufficient to stave off starvation. Reminiscing on his early experiences in Pentonville, he recalled how: 'I used to creep on my hands and knees from corner to corner of my cell sometimes to see if I could find the smallest crumb that might have fallen when I was eating my previous meal.'[7]

He lamented how he would eat rats and mice if necessary, and would readily enjoy their meat due to his hunger while a prisoner, but pitifully found that 'there wasn't a spare crust in any of these cells to induce a rat or mouse to visit'.[8] Unlike the other prisoners, however, O'Donovan Rossa and the Fenian inmates were initially not given regular exercise periods. The standard for ordinary prisoners was that they were taken to the exercise yard where they had to walk the route of a concrete circle emblazoned in the ground.

This was known in the prison parlance as *airing*. Initially, in the case of the Fenian prisoners, they were taken to the refractory yard for exercise and often had to run what was known as 'the wheel'. This was a large tread wheel which included wooden steps built around an iron frame, and was designed in some cases to handle as many as forty prisoners. As the wheel began to rotate, each prisoner was forced to continue stepping along the series of planks generating its power. There was an area within the wheel from which the prisoners could be supervised by the staff, and sometimes the governor would come to observe them, and with his presence, according to prison regulation, he had to be saluted. The wheel was introduced to the British Prison System as a means to instruct prisoners in the value of hard work, parallel to the need for cheap labour. Regarding this treatment as extraordinary, O'Donovan Rossa felt that the Gaol Authorities were taking a pleasure in the punishment of the Fenian prisoners. He did, however, recall that this practice was rescinded and he was later allowed to walk the circle and exercise with ordinary prisoners.[9] With each Fenian grouped between five common criminals, O'Donovan Rossa was initially against association with the criminal classes and debated with himself whether he should kick up a fuss about it, but as he had seen no society since he arrived in prison, he conceded that he would 'take the world as it came'.[10] While still unable to communicate with others, when a prison guard wasn't looking he recalled the Fenian prisoners would wink at each other, this little gesture of defiance keeping their spirits high.

At Pentonville, the religious requirements of Roman Catholics were not attended to. There was no Catholic clergy or provision for Catholic Mass at the institution. O'Donovan Rossa remembered that on Fridays his gaolers would regularly deliver him meat, knowing that as a Catholic he could not eat it. While he initially resisted the temptation to eat the meat, after a while his resolve broke and with hunger getting the better of him, he broke the practice. In terms of hygiene, Pentonville Prison was unclean, and when O'Donovan Rossa had been taken to be washed by the prison guards, he was stripped naked and placed into a communal bath that was divided into compartments by iron sheets. The water was never clean nor changed after individual prisoners, and often the prisoners would touch off each other while in the bath. In many cases the prisoner would come out dirtier than when he went in and O'Donovan Rossa recalled how 'the dirty suds would scum the surface' of the water.[11] Meeting Gambier, O'Donovan Rossa again complained of the treatment of Fenian prisoners and asked for an increase in the food ration to improve their paltry diet. Gambier refused to increase their food ration, and

O'Donovan Rossa suggested that as a political prisoner he had a right to more food when comparable to ordinary convicts. Gambier paused and stared at him and finishing their conversation, he stated 'England has no political prisoners nowadays. You are no more than any other prisoner here.'[12] At Pentonville Prison, O'Donovan Rossa came to a foreboding realisation that as he faced the reality of life imprisonment, 'suicide and lunacy form a very large item in the effect of England's treatment of her convicts, and I don't wonder at it'.[13]

Having come to this realisation, O'Donovan Rossa was concerned for the well-being of Brian Dillon, a fellow Fenian prisoner. While exercising in the yard, Dillon was more melancholy than usual, and continuously gestured, clandestinely, to the ground. O'Donovan Rossa took this as an inference that his comrade was being driven into an early grave resultant from his treatment.[14] While O'Donovan Rossa was concerned about Dillon, his good friend, John Lynch, who was suffering from Tuberculosis, broke the prison rules and when given the opportunity, whispered to O'Donovan Rossa how the prison conditions were extraordinarily difficult for him. Lynch, sent to Woking Prison Hospital to treat his illness, died shortly afterwards. O'Donovan Rossa believed his death was caused by the conditions in Pentonville. Meeting John O'Leary in prison, and breaking the prison rules forbidding conversation, Rossa aptly described Pentonville Prison as 'hell'.[15] Unable to converse with other prisoners, removed from his family and falling into a state of melancholy himself, he mournfully wrote:

> I have no life at present, my life is in the past;
> I have none in the future, if the present is to last;
> The 'Dead Past' only, mirrors now the memories of life,
> The fatherland, the hope of years, the friend, the child, the wife.
>
> Then am I dead at present? Yes dead while buried here –
> Dead to wife, the child and friend, to all the world holds dear;
> Dead to myself, for life is death to one condemned to dwell
> His life long exile in a convict prison cell.[16]

The mundane and noxious reality of prison life at Pentonville Prison was momentarily relived when O'Donovan Rossa secured a meeting with the Prison Board. The Board informed him that a Catholic Priest, Fr Zanetti, would come from Millbank Prison to meet with him and attend to his religious needs. O'Donovan Rossa was delighted to meet with the Catholic priest as it was the first time he had had a conversation with another human being since his imprisonment. Much to his disdain, however, Fr Zanetti refused to speak about Ireland, O'Donovan Rossa's family or his prison conditions. Zanetti explained he was only present to administer religious duties. While their initial meeting was difficult, it is apparent from his writings that O'Donovan Rossa developed a good friendship with Fr Zanetti, and the priest brought him books to read from Millbank. One which O'Donovan Rossa fondly remembered was a book on the history of England. While he had little interest in English history, it was intellectually stimulating and a release from the mundane nature and religious books he had been provided with at Pentonville. Zanetti and O'Donovan Rossa also had regular debates. While Zanetti was forbidden by the prison rules to discuss politics, he regularly implored O'Donovan Rossa to renounce his oath to the IRB and thoroughly embrace his Catholic faith. For his part, O'Donovan Rossa argued that his oath did not impinge upon his Catholicism and the Church's condemnation of the movement was misplaced. When Zanetti asserted that O'Donovan Rossa could not be a good Catholic if he remained true to his oath, the veteran Fenian announced: 'then I fear I will never become a good Catholic... I don't believe God would damn my soul... if all my other sins were forgiven but that of swearing to fight for the liberty of my country, I would face my creator with a light heart'.[17]

After a month in prison O'Donovan Rossa was given a letter from Mary Jane by the Prison Chaplain. Eagerly reading Mary Jane's letter, she told O'Donovan Rossa of her experience at Christmas, lamenting how 'I thought of you all night and cried myself to sleep and dreamland near morning. Two years ago I sat in a circle of father, mother, brothers, sisters and friends, and I did not dream about you. One year ago I sat with you and forgot home and family in your smiles, and this year I sat alone and heartweary, with strange faces in the place of those I had loved and wondered what would the next year bring – more joy or more sorrow?'[18] Mary Jane told him she was pregnant, and how she feared that her unborn child was the only thing she had of her husband. Informing him about his other children, she explained how there had been suggestions that some of the O'Donovan Rossa boys should be adopted, although she was against it and would not support breaking up the family. O'Donovan Rossa was profoundly moved and read Mary Jane's letter several times. Receiving a pencil and paper, he was given permission to reply to his wife, albeit under the strict instructions that he would not reference the prison, his treatment, prison staff or politics. If he did so he was told by prison guards that his letter would be suppressed. Writing to Mary Jane, O'Donovan Rossa asked his wife to win the attention of an English Member of Parliament, as he desired to complain about the manner of his trial in Dublin. The letter was suppressed by the Governor who summoned O'Donovan Rossa to his office. Here the Governor insisted that any reference to his trial needed to be erased from his correspondence or he would lose the privilege of writing to his wife.

Five months later he was taken to see Governor Gambier and was told that he had received another letter from his wife. The letter had been suppressed by the Governor under prison regulations. O'Donovan Rossa protested and on seeing he could get the letter he asked the governor if he could read it to him. Obliging O'Donovan Rossa, the governor read Mary Jane's letter: in his absence she had given birth to their first son, James Maxwell, at Clonakilty on 30 April 1866. Gambier informed him that his wife was ill and confined to bed but their child was well. Mary Jane had attached a photograph of James Maxwell; the governor suppressed the photo, on account of prison regulation, which forbade photographs. It would be returned to Mary Jane. O'Donovan Rossa asked for permission to write to his wife, but his request was refused as prison regulations allowed for only one letter every six months. Protesting against his treatment, O'Donovan Rossa reasonably pointed out that he was now five months a prisoner and as his wife was ill he would like to write her a letter one month in advance. With the gesture of his hand, Gambier dismissed him and the new father was ushered back to his prison cell where he was overcome with fury:

I paced my cell, unmindful of the rules and regulations that forbade me to do so during working hours, but I was soon startled from my meditations by a voice through the keyhole of my door crying out 'what are you doing there? Stop that walking instantly and go to your work'.

   I sat down upon my little stool, the bible and the prayer-book and the other religious book lay on the little table before me, and instead of praying as a good man ought to do, I dwelt upon the hypocrisy of these people that supplied me with such books and trampled under foot all the principles of religion they contained. Here was my wife delivered of a child seven months after I had been taken away from her, and they would not allow me to write a line to her! No, I did not pray on the occasion, but I felt it would be a relief to me if I could curse, and if the high authorities who ordered this treatment toward me were within my reach, I do not know that I would not have pitched their bible in the face and hurled a malediction at them with it.[19]

Breaking the prison rules and discussing his treatment with Fr Zanetti, the priest advised him that he would be best to remain calm, patient and resigned to the prison rules. The experience of not seeing his child and being unable to write a letter to his wife, however, had changed O'Donovan Rossa. He had entered prison determined to remain silent and endure the rigours of prison life. However, his experience had now shown him that this was not tenable; he now resolved to be as difficult as possible and undertake individual acts of resistance against the authorities. For his part, the governor, true to his word, returned the photograph of the newly born James Maxwell to Mary Jane. Recalling the cruelty and spitefulness of this action, she wrote a poem, 'The Returned Picture', which lamented 'cruel cruel jailers… heartless, heartless men'.[20]

On 14 May 1866, O'Donovan Rossa was transferred to Portland Prison in Dorset, just outside of London. As was the case with his arrival in Pentonville, he was handcuffed to a chain gang and escorted by prison guards via a train to the institution. Whereas the conditions in Pentonville were bad, Portland was worse. Greeted by prison staff and Gaol Governor George Clifton upon arrival, the Fenian prisoners were again stripped naked and given new clothes. They were ushered into basement cells, measuring 3½ ft. by 7 ft. and separated by corrugated iron. The cell floors were bare flagstones and the windows were made from a bleak cast iron. When it rained heavily the cell was prone to flooding and it was always cold. O'Donovan Rossa's blankets were damp and the wind howled through his windows. The following day, the Fenian prisoners, unlike at Pentonville, were allowed to speak to each other in the prison yard. This was not necessarily a relaxation of the silent rule, but had more to do with the fact that the governor of Portland had not received adequate instructions about how to maintain the Fenian prisoners. In the yard, the governor announced that he expected the Fenians to abide by the prison rules, and that he governed sternly but fairly, asserting that 'he could be mild or severe according as it was necessary'.[21]

Thinking of Mary Jane and his new son James Maxwell, O'Donovan Rossa asked Governor Clifton if he could write a letter to his wife. In doing so he advised the governor that as a prisoner he was entitled, under ordinary prison regulations, to write a letter upon entry to Gaol. Clifton dismissed his request, asserting that the Fenian prisoners were special men and the privilege of letter writing upon entry was disallowed in their case.

After a week in Portland Prison, the Fenian prisoners were moved to actual prison cells. They were instructed to polish their cells twice a week and had to laboriously scrub the granite flagstone floors. They were also given the task of stitching, parallel to laundry work. Later they were selected for heavy labour and work within the quarries, some 300 yards outside of the prison complex. Being formed into a chain gang, the Fenian prisoners were supervised by heavy security. Their work was hard and laborious, rising at 5 a.m., they began work in the quarries within one hour, although the nature of their labour allowed them ample opportunity to break the silent rule, and O'Donovan Rossa continuously spoke to his fellow prisoners when he got the opportunity. Reported for speaking to others by prison staff, however, he secured from Clifton a concession that Fenian prisoners could speak while at work once they spoke loudly and within earshot of the prison guards. This had been related to his first offence at Portland, where he had been accused of trying to speak to Michael Moore, who occupied the cell nearest him. The governor cited that he must respect the silent rule at all times, the only exception being while at work in the quarries. With hard labour taking its toll on the Fenian prisoners, many of them suffered greatly. Charles Kickham, who was suffering with scrofulous ulcers, was deaf and visually impaired. O'Donovan Rossa recalled that Kickham was regularly shook by prison guards who violently shouted in his ear and forbade him from resting. His comrade, William Roantree, was plagued by haemorrhoids, and he remembered how 'the blood streamed into his shoes while at work'.[22] Martin Carey broke his fingers while kebling a stone. He was taken to the infirmary where a doctor suggested his fingers were so badly damaged they should be amputated. He refused and was sent back to work the following day with his arm placed in a sling.

As part of hard labour within the quarries, O'Donovan Rossa was expected to clean out the toilet. Taking umbrage to this order, O'Donovan Rossa requested a meeting with Clifton to confirm whether this was necessary. Clifton insisted that the prisoner would clean the toilet. Learning that he had been discussing the matter with the governor, one of the prison warders, a Mr Gunning, decided to punish O'Donovan Rossa. The job of cleaning the toilet was rotated every three weeks and maintained by two men. Gunning insisted that O'Donovan Rossa was to clean out the toilet every Monday by himself. Showing the unyielding tenacity which marked his life, O'Donovan refused to clean out the toilets by himself. His comrades had pleaded with him to oblige Gunning and insisted that he should not be a difficult prisoner. Thomas Clarke Luby had argued with him, stressing that as a Fenian, their cause would be better served by acting as gentlemen and enduring prison life with dignity and honour. Making his argument to O'Donovan Rossa, Luby eulogised the Young Irelander John Mitchel, who had equally suffered in Gaol, but did his work like any other convict. He also pointed out to O'Donovan Rossa how Gunning was increasingly singling him out and was using every opportunity he had to report him for insubordination and idleness. Eventually convincing O'Donovan Rossa of the importance of silent endurance, he concluded that his protest could have a counter effect on his fellow Fenian inmates. Resolving to clean the toilet as instructed, he recalled: 'I could never realise to my mind John Mitchel's shovelling the dung out of a privy, and I know I never did it myself without wishing that the Prime Minister of England and the Secretary of State were within reach of my shovel.'[23]

O'Donovan Rossa's resolve to endure harsh prison conditions with dignity, however, was rapidly falling. Having earlier secured a concession from the governor that the Fenian prisoners could speak to each other while at work, the prison guards now began to complain that they were speaking too loudly. Having been approached by a prison guard and bluntly told to stop talking, O'Donovan Rossa angrily answered the gaoler: 'See, officer, I have had warning, and threats and admonitions from you. I know the rules and regulations, you know them too, and when you see me infringing them, just report me to the governor.'[24] O'Donovan Rossa was reported to the governor for disobedience and was punished with bread and water diet and the loss of his existing marks. The bread and water diet was not only a reference to the food – it also entailed a gruelling solitary confinement where the prisoner was forced to sleep on the floor and his cell was cleared of all goods. This became a regular practice when he broke the prison regulations and hardened his resolve to become 'a rebel' against the prison system.[25] Meeting Governor Clifton to discuss his defalcations, he was urged to be disciplined and obedient, or he would be punished further. Examining O'Donovan Rossa's record, Clifton noted that he had been 'fined three thousand two hundred and eighty-five marks'.[26] This had the effect of adding eighteen months to his sentence. Protesting to Clifton, O'Donovan Rossa wanted to know what the governor would do with his corpse, as he had been given a life sentence. For this act of disobedience, he was again placed on bread and water punishment.

On another occasion he had washed his prison cell floor, as instructed by a prison guard. The guard, however, found the floor was not clean enough and insisted he cleaned it again. Cleaning it for a second time he went for exercise but upon returning he was again met by the same guard who insisted he still had to clean his floor. At the same time O'Donovan Rossa was expected to stitch canvass into a bag as part of his sewing duties. Unable to complete the sewing task due to the demands of the prison guards he was punished for being idle and lazy and again sentenced to bread and water punishment. Becoming a regular visitor to the Governor's office, O'Donovan Rossa consistently complained to Clifton and was generally dismissed or punished. While some of his complaints were genuine, others were designed to rile the governor and cause trouble. On one occasion, learning that his wife was to visit him in jail, he had hoped that the authorities would allow her to meet with other Fenian prisoners. This would mean that Mary Jane could convey their messages to their families. Knowing that the prison authorities would not grant this, O'Donovan Rossa planned to rile Governor Clifton, and securing a meeting with the governor, in an interesting, if not bizarre exchange, he asked him whether the expenses of their visitors would be paid for:

O'Donovan Rossa: ' I desire to learn how justly the government mean to act by us. If they left us in Ireland where we were convicted our friends could see us without much expense or inconvenience: they adopt an extraordinary course in bringing us to England; and it is only fair and just that they should pay the expenses of our visitors from Ireland and back again.'

Governor Clifton: 'The government can do what they please with you.'

O'Donovan Rossa: 'I know they can! But when ordinary prisoners are convicted in Ireland they are not brought to England; we should have the benefit of convict law as it stands in Ireland, and if the government cannot afford to keep us there, where our friends could easily see us when the regular visits were due, they ought to pay their expenses to England as they paid ours.'

Governor Clifton: 'The government are treating you too kindly and considerably. Twenty years ago you would have been hanged.' [27]

Dismissing his request, Clifton accused O'Donovan Rossa and his kind of ruining Ireland and stunting its prosperity. O'Donovan Rossa retorted by calmly asking the governor to send his request to the directors of the Prison Board as per his right as a prisoner.

While an inmate at Portland Prison, even his joyful moments were undermined by great sorrow. Mary Jane had been writing to the Prison Authorities seeking permission to see O'Donovan Rossa and had added her name to a visiting ticket in the hope that she could get access to visit him. Their meeting had been facilitated by Deputy Governor Captain Bulwer. Meeting her in Gaol, she introduced him to James Maxwell for the first time. Overcome with emotion, O'Donovan Rossa cradled his new son in his arms, but he was unable to speak with Mary Jane. He feared that she no longer knew him and mourned the fact that he was almost dead to his child, he recalled: 'For the first few moments I kept talking to the wee one, wondering what I could say to the mother: I think we parted without saying much at all. The jailer was right beside us, and my tongue seemed to be paralyzed...'[28]

Mary Jane was horrified by what she had seen of her husband. He was gaunt, malnourished, sunken and shaved. Meeting the governor afterwards, O'Donovan Rossa had learned that Mary Jane had again submitted a photograph of James Maxwell for him. Clifton, however, would not allow him keep it, but would let him look at it before he returned it to Mary Jane. Clifton informed him, that on account of his behaviour, had he been in Portland Prison when Mary Jane had arrived, he would have prevented the meeting and he reprimanded Captain Bulwer for his work in facilitating it. Broken by the experience, Mary Jane wrote a poem, which she called 'A Visit to My Husband in Prison, May 1866':

Within the precincts of the prison bounds,
Treading the sunlit courtyard to a hall,
Roomy and unadorned, where the light
Thro' screenless windows glaringly fall.

Within the precincts of the prison walls,
With rushing memories and bathed breath;
With heart elate and light swift step that smote
Faint echoes in this house of living death.

Midway I stood in bright expectancy,
Tightly I clasped my babe, my eager sight

Restlessly glancing down the long, low room
Held him – my wedded love. My heart stood still
With sudden shock, with sudden sense of doom.

My heart stood still that had with gladsome bound
Counted the moments ere he should appear –
Drew back at sight so changed, and shivering waited,
Pulselessly waited while his steps drew near!

Oh! For a moments twilight that might hide
The harsh tanned features once so soft and fair!
The shrunken eyes that with a feeble flash
Smiled on my presence and his infants there!

Oh! For a shadow on the cruel sun
That mocked my father, Baby with his glare;
Oh! For the night of nothingness or death
Ere thou, my love, this felon garb should wear.

It needed not these passionate, pain-wrung words,
Falling with sad distinctness from thy lips,
To tell a tale of insult, abject toil.
And day long labour hewing Portland steeps![29]

Determined to keep in contact with Mary Jane, and against the rules of the institution, O'Donovan Rossa decided to secretly contact his wife. He had fallen in with an Irish prisoner named Lynch who had facilitated a means of communication with the outside world. For £3, Lynch could facilitate the smuggling of letters to his wife. Lynch was quite industrious and using money within the institution, he was able to secure writing material and pencils, which the Fenian prisoners eagerly bought. When writing these secret letters, one of O'Donovan Rossa's comrades would keep lookout for a prison guard and make a signal if one approached so O'Donovan Rossa could hide the letter. The first letter was addressed to Michael Moore's wife, Catherine, with a letter for Mary Jane hidden inside. He planned to give the letter to Lynch while at Mass, but Lynch had been noticed moving suspiciously toward O'Donovan Rossa and the two were taken away to be searched. Finding the letter, Rossa was charged with attempting to smuggle a letter out of the prison. For this he was again punished with the bread and water diet and was stripped of his uniform and placed into a punishment cell. Eventually meeting with the governor, it had been suggested that he had tried to smuggle the letter to a woman who was not his wife. The governor insinuated that he was having an affair with the wife of fellow Fenian prisoner, Michael Moore, and had it written into the prison books that Rossa was committing adultery.

Circulating this falsehood, Clifton had actually suggested this to Moore when he had requested to write to his wife in Ireland. When summoning him to his office, he asked: 'Moore, do you know that there is another man in this prison carrying on correspondence with your wife?'[30] Moore, who knew the truth, then found it necessary to stage a fight with O'Donovan Rossa while in prison in order to force the issue and allow O'Donovan Rossa to explain the letter was in fact intended for Mary Jane. Meeting with the governor, he explained that the letter was intended for his wife and this had been marked by 'For Mrs O'D' in the corner. Clifton was dismissive of O'Donovan Rossa, however, and instructing prison warders to take him away, the irrepressible Irishman condemned him and the authorities at Portland. 'You have shown us nothing but meanness in your treatment of us since we have come into your hands.' Placed in solitary confinement, he was again brought before the governor the following day, where he accused Clifton of slander. Insulting the governor, Clifton demanded he stayed quiet and listened to what he had to say. The governor admitted he was wrong and claimed he had not seen the reference to 'Mrs O'D' on the letter as the writing was too small. O'Donovan Rossa was fearful that the matter would not be recorded on his record, and it could be claimed that he was having an affair with an honourable woman and asked for leave to write to the Secretary of State. Clifton dismissed his demand, but conceded he would allow O'Donovan Rossa to complain to the director of the Prison Board. Reluctantly accepting this concession, O'Donovan Rossa was returned to his prison cell and fined forty-two marks. When the director arrived at Portland Prison he never got to see O'Donovan Rossa. The prisoner had been reported the previous day for speaking the day before and was again on bread and water punishment in solitary confinement. Under prison regulations, prisoners who were in the refractory wing were not entitled to complain to the director. O'Donovan Rossa believed his punishment was calculated and intended to silence him.

While in solitary confinement O'Donovan Rossa was visited by the prison doctor, but refused to stand to attention upon entry to his prison cell in a small protest for his contemptuous prison treatment. Once again hauled before the governor O'Donovan Rossa vented his ire at the prison regime and telling the governor how the allegation of an affair with Catherine Moore was 'nothing more than a lie', he was again returned to solitary confinement on a further bread and water diet.[31] Released from solitary confinement he remained committed to clearing his name and meeting the governor again he continued to accuse him of lying and that 'the treatment he had received merited nothing but contempt'.[32] He impassionedly held of the letter to Mrs Moore 'I know my feelings towards my wife,' and calling for an examination of the letter insisted 'I venture to say, the man in authority, who after reading it could write an official report to the effect that it was intended any man's wife is either a fool or a rogue.'[33] Similar to previous occasions O'Donovan Rossa was denied satisfaction and 'for this [he] got three additional days bread and water in a cell darker than night'.[34] Visited by the governor and doctor on each day of his solitary confinement, as under prisoner regulations the governor was to inquire whether he had any complaints, he daily complained of his treatment yet his entreaties were ignored. Visited on the final day of his solitary confinement, on this occasion, he condemned Clifton holding 'in coming to ask me have you any complaint, and in refusing to take a complaint from me, you make a mockery of your duties… I will only say that I am your prisoner, and with my body it seems you have the power to do what you please; but my mind or my soul is not yours, and I refuse to pay you in the required salaam.'[35] For this show of defiance, once more he was punished and placed on bread and water diet, reduced to a wasted mass from his treatment he lamented 'obliging the man to salute his punisher is in the civilised word deemed barbarism, but in England 'tis only "discipline". Besides there is in England a doctor to superintend the ruin of a man's health.'[36] O'Donovan Rossa confronted the governor on numerous occasions to lift the accusations of adultery that he was tarnished with. He accused the governor of deliberate falsehoods during many meetings he demanded to have with him and was put on the bread and water diet and subjected to solitary confinement on many occasions as a result.

Despite the governor's allegations that O'Donovan Rossa was having an affair with Michael Moore's wife, he and Moore had developed a plan for escaping from the institution. Moore, who was in the cell beside O'Donovan Rossa, had stolen a chisel from the quarry and was working to secure an escape from Portland. With O'Donovan Rossa, Hugh Brophy and Martin Carey, Moore had planned to burrow a hole in the wall of his prison cell into the prison yard and had hoped to scale the wall to freedom. In his endeavour he had chiselled a hole in the wall large enough to hide the chisel, and had covered the wall with whitening, which he had used to brighten up tins during mundane prison work. The endeavour gave O'Donovan Rossa a glimmer of hope, but he must have known that the plan stood no chance of success. Nevertheless, he recalled how 'once we got out we would die game rather than return to our cells'.[37] Their plan to escape had to be abandoned, however, as when Moore had tunnelled as far as he could, he saw that the stones in the wall were fastened to one another by iron links, impossible to penetrate. But there still was hope – while out working within the quarry, a hole was made which had escaped the officers attention. O'Donovan Rossa and Hugh Brophy had planned to hide in the hole for a couple of days and then make their escape. Smuggling food from the prison, some of the Fenian prisoners had regularly dropped bread into the hole in preparation for the escape attempt. To O'Donovan Rossa's disappointment, however, the plan had to be abandoned as the hole was not safely habitable and the men could not fit inside. For the foreseeable future they were condemned to life as Irish felons. Lamenting his condition, he hoped 'nature comes to the assistance of man when he suffers for what he believes a true and holy principle – liberty! And that the mind sustains the body and its suffering'.[38]

6

The Road to Exile

The authorities at Portland were becoming increasingly frustrated with O'Donovan Rossa. He had refused any of the work which they had set for him, disobeyed their orders and refused any degree of [1]co-operation with the system. They had placed him on bread and water diets, taken the privileges from his cell such as books, beds and stools all to no avail. Having continuously broken prison rules and shown no desire to adapt to the gruelling prison regime, in February 1867, O'Donovan Rossa was removed from Portland Prison and transferred to Millbank Penitentiary, London. Arriving at Millbank, he recognised that from the outset he was a marked man – a prisoner who would be singled out. The greatest indication of this was a notice outside his prison cell indicating his name and stating that he was to be watched at all times with the gas lighting left on in his prison cell at night time. Once again stripped and processed, he contended that this was 'his initiation into the secret masonry of Millbank', but having taken this in his stride, the following day he was again stripped naked and searched, an event which he regarded as a humiliation. This continued throughout his imprisonment in Millbank, and he remarked how even while bathing a prison guard stood beside him, watching him carefully as part of an attempt to break his morale. As part of this system to undermine the Fenian prisoner, he was forced on one occasion to clean his cell three times in one morning. This had the desired effect of making him unable to attend his hard labour task of stitching. Unable to attend his stitching workshop, he was reported for idleness by the prison authorities. Taken away from stitching duties, he was once given the task of picking rope, but his fingers were so sore he could not do the work and he was punished with a bread and water diet, parallel to having his bed taken away. Charged with nineteen offenses at Millbank, he was regarded as the most troublesome prisoner of the institution. In defiance of the Prison System he was regularly punished for shouting *I am a Fenian* and singing Fenian songs. When chastised he would regularly cite how he had to do something to amuse himself.[2]

Despite being a political prisoner, O'Donovan Rossa was put to work alongside ordinary English criminals. He resented this as an attack on his character and cause, yet, as the months passed by in Millbank Prison, he began to welcome their company and found them to be endearing, with good hearts by comparison to his jailers. He befriended many of the convicts; they often kept bread for him and offered him sympathy for the level of punishment he was receiving from the prison authorities. These ordinary criminals found pencils for him and helped him to smuggle letters out of the prison to the outside world. In many cases the letters were discovered which led to more bread and water punishments and increased supervision by the prison staff.

The continuing imprisonment of O'Donovan Rossa had financially burdened Mary Jane. Despite her position as Secretary of the Ladies Committee, she was effectively living on £50 and had sought to maintain her family in Cork and live in Dublin as a political activist raising awareness of her husband's sufferings. Early in 1866, however, the family's nanny, Mrs Healy, could no longer take care of the O'Donovan Rossa children, and Mary Jane was forced to return home to Cork, where she moved her children into her family home in Clonakilty. Returning to Dublin in July 1866, with James Maxwell and two of her stepsons, she again threw herself into the business of the Ladies Committee, earning a sum of £2 per week. O'Donovan Rossa had earlier implored his wife to make for America. He had hoped she could have a better life far removed from associations with an Irish political prisoner. He understood that Mary Jane and their family would be looked after by Irish-Americans and the Fenian network would sustain the family while he was imprisoned. Mary Jane had visited him while in England in May 1867 and seeing him she was horrified by the weight he had lost and how gaunt his face had become. Here she told him that she had resigned from the Ladies Committee and agreed to make for America. She borrowed £20 from the Dublin journalist, Richard Pigott, to help her departure. In the meantime she stressed to Rossa that a Commission of Inquiry was to be held by the British government investigating the treatment of Fenian prisoners. This gave him hope that his experience in British gaols could be improved and his incarceration could become less intolerable. Parting from O'Donovan Rossa, Mary Jane was heartbroken and recalled how 'she turned her face alone to the new continent'.[3] Returning to Clonakilty, Mary Jane told her parents of her plan. She inferred that James Maxwell was too young to travel and he would be better cared for at home in Ireland. Her parents were horrified by her decision to leave for America, and they implored her to rethink her decision as they had no relatives living in the United States. Mary Jane was determined to leave, however, and like O'Donovan Rossa's mother before her, she set sail for New York, leaving James Maxwell and her stepchildren in Ireland in the care of her parents.

Settling into American life she studied elocution, public speaking and learned under the famous Professor Joseph Edwin Frobisher at New York. She supported herself financially through a combination of writing poetry and working with the existing Fenian network in New York. One of her most important contacts at this time was the Civil War veteran General Charles Halpine, who persuaded her to take the lessons under Frobisher. Her time in America was incredibly stressful and lonely, however. She knew nothing of O'Donovan Rossa apart from what she read in the newspapers and was sad to be separated from her family, particularly Maxwell, whom she described as her 'one good angel far across the water'.[4] She was forced to move around New York on several occasions and while initially staying in a Boarding House on 13th Street, she found the accommodation too expensive and was forced to find lodgings in the home of friends of her father on Dominick Street. Describing her first few months in America, she explained how the stress of her life since her husband's arrest had 'left her in a truly lamentable condition', and complained of a 'pernicious effect' on her health.[5] She remained committed to the cause of seeking an amnesty for Fenian prisoners and was active within the Fenian Sisterhood, an ancillary organisation founded to mobilise Irish women in America behind the Fenian Brotherhood. She regularly toured America and Canada and spoke on behalf of her husband to Irish-American audiences and sought to fundraise for the Amnesty Association. On 16 June 1868 she delivered her first address on the theme of her husband's imprisonment at the Coopers Institute in New York City. Introduced by her General Halpine, it was reported by contemporary newspapers that tickets to the public talk were sold out and there was standing room only. Her lectures gave a great impetus to the Fenian cause and also provided her with a platform to raise money and publicise her poetry. She soon became financially independent and her confidence as a speaker and representative grew rapidly. The *Boston Pilot* newspaper reported how 'when she arose before us last night, tall, graceful, handsome, vivacious, we were prepared to be pleased with whatever she might read to us. But great was our astonishment to recognise in the handsome lively lady before us one of the best elocutionists we have ever heard'.[6] It was commented that her talks were an occasion where the warring Fenian factions could come together as one united body.

Being the wife of O'Donovan Rossa, however, it came as no surprise that Mary Jane was sought after by both Fenian factions. With both looking for legitimacy through endorsement, Mary Jane used their internecine fighting to her advantage in securing a better position in America. She was well received upon her job application to John O'Mahony, but the Fenian leader could only offer her a paltry job writing poetry for the Fenian Brotherhood newspaper, known as *The Irish People.* For this she would be paid $10 a week. O'Mahony's counterpart within the Senate Wing, Colonel Roberts, by contrast could offer Mary Jane more favourable work through his connections within the US Senate and gave her accommodation at his luxurious home at Bloomingdale. Staying in Roberts' home for several weeks, Mary Jane wrote a compilation of poetry: *Irish Lyrical Poems.* She was, however, increasingly treading a fine line between both factions and this was no more apparent than within the August Belmont affair.

The August Belmont affair found its origins in the suppression of the *Irish People* newspaper in Dublin in 1863. In anticipation of an Irish rebellion, O'Mahony had lodged $20,000 into a New York bank. The purpose of the fund was to bankroll the IRB, allowing the movement to draw funds in Dublin from the American account. This was dependent on money orders, which were safely secured at No. 12 Parliament Street, the headquarters of the IRB newspaper. When Dublin Castle moved against the newspaper, however, and raided its headquarters, the Dublin Metropolitan Police discovered the money orders and traced their origins to the New York account. Placing a freeze on the money orders, the original $20,000 was now in limbo and there was a dispute between both factions as to who had a right to the money. While the money was never reclaimed, Mary Jane had been advised by the Senate Wing to claim the money and considering that O'Donovan Rossa was owed $8,000 for the establishment of *The Irish People,* a case was taken in her name in September 1869 against August Belmont, who represented the bank.

Overnight, Mary Jane was thrown into controversy and despite her earlier success in America; she soon became a divisive figure within the complexities of Irish-American politics. She was lampooned and condemned by those who had previously celebrated her. Many asserted that she was dishonest and corrupt, holding that O'Donovan Rossa had no claim to any of the $20,000. For her part Mary Jane argued that she had taken the legal action so as to help provide for her family and their education, explaining how 'personally I am uninterested in the success of my suit, except in so far as it benefits my husband and children'.[7] Learning of the suit in America, O'Donovan Rossa was horrified and wrote to her directing she drop the suit as he did not support it. Remembering the Belmont affair, he recalled how:

> Some people say that some things made me mad in prison. Well, if anything made me mad it was that, and I wrote to my living widow to have her nothing whatever to do with the lawsuits about the Belmont money or other Fenian money. I was proud of my life in connection with Fenian affairs, and I did not want to have this pride killed. It was what was keeping the life in me.[8]

Having unwittingly become a pawn amidst the fighting within the Fenian factions, Mary Jane agreed with her husband and dropped the suit. Having re-established contact with her husband, she was increasingly furious with O'Donovan Rossa when she learned how he was acting in prison. Mary Jane believed that he was bringing great difficulty upon himself in acting irrationally. Writing her first letter from America on 19 July 1867, she angrily implored him to think before he acted and remain quiet while in prison in favour of an easier life:

> I must confess to a feeling of vexation and annoyance that you should make yourself so conspicuous amongst men who are supposed to be as sensitive to their condition as you, by the number of complaints you make and by the number made against you. What is the use of bringing so many successive punishments on yourself by impotent defiance of a rule that holds you in its grasp. You can assist you? Or what is to be gained?
>
> ... It is necessary that you should have some incentive to act in a more rational manner... Need I set before you the fact that you have six sons – four of them in my father's house – and likely to remain there if the poor man can keep a house over them, for I have failed in getting any provision for them over here. Need I remind you that you have a wife – a sorely wronged girl whom you took in her inexperience and world ignorance, whom you afterwards with open eyes left unprovided for, and who is at present drudging away her life at writing for a pittance, and wearing away her heart at yearning for an infant who finds a mother at the other side of the great ocean?[9]

In May 1867, the inquiry which Mary Jane had spoken of took place. Headed by Alexander Knox and George Pollock, two staunch conservatives, it came as nothing but a disappointment for O'Donovan Rossa. Examining the conditions and treatment of Fenian prisoners at Portland, Pentonville and Woking, their inquiries included an interview with O'Donovan Rossa at Millbank. Studying O'Donovan Rossa's complaints about Portland, particularly the insinuation that he had been having an affair with Michael Moore's wife, the inquiry concluded that he had brought his difficulties upon himself and was to blame for the rigorous regime of punishment directed against him. Describing his complaints as exaggerated lies and a farrago, the inquiry also supported Governor Clifton's claims about O'Donovan Rossa having an extramarital affair. Finding O'Donovan Rossa to be a dangerous prisoner, the inquiry recommended that he should remain under the closest vigilance by the prison authorities. By now O'Donovan Rossa was near breaking point – the fact that he had partaken in this Commission of Inquiry was now used against him by the prison authorities and his ill-treatment was subsequently worsened. On one occasion, while scrubbing his cell, as mandated by the prison regulations, he finished early and having no more work to do, sat back and relaxed. For this he was punished and placed naked in a cell of solitary confinement. He barricaded himself into the cell and refused entry to prison guards and the senior administration. He was then sentenced to four months of solitary confinement for this act of defiance and on release he resembled a mere shadow of his former self; his body was covered with blisters and hives in addition to significant weight loss.

Against this background, O'Donovan Rossa suffered great mental anguish with the loss of his good friend Edward Duffy, who died on 17 January 1868. Duffy had been a committed Fenian activist since 1861 and was engaged to John O'Leary's sister. A fulltime organiser of the IRB in Connacht, he had spent a great deal of time with O'Donovan Rossa and knew him intimately, having worked with him between March and May 1865. Duffy had been ill for quite some time, however, and was transferred from Pentonville Prison to Millbank House of Detention, where he lay dying in the prison infirmary. Learning of his illness, O'Donovan Rossa had desperately sought to visit him and asked permission to see Duffy before he died, but his request was refused on account of prison regulations. He protested that he had a right to see his friend as he had not been allowed a visit for six months, but they fell upon deaf ears. When a comrade in prison whispered through his cell gratings that Duffy had died, O'Donovan Rossa fell into 'a melancholy mood'[10] and sat in reflection of the times he had enjoyed with his friend. O'Donovan Rossa was determined to pay him a tribute and from his prison cell he wrote his most famous lament, 'Ned Duffy'. O'Donovan's anguish is felt in this powerful verse:

> That whisper through the grating has thrilled through my veins,
> 'Duffy is dead!' a noble soul has slipped the tyrant's chains,
> And whatever wounds they gave him, their lying books will show,
> How they very kindly treated him, more like a friend than foe![11]

Following Duffy's death O'Donovan Rossa was removed from Millbank to Chatham, where the conditions were by far the worst that he had experienced during his imprisonment. Once again he had been processed, shaved, measured, stripped, searched and given a prison uniform. Upon entry to Chatham he was approached by the head guard, a man named Alison, who singled him out, commenting how Rossa's reputation preceded him and that he heard 'he had a pretty bad character but hoped [he'd] become an altered man'.[12] Despite his new surroundings, O'Donovan Rossa was not prepared to be quiet and answered Alison back, holding he was altered, but only in appearance, sarcastically lamenting 'you should have seen… what a handsome man I was when I was in the world'.[13] Alison insisted that he would not find Chatham a welcoming prison if he disobeyed regulations, stressing to his prisoner that it was a military prison and demanded obedience. Taken to his prison cell, he was permitted to write a letter to his wife. As O'Donovan Rossa had written about his treatment in the letter, he was informed that the gaol authorities would not allow the letter to be sent. O'Donovan Rossa concluded that he was a marked man who was branded a bad character by the prison authorities and was being punished for his reputation. This belief, while at Chatham, led him to assume a defiant attitude, which was at odds with the prison authorities.

At Chatham he was allocated hard-labour duties and put to work amongst ordinary criminals. He was left handed, but the prison guards insisted that he could only work with his right hand. Protesting that he could not, the guards effectively forced him to use his right hand at great difficulty to himself and his productivity. O'Donovan Rossa recognised this as a means of punishing him for his reputation and commented how several other prisoners, all ordinary criminals, were left handed and left to their own work, unhindered by prison guards within the hard labour yard.

While working at Chatham, O'Donovan Rossa befriended William Crane. Nicknamed 'Jobler', Crane was a petty criminal originally from Hampstead in England who showed O'Donovan Rossa courtesy while he was imprisoned at Chatham. On one occasion, while working in the yard and forced to use his right hand, Crane gave him support against continued haranguing from the prison guards that he was working too lightly. Eventually summoned by a prison guard, O'Donovan Rossa was challenged for idleness, to which he made motions of his hand as if hammering. This was against the prison rules as he was to keep his hands by his side when talking to a prison officer. The prison guard raised his sword as if to strike the prisoner and ordered him to keep his hands down and show respect. Irked, O'Donovan Rossa answered back: 'The prison rules don't permit me to be insolent to an officer; nor do they permit any officer to be impertinent to me.'[14]

Another prisoner he had met was nicknamed 'Cos', who was the head of the forced labour gang. Cos (shorthand for the surname Cosgrave) was serving time for burglary and was formerly of the British Army. He had a great ability to make O'Donovan Rossa laugh and was accustomed to mischief. Through Jobler, O'Donovan Rossa was introduced to another man called Pratt, whom he later believed was a prison spy. From Bradford in England, similar to Cos, Pratt was a burglar. Pratt supplied O'Donovan Rossa with newspaper clippings, ostensibly to break the mundane reality of his prison cell. This was of course deemed illegal by the prison regulations, and one evening while O'Donovan Rossa was reading newspaper clippings, which related to the Fenian bombing at Clerkenwell, he was caught in his cell by the prison guards. Reported for having prohibited items in his cell, he was also punished for idleness and insolence, the latter two punishments were related to his behaviour in the hard labour yard when he had talked back to the prison guard. For punishment, O'Donovan Rossa was given ten days of isolation on a bread and water diet. When he was released he learned that as a consequence of his behaviour, he was denied the right to write a letter to his wife. Returning to his cell, almost livid, he grabbed a pint glass and smashed it into smithereens against the gas fixture and the wall. For a second time he was punished and given two days on a bread and water diet. When O'Donovan Rossa was released from his punishment, Cos told him he had seen Alison leaving Pratt's prison cell before he had entered O'Donovan Rossa's. Whether or not Pratt was working with Alison to punish Rossa cannot be proven, but the fact that he was labelled a prison spy necessitated his swift removal from Chatham Prison. He had also discovered that the prison authorities had been maintaining a system of divide and rule amongst his fellow prisoners, actively seeking to turn them against him. Thus, while he worked with the prisoners in the hard labour yard, they were not allowed to work outside the prison, but on the occasions that he had been in punishment, they worked outside the prison walls. O'Donovan Rossa speculated that this was intended to facilitate the emergence of a perception that they were being punished on account of him, and if he were not there then their burden could be considerably lessoned.

Returning to his hard labour duties, O'Donovan Rossa remained incredibly obstinate, and desirous of protesting his treatment, he decided that he would cease work within the yard. As a means of protest he downed his tools and with prison guards looking on, he violently threw one of his hammers over the prison wall. Taken to the governor for disobedience and idleness he was again punished with three days on a bread and water diet. On this occasion he stressed to the governor that he would no longer work as part of the hard labour yard and as a protest regarding his treatment he would not salute him under any circumstances. His bread and water punishment was continued for several days afterwards. On 15 June O'Donovan Rossa decided to up the ante and refused to meet with the governor, thus forcing several guards to drag him under protest to the governor's office. Arriving before Governor Powell, he remained obstinate and refused to offer a salute, he furthermore stood leaning against the wall of the governor's office with his arms crossed and one leg crossed over the other in a remarkable show of disrespect. Refusing to stand to attention he was again grabbed by the prison guards and was forcibly held into a position of attention, two holding down his feet, another straightening his back and head, while a further two held his arms. With his anger rising he addressed Powell, recommending how 'it would be a good idea to have a picture of this taken for the edification of those English who are so fond of passing judgements on foreign customs'.[15] Powell refused to acknowledge his demands and O'Donovan Rossa was forcibly taken back to his prison cell.

The following day, 16 June 1868, O'Donovan Rossa would have vengeance on the prison authorities for how he had been treated. Filling his chamber pot in his prison cell, he waited for the governor who was scheduled to do his rounds. With tension almost palpable, O'Donovan Rossa heard the governor enter his prison wing; each prisoner was addressed by a prison guard instructing him to stand to attention as Captain Powell entered his cell. By the minute the voices became closer and the sound of footsteps nearer. On hearing him approach, O'Donovan Rossa grabbed his pail of water and recalled how he braced himself. As the door opened and the governor entered, O'Donovan Rossa threw the contents of his pail upon the governor, and as the water dropped from his face onto his damp clothes, O'Donovan Rossa joyously announced 'that… is the salute I owe you!'[16] Powell's clothes were ruined and the cell door was shut instantaneously as the governor was led away with haste. O'Donovan Rossa recalled his act of defiance:

> I did not pride myself at having done this act, I once thought I could not be guilty of it, but prison life changes a man. And the treatment I received changed me into doing many things I thought myself incapable of when in [the] World. But I should have some satisfaction at the time for the indignities heaped on me and if I could make the Secretary of State or the Prime Minister of England the recipient of the salute I gave the governor, it would have increased my piece of mind. Their treatment of the Irish political prisoners was wanton and uncalled for.[17]

The following day, O'Donovan Rossa was punished for his show of insolence and placed in handcuffs with hands tied behind his back. His cuffs were only removed in order to allow him to be handcuffed in the front so that he could eat or get dressed. Once he had finished eating his bread and water diet and dressed himself, he was again handcuffed from behind. Later his handcuffs were opened and he was given clothes for exercise. After putting on the clothes, however, he was again handcuffed from behind and was taken to a prison yard where he exercised. When exercise was over his cuffs were again opened, he undressed, was placed in a prison uniform and handcuffed from behind again. This continued for thirty-four days, between 17 June to 20 July 1868, and by the first week there were eight blood marks on his wrist. Two warders, Thompson and Brown, used to nip him savagely with the handcuffs every time they put them on him. O'Donovan Rossa reported that this was happening very regularly to him to the prison doctor, who did nothing. When he got the opportunity of being handcuffed from the front, he wrote in blood on his prison cell door 'blood for blood'.[18]

Apart from the physical pain there was also humiliation. He was not allowed braces for his trousers and as his hands were handcuffed he could not secure them and as a result his trousers regularly fell down to his ankles as he walked. This forced Rossa to gnaw holes in his vest with his teeth, so as to affix the buttons of his trousers to his vest, for this he was reported for insolence – he had broken prison regulations by tearing his clothes. His humiliation was not yet over. He was given a book by the Protestant Chaplain, *The History of the Reformation* and the prison warders would not untie his hands from behind his back, nor would they change the pages for him, thus to read he had to place the book on the floor, kneel down and use his tongue and lips to change the pages.

Within fourteen days of his punishment, O'Donovan Rossa was brought before Captain Edmund du Cane, Director of Convict Prisons and was charged with assaulting Governor Powell. Du Cane insisted that the formal punishment for O'Donovan Rossa was twenty-eight days on the bread and water diet, concluding that flogging should not be inflicted on him. This decision was made on 7 July 1868 but his punishment, as instructed by du Cane, did not come into being until 20 July. Throughout the official narrative of his punishment there is no reference to handcuffs, indicating that part of his reprimand was a vendetta by the prison staff, with the possibility that the Director of Prisons also knew. According to prison regulations, only violent prisoners could be handcuffed, and no prisoner could be kept in handcuffs longer than three days without a special order from the Director of Convict Prisons. Unable to flog O'Donovan Rossa, an attempt was now made to psychologically weaken him. His prison cell faced out on to a yard and the warders had built a triangle for flogging so that the scream of convicts could be heard by him. O'Donovan Rossa recalled the lashing of prisoners within his earshot:

> The prisoner's hands were lashed above and, I suppose, his feet – which I could not see – were tied below… the prisoner was naked to the waist. A burley jailer swayed the cat-o-nine-tails – nine pieces of hard cord tied to a stick about a foot and a half long. Every stroke he gave he drew the cords through his hand to clean away the flesh or blood that may be on them, and also to make them even for the next stroke… wasn't my whole flesh creeping and cursing one day as I saw an unfortunate fellow tied up with his head hanging on his shoulder as they were slashing away at him, while the high officials were looking on with umbrellas over their heads and mats under their feet to protect them from catching cold or catching any other discomfort from the drizzling rain.[19]

After being kept thirty-four days in handcuffs, du Cane's sentence was read to O'Donovan Rossa, and despite his earlier punishment, twenty-eight days of bread and water punishment now awaited him. Temporarily taken from his prison cell and lodged in a neighbouring room, he noticed that the prison authorities were making changes to his cell. They had begun a renovation whereby the cell would become damage proof through the installation of an iron water closet. When the work was completed he was removed back to his prison cell and found that the renovations had sought to make his room unbreakable through the use of iron and cement. Examining the renovations to his cell, he noted how the iron closet masked a thick plate of glass which protected a spyhole, allowing constant supervision. O'Donovan Rossa recalled how his prison cell had been turned into a fortress which sought to keep him in. He found, however, that there was a weak point within this supposed fortress and examining his water closet, he discovered that he had control over the tap. To the prison guards' horror, he broke the tap and flooded the cell, imagining himself 'on the banks of a purling stream'.[20] When asked why he had done this, he sarcastically explained how 'he wanted to keep the water closet fresh'.[21]

Again handcuffed for this act of insolence, O'Donovan Rossa was dragged from his prison cell by guards and placed in an isolation cell while they worked to fix the mess he had created. Two days afterwards he was taken back to his prison cell where he was kept in handcuffs; control of the tap was now located outside his prison cell and he was only allowed to use the water tap under supervision with a prison warder in control of the water flow. The prison guards now believed that O'Donovan Rossa's cell was unbreakable and that the Irishman would come to terms with his situation.

No punishment seemed adequate for O'Donovan Rossa as on each occasion he defied the gaol authorities with a one-man war. Having completed his twenty-eight days of bread and water punishment, he was now placed on six months of a penal class diet, but shortly afterwards he returned to bread and water for a refusal to pick oakum. Taken to solitary confinement where he would serve his bread and water punishment for two days, the prison authorities withdrew his bed and took his clothing, forcing him to sleep naked on the floor:

I refused to put my clothes out; Alison came by with warders Hibbert and Giddings. He repeated the demand that I put them out [sic], and when again I refused, the three of them rushed at me. I tried to keep them off by holding them at arms length; made no attempt to strike them; but they struck at my hands with their clubs to make me let go of my hold whenever I caught one of them. I was overpowered and flung on the ground, with Hibbert's knee on my neck. Alison pulled the breeches off me. It was necessary to turn my neck while this was being done. In fact, as I was on my back, he gave me a leap and with his knee foremost, came down on my torso… When the warders had stripped me, they moved to leave; and I attempted to raise myself from the floor, but Hibbert, who was the last to go out, turned, and gave me a kick that threw me against the wall.[22]

Locked into his cell, the prisoner composed himself, but soon afterwards, the spyhole on his cell door was opened and a prison guard examined him. This, in addition to his humiliating treatment, drew his ire and grabbing his pot, he flung it against the cell door as he shouted at the guard.[23] He was taken to the doctor the following day where his wounds were assessed and he was found to have a bruised and swollen chest. No action was taken against Alison, Hibbert and Giddings; in fact, they entered a charge against O'Donovan Rossa, alleging he had attacked them in the course of their regular duties. The charge remained against him for a further two months.

With matters coming to a head, O'Donovan Rossa was visited by Edmund Frederick Du Cane, Chairman of the Board of Directors of Convict Prisons. Du Cane pleaded with O'Donovan Rossa to abide by the prison rules and regulations, citing how obedient his fellow Fenian prisoners had been. Asking him if he could be like them, O'Donovan Rossa stated that if he were treated with dignity he could. Du Cane made O'Donovan Rossa an offer: if he was willing to work within the system and cause no trouble, on behalf of the Prison Board, he was willing to forget the matter and start afresh. This effectively meant that the Prison Board would remit O'Donovan Rossa's remaining punishments. While O'Donovan Rossa was desirous of starting afresh, and was increasingly worn by his prison struggle, he was not yet prepared to stop unless he could get a guarantee that he would be 'treated like a human'.[24] O'Donovan Rossa was returned to an ordinary prison cell, his punishment was cancelled and he was allowed to associate with William Halpin, John Warren and Augustine Costello, the other Fenian prisoners. There was now a marked and recognisable improvement in his behaviour.

On 15 March 1869 John Devoy was transferred to Chatham Prison. Like O'Donovan Rossa, he had been a troublesome prisoner at both Millbank and Portland. In the former he had tried to escape several times, while at the latter he had organised strikes amongst the prisoners against bread and water diets. He had arrived with a new batch of Fenian prisoners including Charles Underwood O'Connell and John McClure, and they quickly bonded with O'Donovan Rossa. O'Donovan Rossa had come across Devoy by chance when he was being brought to see the Director of Convicts. Breaking prison regulations, O'Donovan Rossa grabbed Devoy by the arm and introduced himself to his friend. Devoy did not yet recognise O'Donovan Rossa, and it was only when he announced who he was that Devoy shouted 'Great God, you are Rossa!' Devoy and O'Donovan Rossa were assigned to labour duties which included darning prisoners' stockings. In this task, in which they mended stockings after washing, they were assisted by other Fenian prisoners including Halpin, Burke, Mulleda, McClure and Underwood O'Connell. Resultant of O'Donovan Rossa's prisoner war, however, the prison regime was now increasingly lenient regarding the Fenian prisoners. This was adequately represented by William Halpin, who refused to partake in the work as a result of being denied letter and visiting privileges. While Halpin was punished with forty-eight hours on the bread and water diet, his protest continued and according to O'Donovan Rossa he was left alone, as 'the authorities by this time were tiring of their attempts to civilise us by ill treatment'.[25] With a lighter regime being enforced upon O'Donovan Rossa and his comrades, he came to enjoy the darning work and an atmosphere of genteel banter was noticeably recognisable amongst the prisoners, with the Corkman regularly entertained by stories from William Halpin and jokes by Ricard O'Sullivan Burke. In this vein, John Devoy later recalled an amusing anecdote: he remembered Ricard O'Sullivan Burke poking fun at the Corkman and his ability to charm women, noting he had been married three times. O'Donovan Rossa then unbuttoned his shirt and revealed what he called a *ball searc* (a beauty spot), which made him irresistible.[26]

On 28 June 1869 an Amnesty Association was established at Dublin to secure the release of the Fenian prisoners. Leading figures in the Association included Isaac Butt, who was elected president, John 'Amnesty' Nolan, and J. P. McDonnell, who had been sworn into the IRB by Rossa and John Martin. The association had sought to secure the release of the Fenian prisoners by mobilising popular support in their favour; in doing so they immediately set about organising rallies, petitions, memorials and public meetings in addition to establishing a solid branch network throughout the country. On 10 October 1869 the Amnesty Association organised a significant rally at Cabra in North Dublin to secure the release of Fenian prisoners. In anticipation of the event, the association secured a large thirty-two acre field from a supporter, David Donnelly. Attended by over 200,000 people, the rally was a major success for the association and the wider Fenian movement. Having utilised the force of public opinion, they were saddened the following month to learn of the death of Charles Moore, a Liberal MP who had been vocal about Fenian prisoners. Moore had previously represented the constituency of Tipperary and his death necessitated a by-election to Parliament. Seizing the opportunity of his death, the association decided that they would highlight the experience of Fenian prisoners and their call for amnesty by standing a Fenian prisoner as a candidate for Moore's seat – examining a list of names, the Amnesty Association chose to nominate O'Donovan Rossa in November 1869.

O'Donovan Rossa's nomination had been secured by Peter Gill and T. P. O'Connor and it was celebrated by all who were supporters of advanced nationalism in Ireland. His entire campaign was reliant on two themes: firstly, a nationalist message and secondly, the release of imprisoned Fenian activists. Despite the fact that he was in prison and thus unable to campaign, O'Donovan Rossa topped the poll and defeated the Liberal candidate, Denis Caulfield Heron, by 1,311 votes to 1,028. Celebrating his victory, *The Irishman* newspaper compared O'Donovan Rossa to Henri Rochefort, a French republican who had condemned the Emperor of France.[27] Elected as MP for County Tipperary, O'Donovan Rossa, never one to miss an opportunity to bother the Gaol authorities, requested from Captain Powell a transfer to Millbank Prison in London so as to be closer to Westminster. He hoped that Powell could achieve this as he was desirous of 'attending [his] parliamentary duties at night after picking [his] bit of oakum by the day'.[28] Basking in his new role as Member of Parliament, he joked with John Devoy how, if his constituents allowed it, he intended to appoint him to a tide waitership position. Some debated with him as to whether he would take the Oath of Allegiance necessary to take his seat in Parliament; O'Donovan Rossa claimed that he would deliver his maiden speech in Irish, forcing the state to hire the services of an interpreter: 'I was an Irishman, represented an Irish county, and had a right to be heard in the language of my country… that may be thought ridiculous but it is not a bit more ridiculous than to think the votes of a hundred Irish members can get an independent Irish government…'[29]

Comparing his election to Daniel O'Connell's in 1828, O'Donovan Rossa rather grandly argued that his election was more significant and of greater importance than that of O'Connell. Whereas O'Connell had been a freeman, he was imprisoned, 'dead in law and [was] subjected to every indignity England could heap upon him in his living grace'. Regarding the election as 'a protest against England and a defiance to her ministry', he commended the people of Tipperary for voting for him as a man who 'defied and denounced the most loudly her government, her traitor judges, and her packed juries'.[30] As a convicted felon, O'Donovan Rossa's election was declared null and void and a subsequent re-run of the by-election occurred between the imprisoned Charles Kickham and Heron. Heron won by four votes.

In March 1870, William Ewart Gladstone, the British Prime Minister, resultant from the appeals from the Amnesty Association, had been forced to undertake a further investigation into the treatment of Fenian prisoners in British Prisons. The idea for a Commission of Inquiry had originally been broached by Phillip Callan, an Irish MP for Dundalk, but had been refused out of hand by Gladstone, who cited the 1867 report. Raising the matter for a second time, George Moore, MP for Mayo, again called for an inquiry and went so far as to actually recommend an amnesty.[31] Gladstone, whose government was preparing particularly controversial legislation for Ireland, the Peace Preservation Bill, now agreed to the inquiry as a sop to Irish nationalism, intending it to be short and minor, lasting no more than fifteen days. With the 1867 investigation widely condemned and seen as impartial, Gladstone appointed the widely respected William Reginald Courtney, the Earl of Devon, to head his new commission. Courtney approached his work with gusto, and remained staunchly independent of both the government and prisoners. Courtney was assisted by a team which included George Broderick, a writer for the *Times* newspaper, Stephen De Vere, Dr Robert Lyons, an Irish professor of medicine who had served at the Crimea, Dr Edward Greenhow, and William Ollivant, an English barrister. Becoming known as the Devon Commission, from the start it was apparent that the commission was willing to collaborate with the prisoners and seek their opinions regarding the nature of their imprisonment. While Courtney had dismissed a request by Isaac Butt that he should be allowed to interview the prisoners, suggest witnesses and topics of inquiry, the Earl agreed with Butt to allow friends of prisoners to visit them at reasonable times and periods to assist their preparations for the inquiry. The fact that Courtney had defined assistance to prisoners as appropriate during reasonable times and periods was rather ambiguous and open to interpretation, thus prisoners were now entitled to receive family members or legal advisers in their prison cells, once they were designated as an assistant. Under the terms of the commission, Fenian prisoners could now be interviewed in private in the absence of a prison officer with a guarantee that their statements would remain confidential and not prejudice their continuing treatment within prison. Equally, the remit of the investigation was not to be limited to incarcerated Fenians but was also applicable to former Fenian prisoners and the dependents of current Fenian prisoners. This remit caused tremendous anxiety for the government, who felt that Devon had been naïve by making such terms with Butt. For his part, Butt published the terms and had them printed in *The Freeman's Journal* newspaper, meaning the British government could not renege on the agreement.[32] Horrified at the development of the Devon Commission, Courtney's inquiries took a life of their own and continued for three months. A minor investigation which the government had hoped would only last fifteen days had developed into an intense and methodological investigation. Commenting on the Devon Commission, the Home Office regarded the developments as 'altogether unanticipated'.[33]

Despite the terms secured for the Devon Commission, many Fenian prisoners remained cautious about the inquiry and debated whether they should take part for reasons which included a natural distrust of the British government and the likelihood of a repeat of the 1867 inquiry. After much discussion with his comrades, O'Donovan Rossa agreed to be interviewed by the inquiry. In support of this, O'Donovan Rossa requested Mary Jane to come to England and assist him. Mary Jane was initially testy, however, and argued with her husband about the merits of the inquiry. On arriving in London and securing a meeting with her husband, Mary Jane was told by the Deputy Governor that under no circumstance was she to discuss politics or his treatment. Outraged, she published the details of their meeting in the press. Mary Jane also wrote to the Devon Commission seeking permission to visit her husband and William Halpin. Receiving a letter from William Ollivant, her request was sent to the Home Office on 17 June 1870, and having heard nothing from the commission for five days, Mary Jane returned to her family home in Clonakilty. Receiving a telegram dated 2 July from the Home Office, which had been forwarded to her from her previous London lodgings, she was given permission to see her husband on 4 July. Mary Jane was outraged and believed that the government had actively sought to undermine her husband's contribution to the commission by ensuring that she had been offered permission to see her husband at a time when she could not come to Chatham. She was equally of the belief that her previous meeting with her husband was used against her. Writing a letter to the Earl of Devon, which she had published in *The Freeman's Journal,* she condemned the commission and the British government:

> I feel that I have been treated with cruelty, injustice and indignity.
> Five weeks since I applied for and obtained permission to see my
> husband and obtained permission from the directors of prisons to
> see my husband at Chatham Prison. I took the tedious journey
> from my home here [Clonakilty] but rather to obtain from him
> any instructions regarding the assistance I might be able to render

him in preparing for the expected inquiry into prisoners treatment. My design was frustrated by the deputy governor's strict prohibition during my interview with my husband, that neither his treatment nor politics should form subject of conversation. I resented this suppression of the theme most vitally interesting to us, by writing a truthful account of the interview to the editor of *The Irishman*, which [sic] account brought upon me the displeasure of the Directors of Prisons, and effectually barred me, as I have since proved, the doors of their compassion. Hoping against hope, I hardly knew for what I remained still in London and on seeing some of your correspondence with Mr Butt I, encouraged by its tone, addressed your Lordship on the 17th June, requesting you would grant me an order to see my husband and General Halpin as I wished to assist them in preparing their statement... My Lord this permission granted at the eleventh hour I look upon as an insult; as a crowning proof that while the Government is thus anxious to keep the letter and appearance of its promise intact, it has no regard for the spirit of that promise. It tramples upon the soul of fair play that would be suppressed to have suggested it – it breaks faith in the spirit, and holding to the form, hopes craftily thus to justify itself before the world...[34]

When interviewed by the commission, O'Donovan Rossa gave a frank and detailed account of his prison experiences with particular reference to his treatment following his 'salute' to Captain Powell, when he had been handcuffed for thirty-four days, followed by twenty-eight days on bread and water. Compiling the evidence, the Devon Commission vindicated O'Donovan Rossa and concluded that he was illegally handcuffed for thirty-four days between 17 June and 20 July. The commission recalled his contribution as 'candid and straightforward'.[35] It should be noted that in his prison recollections, O'Donovan Rossa claimed he had been handcuffed for thirty-five days and this had been supported by numerous primary sources, albeit written after the time, indicating that he accidentally miscounted the number of days. Regarding his treatment during his arrival at Pentonville Prison, and the taking of the flannel clothes which he had been given at Mountjoy, the commission found that the governor was wrong to have not returned the flannels as requested. Examining his experience at Portland Prison, where Governor Clifton had tried to establish a belief that O'Donovan Rossa was having an affair with a prisoner's wife, O'Donovan Rossa was again vindicated and the Devon Commission found that 'the Governor acted and spoke under misapprehension... and that O'Donovan Rossa is clear from the imputation of any endeavour to carry on a love intrigue'.[36] Examining his bread and water punishments, it was noted that O'Donovan Rossa had slight aortic disease, and that bread and water punishment was not congenial to his condition and made him, in their opinion, unfit for such discipline. Regarding the continued suppression of O'Donovan Rossa's letters to his family, particularly Mary Jane, the commission recommended that the prison authorities should send his correspondence but censor anything which they deemed offensive to the prison rules. Finalising the report, the Devon Commission concluded that the government could do well to consider a system where political prisoners, which the state refused to recognise as such, could be separated from ordinary prisoners and treated differently within the prison and a separate wing within gaols could be established to accommodate their presence within the prison system.

While the findings of the Devon Commission remained confidential until publication, news of its completion was leaked to the media on 28 November 1870. The *Irish Times* had reported that Lord Devon had finalised his report and handed it to the Home Secretary. Against this background there was increasing speculation about the possibility of an amnesty of Fenian prisoners sometime before Christmas.[37] The report, however, was not published until 16 December and made remarkably uncomfortable reading for the British government. Detailing the experiences of Fenian prisoners in British Gaols, the report indicated a system of brutality, mundane labour and callousness directed towards Fenian prisoners. Of particular discomfort to the government was the fact that Prime Minister Gladstone had been remarkably vocal about prison abuses of political prisoners in Naples and had previously published a pamphlet condemning the imprisonment and treatment of political prisoners in the Italian Kingdom. Now in Britain, under his leadership, a similar style of prison system existed, directed against political prisoners which the state would not recognise.

On the same day as the report's publication, Gladstone offered the Fenian prisoners an amnesty, providing them with an option to leave Gaol. His amnesty proposal was, however, highly controversial on the grounds that it was a conditional amnesty. Under the Gladstone Amnesty, Fenian prisoners would have to agree to absent themselves from Ireland for the duration of their sentence. Under this offer, the government insisted that if a Fenian prisoner accepted an amnesty, and was found in Ireland at any time throughout the duration of their sentence, they would be arrested and re-imprisoned. The choice of amnesty was stark for the Fenian prisoners and they debated amongst themselves what they should do. The possibility of exiling themselves from Ireland was a difficult choice to contemplate. This choice was represented by Harry S. Mulleda, who spoke of the exile in a letter to a friend as perhaps the lesser of two evils, noting how history would judge the British government for their Irish policy as 'wont future generations exclaim what a fearful set of fellows these Fenians must have been, so that a good and liberal government, could not, consistently with its duty to the country, let them out of prison, after five years of penal servitude, lest they should set the Thames on fire!'[38] O'Donovan Rossa was horrified by the offer of a conditional amnesty, but similar to Mulleda he saw it as the lesser of two evils. Mulling over the potential of leaving prison, he regarded the Prime Minister's offer as a meagre swapping of perpetual imprisonment in England for twenty years of banishment in a foreign country. Discussing the matter with Mary Jane, O'Donovan Rossa initially decided to leave for Australia, but after further discussion with his comrades in prison, he made a decision to choose exile in New York.

Released from prison on Saturday 7 January, O'Donovan Rossa was joined by John Devoy, Charles Underwood O'Connell, John McClure and Harry S. Mulleda. As they left Chatham, despite their release, they were incredibly melancholic. Their group was devoid of William Halpin, who had decided that he would not sign the amnesty agreement. Leaving him behind in Chatham was tough on the soon to be exiles, and they had asked to see him before they left. O'Donovan Rossa recollected a painful parting as their coach drove out from the prison yard, leaving Halpin behind in his prison uniform. The five were driven to Chatham Railway Station where they were placed under police protection and boarded a train bound for London. Arriving in London they were accompanied by the authorities on a train to Liverpool where they were scheduled to bound a trans-Atlantic steamer, *The Cuba*, bound for America. In a final tragedy for O'Donovan Rossa, *The Cuba,* was scheduled to dock at Cobh, in County Cork, where it was to receive the Irish mail. Arriving in Cobh harbour, O'Donovan Rossa took in Ireland for one final time. Joined by his wife and James Maxwell at Cobh, some friends of O'Donovan Rossa had come to say farewell. Unable to board the ship, they sailed up to *The Cuba* in small boats and called out to him. Unable to shake any of their hands, O'Donovan Rossa leaped over the deck and onto one of the boats controlled by his friend Davey Riordan.

After a tremendous commotion, with some of the prison guards thinking he was trying to escape, he hugged his friends and climbed back on board. Jeremiah O'Donovan Rossa would not see Ireland again for another twenty-three years. As the *SS Cuba* sailed out of Ireland, he became an exile from his native land.

7

AMERICA

As the Cuba Five made their way to America, *The Milwaukee Sentinel* newspaper broadly welcomed the exiles and wished, in particular, to send a warm welcome 'to the ardent, true hearted Rossa'. The newspaper complimented him on his prison struggle and lamented the pain and suffering he endured while a prisoner of the Queen. Saluting his spirit as unconquerable, the newspaper commented 'never once during his imprisonment has he been known to renounce the faith which brought misfortune upon him'.[1] While O'Donovan Rossa was the most well known of the exiles, there was considerable interest in the arrival of all the former Fenian prisoners to America. This had more to do with political manoeuvring rather than hospitality, however. The Irish-American community was a significant electoral bloc within American politics and the arrival of the Fenian exiles, particularly the well known O'Donovan Rossa, gave an impetuous thrust to politicians eager to capture the hearts and minds of Irish America, and was met with passion and significance. Tammany Hall, a New York political organisation, was particularly eager to welcome the exiles to their new home. The city affiliate of the Democratic Party, under Boss Tweed, it was eager to extend its control throughout the state and saw a golden opportunity for electoral and profitable gain, as being seen alongside the Fenian exiles would 'be productive of great results in way of political capital'.[2]

Tammany Hall helped immigrants in New York City set themselves up in the city and provided the only relief which the poor could receive. The political machine also built New York into a great city; it was under Tweed that the city expanded into the upper east and west of Manhattan. For all of its good work, however, the organisation was endemically corrupt, with many of its leading figures utilising such nefarious practices as bribery, jobbery, judicial corruption, nepotism and embezzlement. This was no more apparent than within the career of Tweed, who had organised a circle of corrupt individuals around him, regularly embezzling city funds and buying votes to secure positions of power within the city. In this Tweed was associated with Abraham Oakley Hall, the Mayor of New York City, Richard Connolly, City Comptroller and Peter Sweeny, New York District Attorney. Since the 1850s, Tammany Hall had shown a great interest in the Irish community and in many respects the democratic machine became a by-word for Irish-America as thousands of Irish-Americans benefitted from the institution and established themselves as a powerful political class.

Prior to the arrival of the exiles, Richard O'Gorman, at a Tammany general committee meeting, raised the issue that the Democratic Party supported Ireland's right to self-determination and 'never fails to sympathise with all men who devote themselves sincerely to the cause of their country's independence'. O'Gorman went on to comment how Fenian prisoners had suffered indignant imprisonment in Britain and deserved a cordial welcome to America.[3] Similar attempts to use the opportunity of the exiles' arrival to America to woo Irish-Americans were made by the New York-based United Irishmen, under the presidency of John McCarthy. They heralded their arrival as 'a new and energetic departure along the path by which our people must advance to the attainment of the liberty they have so long sought'.[4] Both Tammany Hall and the United Irishmen sought to counter the other, having hired two steamers to herald the exiles arrival: *The Antelope* and *The Andrew Fletcher* respectively. A further group, headed by an Irishman called Sweeney, also sought to appeal to the exiles and like his competitors, Sweeney's group had also secured a boat to meet their arrival, followed swiftly by a fraternal Irish-American group called the Knights of St Patrick and a sway of city officials.

Arriving in their new adopted homeland, the exiles sailed past Sandy Hook, New Jersey prior to docking at New York City. In the distance, *The Antelope* and *The Andrew Fletcher* raced to get to them first, and with their parties eagerly boarding the vessel, the exiles were confronted with a political circus as each group tried to entice them to their side. O'Donovan Rossa was horrified and felt he was being used as political capital, not given the time to even leave *The Cuba*. He recalled how 'two phases of the mania were raging – the Irish and the American – and of the two the former was the worst'.[5] He recollected how it was almost impossible to speak, as every time he tried he was interrupted by partisans shouting 'Rossa this way,' and 'Rossa that way'.[6] Reporting the scene, one newspaper recalled how 'O'Donovan Rossa and his compatriots appeared greatly pained at the differences which they recognised among their countrymen.'[7]

In need of retiring from the throng who had rushed *The Cuba*, O'Donovan Rossa was introduced to the collector of New York Port, Mr Murphy. By an incredible chance, Murphy was an Irishman and the two had an interesting conversation in which the collector told him that Irish-America was sympathetic to the Fenian cause, yet as evidenced by his arrival, the movement within the country had become embroiled in American politics and was controlled by 'thieves and swindlers who on every important occasion use them against the interests of our country'.[8] The collector held that this was to the disgrace of the Irish nation and he would be best to avoid all kinds of Irish political movements within America. What the collector refrained from telling O'Donovan Rossa, however, was that he was equally seeking to appeal to the exiles on behalf of the Federal government and was using the opportunity of the exiles' arrival to undermine Tammany Hall. The collector's appeals to O'Donovan Rossa were undermined by the Port's health officer, Dr Carnochan, who having diagnosed a case of smallpox on the boat, recommended quarantine, thus making the collector's offer void. To O'Donovan Rossa's surprise, however, the state quarantine seemingly was not applicable to Tammany Hall. On enquiring why this was the case, O'Donovan Rossa learned that Carnochan belonged to Tammany, and the diagnosis was made as a means of preventing the Cuba Five from accepting the federal offer of accommodation. As the melee was taking place between the Federal government and Tammany, John Moriarity, President of the Irish Republican Association of Pennsylvania, cabled the newly arrived exiles, warning them to 'beware of the New York politicians who [...] woo them but to use them for base and unscrupulous purposes'.[9] Moriarity further advised the exiles of how they should keep aloof of any American political organisation in order to attain respect for their presence in America. Listening attentively to all advice, the exiles privately discussed how to proceed with their arrival in America. Judging that an endorsement of a singular faction could alienate another, they chose to play for time. The Cuba Five agreed that O'Donovan Rossa should read a prepared statement to the assembled interested parties and speaking on their behalf from the deck of *The Cuba*, he explained that it was the hope of the Cuba Five that Irish-America could unite behind a common ground of the dream of Irish independence. He explained how their group could not speak for the other exiles due to arrive in America and would take 'no public step until they arrive'.[10] It was therefore their intention not to endorse one singular party and they would stay in a private hotel. The *Daily Kansas Tribune*, on learning of the statement, added their belief that O'Donovan Rossa was:

By all accounts too shrewd to be a tool in the hands of any clique. We expect to hear of him being a leader, not a follower. In Ireland he was known as one of the most determined and uncompromising of the Fenians: hence his life sentence; hence his defiance of the British government while he was in prison; hence his refusal to ask for clemency or to promise good behaviour, else he might have obtained his liberty a year or two sooner; and hence on his arrival the other day he called upon all Irishmen in America to unite for the regeneration of their country.[11]

Departing *The Cuba* the following day, a large crowd had gathered to celebrate their arrival in America. Escorted by the 69th Irish Regiment of the American Army to Sweeney's Hotel, they were again greeted by throngs of Irish-Americans waving green flags in addition to the American flag. The *New York Herald* recalled their arrival:

The public buildings were gaily decorated, newspaper offices, hotels and banks flaunted the national colours, and Broadway appeared in festive aspect. Throughout the forenoon the streets were thronged with spectators, and in many places flags were hung across the streets. The heads of horses on different lines were decorated with miniature flags of the US and Ireland, while large banners of both nationalities floated from flagstaff's and [gave] the city a holiday appearance.[12]

The exiles arrived at Sweeney's Hotel, where the management had raised a green flag over the building; a large crowd had assembled and there were loud cheers for Rossa in particular. The exiles had chosen to pay for themselves so as not to be in gratitude to any faction in America. They were visited by a veritable who's-who of the Fenian movement in America including Colonel William Roberts, Colonel John Whitehead, John Savage, John O'Mahony and John Mitchel. According to one newspaper, *The Memphis Daily Appeal*, throngs of Irish-Americans had descended on the hotel to see the exiles, many were hoping to 'shake their hands and wish them *caed mille faltha* [sic] to Uncle Sam's dominions'.[13] Soon after they were greeted by a further delegation from the United Irishmen who, despite the exiles' desire not to be in gratitude, presented O'Donovan Rossa with $1,000 and an address welcoming him to America.[14] Shortly afterwards they were visited by the Knights of St Patrick who similarly welcomed them and acknowledged their 'services in the cause of

Irish freedom'.[15] Not to be beaten by the United Irishmen, the Knights of St Patrick, represented by General Frank Millen, similarly presented O'Donovan Rossa with a cheque for $1,100.[16] Meeting so many people left O'Donovan Rossa feeling tired and strained. Considering his prison ordeals, he was the most famous of the exiles and had garnered a considerable degree of public attention. He had met so many people that he complained his hand had been swollen from the abnormal number of handshakes he had provided to well-wishers.

Meeting with representatives from Tammany Hall, the exiles turned down an offer to be put up in a finer establishment, and retiring to the hotel, they declined to see anyone else. To their horror, however, upon arrival they discovered that their rooms had already been paid for. The exiles became celebrities overnight, and daily deputations, letters and congratulations poured in. The greetings extended to the Cuba Five were shown to other exiles who followed in their wake shortly afterwards.[17] Meeting with the other exiles, it was decided that they would have nothing to do with American politics and rise above the factionalism within Irish-America. The House of Congress resolved to welcome them on 'behalf of the people of the United States',[18] and an audience was arranged with the President of the United States, Ulysses S. Grant.[19] Summing up the ludicrous scene of their arrival in America, *The New York Times* aptly noted that the exiles: 'are simply regarded as handy material out of which to make political capital. Neither Collector Murphy, nor Mr Tweed nor Mr Sweeney would care a jot if the "exiles" had all fallen into the river, or had been torn to pieces by the lunatics who quarrelled over them, like vultures over their prey'.[20] This opinion was shared by a Fenian activist, P. M. Gill, who wrote to O'Donovan Rossa, warning him of the duplicity within American politics.[21]

As McGill had suggested, it became painfully clear to the exiles that the Fenian movement had become fractured and intertwined with republican and democratic political machines. As R. P. Gorman contended, unless the movement united its existence, it was hopeless if not worthless. This division would only serve to copper-fasten the British grip on Ireland. He recommended only when Irishmen could work together in the common aim of achieving self-determination could it actually be achieved, informing the exiles:

The Tyranny to which we are indebted for all our misery is not of England, but in ourselves. Here then is the tyrant on whom we must make war. For we confidently believe if the scattered millions of the

Irish race were united and thoroughly organised their demands would be conceded by England, without a blow. If this is true the exiles will see and feel the trying and responsible task they have undertaken, and we hope and believe... through your influence and exertions a new spirit will be infused into the organisation and that you will cement in one powerful and fraternal compact the discordant and diverging elements of our race.[22]

Increasingly, calls were made for the exiles to unite the movement. The exiles lost in the ecstasy of their arrival as 'the acknowledged leaders of their race in America',[23] concluded that they could be a catalyst for change, and upon their call, all other nationalist organisations would collapse into grand coalition. Initially they were supported in this endeavour by the United Irishmen, whose leaders handed over control to them 'in order to secure an immediate and efficient union of all Irish Nationalists'.[24] The exiles held that Fenianism needed to become non-partisan while in America and establishing a directory, which included amongst others O'Donovan Rossa, General Thomas Francis Bourke, John Devoy and Captain John McClure, Devoy wrote how its ambition was:

To create an Irish party in this country, whose actions in American politics will have for its sole object the interests of Ireland. We will also hold aloof from all different sections of the Fenians. I may tell you that most of us are sick of the very issue of Fenianism, though as resolved as ever to work for the attainment of Irish Independence.[25]

It was evident that the exiles were desirous of building a broad-based national movement uniting Irish nationalists in America behind a demand for Irish independence. They favoured establishing a secret and open organisation working in tandem.[26] Dennis Mulcahy, himself a member of the Directory, declared the need for a 'public organisation to be directed by a secret organisation to be in the hands of a select number of the released prisoners'.[27] John Devoy argued that any new movement 'for its object the liberation of Ireland should be so constituted that all the different sections of the Irish people might be included in it'.[28] He argued that existing societies should be ignored as 'none of these represent more than a small section of the Irish people in America and therefore have no claim to be called national organisations'.[29] Devoy saw the open organisation collecting money 'for the purpose of aiding the national movement' while its secret counterpart worked for 'effecting a revolution in

Ireland'.[30] By 8 February 1871 the exiles addressed Irish-America, appealing for support:

> In view of the disunion existing the ranks of Irish nationalists – in this country [...] we the released Irish prisoners appeal to you as Irishmen, loving Ireland and who are desirous of labouring in the hope of restoring her to a position she has occupied and we believe is destined to occupy [...]now propose to unite the whole Irish population of this country into one great organisation, established on so broad a base as to admit all and exclude none.[31]

To achieve unity of purpose the exiles sought to establish a General Council consisting of all Irish separatist organisations operating within America. This was to be achieved through a broad umbrella organisation called the Irish Confederation.[32] Treating all members equally, each constituent organisation would have a share in the confederation funding to the tune of 25 per cent of their income. The confederation, however, would be controlled by the Irish exiles, as neutral affiliates constituting a 'directory of five',[33] to keep secrecy and prevent treachery as 'England will be willing to expend thousands to get an agent into an executive council of such an organisation...'

The Fenian Brotherhood reacted to the Irish Confederation by announcing that its ruling council could not decide on the question of union and had no power to transfer its directory without calling a General Convention to decide upon the issue. The Council decided on 21 March 1871 that 'in the convention there should be a spirit of concession that should actuate men who claim to represent a general fraternity'.[34] O'Mahony staunchly opposed it, as did John Savage, Chief Executive of the Fenian Brotherhood Council. Within a week the convention decided that they would not associate with the confederation as immediate union was impractical.[35] For O'Donovan Rossa it became increasingly apparent that all the Fenian Brotherhood wanted was unity in itself, rather than with others.

The Fenian Brotherhood and the Irish Confederation, while publicly aloof and following a public policy of non-interference in each other's operations, were thus hostile from the very beginning. Behind the scenes, however, as is the case in realpolitik, attempts were made to build a fragile unity between the two, undoubtedly aided by intertwined grassroots membership. This resulted in the formation of an Allied Council of five members, consisting of two representatives from the Irish Confederation, two from the Fenian Brotherhood, and another acceptable to both. It was agreed that the Allied Council would meet on the first Tuesday of each month to discuss 'organisation and important subjects'.[36] This coalition could never deliver stability, and it soon collapsed.

On 9 February 1872 the Confederation had called a general convention for Wednesday 16 May, in New York,[37] to debate and discuss strategy and progress. It would also propose the adoption of a constitution, the Supreme Governing Document, setting out the rules and procedures,[38] declaring that for 'the purpose of assisting the Irish Republican Brotherhood to win the independence of Ireland by armed revolution'.[39] The constitution essentially defined the confederation as the analogous American organisation to the IRB in Ireland, and committed itself to sending 'a regular remittance of money to the supreme council or other governing body of the IRB in Ireland'.[40] The convention agreed that membership of the Confederation was open to all Irishmen who had been proposed to by two members of good standing. So as to keep out treachery, each member would be oath-bound to uphold the Republic.

The Confederation saw many fervent political meetings, and a growth in membership, but its Achilles heel was its inability to unite the wider movement. Its failure to do any real work for Ireland also frustrated O'Donovan Rossa as he found the Confederation was increasingly becoming a bureaucratic farce run by excessive committees and yes men who talked about revolution in Ireland but did very little in practice. Frustrated by their inactivity, he concluded that:

> I cannot find words to express my contempt for these men as Irish revolutionists… I will speak plainer again and say that councils or committees of sixes and sevens to agree on doing something are likely to do nothing. Having bitter experience of their work here, my mind is made up, and I would vote for one man power.[41]

It was looked upon with jealousy and hostility by existing societies, and had collapsed by 1873. The exiles and their supporters, who had come to believe that they were to be a catalyst for change, were left disappointed and disillusioned. O'Donovan Rossa was heartbroken and concluded that his efforts were wasted; he lamented how it had become no more than 'another faction or party where so many existed'.[42]

Apart from Fenianism, O'Donovan Rossa had sought to build a life for his family in America. Since his arrival in 1871 he had sought out the American Dream in the hope of achieving financial prosperity and success. He worked as the editor of the New York-based *Era* newspaper; he had managed the Great Northern and Chatham Hotels and had become a ticket agent for the White Star Line and their counterparts, the National Line of Steamers. The American Dream managed to elude him, however, and he was left in great financial difficulty throughout his life as his spending greatly outweighed his income. O'Donovan Rossa was a poor businessman and he was never one to recoup monies owed to him. In many respects it was common for his customers to take advantage of his good nature and he could regularly be swayed by their political opinions in his dealings with them. That this caused financial distress to the family was evident and writing about his father, Denis O'Donovan Rossa complained to Mary Jane how 'he'll never be a success... Father is particularly unsuited for the business'.[43]

Mary Jane now increasingly faded into the background of their family life and committed herself to looking after O'Donovan Rossa's family. There is an abundance of evidence that he did not get on with his children from his earlier marriages and they resented the fact that he had put his politics before them, necessitating a rather unusual upbringing in Ireland. His son Denis, in particular was incredibly harsh on his father. On 28 December 1871 Mary Jane gave birth to her second child, Kate Ellen. Tragically, Kate Ellen died of cot death within less than a year of her birth on 12 July 1872. The couple had a further child, Frank Daniel, who was born on 26 January 1873. Like Kate Ellen, Frank Daniel died within months on 5 September 1873. Tragedy again struck the family with the birth of Maurice on 19 May 1874; living for two months, he died on Kate Ellen's anniversary. Following Maurice's death, Mary Jane gave birth to Sheela in 1876 and within two years a further daughter, Eileen, was born, followed by Amelia in 1880, Jeremiah in 1881, Isabella in 1883, Mary Jane in 1884 and her sister Margaret in 1887. On two further occasions tragedy again struck the O'Donovan Rossa family as two further children died, Joseph Ivor born on 19 January 1889 and Alexander in 1890, both dying on 29 January 1889 and 28 March 1891 respectively. Coupled with his children from his previous marriages, by the end of the century, O'Donovan Rossa was the father to eighteen living children.

Writing of her father, Margaret remembered him as a devoted family man and explained how 'the general opinion that Jeremiah O'Donovan Rossa was a hot-tempered man of violent tendencies is entirely wrong... Papa was a man of soft speech and courteous manner, who seldom became angry and never was known to swear'.[44] His one idiosyncrasy, according to Margaret, was a profound hatred of chewing gum, which he had banned from the family home, unable to understand why children would put something in their mouth of no nutritional value. This forced the children to regularly smuggle chewing gum into the house and it was later recalled that his opposition to chewing gum was rooted in the experience of the Famine – it had reminded him of the Famine and how people had chewed grass in order to survive. A further peculiarity which he had developed was a marked dislike of bread and water, resultant from his horrific prison treatment. As a supplement to water he drank copious amounts of tea and recalling an amusing family anecdote, Margaret noted that one morning, at 2 a.m., he had arisen from bed in his nightshirt to make some tea but as the milk was outside the house in an icebox he had to walk across the porch. In doing so, however, he accidentally locked himself out and attempting to climb in the window 'chuckling to himself at his success… a big hand grasped him roughly by the shoulder and yanked him back to the porch'.[45] He had been seen by a policeman and suspected of being a burglar was accosted. Bringing O'Donovan Rossa to the front door, the officer rang the doorbell and asked Mary Jane if she had seen 'this queer nut before', to which his wife mischievously exclaimed 'Oh officer… please don't arrest the poor creature. I know him well and I often give him a cup of tea. He's a bit queer at times but perfectly harmless. I'll take him in and put him up for the night.' Satisfying the officer was satisfied with Mary Jane's reply, and on this occasion, the veteran Fenian avoided arrest.

The care of the children was helped by Mary Jane's sister, Isabella, a trained nurse who irregularly lived with the family, but disliked Rossa on account of his need to put politics before family as it was noted that 'Ireland was first in his heart'.[46] Addressing this, Mary Jane commented how it never bothered her as God had made his heart bigger to cater for both his loves – Ireland and his family.[47] A domineering woman, Isabella, known fondly to the children as 'Aunt Anzibella',[48] was a disciplinarian within the household and having lost the sight in one of her eyes was marked by a glass eye, which seemed to follow the children around the room and even left Mary Jane 'terrified'.[49] Their upbringing was also assisted by Lizzie Chadwick, an Irish emigrant from Clonakilty who worked in the family home as a general helper in addition to an Indian woman who was called Hoolie, for she had married an Irishman named O'Hoolihan. The O'Donovan Rossa family were brought up as Roman Catholics and their catholicism was a significant aspect of their family life. Despite his earlier troubles with catholicism on account of his politics, O'Donovan Rossa regularly attended Mass with his family. Equally, Mary Jane was eager that her sense of Irishness should be transferred to her

American family and insisted upon a nationalist education. The children were reared on stories of heroic Irish sagas, rebellions and traditional stories. They were enthralled by the horrors of the Famine and what their parents had seen, and despite the fact that they were born into a country which spoke English, they were taught the Irish language and until school age retained the Irish versions of their names. It should be noted that while the education of the children was entrusted to Mary Jane, she could not speak Irish, and so the teaching of Irish was left to O'Donovan Rossa.

Aside from his family life and attempts to capture the elusive American Dream, O'Donovan Rossa had aspirations to become a politician. This was of course contradictory to the earlier position of the exiles not to involve themselves within the complexities of American politics, but in 1871 O'Donovan Rossa seemingly embraced the New York political scene. His new city was dominated by Tammany Hall, a Democratic Party machine, led by 'Boss' William M. Tweed. The political machine helped immigrants in New York City setup and provided the only relief to which the poor could receive. The political machine also built New York into a great city; it was under Tweed that the City expanded into Upper east and west of Manhattan parallel to the construction of the Brooklyn Bridge. For all of its good work, however, the organisation was endemically corrupt with many of its leading figures utilising such nefarious practices as bribery, jobbery, judicial corruption, nepotism and embezzlement. This was no more apparent than within the career of Boss Tweed who had organised a circle of corrupt individuals around him regularly embezzling city funds and buying votes to secure positions of power within the city. In this Tweed was associated with Abraham Oakley Hall, the Mayor of New York City, Richard Connolly, City Comptroller and Peter Sweeny, New York District Attorney. Since the 1850s Tammany Hall had shown a great interest in the Irish community and in many respects the Democratic machine became a by-word for Irish-America as thousands of Irish-Americans benefitted for the institution and established themselves as a powerful political class.

As previously mentioned, Tammany Hall was a powerful institution within the city, particularly among Irish-Americans. O'Donovan Rossa grew a strong dislike for Tammany as an institution and held Boss Tweed in low regard. Illustrating his view of the Tweed ring he wrote how 'Connolly had the reputation of being the slippery man of this ring; Tweed the rich man; Hall the poor man; and Sweeny the clever man.'[50] He was also infuriated with the relationship between Tammany and the Irish-American community and the association of the Irish in America with base corruption. He recalled how he had met with Connolly at Sweeny's Hotel shortly after his arrival in America and Connolly had implied that if he supported the Tammany machine he could be a very rich man and that he was looking for a replacement of his deputy who had died in Central Park, implying that the position could be tailor-made for the newly arrived Irishman. Rejecting Connolly's offer, O'Donovan Rossa increasingly came to the conclusion that Irish-American politicians had no genuine interest in the affairs of Ireland but were more concerned with achieving and maintaining a position of power in America.

In 1871 Boss Tweed, who was a New York State Senator at the time, was forced to run for re-election. He had suffered a serious blow due to a campaign by *The New York Times* and the cartoonist of *Harpers Weekly*, Thomas Nast, who had exposed the corruption endemic within Tammany Hall. Such was the influence of the campaign against Tammany Hall that it forced an examination of the city's financial books. One step ahead of the media campaign, however, Tweed had his own people lead the investigation and finding no evidence of corruption, Tammany Hall was exonerated. Unwilling to accept this verdict, *The New York Times* continued investigating Tweed and eventually came across James O'Brien, an Irish-American county sheriff, who, unable to blackmail Tweed, sold his information to the newspaper, allowing them to unveil a headline story detailing scandalous levels of fraud and embezzlement within city finances. Forcing Tweed's arrest on 27 October 1871, the scandal undermined the power of Tammany within New York, but despite the great public outcry, he retained a good degree of support amongst Irish-America. Tweed was released on bail shortly after his arrest and seeking to stop the decline of Tammany within New York, it was decided that he would seek re-election to the New York State Senate.

`Determined to challenge Tammany Hall and offer an alternative for Irish-American voters, O'Donovan Rossa decided that he would rival Boss Tweed and run for his seat representing the Fourth District in November 1871. Assessing his candidature, the *New York Herald* described him as 'a strong man against the ring', and celebrated his Irishness as 'a man who ought to get the vote of every Irishman in the district'.[51] That he could challenge Tweed as a republican was aided by the fact that he had taken naturalised citizenship as an American citizen upon his arrival and secured papers on 21 February 1871. Without this he could not have run in the election to the Senate against Tweed and his application was fast-tracked on the basis of his earlier application in 1863. Rossa had justified his campaign on the grounds of Irishness within

America, his belief that 'the Irishman has done as much as any other man to make America',[52] and a perception that Tammany representatives disgraced Irish-America. With a political machine building around the Irishman, his campaign literature increasingly played upon his honourable Fenian past and the questionable character of Tweed:

> The contest in the Fourth Senatorial District is between a man who would elevate the Irish race and a man who would degrade it. William M. Tweed only uses Irishmen that he may build palaces in Fifth Avenue and at Greenwich, and erect stables beside which the finest residence in the Fourth Senatorial District is a hovel. Jeremiah O'Donovan Rossa has proved his love for Ireland and his adopted country and his countrymen in both places. He would make them more powerful by inculcating the virtues that make men noble. He is an honest man; his opponent is not. Rossa deserves the support of every man who can rise above the level of a rum-shop or a brothel.[53]

Portraying himself as a fighter, his election campaign established a narrative of O'Donovan Rossa as 'a true man who will wage determined war against every form of corruption'.[54] His decision to oppose Boss Tweed, however, was remarkably controversial and seen by many as a betrayal of the Irish voice in America. O'Donovan Rossa, it should be understood, had challenged Tammany Hall, an institution perceived to be the only organisation that gave political representation to Irish-America, and this upset a great deal of politically active Irish-Americans. Capturing this sentiment, *The Globe* newspaper condemned O'Donovan Rossa for 'mercenary conduct', going on to assert how:

> His course in this matter has done more damage to Irish nationality, and more to destroy future confidence in so-called Irish patriots, than the treachery of all the perjured informers of hundreds of years! ... O'Donovan Rossa's work for Ireland is over and done, his political career passed... What a name, what renown, what imperishable honours he and his country would have gained if England's bloody government had never pardoned him.[55]

O'Donovan Rossa's election campaign was based on the theme of Tammany's corruption, and he regularly cited how Tammany disgraced rather than benefitted Irish-America. For this he was condemned, ostracised, ridiculed and excluded from Irish-American politics. Losing by 6,000 votes, O'Donovan Rossa claimed that Tweed's election had been a 'gregarious fraud'[56] and was weighted by irregularities in addition to the use of election officials to influence voters in favour of Tweed. O'Donovan Rossa was correct – he had defeated Tweed by 350 votes, but Tweed's people had counted Rossa's votes out. Speaking of Tweed's apparent victory and how he was treated during the campaign, O'Donovan Rossa publically announced:

> The particular thing which met us everywhere was intimidation. The men who were canvassing for me were beaten and driven away and my tickets were destroyed by Tammany agents, and those of Miller, the independent candidate, introduced. Since the election hundreds of people have been to my office to make complaints of repeating, false counting and intimidation... many of my friends went to the polls, but finding that they were endangering their lives, went away without casting their ballots at all. A number of workmen were discharged from the Department of Public Works, yesterday, in consequence of their sympathy with me on the day of election... In the Fourth District Tweed's men were ready to resort to any means, no matter how desperate, to count him in. The only reputation which they seem to have had was ability to count thousands for Tweed if he only had tens. I am confident that, even with all the foul play, as many votes were cast for me as for Tweed, and as to particular instances of fraud, I can produce hundreds of affidavits.[57]

Tweed's election success was short-lived, however; he was again rearrested for embezzling city funds and forced to resign all of his official positions. O'Donovan Rossa claimed his vacant seat but was denied admission to the New York Senate and chose not to put his name forward for nomination again. His only foray into American politics had come to a conclusion.

O'Donovan Rossa had not yet given up on Irish republicanism within America, however. Since his arrival in the United States he had been a member of Clan na Gael, a secretive Irish-American organisation which had been established by James Sheedy at Hester Street, New York on 20 June 1867, the anniversary of the birth of Irish republican Theobald Wolfe Tone. The organisation had been established as a means of providing a common meeting ground for both factions of the Fenian Brotherhood, which had split prior to the Fenian rebellion.[58] While relations thawed between the factions of the

Brotherhood, it was only a shell of its former self, and Clan na Gael remained throughout the 1870s to grow to become one of the most important Irish organisations within America.

The Clan was organised along a hierarchical principle, and at its head was the executive board, known in cipher as the FC. The FC was essentially a committee presided over by a chairman elected annually by a Clan convention. Directly under the FC was a revolutionary directory consisting of a group of six, and was referred to as the RD.[59] The directory's purpose was to consider and organise revolutionary activity. It was marked by 'the autocratic power possessed by its members, about who's [sic] action no detailed information was supplied, and against who's [sic] proceedings there was in consequence, no basis for appeal'.[60] At a grassroots level, the Clan was organised into camps or divisions, led by guardians. Each guardian was ranked in terms of senior, junior and provisional. Only senior guardians knew the identity of the revolutionary directory. Clan members would be kept informed of FC decisions by means of circulars but were requested to dispose of them carefully after reading so as not to allow them fall into the Possession of British Intelligence.

Clan na Gael was slowly becoming the dominant Irish–American revolutionary organisation and was superseding the once mighty Fenian Brotherhood. The America that it emerged within was peculiar to the circumstances of the failure of Fenianism in the previous decade. The once powerful Irish–American base was by now a shadow of its former self, increasingly fractured through internecine sectarianism, distrust and animosity. Resultant from this, the movement had become stagnant and was 'consigned to the melancholic bar room reminisces of the increasingly aged men of '67'.[61] Against this background, O'Donovan Rossa increasingly began to argue that a fresh impetus had to be instilled into the Fenian movement and that America was the perfect base to do so. In this endeavour he was ably supported by one of the greatest Irish–Americans of his generation, Patrick Ford.

Born in Galway in 1837, and like so many others during the Great Famine, Ford emigrated to America in 1845. Educated at Boston at 13-years-of-age, he became involved in journalism and worked with the abolitionist, William Lloyd Garrison, on his newspaper, *The Liberator*. In 1861 he edited *The Boston Tribune* and carried by events leading to the US Civil War he enlisted in the Union Army's 9th Massachusetts Infantry, fighting at the battle of Fredericksburg on 13 December 1862. Settling in New York, Ford established *The Irish World* newspaper as a voice for Irish-Americans. Representative of the American Dream, his new newspaper was incredibly popular amongst Irish-Americans and from humble origins its circulation reached a height of 125,000 subscribers, becoming the most popularly read newspaper amongst the Irish. The *Irish World* championed ideas close to Ford's heart and became a mouthpiece for his arguments in favour of social justice and Irish independence. The newspaper also included trans-Atlantic correspondence, cartoons, reports from every county in Ireland and a section devoted to correspondence amongst its readers.

In 1876 Patrick Ford had received a letter from a subscriber to his newspaper suggesting the establishment of a revolutionary fund to raise money which would be used to attack Britain utilising 'terror, conflagration, and irretrievable destruction',[62] across British cities. Ford found that the idea of a revolutionary fund was a commendable and viable idea; taking the letter to O'Donovan Rossa, the two conferred as to the potential of a Fenian campaign of terrorism against Britain using America as its base of operations. Seeing potential within the idea, O'Donovan Rossa, noting 'a general desire to have more life infused into the Irish national movement'[63] on behalf of Irish-American activists, suggested that a skirmishing fund should be established. In Rossa's strategy, as understood by many within Irish-American Fenianism, this skirmishing fund would provide the means for bombing British cities and public opinion, securing the oxygen of publicity for Fenian grievance while Irish revolutionary organisations prepared for the heavier work of revolution.[64] If such a strategy was undertaken by Irish-Americans, facilitated by a skirmishing fund to maintain bombings within Britain, it was envisaged that 'its bare existence would strike more terror to the soul of England than all the fierce denunciations we could hurl at her from this till dooms day'.[65] This belief that a clandestine campaign would strike terror into Britain was underscored by a perception that a bombing campaign against British cities would so harass and disrupt the common experience of daily life that its own people would force the government to terms on the Irish question. With Ford's permission, O'Donovan Rossa used *The Irish World* to call for the establishment of a skirmishing fund, with Ford publicly commending the idea, explaining in an editorial:

> We heartily commend the suggestions contained in it to the considerations of all men who love Ireland and who earnestly seek to make her a free nation. Rossa wants to raise a skirmishing fund. He wants to see some *action* on foot. The idea is that stagnation will prove the silent destruction of the Irish cause, and that to give strength and vitality to this cause, in fact to keep the very revolutionary

organisations now in existence from dying out and stinking in the nostrils of the people, – it is necessary that the means should be on hand (independent of regular revolutionary funds) which will enable a few intrepid spirits to strike a blow at England, year after year, or oftener as might seem advisable, – *heroic men who will carry on an irregular and incessant warfare against the enemy,* – whilst the regular military organisations are preparing for heavier and more regular war...[66]

In order to support this nascent fund, O'Donovan Rossa became its secretary. Ford also offered the use of his paper to publish returns and the names of subscribers. He further allowed Rossa an independent column within *The Irish World* to highlight political grievance and attract potential supporters, while also keeping current subscribers informed of the fund's existence, thus justifying further subscriptions. In this strategy, successful rhetorical violence and attacks could generate publicity for Fenianism with Fenian bombings used as the language of political grievance. In the long term, this strategy, Ford concluded, could bring the force of public opinion on the British government through the disruption of everyday life, demanding urgent redress of the Irish question. In this spirit, Ford recommended to advanced nationalism a clear adoption of a terrorist strategy holding: '... We must *take the offensive!* Action gives life, action gives health. At present the Irish cause is received with a hiss and a sneer. This is telling against us. A few bold and devoted heroes must spring up and show the world there is still power in Fenianism not only to scare, but to *hurt* England.'[67]

Ford was suggesting a modern manner of warfare never witnessed in contemporary Europe. Using advances in modern travel and the increasing globalisation of nineteenth-century society,[68] he held that in this strategy, 'Spaniards in the days of the invincible Armada and Zulus today could not do what English speaking Irishmen can accomplish. Language, skin-colour, dress, general manners, are all in favour of the Irish,'[69] thus guaranteeing infiltration of British society.

Their appeal to establish a skirmishing fund was rooted within the complexities of Irish-American society and represented a deep political grievance amongst Irish-Americans against Britain. The level of anger amongst Irish-Americans was high enough for many to subscribe to the skirmishing fund. One of these contributors, Michael Ahern of Washington, pledged $20, wondering 'what quantity of dynamite would be sufficient to blow up the

English garrison at Fermoy, and how much would it cost? I am yours until death against the Sasanach'.[70] Thomas J. Kavanagh of Nevada, seeing the fund as a means of injecting life into a stagnant Fenianism, pledged $20 declaring, 'there would be some blood spilt. Then if the young men of Ireland want ... to fight for their country, there they have it. Let them rally round us'.[71] One correspondent, Rory of the Hill, was more to the point, informing Rossa in his position as secretary of the fund that:

> In case you at anytime soon deem it expedient to fit and equip a detachment of secret service whose object will be by the aid of explosives – such as Greek fire, dynamite, dualin etc, to be operated by electricity or fuse for the purpose of blowing up the Parliament in London and some of the forts and castles throughout England and Ireland – if such is mediated by you, I am at your service.[72]

A further correspondent offered the prospect of assassination. B. K. Kennedy of Colorado suggested the termination of Lord Leitrim, noting he was 'born in the county of Leitrim, close to the Lords mansion, would you want a little skirmishing done around there... I have a crow to pick with his lordship'.[73] Indeed, even O'Donovan Rossa's son, James Maxwell contributed to the fund and wrote enthusiastically about the idea of skirmishing, holding that the fund may 'make the light shine so brilliant in England, that you will see perfidious Albion going down and regenerated Ireland rising over her ruins'.[74]

In making their appeal to finance a revolutionary fund, both O'Donovan Rossa and Patrick Ford were aware of great scientific developments which could be beneficial to their campaign, the greatest of which was the invention of Alfred Nobel's dynamite compound, allowing easy transportation of nitro-glycerine through cities or across the Atlantic for use in Britain.[75] Modern scientific development had given the revolutionary a gift of diabolical proportions which could redress the modern conception of warfare; for the first time in history the revolutionist had a tremendous individual and low-cost power at his disposal, supported by the efficacy of modern scientific development, offering unbridled destruction and melodrama, representing in the revolutionary mentality an unparalleled means of victory against tyranny:[76]

> Dynamite held highly idealised associations: It offered new vistas of power, not solely for its potential to wreck destruction but also for its ability to terrify a wide public. The connotations of dynamite for

radical politics are hard to overstate. It was the ultimate weapon of one against the many, of any individual with only a smattering of training... the dynamite bomb seemed tiny in proportion to its capacity to do harm; it could fit easily into a small bag or even a pocket.[77]

Addressing the morality of contemporary warfare, terrorism was seen by proponents as a humane means of conflict, avoiding the bloodshed of open battle, doing the greatest material damage to property, while causing the least loss of life to both sides of conflict. Furthermore, the perceived efficacy of modern science if applied to warfare, tended, as many revolutionists believed, to make conflict shorter. Modern scientific development, along with the dynamite, provided the previously overwhelmed Fenians a way of attacking the powerful British state by means of a small number of men at the least possible expense.[78] James Stephens, the fallen Fenian leader, recognised this when he noted in dismay the emerging strategy of clandestine warfare:

Dynamite was being much talked of in the newspapers; and it was said that the anarchists and nihilists of the old world had at last in their hands an implement of destruction sufficient to destroy all the armies and navies in existence ... it was referred to in glowing terms as the gift of science to the oppressed children of men, whereby despotism could be overcome and the sunshine of liberty would illuminate forever more.[79]

Stephens was horrified with this embryonic strategy, viewing it as 'the wildest, the lowest and the wicked conception of the national movement'.[80] Condemning Rossa for his suggestion of a skirmishing fund to finance bombings, he asked:

Can he be really so moonstruck as to dream that any revolutionary organisations could effectually prepare serious work while his 'skirmishers' kept striking at England, year after year ...? Is his crooning for notoriety so ravenous and insatiable that, to gratify it, he would expose his country to the ban of civilisation? I cannot be calm and think of the injury one reckless scatterbrain may do our cause.[81]

Stephens argued that no revolutionary movement could organise a series of clandestine attacks directed against Britain; such a strategy would only facilitate

British counter-reaction and a loss of support for Fenian grievance. In common with the contemporary conception of warfare, Stephens believed Fenianism needed to mount open battle, shunning what he saw to be a dishonourable means of unfair and secretive conflict. In this view he was endorsed by Thomas Clarke Luby and John O'Leary. Parallel to Stephens, a larger Fenian faction, the IRB Supreme Council, argued that the bombing strategy was premature, the movement needing time to organise, restraining members from committing acts of violence in its name, which it considered counterproductive, and preferring to wait for an opportunity to mount open warfare to challenge the place of British rule in Ireland. Illustrating this point, John O'Leary, a prominent member of the Supreme Council, explained to John Devoy his horror at the notion of a skirmishing fund, holding how he could not support a bombing campaign while Ireland was not engaged in open insurrection against Britain.[82] What defined O'Leary's opposition was the decision that skirmishing was illegitimate, unless accompanied by open warfare. Furthermore, in O'Leary's opinion, the employment of skirmishing even during open warfare was of questionable morality suggesting fenianism needed to wait for a moment of British difficulty to mount a challenge to british rule in Ireland.[83] To this many argued that O'Leary was facilitating revolutionary paralysis. Irish-America agreed that conditions in Ireland were not ripe for revolution, but differed in its assertion that these conditions needed to be fostered by an aggressive campaign of the mobilising and symbolic power of violence. A frustrated O'Donovan Rossa declared against those who wanted to wait for British difficulty rather than take immediate action:

> I'd curse all that platitude people that keep continuing saying out 'wait for the opportunity' they are cods or cowards. There are opportunities and difficulties for England year after year and when they come we are prepared to do nothing, but when they are past we again say out 'wait for the opportunity and do no more'... I'll be burying myself before anything is done if we are to be waiting for those 'wait for the wagon' people to do the work.[84]

Examining the position of the opponents of the skirmishing strategy, supporters of clandestine warfare jeered their contradictory faction, taunting them for waiting and looking for 'some miracle by which they hoped to take the field',[85] against insurmountable odds. In justifying a revolutionary paralysis it was argued that they were shifting the work of establishing the conditions for revolution to later generations, while those of Fenian principles debated the question of legitimacy facilitating the normalisation of colonial rule in Ireland:

> The cry of 'England's difficulty being Ireland's opportunity,' is the 'stock in trade' of many Irishmen in Ireland and America, who do very little for Ireland… Irishmen of the present day should work to free Ireland in their own time, and not be shifting from their own shoulders to the shoulders of the men of the future generations the work they themselves should do.[86]

Proponents of a clandestine bombing campaign against Britain were, therefore, moved by impatience, making the necessity of direct political violence urgent and as a means of survival, holding that the challenge against British hegemony in Ireland could not be left to the future.[87]

This revolutionary paralysis of waiting for the opportunity of future British difficulty, Rossa argued, would allow Britain to set the terms of war, and that if open war was again resorted to, as in 1867, Fenianism would be annihilated by superior British military resources. This view was increasingly justified by an understanding that Britain was strong because she had huge military resources and an ability to rout Fenianism through manipulation or destruction on the battlefield.[88] In Rossa's argument, Ireland had none of these, making the philosophy of the bomb inevitable as a means of retaliation against a more powerful adversary.[89] Therefore, in certain Fenian parlance, bombings were seen as balancing the understanding of power between the mutual nations, compensating for Irish inferiority by rendering British military resources impotent.[90] This understanding tends to indicate that the Fenian adoption of a bombing campaign was a rationally informed choice, underlined by the imbalance between Fenian resources and British hegemony. The perceived imbalance between Fenianism and the British state was a key determinant in their consideration, and given modern scientific developments in explosives and transportation,[91] bombings were seen as the weapon of the weak supported by the perceived efficacy of modern science.

> Ireland is not able to cope with England in the open. With respect to position, resources and weapons, the dualists would be altogether unequal. For us therefore to encourage an 'Erin go Bragh' rising would be criminal… if Ireland means war, let her make war on the

scientific plan. Torpedoes, bombs and Greek fire are now employed by all the great powers. Is Ireland too big a power to despise such little things?[92]

This view was widely advocated by many proponents of the bombing strategy, with Patrick Ford publicly denouncing general insurrection as untimely, ill-advised and leading to horrendous bloodshed, citing the need for small circles of men to employ without intermission, a policy of 'guerrilla warfare', as an invisible army, avoiding a repetition of the defeat of 1867.[93] In this conclusion, Ford had come to an understanding, as followed by the practitioners of terrorism, in later years, that Fenianism had no other choice but to adopt a clandestine strategy following the failure of conventional warfare.[94]

Supported by strong feeling, it was argued that the Irish needed to employ a strategy of direct political violence against Britain, as if 'weak peoples go to war to wrench back their rights from titanic powers, common sense will suggest that they should use *such appliances as physical science puts in their hands*'.[95] Thus, in tandem with modern science, it was believed Fenianism could apply a bombing strategy against British cities, establishing an atmosphere of fear within Britain with the military weakness of Fenianism becoming its strength. In this vein Rossa would conclude within the traditional Fenian understanding of physical force: 'Too fine a sense of honour must be discarded and any means used to attain our end. Justice and right have never had any influence with the British government. They only succumb to terrorism or superior strength, and the former is the weapon we must use.'[96]

Amongst many advanced nationalists it was now increasingly illustrated that dedicated revolutionaries should have no scruples regarding the means of battle, showing no aversion to acts of explosion, assassination and intimidation in their effort to liberate Ireland, given that honourable warfare did not exist. In the 1860s the Irish had fought on British terms and in contemporary modes of warfare, losing humiliatingly to more powerful British hegemony supported by vast military resources. Such a loss demanded a change of strategy, necessitating that in order to avoid defeat, the weaker nation needed to constantly attack by any means possible British cities and property, seeking to terrorise the British state into terms by means of undermining security and demoralising public opinion.[97] Scientific development therefore gave many angry and frustrated Irish-Americans a new impetus, many unwilling to wait for a potential British difficulty in the future becoming embroiled in some far-off European conflict. This impatience, rooted in calculations of the efficacy of modern science applied to warfare, was a key factor in the impetus toward a bombing campaign in Britain. Underlined by Rossa's revolutionary chic, and endorsed by Ford's influence within Irish–America, this impetus 'succeeded in getting together no less than $23,320 dollars by the 14 March following the issue of the appeal – in something less than twelve months'.[98]

Eagerly watching developments in the skirmishing fund, Clan na Gael was interested in what O'Donovan Rossa was doing. The Clan were privately horrified by his bombastic threats and decidedly vocal pronunciations of how a clandestine war could be fought in Britain. John Devoy contended that through his public pronouncements, O'Donovan Rossa had given the British 'ample proof against any man who should fall into their hands'.[99] Devoy had no problem with a revolutionary fund, or the ambition of the skirmishing fund, but could not fathom O'Donovan Rossa's insistence on using the word 'skirmishing' in its title. For Devoy, the use of the word was far too public for a necessarily secret conspiracy, wondering 'why on Earth we should proclaim our intentions to the world'.[100] Devoy's argument was justified by reports in British and Irish newspapers, which lamented O'Donovan Rossa's threats against the British state. *The Irish Times* reported that:

> O'Donovan Rossa... hints darkly in *The Irish World* at the manner in which he will expend [the skirmishing fund] against England. He quotes a description of Russian Cavalry who, 'in a belt around their waist carry a few pounds of gun cotton or dynamite and with this highly destructive explosive they may work incalculable harm.' He adds that gun cotton and dynamite are not very dear and leaves the reader to infer that the fund, thus expended would destroy a great part of England. He adds: 'A small charge of gun cotton placed simply upon a rail and fired with a fuse suffices to blow several feet of the iron to a distance of many yards, thus rendering the railway unserviceable on the instant. A trooper may dismount, place a charge at the base of a telegraph pole, fire it, and be in the saddle again within sixty seconds'.[101]

Another practical worry within the Clan was the likelihood of anti-Irish hysteria in Britain following the experience of bombings in British cities. William Mackey Lomasney, a leading Fenian and veteran of the 1867 Rebellion, himself having no aversion to arbitrary violence, believed that 'before we do anything we must feel that we can justify the act, not only to ourselves in moments of excitement, but before the world, in the dock and with death or imprisonment before us'.[102] Mackey Lomasney believed that if arbitrary attacks were to be taken to Britain, the Clan needed to continue its business of arming Ireland in the wake of potential British reprisals. He privately argued that anything less would be worthless design, and without such a precondition he could not support and undertake the planning of a bombing campaign in Britain. Others, however, welcomed the prospect of reprisals against the Irish with the mobilising power of violence inspiring a British coercive response. This, it was predicted, could result in favourable conditions for an Irish rebellion, legitimising revolutionary aims. Thus, any persecution of the Irish, while unbearable, was but a means to an end, with O'Donovan Rossa holding:

> As to the harm and persecution it would bring on others all I say is this, that there are many of our countrymen in England, in Ireland and in America... if they were persecuted and driven to the wall [they] would fight, and fight bravely when their lives were committed to it. A revolution must be made without them and without any consideration as to what they will suffer or what they think of your work.[103]

The Clan increasingly came to believe that O'Donovan Rossa needed to be restrained and was gravitating toward unilateral action against Britain. Representative of growing anger within the Clan, John Devoy was increasingly furious with the veteran Fenian, and while he understood Rossa's reasonings, believing 'there is no man among us who means better to Ireland, but he will insist on doing just what he likes, irrespective of the wishes of other people who have equal responsibility with him'.[104] Devoy continued to not understand why he would publicly announce his intentions, jeopardising the ambitions of the skirmishing project.[105] Rossa, Devoy held, had given the British ample warning of his plans, through a desire for notoriety and theatricality, thus jeopardising any future or current Fenian initiative. This was obviously debated in the Clan as a source of division, arousing extreme feelings. Doctor William Carroll, Clan president, believed Rossa's opinions and supporters could only lead to 'defeat and disgrace'[106] with the British knowing Fenian intentions, while Rossa was far too unbalanced a character to mount a successful clandestine strategy. Rossa, having taken all of this as a personal attack, savaged his opponents within the Clan, particularly Devoy. He wrote:

Other correspondents say we have no right to talk of dynamite, or power or Greek fire, or guns and bayonets or of anything that would put England on her guard: that it is wrong to say anything about blowing up forts, or ships or castles, of killing anyone in war or peace. Do these people really imagine we are fools, and that in publishing what our contributors say we are giving England notice of the very things we are going to do? She knows as well as you do, that the Irish in America could do a thousand and one things to bring her to her knees, but she knows we are doing very little... we have no spirit to behave like men. There is our mother in chains, and we sit pining and wishing someone else would strike at the rivets that bind her... you must strike England to her knees before she lets go her hold, and it is to strike her in this manner the skirmishing fund is started. Then as to give England warning. We are not doing it, nor will we do it, but without losing one dollar we can have the satisfaction of worrying the life in her, while she is ordering about her ships and her soldiers and her police and working heaven and earth to meet attacks we never planned.[107]

O'Donovan Rossa continued to ignore appeals to be less open as to his plans, framing his argument in an appeal between men of action and inaction. Using *The Irish World* newspaper, he commented:

I am not talking to the milk and water people, I am talking to those who mean fight, who mean war and who know what war is. When an enslaved nation can produce men who are brave and daring enough to risk life and to face death for the mere glory of showing that the national spirit still lives, that nation is not dead and those men should be encouraged instead of repressed.[108]

The Clan eagerly watched the progress of Rossa's skirmishing fund, and threatened by his provocative use of language, least he bring suspicion on their operations, set up a committee to liaise with Rossa, ultimately agreeing that when the fund reached $23,000[109] it would come under the management of Clan na Gael by means of a Board of Trustees including Rossa. Internally, Devoy was still organising opposition to Rossa's public utterances in support of a bombing campaign. Not disheartened by his failure to silence the gregarious Rossa, he successfully manoeuvred allies onto the Trustee Board, calculating that this would be the best security against Rossa's potential for recklessness and unilateralism.[110] In making his selection, Rossa chose Devoy allies Dr William Carroll, James Reynolds and John Breslin to become initial fund trustees. Later, John Devoy, Thomas Clarke Luby and Thomas Francis Bourke were accepted into trusteeship. By 2 December 1877, the trustees, having had enough of Rossa's public eulogy of tactics and strategy, collectively wrote to Ford demanding that nothing should be published in *The Irish World* relative to the skirmishing fund unless it was agreed upon by the Board of Trustees.[111] This letter had the effect of weakening the efficacy of the revolutionary fund as Rossa cut off relations with the trustees, making the undertaking of any clandestine strategy impossible.

On this occasion, Ford defended Rossa against the trustees, sharing similar enthusiasm for bombings and Rossa's bombastic style of journalism, attacking the British State and threatening an unqualified arbitrary skirmishing assault on British cities. Devoy, frustrated and although not in a position to silence Rossa from public expression, was now powerful enough to side-line him and under the direction of the majority of trustees, the fund was renamed a national fund,[112] expanding on the skirmishing programme of political violence, channelling money not exclusively into the propagation of a war in the shadows to mount attacks on British cities but also into lectures, secret trips to Ireland, a potential standing army and the construction of a prototype Fenian submarine.[113] Yet, despite the large sum of money donated for skirmishing by an angry base of subscribers, 'no skirmishing or pretence at skirmishing had actually taken place',[114] this was not the intention of subscribers to the fund, inclined to retribution for past wrongs. Thus, a good many felt cheated, they had not subscribed for the expanded aims of the national fund, and they wanted the promise of imminent attacks against British interest in Ireland, desirous of returning Irish-American vengeance for past wrongs. With increasing anger at the fund's new direction growing ever more problematic for the Clan, the trustees were forced to defend their shift in policy as a result of changing imperial circumstances favourable to British difficulty, thus, when skirmishing was first proposed in 1875, Fenianism was despondent, broken by defeat and recognising no immediate prospect for revolution. Within two years, however, all had changed, with the trustees recognising that:

Circumstances have greatly altered...Old Europe is threatened with a general convulsion. War on the most tremendous scale cannot much longer be starved off by all the artifices and subtleties of all diplomatists in the world. Russia and Turkey are equally resolute to fight the inevitable fight... The rest of the Great powers of Europe will be drawn by an irresistible force into the arena. England above all, whether she likes it or not, must draw her sword once more or meanly confess herself a third class power...England's difficulty... in other words Ireland's opportunity... we propose to enlarge the skirmishing fund, established by Rossa, and of the plans it was intended to further... to aid the work of Ireland's national deliverance. [115]

This analysis of geopolitical difficulty and the possibility of Britain going to war was an understanding rooted in empire. British colonial interests in the Balkans were increasingly threatened by growing Russian influence in the region. To many, this forthcoming imperial crisis signalled the much longed for British imperial difficulty, diverting attention from Ireland. Despite this conclusion, nevertheless, it had not defused opposition to the expanded plans of the trustees. Rossa was furious, contending that the trustees had destroyed what potential the skirmishing fund had and having:

Opposed the skirmishing fund when it started, and when it grew up, in spite of their exertions, they intrigued themselves into its control. How they caught me here was: They asserted they were making final preparations for the struggle with England, and that the success of that struggle would be periled by my bringing on a premature engagement.[116]

Under immense pressure and tension, and with relations between the trustees increasingly untenable, O'Donovan Rossa took to excessive alcohol abuse, with Devoy receiving reports of him staggering in and out of saloons,[117] lamenting that 'he is hopelessly gone'.[118] While Devoy, Breslin and many others had tactically opposed O'Donovan Rossa's public utterance they did respect him as a figurehead in the movement. Of his drinking, Devoy sadly commented that 'he is now so bad that I fear the only way to save him is to put him under restraint. He can't eat or sleep'.[119] Devoy had also discovered that O'Donovan Rossa, in a state of drunkenness, had misappropriated funds from the national collection. His wife noted that in his present state he was a danger[120] and needed to be removed for his own health and the safety of the fund. Devoy agreed, stating that 'he [was] not in a condition to be responsible for what he does',[121] and that he required treatment, finally sending him to convalesce in a convent. At this time the strain on his marriage was immense and Mary Jane was forced to sell her belongings, including jewellery and furniture, to provide for their family. Such was the strain on her marriage that she was forced to return to Ireland with her children and stayed there for a little over a year.

Slowly recovering from his overindulgence in alcohol, O'Donovan Rossa, now sober and again showing signs of frustration with the trustees, a state Devoy concluded was even more dangerous,[122] refused co-operation with his colleagues, to such an extent that Devoy threatened resignation from the fund's trusteeship.[123] Against this tension, extreme supporters had approached Rossa, encouraging him to reclaim the fund from the trustees, reinvigorating its original ambitions and removing others from any involvement in its maintenance and expenditure.[124] This tension between Rossa and the trustees only intensified by comments made by Thomas Francis Bourke and Thomas Clarke Luby, both fund trustees, against the skirmishing strategy and subscribers, stressing the legitimacy of the traditional Fenian argument of waiting for British difficulty in order to facilitate rebellion at home. Bourke furthermore had insulted Rossa by publicly contending in *The Democrat* newspaper that: '[Rossa] has talked of the destruction of cities and arsenals without any regard to the rules of modern warfare or the restraints of modern ideas. All this talk is both foolish and immoral and no one sympathises with it except some ignorant persons who do not know any better.'[125]

As a trustee of the fund, Bourke, Rossa argued, occupied an indefensible position and ought to resign. Not only had he placed himself against the bombing campaign demanded by subscribers through their money, he had also stigmatised as ignorant every subscriber to the skirmishing fund,[126] of which he was one of the managers. Rossa again noted his opposition to the tactical position of traditional Fenianism, endorsed by Bourke and Luby, seeking open, honourable warfare of two recognisable armies, given that waiting for British difficulty could only facilitate revolutionary paralysis. He figured it to be a lazy and abstract doctrine that would probably never come about: 'Well wait till England will let you have it, and you'll wait till you lie down and die.'[127]

For the sake of the fund, by 28 March 1878, an uneasy peace had been agreed between Rossa and the trustees, facilitated by Ford.[128] Patrick Ford, however, was irate at the actions of all involved and summoned Devoy and Rossa to his house, where he was found incensed with the recent behaviour of the trustees.[129] The meeting decided the necessity of concealing the tension between trustees in order to alleviate subscribers' confusion as to the fund's actual intention and usage. Thus it was agreed that *The Irish World* would say 'something vague about inaccurate reports of interviews and something very strong about editorial misrepresentation, and asserting that we are all united and the original object of the fund to be carried out,'[130] namely to undertake a bombing campaign against British cities. As far as the readers and subscribers were concerned, the fund would carry out its intended aim of clandestine skirmishing attacks and there was no dissension whatsoever amongst its management. Despite this agreement, however, the uneasy peace was easily broken[131] by intransigence, and again trustees raised the question of Rossa's misappropriation of funds as a means to side-line him. This time, however, Devoy used what could have become a scandal to oust Rossa from the secretaryship of the fund with the trustees demanding:

> O'Donovan Rossa be requested to resign the secretaryship of the fund and the receivership of the subscriptions, and that if he refuses to comply with this request, the trustees will warn the public to forward no more money – that if he consents to this arrangement the trustees will guarantee, that the deficiency shall be covered up in some reasonable way, so that it cannot reach the public or affect his standing before the public.[132]

Rossa was irate, viewing the trustee's actions as an abandonment of the bombing campaign with the substitution of a strategy of inactivity, which would wait and watch but would not seek to create the opportunity for direct action against Britain.[133] The trustees were now desperate to see Rossa leave the fund, yet he held firm in the face of a total breakdown of relations between him and his colleagues, eventually conceding defeat. As a parting understanding, he insisted that he would only resign if Augustine Ford, Patrick Ford's brother, replaced him as secretary. Augustine Ford was thus co-opted into the secretariat, a role he did not relish: 'In my opinion, these gentlemen would have done more substantial service to the cause... had they selected someone from among themselves... there is not a man in the circle of my friendship – not a man whose ease and comfort I would consult – whom I would advise to have anything at all to do with Irish national funds – not one.'[134] Ford remained secretary for the time being. He became increasingly disillusioned and frustrated with the factionalism of Fenian politics and he took pleasure in the moment to stand down, being replaced by John Breslin.

Devoy and allies now completely controlled the skirmishing fund, while Rossa was reduced to a mere extremist in the fringes of the Clan.

With Devoy now in charge of the skirmishing fund, he increasingly faced a problem of what to do. Devoy, who was more pragmatic than O'Donovan Rossa, came to believe that independence could only be achieved through a combination of public and private means, and sought to form an alliance with Charles Stewart Parnell of the moderate-nationalist Irish Parliamentary Party. Devoy, like many Fenians, had taken 'comfort from the sense of action generated by the Parnellite party',[135] within the House of Commons, viewing it as 'the most viable expression of nationalist sentiment in the country',[136] often harassing and embarrassing the government,[137] on matters of Irish concern. Devoy realised that the inactivity of Fenianism had allowed for the rapid development of a constitutional party, which, under the leadership of Isaac Butt, had championed a federal demand of Home Rule. Parnell contrasted this federal programme with a more dynamic and forceful nationalism, challenging an idle grouping of Irish MPs under Butt. This illustrated to Devoy that there were reliable men in parliament who could be trusted with the national interest before the world. Alliance with Parnell, Devoy hoped, would bring together a united front in a broadly nationalist coalition, placing Fenian resources behind Parnell, harmonising conflicting interests within advanced nationalism.

This was not an abandonment of physical force, but rather a new departure, not diverting from the real object of Irish independence, but reformulating Irish politics by juxtaposing Fenian ideals behind the potential of the Parnellites and creating conditions for Irish rebellion. In this respect, staying true to the traditional anti-constitutionalism of Fenianism, Devoy held that militants should not 'relax their preparations for active work for one moment; for it is by active aggressive work alone that we can ultimately succeed'.[138] Parnell had given Devoy the impression that he supported such an initiative, and Devoy recalled meeting the parliamentarian: 'Parnell tried to convince us that we attached too little importance to the work that could be done in Parliament if the right men were there to do it. He freely admitted that parliamentary work should only play a secondary part, and must be in conjunction with a movement in Ireland.'[139] This strategy, favoured by John Devoy, culminated in the publication of a telegram on 12 October 1878 in which nationalists in America pledged to support Parnell if he set upon:

First – abandonment of the federal demand and substitution of a general declaration in favour of self government.

137

Second – Vigorous agitation of the land question on the basis of a peasant proprietary, while accompanying concessions tending to abolish arbitrary eviction.

Third – exclusion of all sectarian issues from the platform.

Fourth – Irish members to vote together on all Imperial and Home Rule questions adopt an aggressive policy and energetically resist coercive legislation.

Fifth – Advocacy of all struggling nationalities in the British Empire and elsewhere.[140]

It was hoped this New Departure would force genuinely nationalist members of parliament to sit, act and vote together, 'ready to withdraw from the British parliament and meet in Dublin when the time should be ripe',[141] declaring an Irish Parliament, separate to Britain. This was the basis of the new departure policy, with Devoy contending:

> The world judges us – by our public representatives, and in the times that are coming we can't afford to be misrepresented any longer. There is no use sending men to the British Parliament to beg, but we can send men there to protest before the world against England's right to govern Ireland, and when all is right we can command our representatives to withdraw from the British Parliament and meet in Ireland as an Irish legislature. It is only through such means that the whole Irish race the world over can be aroused and their active sympathy enlisted.[142]

While Devoy, Parnell and Davitt talked, events were moving rapidly in Ireland, as the country experienced the worst harvest on record since the Famine, and a fall in the price of Irish agricultural produce from £50 million in 1876 to £37.5 million in 1879, as the market favoured cheaper imports from America, Argentina and Australia. Many tenant farmers could not afford to pay their rent and eviction and starvation loomed. In 1877 there were 406 evictions, compared to 1098 the following year, with the West of Ireland the worst affected. This situation brought about an increasing proliferation of tenants' rights leagues to defend Irish farmers against eviction and starvation and seek fairer rights on the land, eventually resulting in the formation of the Irish National Land League in October 1879. Coming to play a major role in an incipient social revolution, the Land War (1879-82), fought between Irish tenant farmers and landlords, the League was desirous of ensuring the security of tenant farmers and to replace landlordism with tenant ownership and was built on the Fenian organizational network with Parnell as its president supported by Irish-America through Clan na Gael.

While O'Donovan Rossa and his supporters had no objection to the Land League, they viewed the New Departure with horror. The implication inherent within the programme that Irishmen could be elected to London to sit, act and vote together in the British Parliament was perceived as appalling and he wondered if this was a representation of 'the innate slavery engendered in the Irish blood during seven-hundred years of subjection'.[143] Believing that 'England was never going to give up its hold of Ireland until she was beaten to her knees,'[144] he claimed 'it is in that English Parliament the chains of Ireland are forged, and any Irish patriot who goes into that forge to free Ireland will soon find himself welded into the agency of his country's subjection to England'.[145] This for Rossa and his supporters was recognition of British rule in Ireland, and 'the Irish people should no more send representatives to Paris or Berlin', than to London. It was noted that parliamentarism would only serve to corrupt Irish nationalists as 'like Aladdin's visit to the magic cave; there opens up to their vision such beautiful fruit that they are lost in contemplation of these personal treasures and forget their mission', to defend the right of Ireland to a parliament of her own. This sending of men to the British Parliament was also seen as an 'evasion and avoidance of what alone will ever get Irish rights from England – the fight and preparation for the fight', as only the dread of war and the threat of force, rather than the eloquent oration of speeches 'causes more terror and panic to the British heart than a million Irish orators, or all the passive resistance or voting power the [constitutionalists] can bring to bear to solve their impossible demand – a self-governed Ireland under the enemy's flag'.

In Dublin, O'Donovan Rossa's friend Richard Pigott, agreed. Utilising his newspaper, *The Irishman*, the journalist proposed that the New Departure would only destroy the Fenian movement.[146] He furthermore could not fathom the juxtaposition between extremists and constitutionalists holding 'even the very most advanced form of moral-force agitation are as wide apart as the poles asunder', and '[the nationalist is] bound both logically and by the ties of duty to not openly assist or take any part in any public agitation, founded on the admission that the union of England and Ireland is binding'.[147] O'Donovan Rossa, who was by now side-lined, was increasingly re-emerging as a figurehead for those who opposed the New Departure and defining his argument against the new strategy in traditional Fenian doctrine he announced: 'I'm sorry I cannot believe in getting liberty for my Ireland so softly and sweetly; and sorry I forfeit the esteem of my people because of my firm adherence to the principle of all Irish patriots – that it is by the blows alone men strike their strength that the chains of the tyrant can be blown.'[148]

Resolving to undertake a bombing strategy on his own, O'Donovan Rossa increasingly came to believe that Clan na Gael was not an organisation that he wished to belong to. Rossa concluded that Irishmen had to take their fight to Britain on their own terms supported by the efficacy of modern scientific development, compensating Irish military inferiority through a destructive war of reprisal.[149] To do so he further required physical support and seeking to appeal to firebrands within the Clan, he called a convention at Philadelphia where all men 'who mean to do good',[150] in contradiction to Clan policy would be welcomed to discuss new strategy and build a new movement. Rossa had actively canvassed within the Clan for people to attend the weeklong convention, hoping to bring large numbers of the organisation with him. One of those whom he approached was Patrick Ford, who, despite his personal respect for O'Donovan Rossa, would have little parley with the Philadelphia convention. Ford believed that O'Donovan Rossa was making a tactical mistake by breaking with the Clan and was increasingly associating himself with men with little appetite for doing silent work, but seeking self-glorification. O'Donovan Rossa was now expelled from Clan na Gael for having broken its regulations by seeking to organise another society within its ranks. There can be little doubt, however, that Rossa welcomed his discharge, given that it released him from the straightjacket of Clan secrecy and regulation, facilitating independence to follow his own line, and the ability to draw a salary for himself and to speak out as freely as he chose.

On 28 June 1880 at the Philadelphia Convention, a new Fenian faction, styling itself as the United Irishmen of America[151] was established, seeking to force a British withdrawal from Ireland by means of physical force, and attract disaffected advanced nationalists within Irish-America. This position of the United Irishmen of America was aptly captured by a Judge John Brennan of Iowa, who had chaired the Convention when he demanded of the assembled delegates to 'be ready to make any sacrifice of time, any sacrifice of position... any sacrifice of life, in order to lift our desolate and oppressed country to a high position amongst the nations of the Earth. We have come here not so much to talk as to prepare for work'.[152] Delegates, composed largely of former Clan and Fenian brotherhood activists, yet not including well-known Fenian chiefs, with the exception of Rossa, strongly opposed the new departure policy, denouncing parliamentary agitation as a mockery of Fenian principles.[153] They held that any doctrine teaching Irish interests could be redressed or represented in the British Parliament would prove a betrayal of Ireland and a disaster for the Fenian cause. Capturing the belief that the efficacy of modern scientific development had given Fenianism a new impetus following the failure of the 1860s a delegate from Brooklyn, 'Red' Jim McDermott, a firebrand advanced nationalist, member of the order of Saint Sylvester,[154] and a clandestine British Agent, declared:

> I have been actively engaged in labouring for the liberation of Ireland for twenty years... I am compelled to say that the present moment is a most earnest one. 'Our motto is not a cent for blatherskite, but every dollar for dynamite...' We do not mean to meet England on the open battlefield. That would be folly. But we do intend to carry on a warfare on the principle of nihilism.[155]

O'Donovan Rossa was equally vocal and declared his belief that Ireland could only be freed by a resort to violence. In justification of this he cited Lord Palmerston, who forty years before had claimed, if Ireland was a worthless rock in the middle of the Atlantic ocean, the British State would never surrender it unless confronted by force. Arguing that Britain had made the inevitability of an Irish appeal to violence, he suggested to rapturous applause how:

> The freedom of Ireland implies the reduction of England to a position much inferior to that which she has occupied for centuries... England is pre-eminently the hypocrite, the robber, the perjurer, the murderer, the pirate of the universe... a country that has shed enough blood to drown in one great sea all the English on this planet... England cannot consent to Ireland's freedom; violence alone must establish that freedom if it is to exist. Theses propositions I consider axiomatic.[156]

Having been expelled from the Clan, Rossa now became a pariah in advanced nationalism. While he continued to fraternise with grassroots Fenians connected with the Clan, and some important members, the leadership tended to shun him, thus he setup his own sensational newspaper, *The United Irishman,* as a platform for his ideas and fundraising for the resources of the civilisation fund. Through *The United Irishman,* Rossa, increasingly a showman, in what was essentially a 'one man paper',[157] was melodramatic and sensational, claiming responsibility for the smallest British accident. One example of this occurred when Queen Victoria sprained her ankle and was indisposed; through the columns of *The United Irishman* O'Donovan Rossa had contended it was his skirmishers that had soaped the stairs at Windsor.[158] In a much later issue, with the desire to capture headlines, Rossa announced a bounty on the head of the heir to the British throne, Albert Wettin: '$10,000 REWARD FOR THE BODY OF THE PRINCE OF WALES. DEAD OR ALIVE.'[159] Decrying this melodrama, Michael Davitt, a staunch opponent of Rossa, contended that 'anything from the blowing down of a chimney by a hurricane, to the shaking of a part of England by an earthquake, would be claimed by Rossa as a result of the work which he was carrying on in his warfare against the British Empire'.[160] Similarly, John Devoy, who regarded his newspaper with a particular disdain, recalled O'Donovan Rossa's style of journalism as cantankerous and grouchy, describing the United Irishman as 'the queerest Irish paper ever published'.[161]

With the establishment of *The United Irishman,* O'Donovan Rossa had been given an opportunity to air his own political views without the constraints of Clan na Gael's secrecy. He had also hoped that he could use the paper to make money and resolve his dire finances. For all his traits, however, he was a poor businessman and *The United Irishman* was by no means a profitable publication. This was largely of his own doing as he irresponsibly handled money and was incredibly lax with the collection of moneys owed to him. Recalling his business troubles, it was later noted by his daughter Margaret how 'if anyone ordered the paper and could afford to pay for it, Papa was greatly pleased, and if anyone wanted the paper but could not afford to pay for it, Papa was still greatly pleased and sent the paper without the bill'.[162] This greatly annoyed the more business-minded Mary Jane who continuously suggested that the newspaper should be closed due to the cost it incurred on their family. Concluding that it was merely a vanity project for her husband, Mary Jane still remained ostensibly committed to the newspaper out of respect for Rossa, however, there is an abundance of evidence that this was done with great reluctance.

The *United Irishman* newspaper is the closest thing we have today to O'Donovan Rossa's innermost political thought. Its melodrama represented how the Irishman had sought to employ theatrics and deception as weapons in his campaign to terrorise Britain and advocate an Irish Republic. Examining this melodrama, including preposterous claims such as injuring Queen Victoria, some contemporaries held that O'Donovan Rossa was no longer a threat to Britain, and his melodramatic statements and calls for a bombing campaign in the United Kingdom were nothing more than hot air for the consumption of the Irish underclass in America. Examining *The United Irishman*, the *New York Times* commented how it was their opinion that:

> Mr O'Donovan Rossa and a number of lazy patriots are collecting a rich harvest of six pence's from Irish servant girls by pretending to be dynamite fiends. Whenever an explosion occurs anywhere on English soil or onboard an English vessel, Mr O'Donovan Rossa and his pals instantly claim that it was their own dynamite that did the work. In the intervals between accidental explosions they hold secret meetings at which they publicly announce that they are making active preparations to blow the greater part of the British Empire into fragments... Undoubtedly they hate England and would like to produce an occasional inexpensive explosion, whereby a few Englishmen might be killed, but with whiskey and cigars at their present price, they have too much sense to spend their money in such unprofitable work...[163]

By January 1881, these contemporaries were proven wrong when a bomb exploded in Salford, Manchester. The work of O'Donovan Rossa's emissaries, it was the first time a bomb had exploded in Britain for a political cause – claiming the patent of this new type of warfare, O'Donovan Rossa joked how other revolutionists should pay him a royalty for it.[164]

8

'Dynamite' O'Donovan Rossa

Rossa had earlier spoken of the need for silent, secretive bombing campaign grinding away at Britain's vulnerabilities as part of a strategy to wrench control of Ireland. He remained committed to the belief that 'it is fight alone that will compel England to give up Ireland.'[1] He had predicted that given the military resources of Britain open warfare was doomed to failure while Parliamentary agitation could only end in disgrace. Thus seeing how futile and hopeless the levying of conventional war against Britain was, he decided the crippling of Britain by an invisible army should be the future plan of action.[2] While previously he was ridiculed as a showman, out to extract money from credulous Irish-Americans, Rossa's United Irishmen had raised a small amount for money for direct action against the British, but not enough to cause the destruction which he had earlier suggested throughout his involvement with the skirmishing fund, but enough to cause mischief. With his new strategy, and relying on subscriptions from Irish-America, O'Donovan Rossa would now use the money to finance men to go to Britain and mount a bombing campaign, calculating that each attack would generate more funding for future attacks; these men would be known colloquially as skirmishers, taking their name from the earlier skirmishing fund.

Thus, sheltered by fog on the night of 14 January, skirmishers placed an explosive in a ventilating shaft at Salford Barracks, quarters of the King's Regiment. In what would become the first explosion of a bomb in Britain for a political grievance, a nearby butcher's store within the complex, was left 'literally blown to pieces, leaving nothing but the bare walls... the greatest excitement at once prevailed all over the barracks and in the neighbourhood, drawn by the report and the crashing of glass, consequent upon the breaking of numerous houses in the neighbourhood.'[3] The bombers attempted to destroy the armoury of the barracks, which stored in addition to the regiments arms, rifles belonging to four Manchester volunteer regiments – in total between 4,000 and 5,000 weapons,[4] but the police investigation finding 'its authors seem to have been misled as to the part of the building in which the arms were stored',[5] hence the destruction of the butcher's shed. In terms of damage, the bomb, having been placed in the outer wall of the barracks, destroyed a number of shops in the vicinity, injuring a young woman and killing a 7-year-old boy, Richard Clarke.[6] Following the explosion many theories were discussed as possible motivations for it, from practical possibilities of the explosion being gas related, to suggestions that the attack was the work of a mischievous 'practical joke' gone horribly wrong,[7] or intended to divert attention from an arms' seizure. The Salford Chief Constable, however, was convinced all these theories were misjudged, suggesting the attack was not to seize arms, but was 'one of wanton mischief perpetrated for the purpose of intimidation and likely to be repeated in this or similar districts where it is known that numbers of so-called Fenians, Land Leaguers, Home Rulers and the like reside'.[8]

The Chief Constable had correctly concluded a correlation between the government's Irish Policy and the Salford blast. He had recognised that the explosion was a response to coercion, serving to intimidate the government and overawe public opinion for a political purpose. In this summarisation it could be understood that if the explosion were designed and carried out for a political grievance, there was the possibility of further attacks. A great wave of alarm began to hover over major cities, with many wondering if the explosion were a precursor to a new Fenian onslaught. One newspaper calculated that it was the beginning of a predicted Fenian uprising,[9] while *The Press Association*, capturing this mood, could report the emergence of a great state of alarm amongst the public.[10] To meet this state of popular alarm, the government continued to press ahead with Irish coercion with even more determination. This was underlined by localised steps to improve British security, with military and police keeping a vigilant guard over government sites likely to be attacked and with special precautions taken at all places where public arms were stored.[11] While the government undertook increased security precautions, it failed to understand that the Salford explosion was as innovative as it was symbolic. The Salford attack was not just in retaliation to the government's policy of coercion, but fourteen years previously three Fenians had been executed in Manchester for the accidental death of a police sergeant during the rescue of two imprisoned Fenian leaders. The three: William Allen, Michael Larkin and Michael O'Brien became popularly known as the Manchester Martyrs, taking a place in the pantheon of Irish nationalist heroes, having been hung from the wall of Salford gaol. Thus, it was no coincidence that O'Donovan Rossa chose

Salford to inaugurate his bombing campaign. The Salford bombing had proven that, despite the failure of the 1860s and stagnancy of the 1870s, Fenianism had not gone away; it had returned with a vengeance underlined by a new and devastating strategy, seeking disruption of everyday life and employing individuals protected by faceless anonymity, indistinguishable from ordinary civilians, rather than conventional armies.

Salford was the beginning of this new wave of retributive warfare and was a challenge to the contemporary Victorian understanding of war. While Victorians were troubled by the mass phenomenon of modern warfare, either through personal experience or war correspondence, they had never faced a threat like this before. With future battles no longer fought between recognisable armies through conventional warfare, the battleground shifting to British property, the phenomenon of warfare becoming an urban problem, employing unmarked and unrecognisable individuals rather than uniformed armies, relying on new cheap and unpredictable weapons fostered by modern scientific development, the fear of the people grew. Politically motivated violence had been the norm across Europe throughout the 1880s, yet the nature of this threat facing Britain was inherently different. Political activists had attempted to assassinate the German Kaiser twice in 1878. The King of Spain shared similar experiences, as did his Italian counterpart. In Russia the Narodnaya Volya had successfully assassinated the Csar in a politically motivated bomb attack. These political actions against Heads of State, however, were attempted regicides and political assassinations, this was not the skirmishing strategy. By striking Salford Barracks, Irish-Americans had attacked British property for symbolic reasons and to challenge the British State in retribution for its Irish Policy, seeking a reaction in order to solidify its aims. This kind of political agitation was thus far unknown in contemporary Europe.

The Salford explosion also disturbed Clan na Gael and the Supreme Council. The Clan viewed it as an embarrassing attempt at causing terror in Britain. Rossa's hot-headedness, they feared, could have cost them the element of surprise needed for their own clandestine operations, with existing Clan agents coming under the attention of an increasingly vigilant police. Furthermore, the Revolutionary Directory was actively exploring the possibility of a bombing campaign itself and while officially not Clan policy, a leading Clansman, Captain William Mackey Lomasney, had been dispatched to Britain via France to make a reconnaissance of potential targets,[12] with $5,500 to facilitate his mission. Lomasney, parallel to his reconnaissance mission, was also undertaking

1. Jeremiah O'Donovan Rossa, photograph taken in America in 1864. (Image courtesy of the National Library of Ireland)

2. Mary Jane O'Donovan Rossa who married Jeremiah in 1864. (Image courtesy of the Cole/ O'Donovan Rossa family)

3. The wedding certificate of Jeremiah and Mary Jane O'Donovan Rossa, dated 2
October 1864. (Image courtesy of the Cole/O'Donovan Rossa family)

4. The Fenian executive were the most senior staff of the Irish Republican Brotherhood. All men photographed belonged to the Irish People newspaper. O'Donovan Rossa is in the photograph in the bottom right of the image. (Image from author's collection)

5. Dublin Metropolitan Police raid the offices of the Irish People newspaper on 1
September 1865. Following this raid widespread arrests were made including the arres
of O'Donovan Rossa. (Image courtesy of Aidan Lambert)

6. Mugshot of Jeremiah O'Donovan
Rossa taken at Mountjoy Gaol following
his arrest. (Image courtesy of the Cole/
O'Donovan Rossa family)

7. James Maxwell O'Donovan Rossa
who was born on 30 April 1866 durin
O'Donovan Rossa's imprisonment. Thi
photograph had been suppressed from
O'Donovan Rossa on account of prison
regulations. (Image courtesy of th
Cole/O'Donovan Rossa family.)

8. John Devoy, Charles Underwood O'Connell, Henry Mulleda, Jeremiah O'Donovan Rossa and John McClure. Released from prison on 7 January 1871 the five men became known as the Cuba Five. Their arrival in America was a scene of pandemonium as various political parties and Irish–American organisations sought their favour. (Image from author's collection)

9. Dynamite O'Donovan Rossa had spearheaded a bombing campaign against Britain seeking Irish independence. Establishing a new organisation called The United Irishmen of America, their militant wing, known as the skirmishers, had undertaken a number of small-scale bombings in London. (Image courtesy of the Cole/O'Donovan Rossa family.)

10. Red Jim McDermott was Agent Provocateur who had used O'Donovan Rossa to infiltrate a skirmishing conspiracy. He had been responsible for the arrest of several Fenian conspirators between March to April 1883 and had planned simultaneous bombings in Britain and Ireland, clandestinely funded by British intelligence. He was one of the most notorious exposed British Agents of the late nineteenth century. (Image from author's collection)

11. Captain Thomas Phelan was stabbed in O'Donovan Rossa's office. A British Agent, he had been exposed by fellow British Agent John Francis Kearney, who deemed his exposure necessary for his personal protection within O'Donovan Rossa's company. (Image from author's collection)

12. Yseult Dudley, who attempted to assassinate O'Donovan Rossa at Broadway on 2 February 1885. (Image from author's collection)

13. Jeremiah O'Donovan Rossa delivering the oration at the unveiling of the Manchester Martyrs Memorial, Birr, Co. Offaly in July 1894. (Image courtesy of the National Library of Ireland)

14. Jeremiah and Mary Jane O'Donovan Rossa with their daughters at the family home in Staten Island. Note that O'Donovan Rossa looks frail and emaciated by the time of this photograph as he had developed chronic neuritis as a result of his earlier prison treatment, which affected his motor skills. (Image courtesy of the Cole/O'Donovan Rossa family)

15. Jeremiah O'Donovan Rossa died in St Vincent's Hospital, Staten Island on 29 July 1915. In this photograph, taken prior to his death, the once unconquerable O'Donovan Rossa is prostrate in his hospital bed. Suffering from dementia, in addition to chronic neuritis, he increasingly regressed and believed himself to be in prison once more. (Image courtesy of the Cole/O'Donovan Rossa family)

16. Mary Jane O'Donovan Rossa, Fr
Michael Flangan, Eileen O'Donovan
Rossa and Thomas James Clarke
Clarke, a former Dynamitard, believed
the funeral of O'Donovan Rossa could
awaken a national spirit amongst the
Irish people. (Image from author's
collection)

17. Patrick Pearse delivering the oration over the grave of O'Donovan Rossa on 1
August 1915. Note Major General John MacBride, who is standing behind Pearse and
Thomas J. Clarke in the far right of the photo. All three would be shot for their part in
the Easter Rising the following year. (Image courtesy of Glasnevin Museum)

a stockpiling process of explosives for a future bombing initiative against Britain. This was combined with a smuggling operation of large quantities of arms and weaponry into Ireland, in order to oppose tenant evictions. Thus, similar to O'Donovan Rossa's campaign, the Clan initiative would be closely related to the events in Ireland, but Lomasney's strategy was more solidly planned than O'Donovan Rossa's, believing if a bombing campaign were to be implemented, it needed to be properly planned,[13] alongside a determined attempt to arm Ireland and prepare for Irish revolution. Lomasney feared that if the Clan initiated this campaign without proper precautions in Ireland and Britain, the Irish would be susceptible and defenceless in the face of possible British attacks in Ireland and against the Irish immigrant population of Britain.[14] This he wrote to John Devoy, necessitated twenty times the sum of his original funding, $110,000, to mount a concerted bombing campaign in Britain.[15]

While Lomasney was in Europe he was in constant communication with James O'Connor, Secretary of the Supreme Council. It would be incredible to argue that O'Connor knew nothing of Lomasney's activities, in particular his reconnaissance mission, and appears to have supported and financed experiments with dynamite carried out by the Clan emissary.[16] The Supreme Council for the most part were tactically opposed to a potential bombing campaign within its jurisdiction, this was grounded in a similar fear to that held by Lomasney as to the potential for reprisal attacks on the Irish, and a stated opposition to premature action as counter-productive. That James O'Connor was associated with Lomasney appears, however, to indicate that the Supreme Council contained some sympathisers to a potential bombing campaign within their own terms and supervision. It also alludes to a desire by the Supreme Council to acquiesce with its American paymasters and knowledge that support steadily existed within its ranks for the principle of a bombing campaign thus, the Council was not prepared to aggressively oppose suggestions in its favour for fear of alienating supporters. As an organisation, evidence exists that the IRB was by no means a unitary organisation, and within the IRB there was a willingness to co-operate with the Clan on a future bombing initiative. This was particularly strong amongst the Northern England organisation, and James O'Connor, despite his closeness to the council, seems to have supported the idea of bombings in Britain although only with the endorsement of the Revolutionary Directory, safeguarded by the IRB veto checking Irish-American aggression and potential unilateralism.[17] The Supreme Council willingness to co-operate with the Clan was not widely reciprocated with Rossa's skirmishers at grassroots level, however evidence exists that collusion was clearly taking place. There was clear alarm among the Supreme Council at Rossa's maverick streak, and with Mackey Lomasney they sought to counter his operations. In this vein a joint statement was issued under the authority of the Supreme Council and the Clan,[18] warning members of:

> The wild schemes of a certain man, late a brother of the VC who seems to think that by the blackest kind of... rapine and murders he can accomplish enough to satisfy his own petty vindictiveness. We feel it is our duty to ask you to pay no attention to this man, and to warn you against aiding him to carry out any of his insane schemes which can only result in bringing disgrace on our cause.[19]

In order to stop Rossa's skirmishers, a joint IRB–Clan intelligence initiative was launched directed to find skirmishing agents. Writing to John Devoy, the Captain sought information as to the movements of Rossa's people in New York, Boston and along the East Coast, hoping that Devoy, using the Fenian network in America, could trace skirmishers. Posing as an agent recruiting immigrant workers into Britain, he cabled Devoy:

Connolly, Labour Bureau, Castlegarden, N.Y.
Barrow [Devoy] request statistic late shipping emigrants fast as possible with funds can now carry out agreements within time specified, all department working well.[20]

Lomasney's cryptic comment to Devoy that all departments were working well seems to indicate that Devoy, despite later protestations against a bombing campaign, knew of the embryonic Clan operation and supported Lomasney's anticipatory operations.

If the Clan were angry with Rossa for the Salford explosion, they were furious with him for its aftermath. Rossa, never one to be discreet, on 11 February was interviewed in New York by *The Truth* newspaper. The veteran Fenian strongly argued in favour of the bombing campaign, citing that history had shown, particularly in the aftermath of the Clerkenwell explosion, that the British government would only listen to force, and if Britain were to be punished in order to reach terms for Irish independence, only actions like the explosion at Salford could force a conclusion to hostilities, holding 'England isn't the kind of country to ever give up anything until she is absolutely forced to do it.'[21] Drawing on history, couched in ideas of retribution and in support of the view that violence alone could force the Irish Question to the top of the British political agenda, he asked:

> Suppose you found some penniless, shoeless Irishman, who made his way across the channel on the deck of a steamer, found himself in Manchester or St. Giles and collected a number of Irishmen about him and one would ask him 'what news?' to which he would reply 'your father was cut down by a dragoon; your mother was shot by a policeman... how many fires would blaze on the manufactories of England... that is the only way in which he can be brought to grant freedom to Ireland.'[22]

By 15 February, many had come to believe that Rossa had carried out his threat of vengeance as a devastating fire had broken out at London's Victoria Docks. Public opinion immediately came to believe that the fire was arson, and the work of skirmishers designed to attack Britain economically in the name of a political grievance.[23] *The Annual Register* could only concur, contending there was reason to believe that the fire could be attributed to Fenian agency and had cost half a million pounds in damages.[24] While this was all nonsense, and there was absolutely no evidence to substantiate these claims, an anxious public demanded an urgent response and the government was not deterred to grant it.

The Salford attack convinced the government not to deter its planned Coercion Act in Ireland, and by February it had introduced The Protection of Person and Property (Ireland) Act, suspending Habeas Corpus and allowing the government to detain without trial anyone suspected of agrarian offences, treason and prohibiting unlawful gatherings, intimidation and conspiracies regarding non-payment of rent. The Act became law by 2 March. Parallel to coercion, an Arms Bill was introduced into Parliament, The Peace Preservation Bill, giving increased powers of police searching and the prohibition of arms. A controversial and illiberal bill, it represented a division between Harcourt and his liberal colleagues, stemming from a perceived obsession with Fenian conspiracy, and was opposed by Gladstone and radicals within the Liberal Party. Defending coercion and his stringent Irish arms control from internal opposition, the Home Secretary noted how coercion was 'like caviar; unpleasant at first to the palate, it becomes agreeable with use',[25] citing the need to pacify Ireland with a firm hand. In supporting coercion, however, the government had chosen a strategy of punishing the wider population for land agitation. Defending this policy in the wake of land agitation and Fenian conspiracy, at committee, Harcourt had contended that the state had evidence enough to prove a Fenian threat existed, thus necessitating coercive measures but qualifying that his information was not based on informers but on the declared statement of O'Donovan Rossa in the *United Irishman*, and of John Devoy of the American Land League. O'Donovan Rossa had openly advocated the assassination of ministers and the burning of London. He did not assume that members of the Irish Land League held these views, but the Government was bound to take measures of defence due to such statements.[26] Such a strategy, however, risked potentially indicating a profoundly oppressive nature of the state, thus legitimising the aims of the Land League and popularising his objectives, while justifying further inclination to retaliation, particularly from an incensed Irish-America. Despite this risk, almost immediately the government used the powers reserved under coercion to round up significant numbers of Fenians, Land leaguers and activists.

Parallel to developments in Ireland, O'Donovan Rossa was being watched by British Intelligence. From Philadelphia, the British Consulate, headed by Robert Clipperton, informed London that 'Rossa keeps a sort of debtor and creditor account of all monies he sends over to his agents in England and the estimated value of the damage done to Property. By this account he shows that he has expended $ 700... Since the first of October last. Whilst the result of damage done by these men amounts to four millions of dollars.'[27] Clipperton noted that Rossa had claimed responsibility for damage to four sites including Salford Barracks, and the Victoria Docks, 'these are followed by the Mansion House and the Liverpool Custom House, which as he says are not yet accomplished, but may be expected at any moment to be destroyed'.[28] Clipperton believed that Rossa intended to target commercial and political institutions as part of his skirmishing campaign, targeting government buildings in order to inaugurate a serious bombing campaign against Britain. Reporting a New York-based informant, the Consulate suggested all Rossa needed was one great success and a spectacular explosion, bringing him publicity, money and support. Lamenting O'Donovan Rossa's potential for mischief, Robert Clipperton signed off 'there will be no end to it'.[29]

Examining O'Donovan Rossa's capabilities, the British government were increasingly concerned he had organised a system whereby bombs were being produced in America in preparation for attacks in British cities. Supporting this view, British Intelligence had intercepted a letter from Rossa to a colleague suggesting the employment of men in trans-Atlantic steamers for smuggling bombs into Britain.[30] Investigating further, from Philadelphia, Clipperton discovered Rossa employed a number of employees working for various American shipping lines to smuggle explosives into Britain. He speculated that once they arrived in the United Kingdom they would be collected by Rossa's emissaries. Investigating further, this time through the British Consulate at Boston, an employee of one of these lines, Thomas Johnson, offered his services as an informant, and warned of:

> An elaborate scheme of arms importation into Britain from American ports, speculating that along this importation network dynamite could easily be smuggled, 'circumstances have come under my observation... that if continued, and I am more than positive that they will be, may have a very important bearing on the future movements of Rossa in enabling him to carry out his vile intentions. I have made several voyages both in *the Zealand* and *the Anchor* line of steamers and in the vessels of other lines and invariably found that there were amongst the firemen, the coal passers and also the chief stewards' help... men professing to be loyal British subjects, but would sell Queen and country if they found it their interest to do so... while unloading at this side strangers have free access to board the vessels, the men go ashore when they like, and returning again bring with them revolvers which they conceal in the coal bunkers and other places... in this way thousands of revolvers have found their way to Ireland, and if this has been done why cannot the same class of persons carry clandestinely aboard dynamite or any other combustibles... the majority of them are Irishmen, all to a man are Fenians and would not hesitate one moment to blow up a ship.[31]

The government examined each Consul's report with interest, but perhaps the most interesting one was that of Robert Clipperton, who asserted that O'Donovan Rossa was aware of British surveillance at American ports. According to Clipperton, the Irishman had devised a plan where his agents made for Canada and dispatched explosives from there, believing the British would never watch Canadian ports. In receipt of a plethora of Consular reports regarding Irish-American smuggling, the Foreign Office in London unhappily found the opportunities O'Donovan Rossa had for sending explosives across the Atlantic were numerous.[32]

While the importation of explosives into Britain was of a serious concern to the British government, by equal measure they also feared the movement of skirmishers across toward Britain. They particularly feared for Liverpool, the main port of entry for Americans into the State. Given that Liverpool could provide entry and escape to and from Britain, the government were deeply anxious as to Fenian intentions regarding the port city. Robert Clipperton had been reliably informed that an explosion in Liverpool was inevitable, having been planned by O'Donovan Rossa as a potential target.[33] Reports from America seemed to indicate that O'Donovan Rossa had several skirmishers in the city waiting for action, although on this point the government couldn't be certain for fear of misinformation, but the risk of false information could not be ignored given the perceived immanency of the threat. This fear was grounded in an intercepted letter composed by O'Donovan Rossa that claimed the existence of a cell in Liverpool which was preparing a bomb.[34] Investigating the accuracy of the letter, British Consuls in America strongly came to believe a cell was operating in Liverpool and intended to bomb the Customs House using explosives disguised as handbags.[35] According to their information, the cell was well looked after and had ample money, which meant it could easily escape from Britain if required.[36] With mounting speculation as to the presence of a secret skirmishing cell operating in Liverpool, the government speculated that there was a strong potential of more skirmishers in England, and working up a network of informants and spies, they conjectured how O'Donovan Rossa had established a clandestine national cell network, with agents operating in England and Ireland unknown to each other, making infiltration near impossible. All this was nonsense, however; O'Donovan Rossa did not have the funds or resources necessary to establish a clandestine cellular network. This speculation had been fuelled by intriguing informants, who on learning of the government's interest in deflecting Fenianism, invented scurrilous plots and conspiracies for the purpose of extracting money from eager Consul's, who could not afford to avoid information supplied to them. Such was the magnitude of the threat faced by the British State that the government could not take reports from American consuls, no matter how insubstantial or impossible they seemed, for granted, and each rumour and report, whether spurious or factual, had to be equally considered in the event that an actual plot may have escaped unrecognised.

One report that the Foreign Office had received had arrived from a reliable Philadelphian informant to Clipperton, asserting that Rossa was preparing to mount a spectacular explosion in Britain in order to secure his credentials as a man of deed. Clipperton had been informed that the skirmishers had constructed an elaborate series of explosive devices to carry out an event of exciting alarm amongst the general public in furtherance of their aim to force the government to terms. These devices were of two sophisticated designs. According to Clipperton they were:

1.   A Clockwork machine to be used for blowing up buildings.
2.   A similar machine detonated by a spring rather than a clock.[37]

Clipperton also noted the existence of smaller bombs to be carried in handbags, to avoid suspicion, and deposited in selected sites unknown to the public, causing disruption of everyday life.[38] Clipperton believed these bombs were ready to be used immediately, but O'Donovan Rossa and his United Irishmen were divided as how to use them.[39] His information indicated that some within O'Donovan Rossa's council wanted immediate use while others pressed for the passage of the Irish Coercion Bill into law as a clear sign of retaliation and a message of vigour to meet the government's show of force.

As O'Donovan Rossa and the United Irishmen debated how they should use their explosives, on 2 March 1881 the British government passed its Coercion Bill. Further arrests followed with Irish outrage spilling over into further violence and imprisoned Land Leaguers calling upon tenant farmers to pay no rent. Many moderate nationalist agitators continued to argue that government policy would only serve to be counterproductive to the pacification of Ireland, driving more and more people into militancy and desperation, thus establishing conditions for violent action to thrive. This Coercion Act would undoubtedly draw a response from revolutionary Irish-America. Representing this response, the Clan were furious, and an increasing irritation within the grassroots placed heavy pressure on the existing Clan leadership for direct retributive action against Britain. Similarly, O'Donovan Rossa's skirmishers were equally infuriated and from New York, they promised:

Action as remorseless as has been England's conduct toward Ireland, even should we have to lay her cities in ashes, sink her navy and blow her merchant marine from the face of the seas. We will also take cognizance of England's conduct in every particular, and for every outrage under coercion, or Landlord laws, reprisals in the destruction of English property, were to be taken; and for every death in Ireland in which the government was in any way instrumental, the death of an English governmental official was to be encompassed.[40]

Following on from their threat, O'Donovan Rossa's skirmishers made for London where they had sought to blow up the Mansion House – the home of the London Lord Mayor, an Irishman named Alderman William McArthur.[41] The planned bombing was particularly symbolic as not only had McArthur supported Irish coercion, the Mansion House was located in central London, an ideal location to cause maximum destruction and fear. A bomb explosion would prove the vulnerability of the state, sapping British morale while increasing enthusiasm amongst supporters. They had chosen to detonate their bomb on 16 March, the eve of St Patricks Day, when McArthur had invited dignitaries to the Mansion House for a banquet. The skirmishers had found a weak spot in the city's defences, a narrow little thoroughfare known as George Street, which led into a little gateway of the Mansion House, 'leading into the cells in which prisoners are confined during the daily sitting of the justice room.'[42] The east window of the Mansion House looked out onto this street, which was described as a 'dark footpath... much frequented during the day but is quite deserted and lonely at night... the footpath or passage in question is only visited [by police] every quarter of an hour or thereabouts when the constable on patrol goes through on his ordinary round'.[43]

The evening of 16 March was recorded as one of dense fog, offering skirmishers an ample opportunity of clandestine attack. Hidden by darkness and poor visibility, the skirmishers carried with them a wooden box filled with explosives, all the while looking out for witnesses as they made their way to George Street. Outside the Mansion House they carefully laid the bomb, contained in a common deal wooden box, beneath the window of the building's ornate Egyptian Hall. Measuring some twenty-four inches square and five inches high, the device was filled with fifteen pounds of coarse blasting powder. It was strongly bound with iron hoops and pierced in the middle where a fuse had been inserted by the bombers. Wrapped in brown paper, it was placed in a recess fenced in by an iron railing immediately below the east window.[44] The skirmishers lit the fuse, but the hall was empty; the Lord Mayor had unexpectedly postponed the banquet in honour of the Russian Czar Alexander II, who had been assassinated three days earlier. Ironically, the Czar's assassination had saved the Lord Mayor and his guests from a politically motivated explosion.

With this unknown to the skirmishers, they set their bomb and abandoned it at the Mansion House. The bomb was seen by a nearby housekeeper, however, who alerted the police, and was discovered by Police Constable Samuel Cowell. Cowell noted 'smoke and fire issuing from a recess in a built up window beneath the Egyptian hall... On running to see what was alight he found some brown paper which was on fire and which enclosed a flat kind of parcel'[45] placed up against the wall. Cowell grabbed the device and stamped out the fuse before detonation, preventing explosion at the last minute. Cowell brought the device back to Bow Lane Police Station for further investigation,[46] where examining the mechanisation of the bomb, police concluded that 'the burnt outer paper got within an inch of the fuse'[47] and thus despite public and police vigilance alike, on this occasion, the State had averted a bombing, seemingly by accident.

Police discovered 'two American newspapers, one Glasgow and one Irish newspaper of recent date and a linen bag in which the powder had evidently been first kept',[48] with the bomb. This indicated a possible connection with Glasgow Fenianism and the probable existence of a Fenian skirmishing cell in Britain. As the news broke of the foiled Fenian bombing, British newspapers widely reported that the explosive was stopped seconds before detonation, and had it not been for Cowell, Fenians would have exploded a bomb in the centre of London. Despite its failure, the propaganda value was still strong, and it served to illustrate a link between Irish coercion and politically motivated bombing. Attributing the attack to 'Fenian terrorism... [or] the anger of some of the Lord Mayor's Irish constituents in Lambeth, in consequence of the vote he had given in support of the Irish coercion bill in Parliament,'[49] *The Annual Register* recognised this point, and as this was certainly the case, it indicated the skirmishing strategy as a series of reprisals and attacks aimed at intimidating the British government. In the immediate aftermath of the explosion, a rumour began circulating amongst the public and media that some MPs had received threatening letters and that Westminster was to be attacked if security services were to be believed. It was reported that this threat was taken extremely seriously and 'all approaches to the underground rooms adjoining the space under Commons' chamber',[50] were sealed and made strictly private by police posting.[51] Official anxiety was stressed by means of the sewers underneath Parliament, and the possibility of Fenian entry and an explosion from below. This forced the police to deter a Fenian attack from the sewers by placing a heavy iron door at their entry, which was impossible to break through.[52] London, despite the failure of the skirmishing bomb, was seemingly under siege as the Home Office called for increased vigilance to deflect Fenian activity amongst an anxious populace. From New York, in a somewhat botched victory Jeremiah O'Donovan Rossa and his little band of skirmishers were hovering over Britain, the very threat of bombing being enough to arouse panic and anxiety.

By 5 May Rossa's skirmishers had seemingly struck again, moving northwards, their target was the 1st Royal Cheshire Militia quartered at Chester. This attack was an abysmal failure, however, and showed a crude understanding in bomb manufacture. The skirmishers on this occasion had left an explosive device in a bag 'hung on a nail driven into the wall'.[53] The bomb had exploded in the north west corner of the barracks beside the guard's room and washhouses. Rossa's agents, hindered by lack of money, had used a crude substance to attack the barracks, their bomb consisting of 'a cheap, black imitation leather valise, studded with iron knobs... a piece of slow burning combustible fuse, which has the appearance of a cord wrapped in a thin fabric, and is such as is usually employed for exploding combustible materials'.[54] The skirmishers had not drilled deep enough into the wall to undermine its structure, thus doing little damage.[55] This clumsy attempt drew scorn, however, with one newspaper recalling that the Chester attack bore: 'A very striking likeness to the idiotic and wicked attempt to blow up the Mansion House, and is in all probability the work of some fanatical fool, only differing from "Barnaby Rudge" in intensified blood thirstiness.'[56]

Of the Chester attack, Harcourt could only concur with such opinions; the more he heard of Fenian bombing, the less it alarmed him.[57] Despite this bravado, however, the government could take little solace from the foolhardiness of the Chester attack, increasingly the Home Office wondered what Rossa's strategy was, and why he was using such pathetic materials as gunpowder. Many concluded that he was preparing for something spectacular, that the previous attacks were a prelude to inspire anxiety in the public, setting them up for something greater. There was also the possibility that pathetic attacks like Chester were simply intended to draw income from gullible subscribers to his dynamite fund, justifying further and greater attacks in Britain. If this were the case, such a strategy was illustrated in May 1881 when O'Donovan Rossa claimed responsibility for the destruction of the British Warship *The Dotterel*.

With a complement of 156 sailors and six guns, *The Dotterel* exploded at the Straits of Magellen, the impact of the explosion killing all 156 of its crew and scuttling the warship. Considering *The Dotterel* was a new warship, news of the explosion in Britain was met with disbelief and horror, with the government contending the ship had been destroyed by means of gas explosions resultant from badly ventilated coal bunkers. In ordinary times this explanation would have been accepted as valid, but considering the bombing campaign, there was a growing belief that *The Dotterel* had been blown up by skirmishers. This belief had been grounded in the fact that the skirmishers had previously announced that they intended to destroy British vessels on the high seas, using explosives disguised as coal. While the skirmishers had nothing to do with the actual destruction of *The Dotterel*, O'Donovan Rossa was not going to lose the opportunity of association with its destruction. Taking to his newspaper, *The United Irishman,* he wrote how: 'The ghost of *The Dotterel* is still haunting the minds of the English ministers, and cannot be laid while the vengeance of the "Irish skirmishers" lives.'[58] Following on from this, O'Donovan Rossa was interviewed by the American-based *Sun* newspaper, in which he commended the destruction of the warship and warned that 'the Irish people will yet make [Britain] pay dearly for the tyrant game she is playing in Ireland'.[59] Continuing on, he noted how 'any measure that will make England fear for the safety of her own people, and even for her own existence has my strongest approval and hearty support'.[60]

Against this background the British government remained concerned as to the alleged importation of explosives into Britain, firmly believing that if Rossa had intended to launch a dynamite attack, he would have used materials procured in America and smuggled into Britain. Thus the watch was increased at Liverpool Port, the main source of American entry into Britain. From America all reports indicated that something big was being planned by skirmishers and that several bombs were making their way to Britain – the problem for the government was how to locate them, analyse the truthfulness of the information, and if correct, how to arrest those who were to receive them. With this information, customs officials alongside police officers were to be extra vigilant and report any suspicious behaviour or materials discovered. This increased vigilance resulted in a major coup for customs officials, locating hidden dynamite smuggled aboard two American registered vessels.

On 30 June the *SS Malta* arrived in Liverpool, amongst its cargo were several barrels of cement. While there was nothing unusual about this, a customs official noticed a black cross mark on one of the barrels, distinguishing it from the others. Alerting his colleagues, the barrel was examined, discovered hidden inside were 'six zinc boxes, which, upon further examination, proved to be infernal machines, with neatly constructed clockwork and... Dynamite ready prepared',[61] weighing three pounds each. This discovery was matched by the seizure of two more bombs of the same variety aboard the *SS Bavaria*, on 2 July,[62] containing 3lbs of dynamite each and a quantity of nitro-glycerine.[63]

The zinc canister contained in its upper part an inner zinc brass box, or case separated from the lower and larger compartment by a sheet of zinc, which was covered by a moist substance which proved on analysing, to be plaster of Paris and water, with a small quantity of nitrous compound, but not explosive.

The inner case was cemented into the outer case by a layer of similar plaster of Paris, and it is probable that the plaster had merely been spilled when it was being poured between the two zinc walls. The inner case contained clockwork communicating by springs and levers with the nipple of an iron tube which projected down through zinc partition, and if a cap had been placed on the nipple the arrangement would have had essentially the construction of a pistol. The tube was not charged nor was there a cap on the nipple, but the upper end of the tube or the barrel came off easily by unscrewing it so that the tube could be charged in a few moments… the whole arrangement was capable of being converted in a few moments into a most destructive self-exploding bomb.[64]

The devices discovered were recognised to have been of the most sophisticated design produced by skirmishers, all of 'very beautiful workmanship and most effectively designed',[65] employing a time delayed detonation.[66] They were calculated to allow the bomber to set and plant the bomb, and then safely escape before the ensuing panic and destruction. In experiments undertaken to examine the efficacy of the bombs it was noted, in this respect, that having been started, the machines would run for about six hours, when a portion of the clockwork would move a powerful spring, which would be brought into contact with a percussion cap, and so an explosion was caused.[67]

Upon making these discoveries, the customs officers alerted the police, who telegraphed the Home Office. The Home Office was determined that the seizure and subsequent investigation would be conducted under the upmost secrecy in the interest of public safety, and a desire to thwart the psychological effect of the discovery on public opinion by limiting knowledge of the find. However, a discovery such as this, 'the most extensive plot ever by the Fenians for the destruction of public buildings in England',[68] could not stay a secret too long and news was leaked by the media, resulting in strict denials by the authorities, allowing *The Pall Mall Gazette*, in a state of some confusion, to report that the discoveries had received no official confirmation while in some quarters the discovery had been denied,[69] the

Liverpool constabulary going so far as to state that the discovery was an elaborate hoax.[70] *The Press Association,* who had initially released the story, however, stood stubbornly by its claim to the effect that: 'Although its statement had been discredited in several circles, there is no doubt whatever as to the accuracy of the information, but efforts have been made to prevent the disclosure of the information.'[71]

This statement was indeed correct. The State was desperately trying to prevent the information from being confirmed in the interest of public safety. Increasingly the public asked why the authorities were being deliberately reticent, and public opinion was clamouring for clarity. With mounting official caginess regarding the seizure of dynamite, rumours and exaggerations regarding the Fenian threat increased profoundly. Many reading news stories concocted to sell newspapers feared a new wave of attacks were imminent, each more deadly than the last as the skirmishers graduated to first-class bomb construction. 'Any parcel left in a clubroom or forgotten in a railway carriage became an object of fear and suspicion, and in the facts known there was just enough to make the alarm not absolutely fantastic.'[72]

It was in this vein that *The New York Herald* could conclude: 'The Liverpool seizure of infernal machines has at last convinced a credulous British public that the Irish nihilists are fully in earnest in their designs against English life and property, and that the means in their hands are not as crude as has been generally believed.'[73]

This increasing speculation and panic fuelled by police reticence forced the Home Secretary to make a statement in the House of Commons as to what the government knew of the bomb seizures :

The government more than three weeks before had received information that the infernal machines were to be dispatched, and in consequence... sent down a detective and a custom house officer to search the vessels on their arrival at Liverpool... I accordingly communicated at once with the Commissioners of Customs, and a confidential agent of the Customs and a Metropolitan police officer were dispatched instantly from London to Liverpool to await the arrival of the vessels which had been designated in the information I had received. These officers reached Liverpool only a few hours before the arrival of the first of the vessels. The cargoes were accordingly searched, in concert with the police and the Customs authorities at Liverpool; and in the first vessel six of these machines were discovered in a barrel said to contain cement. Four more were found at a later period in the second vessel, concealed in the same manner.[74]

Harcourt held that he would have preferred the seizure to have taken place in complete secrecy, and resented the leaking of the story to the press, holding were it not for the media he would have pursued a policy of absolute silence, so as to allow the police to mount an uninterrupted investigation, while at the same time keeping the bombers unaware of the bombs interception. The Home Secretary also believed that had the government made public the discovery, it would have increased the level of panic amongst the public. This reticence, however, brought the wrath of an anxious public upon the authorities and the Mayor of Liverpool released a statement explaining how: 'The secrecy which was so well preserved was absolutely essential for the ends of justice... the hope of detecting the miscreants lay in the maintenance of perfect secrecy.' [75]

Having seized the explosives, the government were now concerned as to their origin. While the government was aware that the bombs had been manufactured in America, they had little evidence to link it to Rossa's skirmishers. The government were convinced that if they could link the evidence to O'Donovan Rossa, they could then illustrate to the American Administration the international nature of the conspiracy thus forcing the United States government to move against Rossa. A major effort was made by British consuls to locate the manufacturers, and all signs pointed to the state of Illinois[76] where it was held that the bombs were manufactured by a leading United Irishman, Patrick Crowe, personally connected to O'Donovan Rossa. Crowe became the centre of frenzied attention, and more indiscreet than O'Donovan Rossa he openly declared his support for bombing raids in Britain underlined by a constitutional right to produce explosives inherent within American Republicanism :

Dynamite was no more vicious than powder, and with these weapons they could drive from the seas their enemy, destroy her trade, and make profitable business impossible. Some persons would have to die... but war was always cruel and that war was easiest which went straight to the mark, killed the most in the shortest time and compelled nations to make peace.[77]

Crowe's candidacy was met by denials from O'Donovan Rossa, who was advised by associate United Irishman Judge John Brennan,[78] to endorse the aims of the smugglers if he chose, but to deny any knowledge and involvement in their importation to Britain. Decrying any connection between himself and the discovered explosives as ridiculous, he declined to comment when questioned about fundraising for British bombings. O'Donovan Rossa then lamented:[79]

> If those barrels were designed to execute Mr Forster and Mr Gladstone for their murders in Ireland we are sorry they did not reach them in proper fashion. It is our opinion that the Irish in fighting England, could burn down London, Liverpool, Manchester, and other big English cities, and could easily burn down England's shipping, particularly her merchant ships. And we say that the Irish should do it, and hope in God they will do it, if England will not give up Ireland in a lesser sacrifice.[80]

A similar argument was made by several leaders of the United Irishmen denying any involvement in the shipping of dynamite to Britain, holding it was entirely the work of the skirmishers and not done under the direction of the organisation. They noted that while Crowe was connected to the United Irishmen, he was over-enthusiastic in his opinions.[81] Rossa, furthermore, had taken the unusual step of writing to James G. Blaine, American Secretary of State, informing him that the British government were deceiving their American counterpart, holding no Irishman in America had supplied the dynamite discovered in Liverpool, and it was all a ruse by mischief makers in British intelligence[82] designed to discredit the nation in exile and frame innocent men.[83] For many Irish-Americans, the Liverpool discovery was seen as a canard for a number of reasons, particularly because the dynamite was cheaper in Britain and the fuse mechanism could easily be purchased there. There was also a further incredible turn to the story of the Liverpool discovery.

This incredible turn was recognised when it was noted that a number of billheads marked 'O'Donovan Rossa' were discovered amongst the explosives. When this news was publicly released it was particularly uncomfortable for the Irishman as it could serve to indicate his involvement in the plot, meaning he would have broken US Navigational Laws. This would have left him open to a heavy fine, crippling his activities and ability to organise within America. [84] Representing this he denied all knowledge of the explosives and sticking to his earlier story, he insisted on his claim that the discovery was in fact a hoax propagated by Britain. Providing an interview upon news of their discovery, he stated from New York City that:

I do not consider the report true… in my opinion it is a lie gotten up to create further prejudice against those who wish Ireland to be given her freedom. If the machines were really found, then it is likely that it is simply a plot to secure the same end, especially if there were any papers in the barrels bearing my name. It is not probable that I would make machines with anything that would betray me. [85]

The reporter to whom O'Donovan Rossa gave his interview prodded him as to whether the bombs came from America and showed his disbelief of O'Donovan Rossa's statement. The reporter stated to O'Donovan Rossa that if evidence could be established that the bombs came from America, it would undermine his argument profoundly. Seeing this within the context of American Navigational Law, O'Donovan Rossa stayed committed to his denial and reiterated his opinion that the latest discovery of explosives in England was a hoax, but if it was proven real it was his belief that the bombs would have been sent by Irishmen: 'When I say this, I speak from what I know of the spirits that are animating many Irishmen in this country, in Australia, in England, and everywhere. There is a widespread determination of people of our race to teach England that it would be a wise policy to give up Government of Ireland.'[86] O'Donovan Rossa refused to answer whether the United Irishmen of America were involved with the latest discovery. He admitted that he had no fear of being arrested and was willing to speak to the police on any occasion as he had nothing to hide.

Within days, however, O'Donovan Rossa's principle explosives engineer, Patrick Crowe, released a further statement complicating the Liverpool discovery. Again interviewed at Peoria, Crowe, who identified O'Donovan Rossa, Judge Brennan and a number of others as belonging to the Executive Committee of the United Irishmen of America, stated how the executive decided that bombs 'could do better work by depositing torpedoes in British ships which could be done for $73 dollars a piece, and which would bring England to terms by making it dangerous for people to go aboard British vessels'.[87] Describing Crowe and those like him as 'the most desperate agitators', the interviewee went on to state:

Any warfare was good enough for England, who did not conduct honourable warfare herself, and could not expect others to do so. If she didn't do justice to Ireland, every English ship would be sent to the bottom, until people no longer dared to embark in them. Every

Government building would be torn down and a system of terrorism begun.[88]

While there was no evidence to say that O'Donovan Rossa had an opinion on Crowe's statement, it can be speculated that he didn't welcome the introduction of Crowe's more than candid opinions, particularly as there was a possibility that he could be associated with American law breaking.

Despite such candid comments, however, O'Donovan Rossa had nothing to fear while in America. While most people believed he had some involvement with the discovered bombs, nothing could be definitely proven against him. Furthermore, even if he had been guilty of breaking American Navigational Law, and this could be proven, legally, he had not violated the more important American Neutrality Laws, given the contemporary understanding of warfare as an open and honourable conflict between two distinct armies. American Neutrality Law prohibited American citizens from organising warfare against a foreign state with which the United States of America was at peace. There was a strong question of definition regarding the mode of warfare, and the means employed by Irish-American Fenianism. In purely definitional terms, American citizens were prohibited from enlisting within the United States persons to go into the service of a foreign State as soldier, parallel to the prohibition of the fitting out or arming of any vessel to cruise against a State holding peaceful relations with the United States. In this respect, legally, the shipping of the explosives into Britain did not fall within the remit of American Neutrality Laws. Understanding this, the British government sought to extradite O'Donovan Rossa back to Britain. While their case against O'Donovan Rossa was incredibly circumstantial, the British Consulate at Washington had actively examined the possibility of his return to Britain as a prisoner. Making continuous remonstrance to the United States Department of State, the British government ultimately failed in their endeavour to extradite O'Donovan Rossa. The government was burdened by the fact that there was no extradition treaty in existence between Britain and America and it had been unable to prove a definitive connection between O'Donovan Rossa and the bombing campaign which could satisfy the American government. Examining the debate over his liberty and potential extradition, O'Donovan Rossa found the entire debacle rather humorous, commenting how he found deportation to be 'a strange demand on the American government…considering that England paid my passage from an English convict prison to New York, having previously presented me with a parchment paper requiring that I not return to England, Ireland or Scotland during a period of twenty years.'[89]

Despite the inability to provide definitive evidence connecting O'Donovan Rossa to the smuggled explosives, the fact that they had come from America was a considerable source of embarrassment to the United States government. While British remonstrance had failed to make the American government cognisant of the Fenian threat, it had succeeded in securing a pledge that the resources of the State would be used to find the smugglers.[90] In consequence of this pledge, James Russell Lowell, the American ambassador in London, informed the Foreign Office that 'the national state and municipal authorities of the United States are all engaged in the work of discovering the wicked authors of the dynamite plot'.[91] So serious was their concern that James J. Brooks, Chief of the Special Agents of the American Treasury, was instructed to investigate the case, although in the long term his investigations would come to little fruition.[92]

Following on from the Liverpool discovery, in the early morning of 11 June 1881, skirmishers attempted to destroy the Town Hall in Liverpool, damaging glazed windows and offices opposite.[93] When compared to the previous Fenian signature, the bomb had been significantly improvised and improved on its predecessor's style, consisting of more powerful Atlas dynamite, illegal in Britain but widely used in America.[94] The bombers, William McGrath[95] and James McKevitt, each armed with a loaded revolver,[96] had brought the bomb to the steps of the west door of the Town Hall in a large carrier bag. The sight of heavily laden sailors in the port city of Liverpool was not unusual. The bombers' intention had been to detonate their explosive at the Liverpool Customs House in a symbolic economic gesture. They had been disturbed, however, and moved on by police,[97] making their way to the Town Hall. Laying the device for a second time they were again disturbed by a cab driver, John Ross, who thinking they were sailors on account of their large bag, stopped to ask if they wanted a cab.[98] Declining his offer, Ross' intervention had allowed them to lose the benefit of speed and brought them to the notice of a police constable, George Reade, who approached the bombers as they set the fuse.

Hurriedly running across the Town Hall forecourt, Reade followed them, blowing his whistle and raising the alarm; the pursuit continued for half a mile. At the top of Chapel Street, Reade met Constable Creighton,[99] instructing him to return to the Town Hall and deal with the bomb while he continued the chase into Oldhall Street and up Edmund Street, where he met a Constable Casey.[100] While the pursuit of the skirmishers was continuing, at the Town Hall a number of police[101] had removed the bomb to the middle of the road, away from the building and 'before they got more than five yards from it, it exploded'.[102] The force of the blast was seen by onlookers recalling that 'the Town Hall windows... suffered severely from the broken fragments of iron piping, and the stonework in some places appeared as though it had been subjected to artillery'.[103] Such was the force of the blast that it was noted had the bomb been left at the Town Hall, greater damage to the building may have taken place.

With the pursuit of the bombers continuing apace, Casey discovered McKevitt hiding under a lorry trying to evade detection.[104] McKevitt had thrown his gun over a yard wall and when Casey went to find it he discovered it was a ten-chamber revolver with nine chambers loaded.[105] With McKevitt in custody, Casey then 'went over a number of coal yard walls... and found McGrath concealed in the bottom of an empty coal flat, he was very wet and seems to have fallen into the canal'.[106] Casey placed McKevitt's revolver to McGrath's head, demanding to know if he had a gun, and to turn it over at once. Indicating to his pocket, Casey discovered a six-chambered pistol on McGrath, loaded and at full cock.[107] Furthermore, the bomber had on his person a dynamite cap.[108] The first skirmishers of O'Donovan Rossa's bombing campaign had been captured, and Head Constable John Greig attached much importance to their arrest. In this consideration he concluded that their interrogation could serve to unravel Fenian conspiracy, leading to solid intelligence and a very public disincentive for potential bombers.[109]

Greig was partially correct in this interpretation. While the arrest of the bombers would not serve to undermine the impetus for Fenian bombings, their interrogation did provide valuable information as to the actual nature of the Fenian conspiracy. McGrath unhesitatingly told his questioners all he claimed to know of his involvement with skirmishing, implicating himself in an earlier explosion at the Liverpool Police Station the previous month, and how he had been involved in the manufacture of the homemade explosives at his Liverpool home. In McGrath's narrative, his work was supervised by an Irish-American named Gleeson who recruited and provided him with money raised from Irish-America, as the head of a skirmishing cell sponsored by O'Donovan Rossa.[110] According to McGrath, he had been sent to Britain with the aim of bombing public buildings in England, so as to 'inspire confidence'[111] in the bombing strategy by seeking the destruction of government property, rather 'than property that would have to be repaired from the rates'. [112] He was employed by an American steamer, the SS Italy, as quartermaster, which regularly visited Britain, ferrying passengers from New York to Liverpool,[113] and was quite familiar with the city, his employment facilitating a means of communication between Britain and America. McGrath claimed to have received seven and half dollars from Gleeson, who was to be the head of the bombing cell. Arriving in Liverpool, McGrath would take rooms at No. 15 Cottenham Street, establishing a workshop for homemade explosives with Gleeson. Through an acquaintance of Gleeson's, Thomas Carmody, a prominent Liverpool Fenian, McGrath was introduced to James McKevitt, a regular subscriber to Rossa's *United Irishman* newspaper. Police concluded that the ideas of *The United Irishman,* during a time of heightened unrest in Ireland, had facilitated McKevitt's involvement in the conspiracy, and McGrath recruited him due to his strong desire for retribution against Irish coercion.[114]

According to McGrath, both he and McKevitt were the instruments of the skirmishers; the construction of the bombs was left to them, with the planning undertaken by Gleeson and Carmody, who were in regular contact with more senior men in New York. In order to maintain strict secrecy, neither McGrath nor McKevitt were informed as to the details of the plans made by Gleeson and Carmody. Gleeson in particular remained reticent, informing them only of what they needed to know, seeking to reduce the potential of informers or the breaking of conspiracy upon arrest. All Gleeson would note was an intention to destroy public buildings. Such was the importance of Gleeson that the police wasted little resources in trying to find him, but could only lament 'as to the whereabouts of the man Gleeson, or any man corresponding to the description of Gleeson'.[115] There was no information, tending to indicate that Gleeson was a pseudonym. Interrogating McGrath further as to the details of Gleeson, it was discovered that he more than likely had left Britain following the arrests, although McGrath initially held Gleeson was in London engaged in pre-operational surveillance. As to what he was looking at, however, McGrath did not know. Undertaking further investigation of Gleeson, however, it was discovered that he resembled a known Glasgow Fenian named J. J. O'Donnell[116] who had been under supervision in Glasgow but was not viewed as 'a very formidable enemy',[117] to State security. Interestingly, the Glasgow Constabulary had evidence that O'Donnell had visited Liverpool on several occasions prior to the bombings, circumstantially establishing some form of connection to the skirmishing cell and forcing a reappraisal of his character.[118] O'Donnell had, however, as Barton predicted, made for New York following the arrests, leaving Britain from Greenock on 21 April, thus escaping police inquiries into his business.[119]

This skirmishing cell was clearly drawn from a smaller proportion of the existing Fenian network in Liverpool, which provided it with anonymity and assistance. This was further illustrated by the discovery of a pocket book, owned by McGrath, giving the names and addresses of Fenian contacts in Britain and America.[120] The subsequent police investigation indicated that McGrath and McKevitt were not working in isolation but were in contact with known Fenians within the city. The Mayor informed Harcourt: 'I am disposed to think that the action of W. McGrath is not as isolated as his statement would appear to indicate. The Liverpool names are those of well-known Home Rule Fenians, and are referred to in that disjointed way as to suggest that they had been obtained at different times – possibly after interviews.'[121]

The most significant name amongst McGrath's contacts was Tom Carmody. As had been stated in McGrath's interrogation, Carmody was an important figure in the skirmishing conspiracy, in communication with superior men in New York. Carmody a well-known Fenian, similar to McGrath, had been employed aboard a trans-Atlantic steamer, operating between New York and Liverpool, again facilitating communication. According to McGrath, Carmody had left Britain prior to the blast for New York, where he was due to meet O'Donovan Rossa and other members of the skirmishing committee to plan the future of skirmishing work in England.[122] In America, Carmody was extensively watched so that should he return to England he could be arrested upon arrival,[123] but the State concluded that his return was highly unlikely given the arrest of McGrath and McKevitt, and regarded his association with Rossa as significant. O'Donovan Rossa justified the message of the Liverpool explosion as seeking 'to show England that she can't send her armies into Ireland without impunity. It is only the beginning of the trouble.'[124]

Having established this trans-Atlantic connection, the police informed the Liverpool Mayor, William Bower-Forwood, that the recent explosion represented a much wider conspiracy, funded and organised by Irish-America. This conspiracy was underlined by an increasingly globalised world, utilising developments in science and communications, as represented by McGrath and Carmody coming on steam liners connecting Liverpool to America and using that route to smuggle explosives and skirmishers into Britain with ease.[125] Bower-Forwood held that this situation was extraordinarily dangerous to security. It is evident that he understood Irish grievance towards coercion was strong, and explained to Harcourt that a mood existed amongst the Liverpool-Irish to be swayed by Irish-American arguments for retaliation, and that if these sentiments could be found working along the docks he could not 'see that we can do anything to ward off this danger'.[126] If this was the case, Bower-Forwood held that Liverpool was vulnerable at its docklands, as it consisted of large numbers of Irish labourers. The docklands required increased police security and perimeter protection in a difficult but nevertheless hopeless counter Fenian strategy.[127] Against this background, the British government were equally concerned about the possibility of Irishmen leaving the United Kingdom for America where they had learned of the existence of a Fenian dynamite school at Brooklyn. The purpose of this school was to instruct Irishmen in the in the manufacture of explosives. Upon graduation it was understood that they would make for Britain where they would employ their new skills. Students were to be taught by a supposed Russian dynamite specialist, Professor Gazpron Mezzeroff, whom O'Donovan Rossa had allegedly made a five year contract with to instruct pupils in explosive making. While Mezzeroff was in fact a Scots-Irishman named Rodgers continuous consular reports indicated that this dynamite school was a significant threat to British national security. Underlining this threat, O'Donovan Rossa cited how the Professor could train any man within a month for direct action against Britain. Studying the dynamite school the government had discovered that Mezzeroff was teaching students how British policy vindicated violence. Studying one of his lectures the government learned how the Professor held 'it is perfectly honourable and just that Ireland, that has been oppressed for seven hundred years, and had been robbed of all her wealth and means of defence, should use secret devices to obtain her rights and achieve her liberty.' Considering this narrative the government were concerned of further attacks in Britain and the following year there was an increasing upsurge in Fenian violence culminating in the Phoenix Park Assassinations on 6 May 1882. Resulting in the deaths of two of the British government's most important administrators in Ireland, Lord Frederick Cavendish and Thomas Henry Burke, the assassinations had been carried out by a Fenian assassination committee called the Irish National Invincibles.

The assassinations were particularly brutal as the assassins had wielded 11-inch surgical knives, tearing the bodies of Cavendish and Burke asunder. In the immediate aftermath of the killings, there was shock throughout the political establishment and many within the British political elite had laid the blame for the killings squarely at the feet of O'Donovan Rossa. William Forster, whom Cavendish had replaced as Irish Chief Secretary, was on record as noting that 'much inspiration for the deed came from O'Donovan Rossa'.[128] The *London Standard* asserted that 'the brutal ravings of O'Donovan Rossa', needed to be addressed by American law-makers and called for his arrest.[129] In America, the *Galveston Daily News* argued that O'Donovan Rossa had 'the blood of Cavendish and Burke' on his hands resultant from his physical force doctrine.[130] O'Donovan Rossa had nothing to do with the Irish National Invincibles or the Phoenix Park Assassinations. He did, however, support the action and was determined that a plan should be adopted to support the assassinations. This was grounded in the reaction of prominent Irish-Americans within the nationalist movement who were preparing to condemn the assassinations. Regarding this interpretation as 'slavish', O'Donovan Rossa organised a meeting of his associates in New York City, where they agreed to attend a meeting of the American Land League at the Cooper Institute on 12 May 1882, where the association was to be addressed by Charles Stewart Parnell's mother, Delia.

In anticipation of trouble at the Coopers Union, a large police contingent had assembled outside the hall. Noticing O'Donovan Rossa's arrival to the meeting, the police entered the Coopers Union and sat near the veteran Fenian who sat in the middle of the hall with a number of adherents. The first speaker to address the meeting was New York City Mayor William Grace. Originally from County Laois, Grace condemned the assassinations and noted that all had assembled to declare their abhorrence of the assassinations and show condemnation of the Invincibles.[131] This irritated O'Donovan Rossa who, with his supporters, interrupted the meeting as they shouted 'three cheers for the killings'.[132] Grace was followed by Richard O'Gorman, a veteran of the Young Ireland Movement, who similarly condemned the Phoenix Park Assassinations; once again he was heckled by O'Donovan Rossa. Taking to his newspaper, O'Donovan Rossa followed an independent course, and condemning nationalists who judged the Invincibles he asserted that neither he nor his associates could condemn them, writing:

Who can wonder that the indignation of the men of Ireland has been aroused? The wonder is that manhood enough has remained in a few Irishmen to dare to execute well merited vengeance on those destroyers of their kith and kin. We do not wonder that such startling news has reached America. They who sow the wind must expect to reap the whirlwind. Long, long enough, too long, god knows, have all the murdering's been on the English side of the house, all the victims on the Irish side. There is no necessity for us to make any guesses as to the cause of the murder or execution of these men. One thing is certain, the deed was not done by the milk and water Land Leaguers who prate to us of freeing Ireland and ridding the country of landlordism without striking a single blow. The men who struck this blow shall have no word of condemnation from us. They have dared the peril of doing it. They are on the spot where the wrongs of the tyrant are inflicted and felt. There is no fear that we are going to join with the cowardly crowd of politicians here who rush forward with their resolutions of indignation.[133]

The assassinations reshaped the Irish political landscape. In response to the assassinations, the British government established a permanent secret service department at Dublin Castle. Known as the Office of the Assistant Undersecretary for Police and Crime, the new department was mandated with the task of undermining Fenian conspiracy. Initially led by Colonel Henry Brackenbury, within one month the department was in the hands of Edward George Jenkinson, a former Indian official who was accustomed to vigorous unconstitutional usages counter to the established rule of law.[134] Jenkinson established an elaborate web of police, spies, informers and agent provocateurs to monitor Fenian conspiracy, paid through the secret service fund.[135] Describing his modus operandi in the aftermath of the assassinations, he suggested:

We try to find agents in the first instance. Then from them we endeavour to obtain a thorough knowledge of the Fenian organisation in Great Britain. Out of this grows a knowledge of the men who belong to the organisation, and by watching and obtaining information... we by degrees shall find out the groups or sections who are plotting assassinations or explosions.[136]

The assassinations also made a further round of coercion appear increasingly likely, and this impetus was represented by a strong push in government, by Harcourt, with influential Royal support,[137] to establish a new coercion Bill. Privately, Gladstone was horrified, and the introduction of a new Coercion Bill[138] in Parliament was met with hesitation on the part of the Prime Minister.[139] This arose from a private confidence that 'Parnell, Davitt and Dillon will denounce the late murders openly... and that their action will so tranquilise the country that very stringent powers may not be necessary.'[140] Gladstone had thus hoped to avoid the potential of violence, coercing and motivating opposition and popular indignation against the British government, and believed that moderate nationalist denunciation would be enough to pacify Ireland. While Parnell, Davitt and Dillon had denounced the assassinations in a lengthy statement, as predicted by the Prime Minister, Gladstone was reluctantly forced to support the new Coercion Bill through Parliament. Known as the Crimes Bill, the new Coercion Bill was more draconian than the last, allowing the Vice Royalty to establish special non-jury courts of three Supreme Court judges to try cases of treason and murder. Furthermore, within the terms of the Crimes Bill, provision had been made for summary powers of arrest, the suspension of habeas corpus and a power to proclaim entire districts if deemed necessary to public order.

Given that Irish-American Fenianism was schooled in the ideology of American republicanism and the right to resist tyranny by force, it came as no surprise that the Crimes Bill was rejected. As was the case with the earlier Coercion Act, the existence of tyranny as recognised within the language of American republicanism justified a resort to arms in defence of liberty. Thus, the reintroduction of coercion would irritate Irish-America, establishing the inevitability of violent conflict.[141] In this vein, Patrick Ford of *The Irish World* wrote of the Crimes Bill:

> This infamous Repression bill, when it becomes law, will be a declaration of war against Ireland. In this spirit it should be accepted by the Irish people... We on this side of the Atlantic must not stand by with folded arms and see the contest going on without doing what lies in our power to aid our brothers in their heroic struggle... our answer should be such that the English government as well as our brothers will know that we do not intend to stand by as idle spectators whilst Ireland is being trampled underfoot...[142]

These views were easily justified by the mainstream American media, which often incited existing Irish-American impetus. The *Chicago Express* was one such newspaper, condemning the coercion act as 'a savage enactment... borrowed from the jurisprudence of barbarous nations'.[143] The *Baltimore Catholic Mirror,* echoing similar censure, denounced a 'brutal piece of legislation'[144] directed against the Irish people. The *San Francisco Monitor* was more incensed with draconian illiberalism seeing it as:

Fraught with the worst elements of tyranny: it places the lives and liberties of a whole people at the mercy of a few mercenary magistrates by the very government that only awaits a plausible excuse to turn loose its soldiery upon a defenceless people and to shoot them down like dogs.[145]

In this style of journalism, Irish–America was bombarded with sensationalised stories depicting unrelenting tyranny, encouraging tension by means of misconception and exaggeration and increasing Irish-American feelings for retribution against Britain. Compounded with the stories of the previous year, contemporary news and opinion enthused potential Irish-American sympathisers to extremes. In this regard, the Crimes Bill, rather than destroy political violence and agitation, had the opposite effect of inciting more violence and enthusiasm for the bombing campaign.

This impetus for the bombing campaign was graphically illustrated by the discovery of another bomb at London's Mansion House. Having failed to explode, the bomb was largely symbolic and representative of the Fenian response to Coercion. Despite its failure to explode, however, aftermath of its discovery Harcourt lamented in connection to coercion: There is necessarily great alarm as to what these desperados may do next, and London is full of threatening letters and rumours of all kinds. The attempted explosion at the Mansion House was a Fenian scare of the old clumsy kind. I made it a reason for having all the Irish quarters in London beat up last night. My police report very little Fenianism in London but of course it may be imported any day either from America or Ireland.[146]

Such was the effect of the Crimes Bill on Irish-Americans, that one newspaper contended: 'What we have to face is a war conducted in defiance of all moral considerations, by secret conspirators and their tools, with a certain measure of support – be it due to sympathy or terror among the masses and aiming directly at the disintegration of the United Kingdom.'[147]

Within the narrative of the advanced nationalist press in America, the reintroduction of Irish Coercion was seen either as a declaration of war upon the Irish people or an act of draconian tyranny.[148] Underlined by the language of American republicanism, violence was justified in defence of political liberty. This was graphically illustrated in September 1882 when there had been a skirmishing convention at Chicago, where, eulogising the perceived efficacy of modern science and American Republican rhetoric, delegates denounced coercion as tyranny. Pledging themselves to oppose coercion by all means expedient, delegates resolved to support 'the use of infernal machines and dynamite explosives for the destruction of English public property'.[149] In this vein the gathering was addressed by recent graduates of the dynamite school, each more militant than the other in their desire to play a part in the bombing campaign. One Scottish graduate boasted how the dynamite school had trained him in the homemade manufacture of nitro-glycerine, in preparation for his return to Britain.[150] He was followed by an Irish teenager, originally from Donegal, who similarly noted his desire to resist tyranny by promising to 'return to his people in Donegal and blow up at least one British station before he came back to America'.[151]

The very idea that skirmishers were training men in America in do-it-yourself explosive manufacturing[152] was a significant security concern to the British state. The previous year, Rossa had asserted that 'young men have come over from England, Ireland and Scotland for instruction and that several of them have returned sufficiently instructed in the manufacture of the most powerful explosives'.[153] A central objective of the dynamite school was to train men in the do-it-yourself use of explosives in America, and dispatch them to Britain facilitated by advancements in trans-Atlantic communications. In this strategy the individual, facilitated by the efficacy of modern science, was given a low-cost power, a power perceived as a weapon of the weak. Explosives could be built in backrooms, kitchens and workshops using cheaply accessed materials common in every day trade. To facilitate the construction of Explosives, graduates would share their knowledge with Fenians operating in Britain, seeking 'the destruction of British life and property'.[154]

One of the first graduates to have returned to Britain was John Francis Kearney. Kearney lived a seemingly quiet life as an employee of the Caledonian Railway Company,[155] with little or no interest in politics. Despite appearances, however, Kearney was certainly involved with the Liverpool bombings of 1881: significant evidence existed that he had been involved in the recruitment of James McGrath, the imprisoned Liverpool bomber.[156] Operating under the alias 'Glencree',[157] Kearney had recruited an Irish immigrant living in Glasgow, Terrance McDermott, whose connections with men working at a chemical factory at St Rollox facilitated the purchase of small quantities of materials required for the home production of nitro-glycerine.[158] Kearney, having been trained in the production of explosives, shared his expertise in explosive making, using freely available materials, with several Glasgow ribbon men, as an active skirmishing cell. Kearney, however, was one man within a larger network, and another graduate of the dynamite school, Thomas J. Mooney, employing the pseudonym James Moorhead, arrived in Glasgow to work alongside Kearney in training men for the bombing campaign.[159]

Mooney was staying in the home of Sarah Douglas McLachlan, posing as a commercial traveller. He was facilitated by another graduate of the dynamite school, John O'Connor (Henry Dalton), who had briefly stayed with him under the pretence of being a friend at McLachlan home, regularly meeting McDermott on behalf of Kearney.[160] Mooney was now in charge of the skirmishing cell, acting as the principle bomber and planned to mount a spectacular explosion within the city.

In America, O'Donovan Rossa was determined to resist coercion in Ireland and he had instructed Mooney to undertake a bombing in Britain in co-ordination with the other graduates of the school. Mooney had chosen to undertake a bombing on 20 January and had reconnoitred three potential targets. The first of these was Tradeston Gasworks, where with McDermott, he deposited a powerful homemade nitro-glycerine explosive at the base of a large gasometer. They had purposely placed the bomb to the southwest of the gasometer, directing the blast from the densely populated area northwards of the predicted blast. Using a time-delay function, they made their escape, and at ten o'clock, with great force, the bomb detonated, causing a sense of immense consternation. Contemporaries recalled:

> A brilliant glare suddenly illuminated the city for miles round, followed the next instant by a terrific report, so violent in character that homes shook to their foundations, and windows were shattered in all directions. Bright clear flames were then seen to be rising into the air and crowds of astounded citizens sought at once to ascertain the cause. The district and central fire brigades were summoned by the electric fire alarm rung by several startled people.[161]

This consternation was further enflamed by the immense damage caused by the explosion, ensuring public terror in the vicinity. Nearby houses were left wrecked, with enormous financial damage caused. At nearby Muirhouse Lane, a family was dangerously injured and their home destroyed: all had received burns to the hands, neck and face.[162] The homeowner, Thomas Butler, recalled:

> I was sitting by the side of the fire when the explosion took place... I was knocked kind of stupid. The wall was blown in where I was sitting beside the fire. I saw a great light. It blew the windows in... The lamp, which was hanging up by the fireside was blown to pieces,

and I saw a mass of flame around me. My clothes were on fire... my two shirts, and my gallowses, and my waistcoat burned.[163]

The effects of the Tradeston explosion were felt elsewhere, ensuring that this consternation was spread throughout Glasgow city. Resulting from the blast, all artificial light from the streets and places of entertainment[164] failed, plunging the city into absolute darkness, causing a great state of alarm that was recorded to be greater than the actual explosion amongst a terrified popular opinion.[165]

Within half an hour of the Tradeston blast, an off-duty soldier, Adam Barr, discovered another bomb. On this occasion, O'Donovan Rossa's skirmishers had left the explosive on Keppoch Hill Bridge, carrying the Forth and Clyde Canal over the highway, at Possil Road.[166] Barr had disturbed the bomb by moving in from a parapet and putting his fingers into what he thought was sawdust. Barr's disruption was speculated to save the city millions of pounds worth of damage; had the bomb exploded it would have flooded the city for a distance of sixteen miles.[167] Within a further thirty minutes, another bomb exploded at Buchanan Street railway station. On this occasion bombers annihilated an unused coal shed,[168] causing much consternation as two nearby railway workers, Thomas Smith and Simon McStravick, narrowly escaped injury as falling debris rained down upon them. Great damage was done to nearby houses and businesses near the scene of the blast, ranging from broken windows to damaged chimneys.[169] From America, O'Donovan Rossa was utilising the skills of his dynamitards to disrupt daily life in Britain, resultant from this scenario one contemporary mournfully lamented: 'What we have to face is a war conducted in defiance of all moral considerations, by secret conspirators and their tools, with a certain measure of support – be it due to sympathy or terror among the masses and aiming directly at the disintegration of the United Kingdom.'[170]

For three months there was a hiatus in the bombing campaign, but the threat of retaliatory violence was incited by means of the Dublin Invincible trials for the Phoenix Park Assassinations the previous May. In total, twenty-five men had been arrested and charged with involvement in secret conspiracy, with many arraigned on the testimony of an informer, the most notorious being James Carey. Of the American intelligence assets warned London that advanced nationalists were taking a keen interest in the proceedings, likely to lead to some form of retribution for the inevitable outcome of execution.[171] As a representation of interest in the Dublin trials and impending executions, O'Donovan Rossa's skirmishers had determined a further retaliatory attack. Leaving Glasgow on the morning of 9 March with McDermott, they left for London by train, arriving later that evening. As part of their plan for a spectacular explosion in London, linked to the Dublin trials they reconnoitred two pillars of political authority, *The Times* newspaper and Whitehall, the administrative centre of the British government. The bombers sought to undertake simultaneous attacks within the capital, seeking publicity though the use of the media as a vehicle of dissemination of political grievance.

On 15 March, the skirmishers deposited a bomb disguised as a tin japanned lady's hatbox[172] in Playhouse Yard at *The Times* headquarters. The bomb they used, however, was of poor quality, and failing to detonate properly, it engulfed itself in flames which still satisfied the aim of creating great alarm.[173] Its blast was recorded as like the noise of a fog signal to those within its vicinity.[174] Alfred Evens, an eyewitness and employee of a company opposite *The Times* headquarters,[175] recalled the blast:

> I saw the whole of *The Times* office lit up by flames, which were proceeding from an iron box directly under the window. A boy of ours named William Davis brought out a pail of water, which I took from him, and running up to the flames I threw the water over it, and then trod the flames right out... by the appearance of the box it had evidently been placed on the window sill, but the force of the explosion, instead of going into the window knocked the box outwards to the ground.[176]

By nine o'clock that evening the second explosion had taken place, as a sparsely attended House of Commons[177] was shook by reverberations from a nearby powerful blast. Harcourt, in attendance, correctly concluded in a letter to Spencer that the motivation for the blast was the first act of retaliation in London[178] for the Dublin trials:

> You will have heard by this time of the first act of retaliation in London. I was at dinner in the H of C when we heard a loud report, several of them at the table said 'it is an explosion.' I rejoined, 'I have heard so much of explosions I have almost ceased to believe in them.' In about ¼ of an hour the office keeper of the HO came over with the news.[179]

Within minutes the confusion was subdued but it became increasingly clear that a deliberate[180] explosion had taken place at government buildings in Whitehall.[181] On this occasion a bomb had been left on a stone balustrade of the Local Government Board Offices, causing great damage, shattering window panes and wrecking a copy clerk's office.[182] Harcourt noted despondently, 'it is very disheartening to think that all that has happened at Dublin has not terrified them more and that they should still in spite of Carey and co. count on impunity'.[183] Similar to Harcourt, *The Times* concurred, recognising the relationship between the Whitehall blast and the Dublin trials:

The moment has been aptly chosen, in Ireland the law has proved itself too strong for the criminals; the assassins are in safe keeping, waiting for their convictions out of the mouths of their accomplices. It was in England that the next attempt to terrorise the government and Parliament must be made... There are in London, men as desperate, as determined, as uncompromising enemies to England as any of the Invincibles in Dublin... It is hoped that the public will come to know with whom it has to deal. It has to deal with men who hesitate at nothing; with men to whom Human life and the works of human hands, and the fabric of society itself, are as nothing in comparison with the satisfaction of their own wild demands.[184]

In New York, O'Donovan Rossa, while not claiming responsibility for the explosions, acted as a spokesperson for the dynamitards declared that Ireland was at war with Britain and could use any means possible to fight for Irish liberty. Explaining how the explosion took place, he noted 'we could not follow our system unless we used dynamite, and that is what caused the explosion. There was no accident about it.'[185] Justifying the bombings he further explained how they 'were intended to do all the damage possible, and it was done to show England that she had better give Ireland her own Parliament. England is at war with Ireland, and Ireland should be at war with England.'[186] Studying O'Donovan Rossa's message it was reasonably contended that result from the latest bombings was a widespread public fear that affected all from 'prince to pauper':[187]

We have been told loudly and frequently by a certain class of late years that science is the providence of man. If so it seems to be exceedingly blind and wayward... This providence at times appears to infernal rather than divine. The invention of dynamite may be considered to be one of its latest fruits, and a bitter one it is. As yet all we have heard about it has tended to bring the conclusion that a new diabolical agency has been introduced into the world.[188]

Having secured immense publicity for Fenianism, O'Donovan Rossa's skirmishers had also captured the oxygen of publicity in America and Britain. This was represented by increased subscriptions to Rossa's dynamite fund and heavy enthusiasm for bombing campaigns amongst significant cadres of Clan na Gael. One vocal Clan figure in the aftermath of the blast, Edward O'Meagher Condon, commended the efficacy of the blast, noting:

> The evictions daily taking place all over Ireland; the brutality of the soldiery and the police, exercised with impunity on the helpless and unoffending... the contemptuous refusals of the British government to pay any attention to the expostulations and requests of the Irish clergy and representatives... all show the worse than uselessness... of looking to anything but force for redress and relief. [189]

For Condon, peace could only be achieved by British withdrawal from Ireland; he believed that the British government could not be trusted in its Irish policy. This made direct action justifiable in defence of liberty counter to Irish coercion. Condon was endorsed by Congressman John F. Finerty of Illinois, who publicly announced: 'I am sorry it was not more successful. I applaud the Irish in everything they do to get rid of England and her accursed rule. England brought this on herself.'[190] Finerty then commented how 'in this struggle, this vendetta, which England has now distinctly challenged, SCIENCE... must match itself against STRENGTH... In this our battle for vengeance and for liberty, one skilled scientist is worth an army'.[191] Patrick Ford, again toying with the idea of a bombing campaign,[192] noted how the Whitehall explosion had proven that Fenianism would not tolerate injustice in Ireland:

> The blowing up of a public building in the heart of London is a warning to the British government that English statesmen will not ignore if they are wise. In their dealings with Ireland, Gladstone and his predecessors have always acted upon the principle that the brute force at their command made it unnecessary for them to consult the wishes of the Irish people. The explosion that rent the walls of the Local Government Board and shock the halls of Parliament teaches the English statesman the lesson that for the future injustice to Ireland means danger to England.[193]

9

FROM HUBRIS TO NEMESIS

In Dublin, Edward George Jenkinson was increasingly preoccupied with the activity of Jeremiah O'Donovan Rossa as part of his surveillance of Irish-American Fenianism. Jenkinson, as stated earlier, operated an elaborated web of spies, informers and agent-provocateurs. He had established a trans-Atlantic intelligence network in co-operation with New York Vice-Consul William Hoare. The network was useful for infiltration in addition to providing a co-ordinated system for the dissemination of information. This operation was unknown to the British government and facilitated plausible deniability for policy makers in the event of the exposure of British agents in America.[1]

One of his agents was Red Jim McDermott, a Fenian activist who held some of the most militant interpretations of Irish independence. When O'Donovan Rossa had founded the United Irishmen of America in 1881 he had been embraced as a supporter of the new organisation and to rapturous applause had announced from the speaker's podium: 'Our motto is not a cent for blatherskite, but every dollar for dynamite... We do not mean to meet England on the open battlefield. That would be folly. But we do intend to carry on a warfare on the principle of nihilism.'[2] McDermott, who had been a British agent since the 1860s, met with O'Donovan Rossa in his Chambers Street office, prior to the Glasgow bombings in 1883. Here in the company of his half-brother, Matthew O'Brien, also a British agent, McDermott donated $50 to O'Donovan Rossa's dynamite fund. This money was authorised by Jenkinson and Hoare and had come from the British Secret Service Fund on the condition that it would be used to influence an unknowing Rossa. McDermott alluded to the fact that he was going to Ireland to report for *The Brooklyn Daily Argus* on the Irish crisis, and also to find George A.W. Stewart, the absconded secretary of the Brooklyn Board of Education. Securing credentials to work as a correspondent for *The United Irishman,* McDermott received a letter of introduction from Rossa, vague enough to endorse him amongst associates. This letter was used to facilitate the infiltration of Fenian conspiracy on behalf of British intelligence, with McDermott using Rossa's name for his benefit. In this regard, lamenting McDermott, one contemporary recalled:

> Although Rossa had the wildest possible experience of the world, he was one of the most gullible fellows imaginable. Anyone with a little stock of craftiness, who would curse the English government loudly enough, was sure to receive Rossa's heartiest welcome. He was also one of the kindest men, over ready to assist his brother exiles, no matter what section they might belong. Naturally, therefore, McDermott's sly cunning easily imposed upon him, absorbed as he was with what I may call his only 'weakness' – an undying hatred for England and the English.[3]

Following on from his meeting with O'Donovan Rossa, Red Jim sailed for the United Kingdom in late January 1883. Boarding the vessel as Peter Quigley, he arrived in Liverpool in February and travelling to Birkenhead, had a meeting with Edward George Jenkinson.[4] From here he allegedly made his way to London where he met with Matthew O'Brien. McDermott then returned to Liverpool where he set sail for Dublin, provided with money from the Secret Service fund. In Dublin he freely made use of O'Donovan Rossa's name and utilised the letter of recommendation he had intrigued from the Irishman. However, he had little success and a good deal of Fenian activists were dismayed by his at times theatrical militancy. Using his credentials as a journalist, McDermott also visited Dublin Castle where he sought to interview Jenkinson. Ostensibly, this interview was undertaken within the pretext of reporting the Castle response to the Phoenix Park Assassinations but in reality was briefed by his handler by the spymaster.[5]

That evening, McDermott was arrested for drunkenly abusing a police officer near Trinity College. Taken to College Green police station to be held overnight, as was usual with all prisoners detained, he was searched for contraband and the police discovered Rossa's letter of introduction in addition to a letter to Jenkinson at Dublin Castle, seeking an interview on behalf of *The Brooklyn Daily Argus*. The Dublin Metropolitan Police had no reason to doubt that they had a Fenian activist in their custody, but they wondered as to why he wished to see Jenkinson under the cover of being an American journalist. The DMP figured something was afoot, wondering was the undersecretary to be assassinated or had they arrested an informant. Contacting Jenkinson, the station superintendent alerted him of the overt connection between his prisoner and O'Donovan Rossa, but to his surprise he was instructed by the spymaster to release McDermott the following morning. Jenkinson was exceedingly embarrassed; McDermott had acted irresponsibly, his indiscretions bringing attention to his character and forcing intervention from the assistant undersecretary in order to cover-up a connection.

From here, McDermott left for Cork toward the end of February, staying in the Imperial Hotel and living exorbitantly, despite no obvious income. During his sojourn in Cork he actively ingratiated himself in the local Fenian organisation. Making free use of Rossa's letter of introduction, he styled himself himself as a skirmishing emissary, fulfilling Jenkinson's strategy of entering into conspiracy proactively and seeking to break it from within. As part of this scheme of penetration, he went out of his way to ingratiate himself within the local Cork nationalists, making sure to be seen every day with like-minded Fenians, and attending Land League meetings and speeches. The Irish-American built up a strong list of contacts in Munster, which he compiled in a pocket notebook, listing names and addresses of confederates, visiting each one in order to become familiar with them and their activities. Through one of these confederates, McDermott learned of William O'Riordan (alias James O'Malley), an active Fenian since 1865, who had also remained active within the IRB as a supporter of O'Donovan Rossa, and as a member of the skirmishing cell based in Cork headed by Irish-American Timothy Featherstone.[6] Initially, McDermott was unaware of the existence of a skirmishing cell in Cork. Learning of the skirmishing cell by chance, however, when he intercepted a letter bound for Featherstone, McDermott infiltrated the conspiracy through his letter of introduction by O'Donovan Rossa. This was against the background of consistent objection by O'Malley, who intensely mistrusted the Irish-American. Claiming to be an active dynamitard and a supporter of O'Donovan Rossa, he was introduced to other members of the conspiracy including Richard Short, Timothy Carmody, Daniel O'Herlihy, Denis Deasy and Henry Morgan. Red Jim learned through his Cork connections that O'Donovan Rossa had another man living in England, Patsy Flanagan, a railway guard at St Helen's junction.[7] The Cork skirmishers were actively working alongside Kearney and John O'Connor (Dalton) in Glasgow. Featherstone and Dalton had been in Glasgow as early as October and November 1882.[8] That both visited the existing Glasgow cell illustrates a degree of co-operation was emerging in the Cork–Glasgow–London skirmishing axis. The conspiracy ran into all three countries of the

United Kingdom, and in this vein there is strong evidence to indicate that they had plotted to hold almost simultaneous explosions in Scotland, Ireland and England. McDermott was thus introduced into an extensive skirmishing operation and further learned of Dalton's existence in London.

Making his way to meet with Dalton on behalf of Featherstone, McDermott found the skirmisher 'without a pound of the stuff or a companion'.[9] Showing him O'Donovan Rossa's letter of introduction, Red Jim befriended the skirmisher and with him planned bombing attacks in London, reconnoitring Big Ben Clock tower, Westminster Palace and Westminster Abbey. Examining the wreckage of the Local Government Board, the two were seen to be heartedly laughing. During their reconnoitring, however, they were being watched by the Special Irish Branch, one detective commenting how:

> Dalton and [McDermott] met at Charing Cross Hotel at 5pm on Saturday 24 March last. They went to several hotels and to the Houses of Parliament. On their way they passed the Local Government Board Offices... they went round the railings of the House of Lords and Commons and stopped at the Clock Tower for about ten minutes. Dalton raised his hands, and I heard him say 'up'.[10]

Under the pretext of McDermott's skirmishing activities, and posing as a skirmishing emissary, he would continuously visit London in order to contact Dalton. In the course of his London visits, McDermott made secret contact with Jenkinson and continued to brief him on developments. This was particularly relevant following the Whitehall bombing, with the spymaster travelling to London to examine the scene and making enquiries for his own largely secretive investigations, unknown to the police, using intelligence assets and the RIC stationed in London. In a letter to Harcourt he wrote:

> When I was in London I told you I was trying to find out the men who were concerned in the explosion at the local govt. Board and also the names of Rossa's agents in England and Ireland. I succeeded in a great measure and before I left London I put Mr. Williamson on a clue, which if... followed out, ought to lead to important results.[11]

What this clue was remains unclear, but could possibly have been a reference to a rival cell then functioning in London. The cell was under the auspices of Clan na Gael but was loosely connected to O'Donovan Rossa, under an Irish-

American doctor using the alias of Mr Fletcher.[12] Jim McDermott knew of the Clan cell and had actively searched for Fletcher; whether he met with him remains unclear, but he almost certainly informed Jenkinson of their existence. In London, McDermott would work out with Jenkinson a means of advancing the skirmishing plot; the skirmishers would sail for Britain from Cork, for active work. Upon departure, McDermott would telegraph Jenkinson as to the departure of the explosives, with the spymaster alerting the police, having received information from a source that he could not divulge, as to their arrival in order to follow the bomb and those with it. This would facilitate wider arrests and break the skirmishing cell. The spymaster hoped the police would not move too rashly and spoil an excellent intelligence operation.

As part of this scheme of entrapment, McDermott had devised with Featherstone a conspiracy whereby dynamite would be smuggled into Liverpool for a skirmishing attack against St George's Hall. McDermott, who possessed the explosives, passed them on to Denis Deasy, whom he instructed to smuggle the bomb into Liverpool. However, Deasy failed to smuggle the box of nitro-glycerine to the City. He was then persuaded to accompany a further consignment soon after, and McDermott personally gave him a note signed in Featherstone's name and addressed to Patsy Flanagan, alluding to the plot and implicating others in the conspiracy.

Deasy boarded the SS *Upupa* at Cork, bound for Liverpool, at the end of March.[13] The police knew nothing about his departure and he was not observed at Cork Harbour. As he arrived at the terminal, the Liverpool constabulary were waiting, however, watching his movements in consequence of information received from Jenkinson, despite the fact that his movements in Cork were unwatched. By alerting the police, Jenkinson had hoped that they would not move too rashly against Deasy, thus allowing maturation of the plot facilitating Deasy meeting with accomplices, a great advantage being made by 'dogging Deasy to his destination',[14] collecting information as to whom he was meeting in a slow and patient operation. Leaving the boat, Deasy had hired a porter, Thomas Shannon, to take his luggage, a heavy black trunk, to No. 34 Regent Street, Liverpool.[15] Deasy was going to a location with his explosive, who was there or what he would do with it was still unknown, but Jenkinson's scheme of entrapment was working well. However, it still depended on the action of the normal policing operation being delayed. Yet, to the spymaster's horror, Deasy was arrested by overzealous police before he could make it outside of the port: 'The Liverpool police were a little bit to [rapid] in their action, I told them to follow Deasy... and find out the men who were to act with him and to whom he was to consign the box. It is a great pity they did not allow him to meet Flanagan...'[16]

Searching Deasy's luggage, police found a packet of chloride of potash and a packet of powdered sugar, all patented with the mark of 'T. R. Lester Chemist Cork', alongside a bottle of acid and several brass tubes of a peculiar construction, wrapped in paper.[17] Each tube was carefully stitched into the canvass of the inside fabric, designed to hinder vigilant customs officials from discovery:

> There was a hole in the tin canister and a corresponding hole in the canvas in which they were covered. The hole in the tin canisters led up to a tin cylinder... The canister was filled with sawdust and nitro-glycerine, with the exception of the tin cylinder. The stuff, which was in the canister, was known by the name of lignin dynamite. It was very strong containing 75 percent of nitro-glycerine on average. It was a highly destructive article.[18]

Each tin canister had a carefully drilled hole at the top which was uncovered by the canvas and loosely plugged by paper, over sawdust. Parallel to the tin canisters were brass taps, to be used in the detonation process. Police also discovered the forged Featherstone letter implicating Flanagan and others. Flanagan had been identified by Jenkinson as a Rossa emissary in Liverpool.[19] The spymaster would have preferred that Deasy had made contact with Flanagan, thus expanding the conspiracy, but the letter of introduction was enough to draw suspicion as to his person, and Deasy's arrest now required immediate action against the Irishman for fear he would disappear, believing the operation compromised having heard nothing from Deasy. In this vein, using Deasy's letter of introduction containing Flanagan's address, police immediately swooped on the Irishman, raiding his lodgings at Sutton. While Flanagan was not there at the time of the policemen's arrival, detectives gained entry into his quarters and discovered a locked tin box. At 3 a.m. Flanagan was found and taken back to his room. The tin box was opened in the presence of Detective Constable Samuel Johnson, inside the box was a leather bag containing a loaded six-chamber revolver, a number of cartridges, a false beard, moustache, a small tin can containing white powder (chlorate of potash and sugar) and a bottle containing liquid, later discovered to be vitriol acid. Flanagan claimed the powdered chemicals were being used as tooth powder, while the liquid in the bottle was medicine for a liver complaint, asserting he knew nothing of Deasy and the dynamite. In this regard, while Flanagan was certainly connected to the skirmishers, the police had difficulty establishing a connection between the Irishman and Fenianism.[20] The evidence, however, was mounting against him and he was relentlessly interrogated, with the official conclusion being Flanagan was 'an instrument rather than an active agent in the conspiracy'.[21]

The letter, which McDermott had given him, signed in Featherstone's name, became the link from Liverpool to Cork, and later expanded to Glasgow, with a search mounted for the Cork skirmishers. Within hours, Featherstone was discovered in a police raid.[22] Searched by the RIC, he was found in possession of a recipe for Greek fire given to him by Jim McDermott. An investigation of his house revealed a large portmanteau, containing a small glass test-tube, which had recently contained liquid. It was discovered that the contents were intended to be of an incendiary nature.[23] The RIC, contending they had made an important arrest, concluded that Featherstone was a leading agent of the American dynamite party in Cork, and through the captive, further arrests were made, with known associates O'Herlihy and Carmody taken into custody. Only O'Malley and Short escaped the police net, while Jim McDermott disappeared – disguised as a priest he made his way to Dublin. By 30 March the police had raided several homes of known Featherstone associates and Fenians.[24] Captain Plunkett, Cork Royal Magistrate, summed up the scenario when he alerted the public: 'The government had information of the existence in Cork of a very formidable and dangerous conspiracy,'[25] asserting that Featherstone and his associates were formally remanded on the charge of being 'members of a secret society, whose objects were to murder and to blow up public buildings'[26] in Britain and Ireland. Jenkinson's methods, despite the hasty action of the Liverpool constabulary, and clear illegality, had succeeded to a great degree in breaking the skirmishing conspiracy. In London, Harcourt was jubilant, commending the spymaster's prudence:

> I think Jenkinson has done splendidly and shown marvellous resource. His information appears the first rate and altogether we are indebted to him for what security we possess against these fiends. It is of immense service to have seized them… What we want is a second Jenkinson. But where is he? Jenkinson was a happy accident. Can we hope to reproduce him?[27]

By 31 March, Deasy and Flanagan were tried in Liverpool while Featherstone, O'Herlihy, Carmody and Morgan were tried for treason felony in Cork. The prosecution defined their strategy to ensnare Featherstone, as he was the chief manufacturer of explosives, making continuous reference to McDermott's dynamite recipe, which had been described by Featherstone as 'a cure for gout'.[28] The prosecution also produced correspondence between Featherstone and O'Herlihy, proving a connection existed between the two as explosive maker and known Fenian.[29] Featherstone and O'Herlihy were then transported to Liverpool for trial with Deasy and Flanagan; O'Herlihy was the only acquittal, with insufficient evidence of his part in the conspiracy to try him. Deasy would die incarcerated, and Jim McDermott was not detected.[30]

From Ireland, the agent-provocateur made his way to France where he settled in Paris in the company of Patrick Casey and Eugene Davis, two Fenian supporters living in the French capital. From here, McDermott wrote to O'Donovan Rossa, explaining the disaster in Cork and claiming detectives were watching him very closely, necessitating a speedy escape.[31] He further discussed his belief that there was an informer amongst the Cork skirmishers and pointed the finger at Timothy Carmody, pointing to the non-publication of his evidence during the Cork trial as testament to his accusations, serving to indicate he had provided information to state authorities. McDermott, however, was still the subject of immense suspicion and his accusations of Carmody's treachery did not serve to divert attention from himself. In Ireland, James O'Malley was furiously looking for Red Jim and believing him to be a spy, had pledged to kill him. Through the Fenian network, O'Malley, who had also been in contact with O'Donovan Rossa in New York, discovered McDermott was in Paris. Travelling to France with the intention to interrogate and kill him, he arranged a meeting with the Agent-Provocateur at Le Havre through Eugene Davis. Davis had accompanied McDermott to Le Havre, recalled when introduced to O'Malley, 'I must say candidly and above board... that Mr McDermott's manner underwent a rapid change when he shook hands and kissed his Cork acquaintance. He was as nervous, cautious and reserved in his conversation with us as up to that time he was frank and unsuspecting.'[32]

At Le Havre, O'Malley drugged and interrogated McDermott relentlessly. The agent-provocateur escaped, however, and safely boarded a trans-Atlantic steamer to New York City. As America was not safe for McDermott, however, he made his way to the New York Counsel where he met with Hoare who had him shuffled in disguise to Canada. Consul Hoare again supplied him with money from the Secret Service Fund. For the purpose of fostering dynamite agitation and the establishment of dynamite cells within Canada, British Intelligence were once again employing the Irish-American for entrapment, operating outside the established rule of law. Knowing the possibility of McDermott being killed, Jenkinson panicked and, with Hoare, unsuccessfully tried to have him extradited to Britain to face a show-trial for his involvement in the Cork Skirmishing plot, have him found innocent due to lack of evidence and then to disappear.[33] Jenkinson had written to Harcourt noting that if McDermott were killed 'it would be a most disastrous thing for me. I should get no informers and the sources of my information would be dried up'.[34] His death would prove a disincentive for existing and potential informants and place a gap in the intelligence cycle. Jenkinson was so nerved at this possibility that he revealed McDermott to be his agent within the conspiracy, a desperate step by a man valuing total secrecy. He suggested that show trial could definitely be arranged as:

> We have plenty of proof that he, when at Cork, associated with Featherstone and was mixed up in the dynamite business... When he was down in Cork he was in constant communication with me, and as the arrests came immediately afterwards, the Rossa party naturally came to the conclusion that he had betrayed them... Would you therefore be so good as to have a telegram sent over from the colonial office asking the Canadian government to arrest him – it need not be kept a secret, indeed the more publicity given to it the better.[35]

Jenkinson held that publicity generated around British attempts to extradite McDermott would bolster his revolutionary credentials and confuse Irish–American interest in him.

While this was taking place, behind the scenes, McDermott had been contacted by O'Donovan Rossa through his personal secretary, Patrick Joyce. Joyce had led McDermott to believe that O'Donovan Rossa trusted him and believed that allegations of his duplicity were simply British mischief making.[36] At the same time, O'Donovan Rossa had been in contact with the IRB in Ireland who had dispatched two assassins to New York in order to kill McDermott. As McDermott returned to America, O'Donovan Rossa had met with the assassins and helped to co-ordinate their activity in New York. Indeed, Red Jim narrowly avoided execution when his assassins feared they could injure an innocent party.[37] Co-ordinating their activity with O'Donovan Rossa, the Irishman arranged a meeting with Red Jim in his Chambers Street offices. In this meeting, McDermott defended all of his actions, and continued his theme of Carmody's betrayal. O'Donovan Rossa listened inventively, hiding his anger that the British agent had used his name to entrap Irishmen. Withdrawing to a nearby pub, Ryan's Saloon, O'Donovan Rossa ushered McDermott to the back of the pub and sat him down with a wall behind him. As O'Donovan Rossa walked to the bar to order drinks, the two assassins burst into the pub and one of them shot at McDermott. The gun jammed, however, and the assassin, who was visibly shaking, struggled with his trigger – when the gun actually fired it only grazed McDermott and the agent-provocateur fought his way out of the bar. Making their escape, one of the IRB agents, James Gaynor, was arrested, but no charges were brought against him as no one in the saloon saw, heard or remembered the event in the subsequent police investigation.[38]

With Hoare's consent, McDermott was quickly shuffled out of America and placed aboard a trans-Atlantic steamer for Liverpool. Again utilising the alias of Peter Quigley, he was arrested upon arrival by waiting police and charged with 'conspiracy to murder public officials in Ireland and Liverpool'.[39] McDermott protested against his arrest and the newspapers maintained a story of how an Irish conspirator had been arrested in the maiden city. Encouraging their interest in the story, Jenkinson leaked a fabricated plot to the press, insisting that Red Jim had arrived in Liverpool as part of a conspiracy to release the men he had allegedly entrapped from custody. This story ran parallel to the stories of McDermott's duplicity, and it was Jenkinson's intention to muddy the waters, confusing Irish-America as to whether Red Jim McDermott was an informer or not. Jenkinson's strategy was a resounding failure, *The Brooklyn Eagle* noted:

> McDermott is not such a fool as to play fast and loose both with the English police and with the Irish secret societies here, and after being shot at by the one party runs rush into the prison of the other. Such a course is inconsistent with his well-known acuteness and diplomacy and certainly gives colour to the suspicion that after being shot at in New York, he crossed over to Liverpool because his life would be safer in a British prison.[40]

For many it became increasingly clear that McDermott had sought protection in England from Fenianism. Examining the nature of his arrest, *The Irish World* commented how:

> They will go through a farcical trial over there in Liverpool: McDermott will bear himself very dramatically in court, he will be 'called to order,' by the big wig on the bench; will be 'convicted' and

solemnly 'sentenced' for, say, a term of ten years; and then on some fine day, his jailers will shut their eyes and allow their 'prisoner' to steal away noiselessly and go whithersoever he will. But, as the boys say, it is all 'too thin' – England will deceive no one.[41]

O'Donovan Rossa would go further than this article did and he wrote to the British Prime Minister, William Gladstone, asking him to intervene in the charade and put a stop to all this nonsense. In no uncertain words, *The New York Times* reported how the Irishman telegraphed the Prime Minister with the advice: 'abandon mock trial of your spy Jim McDermott. When the British Empire plays such a farce as this you must be hard driven'.[42] The British government did not justify O'Donovan Rossa's advice with a response, and it became clear that McDermott's arrest had been hastily arranged to restore legitimacy to his revolutionary credentials. Jenkinson's plan had spectacularly backfired and wrought increased suspicion on McDermott, confirming his status as a British agent, with his arrest and trial seen as 'a put up job'.[43] As predicted, his trial had collapsed due to a lack of evidence and having been remanded by the Liverpool Stipendiary Court three times, McDermott was released from custody, leaving the court in jubilation. McDermott now disappeared from the public eye and was not to be seen publicly again. The informer was shuffled to Europe where he settled in France. In France, McDermott would marry and adopt his new wife's name, referring to himself as the *Count de Neonlier*. According to Jenkinson, he had 'married well and was very well off'.[44]

As O'Donovan Rossa was undertaking a bombing campaign against Britain, Clan na Gael were afraid of being side-lined within the complexity of Irish-American politics. In the fall of 1882, inspired by O'Donovan Rossa's campaign, the Clan began taking tentative steps towards a bombing campaign in Britain. This was represented by the employment of Dr Thomas Gallagher, a medical doctor from Greenpoint, Brooklyn, who was entrusted with the responsibility of creating a dynamitard cell under the auspices of Clan na Gael. Unbeknownst to the Clan, however, Gallagher had entered into an operational alliance with O'Donovan Rossa and was eager to recruit some of his skirmishers for the Clan cell. Gallagher was offered the employment of William Lynch, a resident of Bergen Street, Brooklyn. Lynch lived with his mother and sister, and worked as a coach painter. He had been instructed in the manufacture and transportation of explosives at Rossa's dynamite school in New York and was purposely selected for his understanding of explosive making and transport. On 6 March 1883, Lynch was approached by his Fenian

Club President, Thomas Burns, who told him he was going to Britain and gave a letter of introduction to Thomas Gallagher, despite his being a member of a competing organisation.[45] Meeting Gallagher at 420 Manhattan Avenue in Greenpoint, Lynch was informed he was selected for active work, and given $150 to purchase a steamer ticket for Liverpool.[46] Lynch was initially apprehensive of travelling to Britain, explaining to the doctor that he was the sole provider for his mother and sister. The doctor, however, had set his mind at ease by promising that in his absence, his family would be taken care of. This guarantee was also supported by Thomas Burns who explained to Lynch that 'the old man will see you righted',[47] Lynch understood this as a reference to O'Donovan Rossa.

Establishing a bombing cell with the support of O'Donovan Rossa, Gallagher chose James Murphy as his deputy. Originally from Cork, Murphy had arrived in Britain in February 1883 and established a sham paint shop at Birmingham. This facilitated the purchase of large quantities of nitric and sulphuric acid in addition to glycerine without raising suspicion. Establishing a bomb-making factory in the back of his shop, Murphy adopted the alias of Alfred Whitehead. Gallagher had also employed his brother Bernard in Glasgow, John Kent (alias Curtin), for whom he secured lodgings in Glasgow and Thomas James Clarke, the future signatory of the Easter Proclamation in 1916. Gallagher had intended his bombing cell to be based in London but transport explosives from Birmingham and both Lynch and Clarke, who for reasons of secrecy at no point met each other, were instructed to collect explosives from Murphy's shop and travel to London via public transport. Murphy had, however, purchased a suspicious amount of nitric acid and glycerine from the same source, Harris and Co., on multiple occasions, arousing the suspicion of shop employee Gilbert Pritchard. Pritchard, who could not understand why a small shop keeper was purchasing so many chemicals, brought the matter to the police. They were troubled by his concerns and the Birmingham Chief Constable, Joseph Farndale, authorised an intensive surveillance of Murphy's shop. This resulted in the identification of Clarke and Lynch as potential suspects in the bombing conspiracy.

On 4 April 1883, Tom Clarke had arrived at the Ledsam Street paint shop and left with a large trunk. He was followed by police but was lost sight of. Later that evening, however, Lynch also arrived at the Birmingham shop and similarly leaving with a large trunk, he was followed by detectives to London where he was traced to De La Motte's Beaufort Hotel. Arrested at 12 a.m., police discovered a box containing a £5 note stamped with the mark

'1883 New York', some of his own photographs, a map of London, and an envelope bearing the name 'Mr Thomas Gallagher'.[48] Amongst these personal belongings detectives found a letter instructing Lynch to go to Charing Cross Hotel and ask for a Mr Fletcher. The police concluded that this Fletcher may be an accomplice. Furthermore, they discovered what Langrish considered to be explosives: two hundred pounds of nitro-glycerine poured into rubber bags tied tightly so as to prevent spillage, and resembling an air pillow, parallel to a short tube closed by a plug yet revealing a strong chemical odour. That these materials had come from Whitehead's Birmingham shop was abundantly clear to detectives. Rees thus telegraphed Farndale, informing him of the 'man whom I followed arrested. Contents of his bag believed to be nitro-glycerine'.[49]

With the arrest of Lynch in London, the Birmingham Constabulary raided Murphy's paint shop where they discovered 170 lbs of undiluted nitro-glycerine, and 30 lbs of a similar undiluted substance found floating in acid undergoing fermentation, while the kitchen boiler was filled with liquid. Furthermore, detectives recorded a number of carboys containing 680 lbs of sulphuric acid, 450 lbs of nitric acid, and two tins of pure glycerine weighing 50 lbs each.[50] The scullery furnace had been improvised with a copper funnel, used to carry off fumes from the mixing of chemicals so as to avoid suspicion by unsavoury smells.[51] The Birmingham police were lucky, however: they discovered hidden amongst Whitehead's papers a letter from Henry Hammond Wilson, and his signature written four times in a notebook. More importantly, the letter contained his address at Nelson Square London.[52] Thomas J. Clarke had been discovered and the police now set about to arrest him. Raiding his lodgings they discovered Clarke in the company of Gallagher and arrested both dynamitards. Within days they were joined in custody by Bernard Gallagher, who had been arrested in Glasgow and transferred to London, John Kent who had been arrested without warrant at Euston Station on Saturday 7 April, and an American man, William Ansburgh.

As for the final remaining members of the cell, both Curtin and Ansburgh were arrested in weak circumstances; Curtin was evidently involved in the conspiracy and had been summoned to London by Gallagher through his brother Bernard for active work. The police had been deliberately reticent in the aftermath of the London arrests and Curtin did not know that Gallagher had been detained and waited on him outside the Charing Cross Hotel. Curtin, by now supervised by police, was followed to No. 11 Woburn Place, Bloomsbury by William Melville, posing as an Irish tourist who had befriended him.[53] Melville and John Littlechild would arrest him. They feared further delay could be dangerous, suspecting he was about to make for America. Without circumstance and without warrant they arrested him at Euston Station on Saturday 7 April, taking him to Bow Street police station for interrogation. The letter found in the Charing Cross Hotel was central to the inquisition and the police became interested in the Irishman's connection to Gallagher. Curtin denied all knowledge, to which the letter in his handwriting was produced. Curtin, stunned, claimed it was a forgery and had never met the Brooklyn doctor.[54]

Ansburgh was arrested on exceptionally weak grounds: when the doctor's room at the Charing Cross Hotel had been raided, a name card with his address at the Savage Hotel London, Blackfriars was found, indicating a connection, substantiated by the fact that Gallagher had only visited him, and following his arrival, Ansburgh paid his landlord, Walther Savage, a week's rent in advance. A further connection was established when a clerk at the American exchange, George Glanville, recalled, although he could not be certain, that Ansburgh received at the American Exchange in London a telegram under the name Daniel Galer, in Gallagher's presence. It did not also escape the notice of the police that Ansburgh was living in very close proximity to Clarke at Nelson Square, and that if he were involved in the conspiracy this would have been very convenient for the bombers. While this may have been a coincidence, no connection could be made between Clarke and Ansburgh as similar to Lynch, they had never met each other.

The Gallagher Cell was christened the 'disciples of O'Donovan Rossa'[55] by the media and were tried alongside Henry Dalton at London's Old Bailey on Monday 11 June, accompanied by a heavy security entourage including mounted constables with drawn swords.[56] The heavy security detail was both to prevent a rescue attempt and protect the prisoners from an angry London crowd. Charged under the terms of the 1848 Treason Felony Act, they were accused of levying war upon the Queen. Unveilling Lynch as their star witness, having struck a deal with the police, he told the court of an extensive conspiracy. Lynch's testimony in the Central Criminal Court noted that Gallagher had taken him to the scene of the Whitehall bombing where the Brooklyn doctor had scoffed at the destruction as 'mere child's play',[57] which was to be repeated on a much greater scale by his dynamite cell. On Lynch's evidence, Gallagher, Clarke and Curtin were sentenced to life imprisonment. Only Bernard Gallagher and William Ansburgh were released.

The news of the arrests in London of the Gallagher Cell had sent shockwaves throughout Irish-American Fenians. Clan na Gael were incredibly disappointed with Gallagher and blamed the failure of his mission on his organisational alliance with O'Donovan Rossa. The failure of the Gallagher Cell, however, did not undermine the activity of Clan na Gael, who increasingly undertook a sustained bombing campaign in Britain, detonating explosives on the London Underground Railway in October 1883, injuring seventy-two people. By February 1884, these bombings were followed by an explosion at Victoria Station which had been planned as part of a spectacular bombing plan, targeting London rail termini. The plot failed somewhat when other bombs failed to detonate. Within months, dynamitards destroyed the headquarters of the Special Irish Branch at Scotland Yard and maintained multiple explosions at London's Pall Mall in May 1884. In January 1885, the dynamitards undertook the pinnacle of their bombing campaign: the infamous Dynamite Saturday when dynamitards detonated almost simultaneous explosions at the Tower of London and in the Chamber of the House of Commons.

Despite O'Donovan Rossa's inability to continue with the dynamite campaign, his newspaper remained extremely vocal regarding the bombing strategy. As part of this initiative, he regularly claimed responsibility for Clan initiatives. Following the bombing at Victoria he acted as a spokesman for the dynamitards and despite having no idea who was behind the explosions, stated to the media:

> We've been very quiet of late, but I think the work will go on faster than ever in a little while… In spite of all the laws that England can make the chemical agents necessary can be produced [in England]. We are learning simpler and better ways of making the explosive stuff all the time and we have men ready and willing to carry out the plans amongst themselves… Our aim is to convince the commercial classes of England that it is cheaper to give up than to hold England. Therefore any means by which we can attack the wealth of the country comes within our lines.[58]

Against this background, one of O'Donovan Rossa's most vocal critics was John Daly. A veteran Fenian, Daly had been born in Limerick in 1845 and was involved both with the Fenian rebellion in 1867 and the subsequent reorganisation of the IRB. In 1881 he had come to New York City where he remained until 1883, and he associated with Clan na Gael. Daly, who supported the concept of a bombing campaign, was vocally critical of O'Donovan Rossa and his disposition for journalistic sensationalism in addition to deriding the skirmishers as lacking ambition. Associating with John Devoy and John Breslin, it came as no surprise that he disliked O'Donovan Rossa. He met the Fenian on several occasions at his Chambers Street offices in a series of meetings, which can only be described as uncomfortable. Growing to detest Daly, O'Donovan Rossa took to his *United Irishman* newspaper to decry the Fenian activist. Outraged, Daly wrote to O'Donovan Rossa on 8 January 1883, stating: 'Owing to the position you once held in the cause of our country I have given long and deep consideration to the false, treacherous and felon setting statements which you have of late published in your newspaper about me.'[59]

Demanding an apology from O'Donovan Rossa, Daly challenged him to a duel: 'I hope to prove that I can stand powder if you have any courage left in you.' This challenge was acceded to by O'Donovan Rossa, who refused to stand down despite the threat to his life from Daly, and he instructed his acolyte, John Francis Kearney, to arrange the duel, condemning Daly as a man who 'deserves to be kicked and he will have satisfaction out of me the next time he will meet me'. Responding through Kearney, Daly gave Kearney the impression that he was determined to kill O'Donovan Rossa and penning him a note, which he gave to Kearney, he angrily noted 'I'm glad you agreed to meet me. It shows you have some of your old pluck left.' Daly, who was in the presence of another Clan member named McInerney, was regarded by Kearney as cool and level-headed in what can only be described as an intense meeting. Withdrawing to a nearby saloon, Daly had refused to drink with Kearney. The Rossa acolyte, goading the Limerick Fenian, suggested: 'don't refuse any luxuries, as it may be your last opportunity, Rossa is a dead shot'. Forcing a smile from Daly, the Irishman now joined Kearney in a drink to good health and the two men parted. Having agreed to the duel, representatives for O'Donovan Rossa, led by his personal secretary Patrick Joyce, met with McInerney on behalf of Daly. At this meeting the representatives discussed the weapons to be used for the duel, discussing suggestions as varied as the use of hand grenades, pistols and the placing of both men in a darkened room with revolvers. Finally agreeing to pistols at dawn, it was decided that the duel would take place at New Jersey, where they would be placed twenty paces apart. In New York, O'Donovan Rossa was preparing himself for the duel, regularly practising shooting and preparing a will. The duel was scheduled for 11 January in a field near Fort Lee, New Jersey, amidst much public anticipation. However, neither man arrived for the duel. John Daly had left America on a Fenian errand, while O'Donovan Rossa had mistakenly believed that the duel was in Weehawken, New Jersey, the site of the famous Hamilton–Burr duel, where he had waited upon Daly. O'Donovan Rossa condemned Daly as a coward 'who did not mean fight'.[60] While O'Donovan Rossa continued in his condemnation of Daly, John Daly had arrived in England, where he was intensely watched by the British Secret Service. He facilitated the passage of explosives into England, through one of his confederates, a British agent named Big Dan O'Neill. Daly was arrested in possession of the explosives on Good Friday 1884 and was sentenced to life imprisonment as it was suggested that he had intended to assassinate the British government in session, by throwing the bombs from the visitors' gallery of the House of Commons onto the government front bench. Regarded by O'Donovan Rossa as a coward, the British Secret Service described him as 'the most bloody minded fanatic since the days of Guy Fawkes', finding him to be 'a plucky dare devil man, and was one of the few who had the courage to fight'.[61]

After the Whitehall explosion in 1883, O'Donovan Rossa was confined to endorsing Fenian bombings through his newspaper. He was still associated with a number of dynamitards in New York City. One of these was Thomas Phelan, who was originally from Ireland and was a founding member of the United Irishmen of America and gravitated toward the reconstituted Fenian Brotherhood. Portraying himself as a militant supporter of the earlier bombing campaign, Phelan had been a British agent employed by Edward George Jenkinson. The spymaster had earlier used Phelan to investigate the Glasgow bombings in 1883 and found him to be a pleasant, modest man whose singular motivation was to undermine the Fenian conspiracy of which he belonged. Developing a friendship with Jenkinson, the spymaster saved his life on a number of occasions.

Phelan had been exposed by John Francis Kearney, who by this stage was himself employed as a British agent. The exposure was necessary to protect Kearney from suspicion within the movement and there is a swath of conjecture suggesting that Phelan was preparing his exposure as a spy also. This was graphically represented by an article which appeared in the *Kansas City Journal* revealing a number of potential skirmishing plans including an attack on the British ship, *Queen* while docked at Liverpool and his involvement with Kearney, whom the article acknowledged as behind the Glasgow explosions of 1883 and the attempt to blow up the SS *Queen*.

Phelan had received a letter from O'Donovan Rossa asking him to attend his office in New York to explain himself. When Phelan arrived, O'Donovan Rossa was not there, and entering the office he was met by Richard Short, one of the conspirators Red Jim had earlier deceived, in the company of two other men, one of whom was Kearney. Phelan was challenged as to his duplicity and having asked Phelan if he wanted a priest, Short audibly shouted 'now I've got you'[62] and in a fit of rage short-stabbed Phelan. As the pair scuffled, he was stabbed thirteen times in the breast and back and received a broken arm. Bursting out of O'Donovan Rossa's office, Phelan continued to scuffle with Short, as they made for the stairs. In a remarkable scene, with blood streaming down Phelan's body, an eyewitness recalled:

> Four men ran down the stairs, each trying to push the other out of the way. Blood was trickling down the face of the last man. They were half way down the stairs when the man with blood [Phelan] got the lead of the others. I then ran too, and opened the window of our office which looks out to Chambers Street. Then I saw the man with blood on his face on the sidewalk put his hand to his hip pocket and pull out a revolver and fire at one of the three men.[63]

The police soon arrived and opened fire on Short. They arrested him and brought him before Phelan, asking if this was the man who stabbed him. Phelan confirmed it was and reaching for his pistol, declared that if he were to die he would take Short with him. Wrestled by police, Phelan was taken by ambulance to Chambers Street Hospital. Short was held in remand at the Tombs, New York. O'Donovan Rossa, who arrived at his office shortly afterwards, was interviewed by the media as to his opinion of the attempted assassination. Recalled by the press as appearing astonished, he did not give a statement and refused to answer questions about the stabbing. While O'Donovan Rossa did not enter a statement, some of his associates noted that it was important to recall how he had not been in his office at the time of the stabbing and therefore did not know about the attempted killing. This narrative, however, was contradicted by the fact that Phelan had come to O'Donovan Rossa's office at his personal request, indicating he had knowledge that Phelan was to be interrogated at the least. Against this background one of his friends explained to the press how 'I have known Rossa for a long time and in my opinion he is too honourable a man to stoop so low as to act as a decoy in a prearranged plan to outrage anyone.'[64] It was not until 12 January that O'Donovan Rossa finally made a statement regarding the stabbing of Phelan. Denying he knew anything of the conspiracy to assassinate the informer, he claimed that the reason he was not in his office on the day of the attempted killing was due to the fact that he was in the bank cashing a cheque which had been given him by a friend. This alibi was taken for granted as it was known that O'Donovan Rossa's finances were incredibly unstable, and so no action was taken against him, despite the fact that an attempted killing had taken place in his office.

Resultant from his poor finances, O'Donovan Rossa was desperate for money: he needed it both personally and politically. By chance, with financial difficulty hovering over him like a spectre, he received a message from an Englishwoman called Yseult Dudley. Dudley was eager to donate money to the bombing campaign. A mysterious character, she was born in England and at 24-years-of-age had trained as a nurse at Queen Charlottes' Hospital, London. Showing an interest in education for a time, she was a governess who specialised in English and French for privileged children. Dudley was recorded as eccentric and prone to melancholic periods. In July 1883 she had tried to kill herself by inhaling chloroform on a train track; laying on the track she had waited for a train to come but was found by a rail worker, 'with a handkerchief over her face and in her hand was a bottle labelled poison'.[65] Dudley was then tried for attempting to kill herself, and while in the charge of the Court she had tried to poison herself using opium, which she had smuggled into the court on her person. Dudley had claimed that she was driven to desperation through the loss of her two children and kept a lock of hair in a locket around her neck alongside a letter reading 'I cannot stay longer from my dear little blue eyed darling, and I hope and expect to meet her soon in Heaven.'[66] Trying to poison herself again, as she travelled between London and Brighton, she was taken into custody at Hayward's Heath Asylum in Sussex, where the Resident Superintendent asserted that 'she was suffering from suicidal mania, and during the first six months of her stay, she was subject to very violent paroxysms and while they lasted no one's life was safe'.[67] Remaining at Hayward's Heath for twelve months, she had apparently been cured of her mental instability and was released into the custody of friends and made for America, settling into boarding accommodation at No. 60 Clinton House, New York.

Eventually meeting with Dudley in his Chamber Street office, to his great delight she offered him money and financial stability, proposing to give him $1,000 in monthly instalments, some of which he could draw upon himself for income. When she had met him, like so many before her, she professed an undying hatred of British rule in Ireland and despite her nationality insisted that she was eager to see the Irish people rise up as an independent nation. Like Red Jim before her, Dudley had played upon his naivety and willingness to accept anyone who professed a dislike of British governance in Ireland into his company. Gregariously eager in her desire to give O'Donovan Rossa money, she arranged to meet him at Chambers Street near Broadway at 5 p.m. on 2

February, where she told him she would have a substantial cheque for him.

Meeting O'Donovan Rossa at Sweeney's Hotel on 2 February, Dudley was extraordinarily militant and stressed to him that she hoped the money which she would give him would be used to fund the bombing campaign. According to O'Donovan Rossa, she was 'rabid in her views on dynamite. She said the London explosions were no good and wanted a horrible sacrifice of life to strike terror into the heart of Ireland's enemies'.[68] O'Donovan Rossa was horrified by her militancy and stressing how he was 'not engaged in that business and received no money for such purposes', he explained that he only received money 'to help the Irish cause'.[69] Concluding their meeting, Dudley and O'Donovan Rossa left the building together, but as Rossa turned to make his way back to his office, Dudley called after him and unveiled a pistol. Rossa stood silently looking at Dudley and it was reported by witnesses that his last words to her were: 'Great God has it come to this?'[70] Out of instinct he placed his hand in front of his face as he was gunned down. It was recalled that Dudley: 'Stood perfectly still and fired three more shots at Rossa... neither her face nor her manner betrayed the slightest excitement or emotion. She cast one glance at the form of her prostrate victim, before she turned to walk away.'[71] Initially it had been speculated that O'Donovan Rossa was killed, however, it soon became clear that Dudley had failed to murder him. She had only injured him and his wounds were not fatal. Rossa had been gunned down in open daylight and witnesses flocked to his assistance. A New Jersey man, Peter Y. Everett, rushed to help him, cradling his body. O'Donovan Rossa's head had drooped on to his breast, and for a few seconds he seemed quite overcome. O'Donovan Rossa had been the victim of a number of poison pen letters regarding his involvement in the bombing campaign. One such letter delivered to him in January threatened his assassination by vengeful Englishmen:

Fiend: I and my four companions have vowed to rid the Earth of your loathsome presence. Three of my friends have been tracking your footsteps for the last 28 hours, and I shall arrive in New York Monday, and I pledge my word as an Englishman that whatever and whenever I meet you, either in public or in private, I will send a bullet through your cowardly heart. If you had the courage of a man I would meet you pistol to pistol... I and my Friends and England shall no longer suffer at the hands of a viper who is afraid to strike like a man, and who, by Gods help, shall be shot as a venomous reptile.[72]

O'Donovan Rossa often took threats such as these in his stride and paid little heed to them. He would surely have happily met the author pistol to pistol. Rossa's weakness, however, was his recklessness, and taking few measures to counteract threats against his life, he left himself open to Dudley's attack.

Dudley was arrested by City Marshal James McCauley and taken to City Hall police station where she declared her name, announcing: 'I have shot O'Donovan Rossa, I am an Englishwoman, and I shot him because he was O'Donovan Rossa, you know the rest.'[73] Dudley was extensively questioned by the police as to her motives, and she sat silently staring at the wall in response. She was moved to the fourth precinct station in Oak Street where again the police tried hard to elucidate her motives, to which she gave basic, monosyllabic answers already given at City Hall. Given this soldier-like strategy, the police had great difficulty in discovering her motivation. A number of theories were advanced including that some of her family were killed in the course of the dynamite war, but given that less than several individuals were killed in the conflict, three of them dynamitards, this theory was soon quashed.

On 3 February 1885, *The Brooklyn Eagle* spoke to Dudley in an effort to illuminate her motives and reasons for an attempt on Rossa's life. Evidently, the paper had more success than the police as Dudley told all. *The Brooklyn Eagle* was concerned that Dudley was part of an assassination team specially sent over from Britain to kill O'Donovan Rossa and leading dynamitards. She admonished the assertion and claimed to be working alone, justifying her attempt to kill him as 'he had been murdering innocent Englishwomen and children and it was fitting that he should die by the hands of an Englishwoman'.[74] Throughout the course of the interview she showed no emotion, remaining remarkably calm, she was almost vacant. She stressed that she would not give much detail regarding the attempted assassination until the trial and gave the impression of being questioned on a subject that she 'desires to say nothing about'.[75] Despite her promises to reveal all in her pending trial, when she took to the Tombs Police Court in New York on 16 February, she remained mute and gave no details as to her motives. She was, however, interviewed by the *New York Tribune* and she provided a detailed statement as to why she had shot O'Donovan Rossa:

> That man ought to die. He is a villain. I did not believe what the newspapers said of him. It was all too horrible, but they have not told half the truth about him. He has convinced himself out of his

own mouth. I determined to satisfy myself about him… he answered my letter and made an appointment with me. We met on Saturday in Sweeney's Hotel. I asked him if it were true that he was at the bottom of the dynamite explosions in England. He said he was. Then I said to him 'but think of the awful wrong you are doing in killing innocent women and children.' 'What is the death of a few women and children compared to the wrong that Ireland has suffered at English hands?' he said. Then I made up my mind that he was the worst villain on the face of the earth. I determined to kill him.[76]

Dudley asked the *Herald* reporter if O'Donovan Rossa was going to die, but on learning that his wounds were not fatal, she became markedly disappointed. The reporter told her that the doctors had difficulty removing the bullet from his body, however. Dudley's mood changed and buoyantly she declared 'there's hope yet'.[77]

In Britain, Dudley seems to have become a public sensation, and all of the major newspapers celebrated the assassination attempt. Accordingly, a good many Britons were jubilant over Rossa's near-death experience, and the papers that carried the story were 'selling like wildfire'.[78] *The Times,* in a remarkably rancorous note, exclaimed how 'he richly deserves to be killed',[79] and similarly reporting the reaction of the Canadian Parliament upon news of the shooting, the newspaper recalled 'when the later reports said that the wound was not dangerous there was a marked exhibition of disappointment'.[80] *The Birmingham Daily Post* found him to be a man who circulated 'articles inciting violence and intimidation'.[81] *The Aberdeen Weekly Journal* similarly favoured Dudley, describing her in blissful language as 'calm and placid', finding 'her good looks and youthful appearance enlisted very general sympathy on her behalf'.[82] The newspaper concluded that the attempt on O'Donovan Rossa's life was long-awaited and expressed 'the liveliest satisfaction that the attempt had been made and the strongest admiration for the woman who made it'.[83] *The Northern Echo* lamented how British newspapers bore 'striking testimony to the hatred which is felt towards Rossa'.[84]

Rossa was rushed to Chambers Street Hospital in great pain, 'looking pale and frightened'.[85] Dudley's bullets had penetrated his body under his left shoulder blade and had travelled upward for 4 inches. Thinking himself likely to die, he demanded to see the coroner and made an ante-mortem statement, explaining his relationship with Dudley for the benefit of a future prosecution:

Saturday January 31ˢᵗ at about 3 p.m. I received a letter at my office, Chambers Street. The message was in writing and was delivered by a messenger boy. The note stated that a lady wished to see me: that she was interested in the Irish cause and desired to assist it. She did not care to come to my office and remain waiting there until I came. She only would ask for ten minutes time. The boy told me the lady was at the telegraph office in the Stewart building, Broadway and Chambers Street. I went with him and I met her. I told her it would be well to go to some hotel as the telegraph office was no place to talk in. We came out and went into Sweeney's hotel. We went into the ladies parlour and she said she would be able to give me considerable money if anything good was done. She then said she would call Monday, February 2ⁿᵈ at 4 o'clock. Today she sent a telegraph to my office and there I met the lady. She showed me a paper which I was to sign. She then suggested that we go to some place. We walked down Chambers Street toward Broadway, and we got a short distance toward Broadway, when the woman stepped back and fired two or three shots at me. One of the balls entered my back.

(Signed) Jeremiah O'Donovan Rossa. [86]

Beginning to recover, however, O'Donovan Rossa was given permission to see a reporter and gave him a further statement. To the reporter he explained his belief that his would-be assassin was a British agent who had been chosen specially to assassinate him. Describing her to the reporter as 'nothing more or less than an agent of the British government employed to assassinate me', he continued: 'It was a premeditated affair, and this woman was simply the engine by which the dastardly work was to be accomplished... It is the work of the English government whose policy has always been to assassinate men they could not otherwise reach.'[87]

Ironically, Rossa was placed in a hospital bed near Phelan, who according to one source seemed pleased that O'Donovan Rossa had been shot. Phelan was swiftly placed under strict supervision by police for fear of further attack. Visited by his family and secretary Patrick Joyce, O'Donovan Rossa released a statement holding that Dudley was a British spy and had been sent to murder him on behalf of the British government. Speaking with the press in a personal capacity, Patrick Joyce, O'Donovan Rossa's secretary, declared O'Donovan Rossa 'the great dynamiter', and stated his belief that:

It was some conspiracy on England's part to rid the world of Rossa, whom she dreads and fears. There is no question but what the agents of England in New York know all about the plot and the woman was the tool to carry it into execution. They selected a woman for the deed because they had not men among them brave enough to attack him... he is not dead and England will find it out to her sorrow soon enough.[88]

The British government denied this, however, and its consulate in New York stated that Dudley was working on her own responsibility. As a British citizen, the British government would be anxious to help her throughout her trial.

On 30 June Yseult Dudley was acquitted, on the grounds of insanity, of the attempted murder of O'Donovan Rossa. It had been suggested that she suffered from epilepsy and congenital moral insanity.[89] Her defence had argued that her epilepsy had been the cause of 'the mental disturbance that prompted the criminal act of shooting Rossa'.[90] Support by medical evidence asserted that 'her mind was generally so impaired that she was seemingly incapable of controlling the feeblest impulses of passion'.[91] Interviewed by the media, Dudley remained defiant and exclaimed 'she was highly grateful at the opportunity afforded to her to give Rossa a dressing out. This she said pleased her more than the fact of her acquittal'.[92] O'Donovan Rossa was outraged with the verdict and continued to argue that Dudley was a British agent who had been sent to kill him. As was the case in 1865, he decried the court and labelled the handling of the Dudley case as 'a farce from the beginning to the end'. Describing Dudley's trial as a 'burlesque on justice', he questioned whether she was actually insane and pointed to the fact that Dudley was reasonably well-balanced throughout her trial and their subsequent meeting at Sweeney's Hotel. Questioning her bona-fades O'Donovan Rossa expressed his belief that Dudley 'was no more insane than he was and that her attack on his life was the outcome of a well-planned and deep laid conspiracy in this country to take his life'.[93]

Released from hospital, O'Donovan Rossa continued to support the concept of a bombing campaign, but in 1886 he was ousted as head of the Fenian Brotherhood, an organisation which Rossa had earlier revived, by Patrick Sarsfield Cassidy. Cassidy had used O'Donovan Rossa's earlier misappropriation of the skirmishing fund against him and cited that it was in the best interest of the movement for the Irishman to become a mere figurehead. The advent of Cassidy to the leadership left O'Donovan Rossa marginalised within his own organisation. Speaking of the change of leadership against the backdrop of increasing plans to undertake a bombing during the Queen's Jubilee in 1887, Luke Dillon noted O'Donovan Rossa's isolation when he explained to John Devoy how at a council of the Fenian Brotherhood, poor Rossa was left out in the cold, but was caught by one of the council peeping through the keyhole. Cassidy and O'Donovan Rossa despised each other and amidst much antagonism there were increasing denunciations of Sarsfield Cassidy as a spy amongst followers of O'Donovan Rossa. Indeed, O'Donovan Rossa denounced Cassidy on several occasions, through the *United Irishman*, as the heir to Red Jim and a villain worse than Pierce Nagle. These accusations irked Sarsfield Cassidy, who threatened O'Donovan Rossa and anyone associated with him with legal action, increasingly isolating Rossa and breaking his connection to the *United Irishman* printer, Patrick Farrelly. Unbeaten, however, O'Donovan Rossa hired a new printer, Wilber Hendrickson, who was willing to print anything that the Irishman gave him, giving his word to print the *United Irishman* 'at all hazards'.[94] Like Farrelly Sarsfield Cassidy visited Hendrickson on several occasions and regularly threatened him with legal action, but unlike his former printer, O'Donovan Rossa's new man refused to be intimidated.

The bitter acrimony between O'Donovan Rossa and Sarsfield Cassidy, came to a head in 1889 when the latter bought a libel case against O'Donovan Rossa and Hendrickson, citing how O'Donovan Rossa had been using his newspaper to defame his character. This was graphically represented on 22 May 1889 when O'Donovan Rossa had used his newspaper to denounce Cassidy as 'an English spy',[95] and again associated him with Red Jim McDermott, indicating he had taken the agent-provocateur's place and had 'been on duty for England since'.[96] Writing to James Maxwell, Mary Jane asserted how he felt 'quite confident of his ability to prove Cassidy all he has called him'. But, expressing her fears to James Maxwell, she further stated: 'I have seen none of his proofs and have a horrible fear he will find himself over matched and in the grip of the national law.'[97]

Similar to Sarsfield Cassidy, O'Donovan Rossa had also initiated legal proceedings against the Fenian leader for libel. This had been inspired by allegations of treachery and pilfering, which Sarsfield Cassidy had made against him in the *Catholic News*, which had angered O'Donovan Rossa so much that he charged its editor, Herman Ridder, with criminal defamation and sought damages of $100,000. Losing to Ridder, he was still not deterred and meeting at the Court of Sessions in New York City, Sarsfield Cassidy was accused of branding O'Donovan Rossa a spy. In doing so, Sarsfield Cassidy had made continual reference to O'Donovan Rossa's relationship with Red Jim McDermott and had made a convincing argument about the $50 donation, which the informer had paid to his Resources of Civilisation Fund. This was supported by the powerful Henry Labouchere, a liberal editor, politician and high-profile supporter of Parnell, confirming how O'Donovan Rossa had stated he knew McDermott to be a spy. Using parliamentary privilege, Labouchere had asserted in Parliament how 'secret service money was... actually given to O'Donovan Rossa', alleging his funds to maintain the dynamite campaign were 'supplemented by contributions from Her Majesty's government themselves'.[98] It is important to note that at no point did Labouchere allege that O'Donovan Rossa was directly in receipt of Secret Service funding. His reference to intelligence funding was largely confused with the activities of Red Jim McDermott.

Indeed, McDermott's legacy came back to haunt O'Donovan Rossa during the trial, as Cassidy's lawyer recalled O'Donovan Rossa's previous admission in 1883, that he knew McDermott to be an informer and never trusted him. This was factually inaccurate, as all the evidence suggests O'Donovan Rossa was duped by the mischievous Irishman and all the evidence points towards O'Donovan Rossa making a rash, ill-thought decision to justify his association with Red Jim some years previously. In trying to save face by claiming to have known he was a spy, however, he gave great opportunity to Sarsfield Cassidy, who, reaching into his pocket following O'Donovan Rossa's announcement, revealed a brown envelope, which he produced to his defence. Carefully opening the envelope, Sarsfield Cassidy's solicitor dramatically produced a cheque, signed by Rossa and McDermott. Observing the scene, one contemporary noted how 'his expression became pitiful'.[99] Visibly thrown, O'Donovan Rossa was brutally interrogated by O'Byrne, who refused to let go his admission that he knew McDermott to be a spy. To this, O'Donovan Rossa stumbled through evidence, bizarrely asserting how he 'knew the money did not come right and thought [he] might as well have some of it as anybody else'.[100] Seizing this, the prosecuting lawyer, much to Sarsfield Cassidy's obvious delight, asked O'Donovan Rossa to clarify his remarks, stating 'do you mean that it should go out to the world through the newspapers that you were secretly in the receipt of money from this man when you knew him to be an informer, engaged in betraying men into penal servitude for life and to the gallows?' Obviously flustered and anxious, O'Donovan Rossa meekly responded 'I mean that I knew the money didn't come right, but I thought I might as well take it,' for the good of the republican cause. In addition to the McDermott cheque, Sarsfield Cassidy's lawyer also possessed a letter from British MP Henry Labouchere, written to Sarsfield Cassidy, stressing his belief that Rossa knowingly accepted money from Red Jim McDermott which had been supplied by the British Secret Service. Labouchere's letter indicated that this occurred on several occasions, including the day that McDermott was shot at in Ryan's Saloon, 21 July 1883.[101] Further damning evidence was provided by Richard Short, the dynamitard who had been associated with Featherstone and stabbed Phelan in O'Donovan Rossa's office, who claimed O'Donovan Rossa owed him money which he had promised for his defence. This had the effect of casting doubt on O'Donovan Rossa's honestly and was supported by John Murphy, the Treasurer of the Fenian Brotherhood, who claimed that he believed O'Donovan Rossa had appropriated money from Brotherhood funds. On this evidence, and coupled with the stubborn refusal of Labouchere to withdraw his remarks in London, the case for libel was thrown out of court and O'Donovan Rossa had not been vindicated. Talking to the press in the aftermath of the trial he released a statement defending his character and answering the charges raised during the trial:

> You ask me about the Labouchere letter and getting the money from McDermott, and McDermott being a spy... I knew for some months before that McDermott was a spy. My council of ten United Irishmen knew it. I knew McDermott was watching me and sounding me to see if I suspected him. I knew our committee were on his track and I knew my place was to pretend I had not the least suspicion of him. If I had refused to take the cheque he offered me that morning I should have aroused his suspicion... Rocky Mountain O'Brien, Pat Joyce and the United Irishman council and everyone who were around me knew I got it that cheque. There was no secret in it. I was laughing at how I tricked Red Jim while he tried to trick me.[102]

Privately, O'Donovan Rossa still believed that Sarsfield Cassidy was a British spy. He stressed this belief to his family and held that the Fenian leader was being directed by London to ruin him within Irish-American circles. This was evident in a letter written by Mary Jane to their son Maxwell, where she asserted: 'Having failed in their efforts to hold or to kill him, knowing the impossibility of bribing him, they lure a crafty scribe and spy to spin a web of lies with distorted threads of truth to strengthen it...'[103]

On 20 June 1889, O'Donovan Rossa was arrested in the company of Hendrickson by the New York Police Department on account of Sarsfield Cassidy's counter libel suit. He was imprisoned at the Tombs, New York. Recalling his arrest, the *Pittsburgh Dispatch* celebrated his jailing, holding how while it was 'easy enough to put Rossa in Jail. Hitherto the difficulty has been in keeping him there'.[104] As the newspaper had predicted, the following day O'Donovan Rossa was released from the Tombs and with Hendrickson, provided bail. Despite his arrest for libel and the earlier collapse of his trial against Sarsfield Cassidy, he was more determined than ever to prove his accusations of the duplicity of the Fenian chief. On this occasion he was found guilty of libel by the court and was instructed to print a retraction in the *United Irishman,* indicating that his accusations against Sarsfield Cassidy were wrong. This was agreeable to Sarsfield Cassidy's legal team, who expressed their willingness to advise remission on any penalties agreed upon by the Court. Refusing to do so, O'Donovan Rossa was now faced with the possibility of being held in contempt of court. Judge Andrews, however, showed leniency on account of O'Donovan Rossa's large family and financial difficulties. Pronouncing him guilty of libel, O'Donovan Rossa was fined $100. Unable to personally pay the fine, a supporter, J. D. O'Brien, paid the charge and O'Donovan Rossa was released from Court accompanied by his supporters. John Boyle O'Reilly, who knew him personally, found the entire scene to be somewhat of a spectacle and finding humour in O'Donovan Rossa's refusal to retract his allegations, commented:

> Rossa refused to retract and save the fine. The stubborn old savage! We have known that same Rossa, a quarter of a century ago, to repudiate all authority used against him in an English prison... They drove Rossa a little mad, we think; and now the stiff neck will not bow even to the verdict of twelve men. But for the heroic heart of old, we must be lenient with the old savage.[105]

Following his defeat, O'Donovan Rossa was forced to quit his Chambers Street office and his already meagre finances dwindled further. In dire straits, he became a travelling salesman of sorts and formed a relationship with Thurber, Whyland and Co., importers, manufacturers and grocers. He had been given the job by Frank B. Thurber on a commission basis and travelled throughout New York on behalf of the company selling cigars, liquor and facilitating the purchase of groceries. He was, however, still unfree of Sarsfield Cassidy, who demanded O'Donovan Rossa pay him $130 dollars, which he claimed to be entitled to for past service to the Fenian Brotherhood when O'Donovan Rossa was its leader. Unable and unwilling to pay Sarsfield Cassidy, the latter again took him to Court. In Court, Sarsfield Cassidy argued that he was entitled to the money owed him and this could be provided through the income raised through O'Donovan Rossa's *United Irishman* newspaper. As part of the court case, Sarsfield Cassidy had successfully argued his point and a judge had demanded to see the financial accounts of the *United Irishman*. Refusing to do this, O'Donovan Rossa was placed in a precarious position, and despite the previous libel case, implied that Sarsfield Cassidy was a British agent and only wanted to see his financial books as they contained the names of Fenians in Ireland, America and the United Kingdom. This implication, however, confused the judge, who believed that O'Donovan Rossa considered him to be a British spy. Clarifying the matter for the judge he again directly denounced Sarsfield Cassidy as a spy. In a remarkable scene in the courtroom, Sarsfield Cassidy charged O'Donovan Rossa and as both men physically fought each other, the judge and his counsels fled the courtroom as police frantically tried to pull them apart, O'Donovan Rossa tearing Sarsfield Cassidy's shirt and ripping his collar as he grabbed him by the throat.[106] Seeking revenge against O'Donovan Rossa, Sarsfield Cassidy printed copies of the cheque O'Donovan Rossa had received from Red Jim and had them sent throughout political Irish-America and printed in newspapers as a means to destroy his name. Indeed, a box containing multiple copies of the cheque was sent to his boss, Frank Thurber, with the implication that he could not be trusted. Horrified, O'Donovan Rossa sought to answer the charges through continued insistence that Sarsfield Cassidy was a British spy and the only way he could have received that cheque was if he, his enemy, was in communication with the exposed agent-provocateur.

Financially burdened by the entire debacle, O'Donovan Rossa's financial problems were only exasperated by his inability to defeat Sarsfield Cassidy. This was represented by a reduction of his newspaper to a fortnightly publication and was compounded by a decline in subscribers, resultant from Sarsfield Cassidy's allegations. His friends rallied around him, however, and denounced the court's findings and supported his claims of Sarsfield Cassidy's duplicity. They had raised a testimonial in his honour in order to maintain him and his family and provide funds for an eventual return to Ireland. This was supported by the fact that his term of exile was due to end in 1894, and O'Donovan Rossa was desirous of returning home and wished to see his old towns of Roscarbery and Skibbereen. He was equally anxious to connect with the IRB, examine the likelihood of a potential rebellion in Ireland and assist the movement at home. Beginning correspondence with the American government as early as 1891, he requested an American passport and protection from Britain as an

American citizen. This reflected concerns amongst his family and friends that once he arrived in Ireland he would be arrested by the British government on account of his activities during the bombing campaign and his endorsement of Irish revolutionary politics through the *United Irishman* newspaper. On 13 January 1891 he wrote to US Secretary of State James G. Blaine and officially requested a passport and protection, noting:

> I apply to you for a passport to Europe. I am an Irishman. I tried to drive England out of Ireland; England arrested me in Ireland in the year 1865 and sentenced me to penal servitude for life. In 1871 she gave me a patent of conditional pardon, a copy of which I enclose. She shipped me from Chatham Prison to America and forbid me to return for twenty years. The twenty years are now up and I desire to take a trip to Ireland and other places in Europe.
>
> My friends here say England will arrest me and put me in prison again, and keep me in prison for life; more of the friends say she will not, because James G. Blaine is the Secretary of State now and he will insist that England cannot arrest an American citizen for any act of his, or any speech of his inimical to England in the United States. Of course if I break the law in England I'll be arrested, as you or anyone else would be arrested.
>
> But the passport I want is one that will save me from arrest on my landing in the Cove of Cork – provided I commit no crime on shipboard during the voyage.
>
> I don't or won't deny that as an Irishman and an American, I have, while in America, done all I could to help Irishmen to free Ireland from the tyranny of England. You, by your speeches and contributions have helped in that direction yourself.
>
> I enclose the necessary papers for the passport, with the legal fee.
>
> Yours very respectfully,
>
> Jeremiah O'Donovan Rossa[107]

Receiving a response from the US Department of State, it was apparent that the American government was keen not to anger their British counterparts. On providing him with a United States passport, he was told that the American government could not and would not protect his liberty while he was within the United Kingdom and should the British government choose to arrest him that was to their desecration as a foreign power.

While O'Donovan Rossa was securing his passport and preparing for his future visit to Ireland, his son Alexander died on 28 March 1891. Alexander O'Donovan Rossa was seven months old when he had developed pneumonia and died within ten days. O'Donovan Rossa was heartbroken at his loss and recalled in a letter to James Maxwell how 'he was such a beautiful, healthy, active little fellow... the look he gave me and Mother a few minutes before he died will never leave my mind... he was such a beautiful child'.[108] Alexander O'Donovan Rossa was buried at St Peter's Cemetery, Staten Island, in a small, family-only ceremony. The O'Donovan Rossas were not spared all tragedy yet as two years later James Maxwell joined his brother and the family lost another son.

The arrival of the exiles in 1871 was a significant moment in the evolution of Irish-American politics. O'Donovan Rossa had captured media headlines resultant from his sufferings in British Gaols. As he departed the *Cuba* he proudly held his son James Maxwell in his arms and the young boy became something of a media sensation, representing the human side of the great Irishman. When O'Donovan Rossa had been tried in 1865, he had famously declared he was an Irishman since the day he was born. This was an indication, within his own mentality, of the reason why he was being tried by a British court in Ireland. Similarly, when he was exiled he had noted his desire to return to Ireland from the deck of the *Cuba,* announced that he could not return home and liberate Ireland, and so his son would return to Ireland to continue his work. Seeing the media value in this, the press reported on James Maxwell O'Donovan Rossa, describing the young child as the personification of his father's spirit and temperament. Thrown into a media and political frenzy with the arrival of the exiles in 1871, the young boy was declared to be 'the youngest rebel of the lot', and an 'Irishman since he was born', who would likely return to Ireland and 'do good work'.[109]

Rather than follow his father into the business of revolution, however, James Maxwell chose to join the United States Navy and, enrolling with the institution, graduated to the rank of engineer and was stationed at New Orleans. There is an abundance of evidence which indicates that James Maxwell was the darling of the O'Donovan Rossa family and his father was enthralled with his new career. O'Donovan Rossa admired how his son presented himself in his United States Navy uniform and often dreamed how if Ireland could be different James Maxwell could have served his own country rather than don the uniform of another nation. This was graphically illustrated by his daughter, Margaret, who recalled a wonderful childhood scene of her father walking into the room as the children playfully followed James Maxwell, dressed in his military uniform, in a military march throughout the family dining room. Grabbing James Maxwell's sword, which her father buckled around his waist, the veteran Fenian joined in the childish march and led it, lovingly calling his wife to 'Come along, my own, and join the Irish Navy'.[110]

On 27 March 1892, Mary Jane received a letter from James Maxwell, who had been serving at South Carolina. He been involved in an accident aboard the USS *Seward* and was hospitalised in New Orleans. He had been severely injured and received face, neck, wrist and scalp burns in addition to suffering serious lung damage following an explosion in the ship's boiler room in the hull. According to his commanding officer, who had written to O'Donovan Rossa, his behaviour aboard the *Seward* during the boiler room explosion was one of great heroism and he had saved the lives of many of his comrades, particularly an engineer named Patterson, who had been directly injured in the explosion. It was noted how 'Maxwell without a thought for himself, had rushed into that boiling inferno, shut off the engines, and dragged to safety the unconscious man,' thus saving his life. Extolling his bravery, O'Donovan Rossa must have reacted with pride when Maxwell's commanding officer noted: 'Great glory has been added to your reputation by your son, James Maxwell.'[111] Recalling the incident to his mother, James Maxwell played down his bravery and noted that from now on he would no longer have the fear that he wouldn't carry himself as a man when faced with peril, commenting how 'but I know now, and I give thanks to God in this regard, that your son is similar in manner to his famous father'.[112]

In July 1892, James Maxwell returned to the family home; he had been released on indefinite leave from the Navy to facilitate his recovery. Largely confined to bed, his sister Margaret remembered an almost idyllic scene of how Jeremiah and Mary Jane were 'so proud of his splendid record',[113] and he was treated as a hero within the household. While his burns were healing, his lung damage was causing him great pain and the family had taken him to several doctors, as he had also developed a troublesome cough. During one of his many visits to the doctor it was recommended to the family that the environment in New York City was not conducive to his health and that perhaps a sea trip could be arranged to a more favourable climate with cleaner air. Choosing to visit Ireland, it was decided that he would stay with Mary Jane's parents in Clonakilty. Staying in Ireland for less than one month, there was no improvement in his health and his cough became noticeably worse. His doctors next sent him to Tennessee – still there was no recovery, and returning to New York, 'his body was thin to emaciation, his soft eyes were clouded with pain, and the cough racked his body day and night'.[114] In October, O'Donovan Rossa was travelling around Massachusetts giving lectures. He spoke in East Cambridge, Charlestown and in West Quincy about his prison experiences and struggle for Irish independence. He was then invited to give other lectures throughout America; he was to speak at the Sheares Club in Philadelphia to a celebration of the Manchester Martyrs on 29 November. Dispensing with all other business so that he could spend time in his own home in Hancock Street with Maxwell, O'Donovan Rossa cancelled his lectures. His son died on 22 November 1893. His final words to Mary Jane were 'let the fires out, Mother'.[115] His sister Margaret recalled how she had been awoken with her siblings by Lizzie Chadwick, who she noticed had tears streaming down her face, and as the children descended down the stairs:

> To our eyes the strange scene before us was like a tableau in a play. Father Cherry, our parish priest, was standing at one side of Maxwell's bed and on a little table stood two lighted candles, a gleaming crucifix and holy water. On the other side knelt Mamma and Papa and Aunt Isabella, Mamma's lovely features contorted with grief and Pappa's arm thrown protectingly across her shoulders. Between them lay Maxwell, still and white, but with a sort of gladness shining from his face.[116]

James Maxwell was buried at St Peter's Cemetery, Staten Island, with full military honours amidst scenes of a devastated family. The toil of burying his son weighed heavily upon O'Donovan Rossa, who was left heartbroken by the death of James Maxwell. Capturing the sense of tragedy, his daughter Eileen recalled how she stumbled upon her father some days after her brother's funeral, and seeing him sitting on the top step of the staircase, she lamented a broken man whom she saw with 'fine head buried in his hands and tears streaming through his fingers, while his body shook with convulsive sobs. Papa, our hero, who had laughed at prison tortures, who had never bent his head to English rule!'[117]

10

A Journey of Personal Discovery

In the month that James Maxwell had died, O'Donovan Rossa had received a letter from James Corbett Connolly inviting him to return home on a speaking tour of Ireland. Corbett Connolly was desirous of hearing a narrative about the Fenian movement in the 1860s, O'Donovan Rossa's prison experiences in addition to his thoughts, and reflections on the Irish Republic.[1] Corbett Connolly believed that O'Donovan Rossa's arrival in Ireland would come at an opportune time as nationalist Ireland was greatly divided over the legacy of Charles Stewart Parnell, who was exposed as maintaining a relationship with a married woman in 1890 and died in disgrace the following year. Tearing his Irish Parliamentary Party asunder, even after his death, political Ireland was divided between Parnellites and anti-Parnellites, both of whom ostensibly remained committed to self-governance through Home Rule. In the void that Parnell had left, Corbett Connolly had hoped that O'Donovan Rossa's visit could increase interest in Irish republicanism through his recollections of the recent Fenian past. Jumping at the opportunity of coming home to Ireland, O'Donovan Rossa secured another passport from the American government and was eager that James Corbett Connolly could provide for his family while he was in Ireland. Securing a payment of $1,000 for his family, O'Donovan Rossa agreed to come to Ireland and engage in the speaking tour. He booked tickets for the trans-Atlantic steamer, *the Campania,* and departed New York on Saturday 19 May 1894. Having left for Ireland, Mary Jane's sister Isabella permanently moved into the family home to take care of her following James Maxwell's death. Incredibly angry with O'Donovan Rossa for leaving Mary Jane for Ireland, Isabella seems to have brought her sister out of a deep depression following the death of her son, and it was during this time that Mary Jane made the decision to move the family home from Hancock Street to Mariners Harbour, Staten Island, which became a retreat to Mary Jane. Recalling her mother at this time, Margaret O'Donovan Rossa recollected how:

Not without a bitter struggle did my mother recover from the overwhelming shock of Maxwell's death, but day by day she fought her battle, throwing herself wholeheartedly into anything that might occupy her mind and tire her body. She studied books on the cultivation of grapes and built a beautiful latticed arbour to shade the little red brick path in the back of the house which she used to grow fruit. She adored the new home and loved the fact that there were few Irish in the area, thus no one knew the family name and could not bother her about James Maxwell. From the front porch of the house the family could see Shooters Island where ships were left in dock in addition to stunning views of Newark Bay and the Kill van Kull tidal strait. In her husband's absence 'when grief would threaten to overwhelm her' she would regularly sit on the porch taking in the view and 'scribbling furiously on sheet after sheet of rustling paper, stopping only to gaze with wistful eyes at the ships that sailed the Kill van Kull.'[2]

Across the Atlantic Ocean, in anticipation of O'Donovan Rossa's arrival, the small harbour town of Cobh became incredibly cosmopolitan as journalists from all over the world descended upon it to report on the arrival of the notorious Jeremiah O'Donovan Rossa. The journalists were joined by a huge crowd that had assembled from all across the country and included some of the Irishman's friends. Amongst the crowd was a significant IRB party for the protection of O'Donovan Rossa as he disembarked from the trans-Atlantic steamer. While the crowd was gathering the Royal Irish Constabulary (RIC), assisted by a number of G-men (intelligence officers) especially sent down from Dublin, also assembled and an uneasy tension ran between the police and IRB. For *The Freeman's Journal* newspaper, the entire scene was sensational[3]

O'Donovan Rossa's arrival into Cobh was almost triumphal and one newspaper recalled the scene as resembling 'the march of a conquering hero'.[4] He was greeted by a large crowd waving green flags, singing patriot songs and loudly applauding him as he disembarked into Ireland. Commenting on the scene, one newspaper noted how it was apparent by the reception he was afforded 'that the old teachings and the fiery spirit of patriotism instilled in the minds of the young men of thirty years ago by Rossa and the other leaders of the Fenian movement still remain as fixed and as undying in their bosoms as ever'.[5] This scene forced another journalist to consider the career of O'Donovan Rossa and the love the Irish people bestowed upon him, recollecting that he was perhaps 'the most curious product of Irish Revolutionary politics'.[6] Walking through the throngs of onlookers, many of whom eagerly waited with outstretched hands, he was quickly ushered into a waiting car by Corbett Connolly and taken to Cork where he met with Lord Mayor Roche, who welcomed him home on behalf of the people of Cork city. Interviewed by a reporter, he explained his delight to be home and did not intend to take part in politics; this was specifically for the benefit of the British government in case they thought about arresting him. He happily exclaimed how during his exile he had 'an irrepressible desire to see the old sod again. I believed it belonged to my very life to come back and back I came'.[7] Explaining how his Irish nature had not changed, O'Donovan Rossa described to the journalist how he wished to stay in Ireland for two months and reacquaint himself with old friends, reminiscence about old times and rediscover his country. To another reporter he spoke freely about Irish politics and decried the years of banishment which had been bestowed upon him by the British government, the reporter recalling him to be vigorous on the national question.[8]

He then began a lecturing tour and next arrived in Skibbereen, where he was welcomed back to his home town by a large crowd. Moving throughout the country he delivered speeches in Counties Kerry, Laois, Tyrone and Kilkenny. He then delivered a lecture in Clontarf, Dublin, at Costigan's hotel on 28 June 1894. He was welcomed by the hotel owner and arose to great chanting and applause. Delivering his speech, O'Donovan Rossa announced that 'during his life he tried to do his best in his own way for Ireland and he hoped he did it in a manner that reflected no discredit on their race or country'.[9] The Dublin IRB had hoped that O'Donovan Rossa could be rewarded for his services to Irish nationalism and the IRB was eager to secure him a sinecure at Dublin Corporation. This scheme had been facilitated through the recent death of Dublin City Marshal Charles Kavanagh. Establishing a committee to secure his appointment to the Council as the new City Marshal, a position worth £1,000 a year, the IRB were eager to use his future appointment as a means of embarrassing Dublin Castle and winning publicity for the Fenian ambition of Irish independence from Britain. This had also been representative of a change within IRB policy, with Fenians willing to stand for election to Dublin Corporation and other county councils. The IRB committee met for the first time in D'Olier Street, Dublin on 5 July 1894, a stone's throw from Trinity College and the Brunswick Street Police Station. Styling themselves the O'Donovan Rossa Election Committee, it was the initiative of Michael

Lambert, James Boland and James Bermingham, three prominent Fenians within the Dublin IRB network. They released a statement to the press outlining its intention to nominate O'Donovan Rossa, holding: 'The vacant position of City Marshal presents an opportunity to the patriotic members of the Corporation of satisfying what, we are certain, is the strongest wish of the majority of their constituents by bestowing this important trust upon the man who wrought the rugged paths of life that others might walk in the smooth.'[10]

Illustrating the depth of Fenian influence within civic society, the committee used the Fenian network to secure support from the Dublin Workingmen's Club, the Bricklayers Union, the St James' Band, the United Labourers Brass Band and the Pavers' Association. Eventually establishing a Headquarters at No. 41 York Street, Dublin, which was the head office of the Workingman's Association, they had agreed to hold a rally to support O'Donovan Rossa's candidature in the Phoenix Park on Sunday 15 July. Having announced their intention to support O'Donovan Rossa's candidature, the O'Donovan Rossa Election Committee received a flood of support from the municipal government and civic society around the country. From Ulster the committee received a rousing endorsement from the Irish National Federation, declaring: 'We strongly recommend the Dublin Corporation to appoint Mr Jeremiah O'Donovan Rossa to the vacant post of City Marshal, in order that the veteran patriot may have means of proper support in his declining years.'[11]

In Tipperary, the Rossa Reception Committee mustered support for a public meeting to similarly support the initiative to have O'Donovan Rossa appointed to the City Marshalship and called upon the nationalist representatives in the Corporation to vote for O'Donovan Rossa and 'show that the people of Dublin are not unmindful of the debt they, in common with the Nationalists of Ireland, owe him, and the cause with which he was identified in '65'.[12]

Similar to Tipperary, the Cork O'Donovan Rossa Committee called upon the Corporation to show respect to a cause which O'Donovan Rossa had championed and asked the Corporation to consider his 'unselfish sufferings for Ireland both in and out of prison'.[13]

Representing the Municipal Government, Cork County Council proposed a motion that it should call upon its Dublin counterparts to elect O'Donovan Rossa to the position of Marshal. This motion was viciously opposed by the Unionist bloc within Cork County Council, who held that local government should not be associated with a known advocate of the previous bombing campaign in Britain. To this allegation the Mayor of Cork announced that he had no evidence of O'Donovan Rossa being involved with dynamite conspiracies. Amidst rapturous Unionist disbelief, and tying the council vote to European affairs, particularly the assassination of the French President Sadi Carnot, Alderman Julian, and a prominent Unionist announced:

> As a member of a Christian Church he considered he would not be doing his duty if he did not raise his voice against the Council's disgracing themselves by supporting in the manner proposed a person of Rossa's record. Councillor Rowe seconded the amendment. At their last meeting they passed a vote of sympathy with Mme. Carnot and the French Republic upon the assassination of the President, and now they were asked to vote in favour of a man who, he firmly believed, was in sympathy with the men whose conduct led up to that assassination.[14]

To illustrate his point further, Julian called for a motion of support, which he knew would not be accepted, endorsing Sante Geronimo Caserio, the assassin of the French President. Despite Unionist opposition, the motion was carried and Cork County Council endorsed the plan to elect O'Donovan Rossa to a position in its Dublin counterpart. Despite their endorsement, and the support of nationalist Ireland, on 16 July 1894 O'Donovan Rossa only received three votes and was eliminated from the contest. The position was given to William E. Clancy, son of the City Sub Sheriff.

Undeterred by his failure to win a position at Dublin Corporation, O'Donovan Rossa arrived at Birr, Co. Offaly on Sunday 22 July where he was scheduled to speak at the unveiling of a monument in the Town Square for the Manchester Martyrs. In anticipation of his arrival the IRB had organised a show of strength and bands were brought in from Athlone, Tullamore, Nenagh, Borrisokane and Templemore to name a few. These bands from the midlands were consolidated by bands that had travelled from Dublin by train. Arriving in the town to a hero's welcome, he was greeted by 12,000 people. Unveiling the statue alongside the playing of the Fenian anthem 'God Save Ireland', O'Donovan Rossa was introduced by John Powell, the editor of the *Midland Tribune*, who condemned Dublin Corporation of the 'vilest corruption' in the appointment of William E. Clancy over O'Donovan Rossa. Taking to the stage at 2 p.m., O'Donovan Rossa delivered one of his most fiery speeches, denouncing British rule in Ireland and remembering his friendship with William Philip Allen and Michael O'Brien, both of whom were hanged with Micheal Larkin in 1867. Describing the Manchester Martyrs as decent, honourable and patriotic men, he concluded his speech with religious tones and explained amidst rapturous applause that 'the blood of the martyrs is the seed of the church, and blessed are they who suffer persecution for justice sake, for theirs is the Kingdom of Heaven. In like manner the blood of their martyred countrymen was the life of its nationality'.[15]

On Saturday 18 August 1894 O'Donovan Rossa gave a farewell lecture to Dublin. The lecture, which had been organised by the IRB, took place in the Rotunda Hall at the top of O'Connell Street, Dublin. Well attended by advanced nationalists in the city, it brought together O'Donovan Rossa and James Stephens as both men reminisced about Fenianism in the 1860s and their experiences. Musical entertainment was provided by the St James' Band and the band of the Bricklayers Society of Ireland, while the front row of the audience consisted of a veritable who's who of the IRB including James Boland, Michael Lambert, James Bermingham, Fred Allen and James Stritch. Introducing O'Donovan Rossa as his comrade, James Stephens spoke of the 'dark days' of the 1860s and O'Donovan Rossa recalled his first meeting with the former Chief Organiser of the Irish Republic. He went on to explain the rationale of Fenianism and what they had hoped to achieve prior to the Fenian rebellion, explaining how: 'At that time we worked energetically to unite the Irish people for one more struggle for Ireland. The aim was to have in every parish in Ireland men of good reputation and of influence so that when the proper time came they would be able to bring the whole parish with them.'[16]

Condemning constitutional nationalism as a charade he asserted how, 'with the education the traditions, and the mothers mill he had he was not able to teach himself that the independence of Ireland could be gained peacefully'.[17] Continuing his speech, O'Donovan Rossa delivered an unexpected and scathing denunciation of fellow Fenian Michael Davitt as a 'scoundrel'.[18] This was related to statements which Davitt had earlier made about his connection to Red Jim McDermott. Such was the narrative of his denunciation that Davitt was forced to write a statement for publication in the press lampooning O'Donovan Rossa as 'a revolutionary Bob Acres',[19] who did not have the courage to face him.

Leaving Dublin via Kingsbridge (Heuston Station) the following day, O'Donovan Rossa was accompanied to his train by James Boland. Giving Boland a signed copy of his *Prison Life,* O'Donovan Rossa boarded the train for Waterford where he was next to address a meeting at the Theatre Royal. Arriving in Waterford that evening the returning Irishman was met by a brass band that played nationalist songs amidst the cheers of a large crowd who had gathered to pay their respects. When he arrived in Waterford City, he delivered an impromptu speech at the entrance of the town hall where he thanked the people for such a rapturous welcome and acknowledged his great desire to return home after so many years of exile. Lecturing on his prison experiences it was recalled that the audience of the Theatre Royal were engrossed in his discourse. His speech came to an end with the playing of 'God Save Ireland'.

O'Donovan Rossa returned to America on 25 August where he was again met with a hero's welcome as Irish–American societies had assembled. Arriving to his new home at Mariners Harbour, Staten Island, he was accompanied by a brass band who had met him upon his return to New York City. Marching to his home in the presence of a large Irish-American contingent, O'Donovan Rossa was eager to see his family despite the bizarre nature of his return. And seeing Mary Jane waiting for him at the door of their home he ran towards her and hugged her:

> and kissed her fondly before them all, while the band played louder than ever and the men of the party cheered in wild approval; but as mamma looked at the band and the carriages and all the cheering crowd a sudden gale of helpless laughter shook her slender body 'well children' she gasped brokenly when at last she could catch her breath 'what do you suppose the neighbours think NOW!'[20]

O'Donovan Rossa remained in America for five months and then made for Britain aboard the SS *Majestic* on 30 January 1895. Bound for Liverpool, he intended to carry out a lecturing tour in scattered Irish hamlets in the North of England (Wigan, Bradford, Burnley, Jarrow and Newcastle) then on to Cardiff in Wales and then London. Like in Ireland, this had been arranged by the IRB network, which was eager to build upon Irish sentiment in England. O'Donovan Rossa was greeted as one of the most controversial Irishmen of his time. Staying at the home of Dr Mark Ryan, a member of the IRB, Rossa had made a point of highlighting the charges which Sarsfield Cassidy had laid upon him of being a spy and announced his desire to clear his name by challenging the source of those accusations made by Henry Lebouchere. Addressing a public meeting at St Martin's Hall, London, he denounced the allegations amidst rapturous applause and denounced Lebouchere for 'more infamous and treacherous work than the English bullet that was sent to his body in America'.[21] Decrying Labouchere as a 'liar and scoundrel',[22] he then proceeded to give a graphic description of his prison experiences. O'Donovan

Rossa then called for unity within Irish nationalism. Appealing to the factions of the divided Irish Parliamentary Party to unite for justice for Ireland, he announced he could never support constitutionalism and believed that debate, discussion and ultimately consensus could never achieve an independent Ireland. Explaining to the assembled crowd how he remained committed to the idea of physical force, he contended: 'It had been instilled into his spirit that until Irishmen convinced England that she was losing more than she was gaining by keeping Ireland under her dominion. She would continue to remain in subjection to the English government.'[23] From London he made his way to Cardiff where he stayed from 19 to 23 March. In Cardiff he made a similar speech, where, recollecting his prison experiences, he accused the British government of attempting to 'starve' him while in custody.[24] Pressed as to his beliefs in physical force, again he wished the IPP factions could achieve unity and secure independence by force, but as in London, condemned constitutional nationalism as a fallacy destined to failure. Commenting how Ireland could only be liberated by physical force, he stressed that England had made it necessary for Irishmen to fight as the British state could not consider the right of Irishmen to choose their own destinies as a neighbouring island nation. O'Donovan Rossa arrived back in London on Tuesday 7 May and secured admission to the British Parliament, where he met with a number of Parnellite MPs and sat in the Visitors' Gallery of the House of Commons. In anticipation of his visit he had sent a number of business cards to political leaders who had traditionally opposed him, including Arthur Balfour, former Chief Secretary, requesting a meeting. Taking the opportunity of writing to the leader of the Unionist Bloc in Parliament, Colonel Saunderson, he sardonically noted how he was desirous to meet a fan, considering the Unionist leader to have been 'a most devoted student of his speeches and writings'.[25] Saunderson declined the invitation to meet with O'Donovan Rossa.

Arriving at the Houses of Parliament, O'Donovan Rossa attended a debate on the second reading of a bill authorising the repeal of the Irish Coercion Act (1887), which had been justified by the government on the basis that 'the state of affairs in Ireland was such as had not existed within the living memory of man', as there was an absence of political agitation.[26] This was overwhelmingly connected to the relative weakness of the IRB and the internecine factionalism of the IPP, which had been divided over Parnell's legacy. Attending the debate, O'Donovan Rossa was seen to scoff at the British government's attempts to legislate for Ireland and was noticed to be rather anxious within his seat. As the government representative John Morley stood up to speak on the Repeal Bill he was joined by O'Donovan Rossa who announced from the Visitors' Gallery that he was attending Parliament to clear his name from the allegations which had been made against him by Henry Lebouchere. Denouncing Lebouchere and British governance in Ireland, he exclaimed 'Mr Speaker! An assassin's blow has been aimed at me in this house. A stain has been put on my name.'[27] Before he could make any further statements he was quickly grabbed by police and led by the Deputy Sergeant at Arms, out of Parliament. Followed by the Parnellites out of the chamber, led by Parnellite leader John Redmond, O'Donovan Rossa asserted that he was not surprised by his expulsion but was surprised that he had not been arrested. The fact that he was supported by the Parnellite Members of Parliament was not lost on the media and their parliamentary colleagues. Reporting their support, one newspaper lamented how this would be Ireland's future if the nation were to receive Home Rule considering how:

> The incident illustrates the sort of thing that might be expected in a Dublin Parliament. In that Assembly, if it should ever be established, such men as Rossa would be predominating spirits, and after this example of his ideas of Parliamentry decorum we might be tolerably correct in assuming that procedure in the Dublin Legislature would be at all events extremely lively and diverting, though perhaps not very calculated to promote the despatch of public business or the peace and prosperity of the country.[28]

Seeing the comedy of his appearance at Parliament, however, the *Pall Mall Gazette* commented how O'Donovan Rossa had achieved the impossible by enlivening Parliament on a Wednesday afternoon and found him to be 'if not an itinerant lecturer', perhaps 'one of the best advertisers who will be celebrated when the epic of Fenianism comes to be written'.[29] Becoming a media sensation overnight, the story of his expulsion from Parliament captured the public's imagination and was met with rapturous support among advanced Irish nationalists. One contemporary, examining his resolve in Parliament, described him as 'a veritable modern Guy Fawkes'.[30] Despite the support of the Parnellites, O'Donovan Rossa remained his own man and at a subsequent lecture in Bermondsey, London, on 13 May he addressed the nature of his expulsion from Parliament and announced his belief that Home Rule was a fallacy which could never be granted by peaceful constitutional means.[31] Declaring himself to be committed to the values of Fenianism, he contended that he was ready to shoot Lebouchere as a means of satisfaction to clear his name. Bermondsey would be his final lecture in London prior to his departure to America. Having made the headlines for his expulsion from Parliament, he was visited by an unusual guest at Dr Mark Ryan's home who had travelled from Paris to see him. Her name was Maude Gonne.

Born in England, Gonne was the daughter of a British Army Officer and was an intimate acquaintance of W. B. Yeats, who had fallen in love with her. Despite her upbringing, Gonne was a committed Irish republican and desired a meeting with O'Donovan Rossa. She engaged him in conversation and offered him an invitation to her home in Paris and desired to keep in contact. Taking her offer he briefly visited Paris prior to leaving for America but Maud Gonne was not in town and did not have the opportunity to see him. They did, however, maintain a correspondence regarding national affairs. Returning to England he learned that a committee of Irish Americans, standing with the Republican Party in America, had been established to secure him a job in the civil service. This was a remarkable position for a man such as O'Donovan Rossa and it is difficult to imagine how he considered taking the position considering his self-independence. Applying for the position in his application he described himself as an Irishman who had been arrested in 1865 for the 'trying to free Ireland from English rule'.[32] Asked as to whether he had been found guilty of any crime while in America he cited his accusations against Sarsfield Cassidy and explained that he had been found guilty of libel, was unable to withdraw his charges and was fined $100. Within two weeks of his application, O'Donovan Rossa received a letter from William Briscoe telling him that he did not meet the criteria for entry to the United States Civil Service as he did not meet Rule 22 of Civil Service regulations, stating: 'No applicant will be admitted to the examination unless he/she is in good health, and no applicant will be placed on the list of qualified persons, unless the Examination Board is satisfied that the applicant would be fully satisfactory in terms of being qualified for the position.'[33] Using his newspaper to condemn the United States Civil Service, the failure of his application captured a number of headlines in America, and a reporter from *The Daily News* actually interviewed Briscoe. In the interview, Briscoe stated that the reason his application had been rejected was because it was the opinion of the civil service that he had not sufficiently answered why he was arrested in 1865 nor explained adequately his involvement in the Sarsfield Cassidy trial for libel. While Briscoe had not made O'Donovan Rossa's application public, the veteran Fenian took umbrage with the interview and accused the Civil Service of insulting his honour. He suggested that his application had been rejected due to one particular commissioner whom he claimed was opposed to his candidacy and claimed it was his views that had prevented him assuming a position.

Not to be beaten, however, he continued to apply for Civil Service positions and in 1898 he successfully secured the role of Inspector of Weights and Measures for the 10th District of New York City. A position which came with a salary of $1,500 dollars a year, his employment had been authorised by Robert Anderson Van Wyck, the first Mayor of New York City. Causing something of a stir in New York politics, the appointment was met with disbelief amongst some of the politicians who condemned the appointment of 'Dynamite Rossa',[34] as a plum job awarded through the patronage of the Mayor. The appointment had caused a considerable stir particularly amongst grassroots Democrats who complained that O'Donovan Rossa was previously a republican and never worked for the Democratic Party and that the appointment should be made amongst men who had worked tirelessly for the Democrats.[35] O'Donovan Rossa held the position for a little under a year, however. He was an unfortunate victim of New York State politics and of a disagreement between Van Wyck and the new governor of the State, the future President Teddy Roosevelt. When Roosevelt, a Republican, had been elected State Governor in November 1898 he had the power to cancel the appointments of the New York City Mayor, and in doing so he insisted upon O'Donovan Rossa's removal from office. His removal was largely on account of his failure to pass a Civil Service exam, and despite appeals from Van Wyck to maintain Rossa's employment Roosevelt was not for moving. Dismissed from office, O'Donovan Rossa suggested that he had been the victim of political bias.

11

'THEY HAVE LEFT US OUR FENIAN DEAD': A REVOLUTIONARY'S EPITAPH

In summer 1904 O'Donovan Rossa received an invitation from The Young Ireland Society to return home and tour Skibbereen. The Young Ireland Society was a nationalist debating and literary club led by Fred Allen which had been established in 1881 and quickly came to be dominated by the IRB. The Skibbereen branch of the society had been active in West Cork and attracted a high calibre of republicans to town including Maud Gonne, Rocky Mountain O'Brien and John Daly who had been imprisoned during the Fenian dynamite campaign in 1884 for having allegedly been involved in a plot to assassinate the British government in the House of Commons by throwing bombs (given him by an agent-provocateur) from the Visitors' Gallery of the House of Commons. Led by prominent republican Geoffrey Wycherley, the committee of the Skibbereen branch had hoped that O'Donovan Rossa could unveil a new national monument in the town centre celebrating the Irish Revolutionary tradition. Known as the Maid of Erin, the statue was crafted to be 18 ft. tall and was engraved with the years 1798, 1803, 1848 and 1867, in homage to the Irish rebellions of those years and the movements that inspired them. O'Donovan Rossa eagerly accepted the offer to return home and unveil the statue in a great public demonstration. Prior to leaving New York, the Young Ireland Society organised a reception in his honour in New York City. Taking place at Saengerbund Hall, on Smith and Schermerhorn Street, the event, chaired by P. J. Hynes, celebrated O'Donovan Rossa's life, and the unrepentant Fenian was introduced as 'a grand old warrior of a glorious and still living cause'. O'Donovan Rossa was visibly moved by the display. Addressing the assembled he commended their sense of nationality and urged them to remain steadfast behind the republican cause, holding that 'England would never relinquish what she had unless it was shown to her that she would lose more by keeping it.'[1] The following day O'Donovan Rossa was accompanied to the New York docks by Irish-American republicans in a procession led by a brass band, where he boarded the SS *Etruria* bound for Cobh, Ireland. Recalling the scene one contemporary noted how: 'The sailing of Rossa was a rather lively affair… the band played, and until long after the *Etruria* had started down the river the strains of "The Wearing of the Green" floated out from the end of the cunard dock and the Irishmen kept up their cheering, until Rossa, who was at the rail, could no longer be distinguished.'[2]

The Ireland that O'Donovan Rossa was returning to in the twentieth century was engulfed by new social and political movements which would bring great change to the island. Nationalist Ireland was dominated by constitutional nationalism and a desire to achieve Irish devolution in the form of Home Rule. Since 1900 the divided Irish Parliamentary Party had united under the leadership of John Redmond and had sought to achieve some degree of Irish devolution from London. Returning seventy-seven MPs in 1900 the party sought to emulate its former self by showing how a third party could work at Westminster and capture the balance of power. Despite unity, however, its ambition of Irish devolution, in the form of a Home Rule Parliament, remained a distant aspiration. Internally, the IPP was under considerable strain as factions and personal rivalries emerged between several leading figures, effectively hindering its organisation and electoral strength. The newly united party faced almost impossible odds. Firstly, their influence in Parliament was weak as neither the conservative or liberal Parties needed the Irish bloc to form a government at the turn of the twentieth century. This had the effect of consigning the party to the wilderness of parliamentary politics. Parliament was also largely disinterested when it came to Ireland, making it very difficult for Irish issues to come to the fore. There was also recognition amongst British political elites that the question of Irish Home Rule, whatever that could mean, was dangerous for political ambitions. It was well understood that previous liberal governments in 1886 and 1893 had positively embraced the Home Rule question and were punished by the electorate for it: the most significant casualty being former Prime Minister William Gladstone. Finally, and perhaps most practically, the Conservative Party had been in power since 1895 and refused to countenance Irish Home Rule. Their opposition had been long standing since 1886 and represented a desire to maintain the Union between Britain and Ireland.

At the end of the political spectrum, representing a fringe within the wider nationalist movement, Fenianism, a movement deeply rooted in Rossa's heart, remained moribund and stagnant. Capturing the decay of Fenianism at the turn of the twentieth century the historian Matthew Kelly has asserted that the activities of the Irish Republican Brotherhood were 'consigned to the melancholic bar room reminisces of the increasingly aged men of '67'.[3] Horrified by the miserable state of Ireland's revolutionary underground, a small cabal of revolutionaries living in Belfast decided they had to begin a process of reorganisation. In March 1905 Denis McCullough and John Bulmer Hobson formed the Dungannon Clubs, seeking to promote the concept of an independent Irish Republic. Such clubs were on the surface cultural and commemorative organisations, dedicated to gathering nationalists together for discussion and debate. The following year McCullough and Hobson made the acquaintance of Seán MacDiarmada, whom Hobson recruited into the IRB. Although initially reluctant, MacDiarmada would soon become one of the most important figures within the IRB revival. Around the same time, a new movement, Sinn Féin (Ourselves Alone), had begun to emerge, seeking to challenge the electoral dominance of the IPP. Founded by the journalist Arthur Griffith and led by a national council, Sinn Féin sought economic and cultural self-sufficiency and also represented the growing self-confidence that the Irish cultural revival had encouraged. Officially established on 28 November 1905, the Sinn Féin policy was defined by Griffith as a serious alternative to that of the IPP and decried British governance of Ireland as tyrannical, holding that 'Irish people were a free people, and must continue to possess the rights of a free people.'[4]

Sinn Féin sought to achieve 'a national legislature endowed with the moral authority of the Irish nation',[5] sitting in Dublin. This national legislature, according to Sinn Féin, could only be formed by passive resistance, with Irish MPs withdrawing from London to Dublin and establishing their own parliament. It condemned the IPP for taking its seats in Westminster, holding that they were making a tactical error in giving recognition to the British claim to make laws for Ireland. Despite its radicalism, however, Sinn Féin was not advocating total separation from Britain. What it had sought was the reestablishment of the former Kingdom of Ireland, which had ceased to exist with the passage of the Irish Act of Union on 1 January 1801, and a restoration of an agreement by the British government, the Renunciation Act of 1783, that the Irish Parliament had the exclusive right to legislate for Ireland. In justification for this strategy, Griffith had pointed to the Austro–Hungarian

Empire. In 1867, after Hungarian MPs refused to sit in the Austrian Parliament, direct Austrian rule in Hungary became impossible and both countries, although co-operating in matters of finance, taxation and war, were given separate legislatures, armies and institutions of state unified by the common Crown. While remaining the Emperor of Austria, Franz Josef was recognised only as the King of Hungary. Arthur Griffith and Sinn Féin advocated a similar policy, envisaging the transformation of Ireland and Britain into two separate states united by the one king. Sinn Féin was quickly infiltrated by the IRB with MacDiarmada, Bulmer Hobson and McCullough bringing in significant numbers of radicalised members. This was partially due to pressure from Irish-America, where the IRB's sister organisation, Clan na Gael, had been actively pressing for uniting the many advanced Irish nationalist groups, going so far as to threaten the withholding of funding to the IRB unless a unified body was created.

Amidst all this change in Irish politics, O'Donovan Rossa arrived at Cobh Harbour for his second visit to Ireland on 19 November 1904 and met with Charles Doran. Like O'Donovan Rossa, Doran had been involved in Fenianism since the 1860s and both men were close friends. Doran, who had been second in command to William Halpin during the Fenian Rebellion, was prominent in Cobh and was one of the leading Fenians of his generation; he had been instrumental in the planning of O'Donovan Rossa's second visit to Ireland. Doran was accompanied by Geoffrey Wycherley, President of the Skibbereen Young Ireland Society and himself a Fenian activist. Both Doran and Wycherley accompanied O'Donovan Rossa to Cork city by train and when he arrived in the city, as with his previous visit, he was met by a sizable crowd who had assembled to catch a glimpse of the returning Irishman. Indeed, such was the size of the assembled crowd that the train station had to be closed with staff insisting on admittance by ticket only. Leaving the train station with great difficulty, O'Donovan Rossa boarded a wagonette and drove in the direction of the city centre; as he approached King Street and onwards to Patrick Street, the South Mall and the Parade, the streets were dense with an assembled crowd cheering him home and waving green flags in his honour. O'Donovan Rossa was visibly touched by the welcome and acknowledged the crowds as a returning hero.[6]

Arriving at Cork City Hall for an official reception, O'Donovan Rossa was again met by a significant crowd, to such an extent that he was delayed entering the building due to the high volume of well-wishers desirous of shaking his hand and welcoming him home. Describing the number of well-wishers as 'one of the greatest demonstrations that Cork had ever seen', Charles Doran brought O'Donovan Rossa into City Hall. Receiving an address from Cork County Council, O'Donovan Rossa was welcomed home by the elected representatives of the County who expressed their 'sincere admiration of the grand principle which has ever been your guiding star, and for the many noble and courageous actions with which your name was coupled in dark and evil days. You have ever kept before you the watch word of "Ireland a Nation".'[7] At the end of the evening O'Donovan Rossa was interviewed by a journalist who asked him what his idea of an independent Ireland was. Receiving an answer, which he gave 'with readiness and a degree of energy', O'Donovan Rossa noted that he supported absolute separation from Britain and the establishment of an Irish Republic. Condemning constitutionalism, he cited his belief that Britain would never give Ireland Home Rule and that even if the British government did; he would consider it an inadequate solution to the Irish question.[8] Bringing his interview to a conclusion he commented how 'trusting England is like trusting the devil for your heavenly salvation', declaring himself the 'same Irishman that he always was, and would continue to be so to the end'.[9]

Leaving Cork city that evening, O'Donovan Rossa, accompanied by Doran and Wycherley, made his way to Skibbereen by train. Once again he was the subject of a rather large crowd who cheered his departure and as the train left Cork city he was greeted at every major train station by significant crowds who had gathered on the platforms to see him. Arriving at Bandon he was greeted by a crowd headed by Mr E. Burke, the Honorary Secretary of the Bandon 1798 Centenary Committee. When O'Donovan Rossa departed the train to address the crowd Burke presented him with an address signed on behalf of the Centenary Committee 'hailing him as a pioneer of a movement as glorious and noble as ever adorned the annals of our country's history'.[10] Again visibly moved, O'Donovan Rossa thanked the people of Bandon and embraced Burke, explaining how all that he had done throughout his life was to try and 'rid Ireland of foreign rule and for that he did not think he merited any praise. He had only done what was in his nature to do and what was a pleasure to him to do'.[11] Unable to stay in Bantry he left the platform and again boarded the train to Skibbereen. The next station following Bantry was Ballineen, where again he was greeted by a sizable crowd on the platform. On this occasion, however, he chose to address them from the window of his carriage, holding that he was 'glad to see that the old spirit was alive in the people of Ireland still'.[12] From here the train arrived in Dunmanway where he was greeted by a further crowd. On this occasion he was addressed by James McCarthy, who had fought during the 1867 Rebellion. From Dunmanway he arrived at Drimoleague where a similar scene was witnessed, while at the following train station, Madore, he was greeted by veterans of the 1867 Rebellion who addressed him in Irish.

From Madore, O'Donovan Rossa finally arrived in Skibbereen, where a large crowd led by a brass band and torch bearers had assembled at the train station. Departing the train, he was besieged by old friends and neighbours in addition to people whom he had never met before, some of whom had travelled from throughout the province of Munster. Introduced by Wycherley to his wife, O'Donovan Rossa received a bouquet of patriotic flowers and boarding a waiting wagonette, announced his delight to be home in Skibbereen and begged to thank them for their warm welcome. He went on to note:

Although he had spent many of his years in a foreign country he could assure them that he never changed one bit. He was always an Irishman. They knew his principles and convictions about his country when he left Ireland forty years ago; he always held the same principles since; they were his principles now as they were then, and they would be his principles to the last.

O'Donovan Rossa made his way to Skibbereen Town Hall, where the Young Ireland Society had prepared the Hall for a lecture he was to give that evening. The hall had been specially decorated for him and included portraits of famous Irish republicans in addition to green flags and banners. Here he received a further address from the people of Skibbereen, who asserted 'we believe we are free born men, entitled to own and govern our country by all the laws of God and men, and for the absolute freedom and absolute independence of our country we shall ever strive'.[13] Receiving further addresses from the Gaelic Athletic Association and the Skibbereen Urban Council, he then commenced a lecture recalling his youth in the town, the experiences he had endured during the Famine and how the Phoenix and IRB Societies came about in the 1850s.

Addressing the rather large crowd, he spoke bilingually on the importance of the advanced nationalist movement within Irish history. Received with loud cheers, he denounced constitutional nationalism and the place of British Rule in Ireland, and openly declared 'men of action were wanted not men of words if the unconquered heirs of the murdered and plundered owners of

Ireland were to attain their inheritance. England's policy is tyranny maintained by force and fraud [and] force was required to overthrow it'.[14] To rapturous applause, he commended the assembled crowd, announcing how 'the people, if directed properly could drive the English out of Ireland'.[15] Eulogising the dead of previous Irish rebellions, he justified his belief in Irish republicanism metaphorically by referencing Robert Emmet, Joe Brady and Michael O'Brien as ghosts who implored continuation of the struggle. Appealing to the dead generations of Irish rebels he held that it was the mission of this generation to achieve an Irish Republic. Addressing the importance of commemoration to republicans, he asserted how he was glad to see Irishmen and women openly endorsing the policy of the dead generations through commemoration, holding that commemorations would 'inspire a young generation and make them rebellious to English rule'.[16] Eulogising the youth and the need to nurture them against British rule as the generation that could achieve an Irish Republic, he commented how:

> England did not care very much about talk at anytime, and did she now? ('No! No!') She had made every effort both by fire and sword to exterminate the Irish race, but from what he saw since he landed in that country, he could say, thank God that she had not succeeded. She murdered and plundered them, cast them into prison, sent them into exile, but it was cheering to find that despite all that, good Irishmen remained, and the young blood of the country was there to continue the fight in which their fathers had made so many sacrifices. Let that spirit always remain!... If it does the future of our country is a bright and encouraging one. Our people are scattered over the four corners of the globe, and under whatever clime an Irishman's pulse beats, it must beat with vengeance in his heart.[17]

Concluding his rousing speech with a call for Irishmen and Irishwomen to be 'be true to the principles for which their best and bravest countrymen sacrificed their lives and liberties',[18] he then unveiled the Maid of Erin to rapturous applause and cheering. Staying in Ireland until Christmas Eve, he left for America aboard the SS *Campania*. He would return the following year, however, for his final visit to Ireland, as prior to his departure he had shown the letter from the state service to Doran and a number of friends. Resolving that if America could not find O'Donovan Rossa work, Ireland would not let him down. His friends decided it was time for O'Donovan Rossa to permanently return to Ireland and with James O'Neill and John Ronayne, Charles Doran actively campaigned to secure him a position in Cork County Council and purchase a house for his family.

Returning to Ireland on 19 November 1905, this time with Mary Jane and daughters Jane and Margaret, he was presented with a furnished bungalow at No. 9 Chapel Lane, Blackrock, County Cork in receipt of his services to the Irish nation. In addition to this, the clerical position which Doran had spoken of in Cork County Council had been secured for the returning Irishman. Doran had utilised the Cork Young Ireland society to influence the council to create a job for O'Donovan Rossa as Correspondence Secretary to the local government. In creating the position, Cork County Council had voted that O'Donovan Rossa would be in receipt of a yearly salary of £1,000 for the duration of his permanent employment. Settling into his new life in Ireland, he remained actively committed to Irish republicanism and rather than rest following a gruelling trans-Atlantic voyage, the day after his arrival to Cork he addressed a large commemorative rally in honour of the Manchester Martyrs. Attending the rally, with his erstwhile adversary John Daly, as a joint guest of honour, it was recalled that O'Donovan Rossa had represented a direct link to the Fenianism of the 1860s and was 'the embodiment of the aspirations of the youth '.[19] Following on from Daly who decried the cynicism of constitutionalist politicians commemorating the patriot dead, O'Donovan Rossa delivered a broadly militant speech. Commending the bravery of the Manchester•Martyrs and the ideal of an Irish Republic which they, and his comrades of the 1860s represented :

> The English used every means in their power to impress upon the Irish people the impossibility of ridding Ireland of English rule. He had not been impressed with that opinion. He believed that it was possible for the Irish people to free themselves from English rule. He believed it was possible for them to convince England that she was going to lose more than she was going to gain by holding Ireland, and when they convinced England of that the day of Ireland's freedom was at hand. But they must use against England the weapons that England herself used to conquer any country she was fighting against.[20]

Having made a stirring speech advocating physical force in Cork, the following week he repeated his militancy in Dublin. Here, at another commemorative rally which progressed through O'Connell Street and past the iconic General Post Office, he condemned the British government for murdering Irishmen and lamented the memory of his former comrades, particularly Michael O'Brien, whom he had personally known. As the parade went to Glasnevin Cemetery, where wreaths were laid at the Manchester Martyr memorial, he brought the crowd on an impromptu tour of the cemetery where he visited the graves of James Stephens, the Fenian plot containing the remains of John O'Mahony and Terence Bellew MacManus, Dennis Duggan, John 'Amnesty' Nolan and Anne Devlin, to name a few. Arriving at the back of the cemetery under the former entrance at Prospect Square, he delivered a fiery speech to the assembled crowd announcing:

> Fifty years ago the *London Times* said that the Irish were gone with a vengeance (hisses). They were scattered over the habitable world, but vengeance was inscribed in their hearts and if they were true to themselves and their country it might yet wreck destruction on that tyranny which had deprived them of home and livelihood in the land of their fathers (cheers).[21]

Commencing to describe his prison experiences to the assembled he gave a graphic description of British brutality within prisons when he spoke of how the wardens sought to undermine his dignity by stripping him naked, 'jumping on him naked when he was in his cell with the intention of murdering him', and describing his thirty- four days of punishment for his salute of Governor Powell in 1868, he lamented with graphic detail how he was 'nearly starved and the flesh began to rot off his bones'. He then finished his address by dramatically announcing to the large crowd that he would 'do all in his power to rid Ireland of the curse that had cursed its people for the last 760 years!'[22]

O'Donovan Rossa enjoyed his new life in Ireland, and he regularly visited towns throughout the country, lecturing on his prison experiences and occasionally made visits to England where he again lectured to republican audiences. Seeing his position with Cork County Council as nothing more than a sinecure, he would joke about his importance to the local government, holding that he was much more than the correspondence secretary but was in fact 'an advisor', to the city's politicians.[23] In January 1906 O'Donovan Rossa's daughters returned to New York City, leaving their parents in Cork. Within months of their departure, Mary Jane O'Donovan Rossa fell ill with pneumonia and was advised to return to America on doctors' orders. It was noted how her 'heart had been effected by the strain of her illness, that spells of uncontrollable weeping would come upon her, and that her body bore small resemblance to the lovely form' her family remembered.[24] Making 'the greatest sacrifice of a life of self-denial',[25] O'Donovan Rossa resigned his position with Cork County Council. Lamenting her sickness he recalled how the separation from her children played a part in her decline.[26] While it is generally accepted as the reason for his decision to return to America, another factor was at play in his decision – the rise of constitutional nationalism.

O'Donovan Rossa deplored the Irish Parliamentary Party and longed for a rebellion against British rule in Ireland, believing that violence or the threat of violence remained the only strategy that could force Britain out. In 1906, however, there was no desire for a violent revolution against British rule in Ireland, and the IRB was a shadow of its former self led by older men like O'Donovan Rossa, but by far more conservative in their aspirations to undermine British rule. It was maddening for him to see the Irish people rally behind the recently united IPP and its desire for limited independence in the form of Home Rule. Returning to America in June 1906, upon his arrival he lamented the rise of constitutional nationalism and the IPP, stating: 'I don't want to say this too loud but Ireland is going to the bad. The poor deluded people – God help them, but it will never come.'[27]

In October 1910 *The Gaelic American* newspaper, controlled by John Devoy, lamented how Jeremiah O'Donovan Rossa 'lies stricken in his latest illness at his home in Staten Island'.[28] Within four years of his return to America he had developed chronic neuritis, an inflammation of nerves, which affected his motor skills causing pain, loss of reflexes and muscular degeneration. His condition was resultant from a combination of the harsh effects he had experienced in prison and increasing old age. He could also not sleep and had developed troubling dreams and nightmares in addition to increasing fatigue. Knowing that his life was nearing an end, O'Donovan Rossa was eager to make amends for past wrongs. He had decided to make contact with his erstwhile friend John Devoy, whom he had fallen out with in the 1870s, following his takeover of the skirmishing fund. Their reconciliation was facilitated by Mary Jane, who despite the acrimony between her husband and Devoy, maintained a deep-seated respect for the latter. Writing to Devoy in February 1913, having given up hope of O'Donovan Rossa's recovery, she noted how the unrepentant Fenian was confined to bed 'through lameness and general debility', and encouraged him to meet with O'Donovan Rossa before he died. Lamenting her husband's 'simple heart', she noted that 'you were very dear to it long ago. Bury the between times and again be the younger brother'.[29] Writing a letter to Devoy, O'Donovan Rossa also lamented the friendship they had lost and offering an olive branch to him, suggested how he hoped his former friend could visit him as he was suffering from 'a lonesome kind of life'.[30] By the 17 March, Devoy had visited O'Donovan Rossa and to his great joy, the two bonded as Rossa, upon seeing him 'at once lifted his enfeebled hand... and said "John I'm so sorry we ever quarrelled".' Devoy was greatly moved and apologised for his part in their quarrel. Devoy was accompanied by Colonel Ricard Burke, whom the aging O'Donovan Rossa did not recognise. Asking Mary Jane who Burke was, Burke looked at O'Donovan Rossa and said 'what, you scalawag, don't you know Ric. Burke!' Still confused, O'Donovan Rossa stared intently at Burke, 'I know Ricard Burke but I don't know you!' Much to O'Donovan Rossa's surprise, Burke began to tell his Kick Zie Bucket story, which used to entertain O'Donovan Rossa in his lighter days in Chatham Prison, leaping up in his bed he embraced Burke.[31] Seeing the delight in her husband during the visit of Devoy and Burke, Mary Jane took the time to write to Devoy, thanking him and commenting how Rossa's 'face is still wearing the smile of satisfaction that greeted your coming, and he has pleasant food for thought for many days to come'.[32]

O'Donovan Rossa's satisfaction, however, was not to last long. Mary Jane was increasingly unable to cater for his needs as he was becoming increasingly burdened by the chronic neuritis and bouts of memory loss. Indeed he increasingly came to believe that he was still imprisoned and became incredibly anxious and troubled. Breaking under the strain of caring for her husband, Mary Jane reluctantly agreed to hospitalisation and the transfer of O'Donovan Rossa to St Vincent's Hospital, Staten Island. His condition upon entry to the hospital was lamentable and accordingly he was unable to sit up straight in bed, take food or grip anything, while 'his memory that was so wonderful is so much impaired, noticeably so from week to week'.[33] Mary Jane had hopes of bringing him home, but she soon realised that he could not return back. This was painfully apparent to her in October 1913, when she lamented how her husband, the once unrepentant Fenian leader, who had relentlessly defended himself in Dublin in 1865, underwent incredibly harsh prison treatment between 1867-69 and always followed his own way in the complexities of Irish-American politics, was confined to a wheelchair being 'wheeled around the halls and wards'. Still thinking himself to be in prison, despite variable bouts of anxiety, Mary Jane commented how he was relatively happy, describing his new prison as 'a very healthy place', with kind staff. She did note, however, that often 'his talk rambled from reason', and she found it to be an incredibly depressing experience.[34] Mary Jane recalled that St Vincent's Hospital was a welcoming place with a large population of Irish patients and staff. She remembered how a man in the bed next to O'Donovan Rossa would speak Irish to him and how the Irish nuns would treat him with the kindest respect, often sharing food with him. Despite this, however, and supported by his belief that he was still in prison, he was eager to return home at once. Mary Jane, unable to care for him, had to continuously come up with excuses as to why he could not come home. Writing to Devoy, she lamented how 'he is so persistent in his craving that I am afraid to pronounce a refusal lest it might have too depressing an effect on him. So every visit I think of some plausible reason for delay that will satisfy him for a time'.[35] Mary Jane lamented how he had to be restrained in his bed as he tried to get out on multiple occasions, be it to escape his imprisonment, write to subscribers of his newspaper and deliver letters to friends in Roscarbery and Skibbereen who were long dead. He also developed a habit of picking his clothes to pieces as he imagined himself again picking oakum as a prisoner. On a further occasion he stopped a patient walking down the corridor shouting 'Governor, Governor! This lady is my wife. She wants to take me home. Stop the car for us!'[36] Visited by his daughters, he was found to be full of delusions and had become deaf in addition to experiencing blindness. He knew nothing of politics and increasingly lived in the past as if it were the present. The tragedy of his final years was captured by his wife who lamented how 'I could sit and cry for him, poor faithful banner-bearer, poor old wolfhound of the cause of Ireland, fading away slowly in mental decline.'[37] As O'Donovan Rossa was declining in St Vincent's Hospital, Staten Island, Ireland was beginning to undergo a process of monumental change.

In April 1912, Herbert Asquith introduced the third Home Rule Bill. Under Asquith's plan, Ireland was to be given a devolved local assembly which consisted of two chambers including a House of Commons with 164 representatives of the Irish people and an Upper House known as the Senate that was made of 40 members. The Home Rule Parliament would have the power to elect an Irish government and this would run parallel to the abolition of Dublin Castle as the centre of British administration. Despite this revolutionary proposal, however, the Local Assembly had extremely curtailed powers with taxation, the monarchy, war and peace, treason, religion and the army. There was also a provision within the bill giving authoritive power to the British Privy Council over the implementation of Irish law. This meant that senior British politicians and lawmakers could block any bill that was passed by the Irish assembly, making Westminster superior to its Dublin counterpart.

The bill passed the House of Commons by a slim majority of ten votes. Passed on to the House of Lords for consideration, the third Home Rule Bill was defeated by 326 to 69 votes. Home Rule was now imminent for Ireland; the House of Lords could only postpone the passage of the bill for two years. Twenty-six years since the introduction of the first Home Rule Bill in 1886, nationalist Ireland rejoiced as Ireland now had a chance to govern its own destiny. By contrast, however, unionists continued to reject Home Rule as illiberal, impractical and an affront to their rights as British subjects. Determined to resist Irish devolution, many unionists increasingly considered a concept of partition, where the province of Ulster would remain part of Great Britain, rather than becoming part of an Irish state. While the concept of partition appealed to some unionists as practical, considering Ulster's thriving industry and the large density of protestants within the province, for other Unionists, such as Edward Carson, the concept was appalling. Carson, a Dublin barrister, had viewed partition as a threat to southern protestants and desired that Ireland as a whole remained part of the United Kingdom. Considering that Ulster had the highest proportion of unionists in Ireland, however, Carson was willing to exploit Ulster unionist opposition as a means of maintaining the Union with Great Britain within the entire island. Carson believed that the unionist minority in Ireland was a powerful bloc of British governance in Ireland, and that the British government would be forced to abandon the legislation for Irish home rule in the face of Unionist protest. To demonstrate this, Carson organised a series of rallies and parades, culminating in Ulster Day, when on 28 September 1912, nearly half a million people signed a document called the Ulster Solemn League and Covenant, holding:

Being convinced in our consciences that Home Rule would be disastrous to the material well-being of Ulster as well as of the whole of Ireland, subversive of our civil and religious freedom, destructive of our citizenship and perilous to the unity of the Empire, we, whose names are underwritten, men of Ulster, loyal subjects of his Gracious Majesty King George V, humbly relying on the God whom our fathers in days of stress and trial confidently trusted, do hereby pledge ourselves in solemn Covenant throughout this our time of threatened calamity to stand by one another in defending for ourselves and our children our cherished position of equal citizenship in the United Kingdom and in using all means which may be found necessary to defeat the present conspiracy to set up a Home Rule Parliament in Ireland. And in the event of such a Parliament being forced upon us we further solemnly and mutually pledge ourselves to refuse to recognise its authority. In sure confidence that God will defend the right we hereto subscribe our names. And further, we individually declare that we have not already signed this Covenant.[38]

By January 1913, Carson, with the support of James Craig and other influential unionists, established the Ulster Volunteer Force to stop Home Rule and defend the position of Ulster as part of the British state. Appointing Sir George Richardson, a retired British Army Officer, as the commander of the paramilitary force, the UVF was supported by powerful elements within the British establishment and had received £1 million to establish a secret arms fund to collect weapons from Germany. This would culminate in the famous Larne Gun Running, when the UVF, with the support and knowledge of the British Army, secured 25,000 rifles and three million rounds of ammunition at Larne, Bangor and Donaghadee. These developments were wholeheartedly supported by the British Conservative Party, and *The Penny Illustrated Paper* reported Bonar Law, exclaiming 'Ulster will never surrender.'[39] F. E. Smith, later Lord Birkenhead, was also a regular participant at UVF rallies, and speaking at a Conservative meeting in England he defended the UVF and the strategy of 'openly arming to resist' Home Rule.[40] With the support of the British Conservative Party, Carson could openly declare:

We have the declaration of our leader Mr Bonar Law, that under existing circumstances we shall be backed up in any course we are compelled to take, and we will call upon the Unionist Party in England, and there will be no difficulty about it, to carry out to the bitter end, the pledge and the promise that they have given us, and the government will soon find that the quarrel, which looks to them in the distance, to be a local one, in a comparatively small part of his Majesty's Dominions, will very soon grow until it permeates into every village and hamlet within the United Kingdom... I send our fellow citizens across the sea in other parts of the United Kingdom this simple message: – 'we are preparing and prepared to do our part; we call upon you to do yours. We are prepared, as we were always prepared, never to betray you; and we call upon you to see that we are not betrayed.'[41]

Increasingly, Unionist opposition to Home Rule had reintroduced the threat of violence in Irish politics. The formation of the Ulster Volunteers forced the Irish Republican Brotherhood to consider the establishment of a similar nationalist organisation. According to the historian Owen McGee, Bulmer Hobson had recognised the importance of the establishment of the UVF and the reintroduction of violence into Irish politics, suggesting that the actions of Ulster unionism should be used to persuade the public of the importance of nationalist Ireland arming itself.[42] Representative of the IRB perspective since January 1913 and buoyed on by Ulster Unionism, the IRB had been training an officer corps at No. 41 Parnell Square, Dublin. This work was undertaken by James Stritch and James Boland on behalf of the brotherhood. As the IRB continued to prepare for the inevitable emergence of a nationalist volunteer force, on 1 November 1913 an *An Claidheamh Soluis* published an article by Eoin MacNeill entitled 'The North Began'. The article encouraged the establishment of a nationalist volunteer force as 'there is nothing to prevent the other twenty-eight counties from calling into existence citizen forces to hold Ireland for the Empire. It was precisely with this object that the Volunteers of 1782 were enrolled, and they became the instrument of establishing Irish self-government'.[43] MacNeill, originally from County Antrim, was by no means a proponent of violent revolution and evidence exists that he viewed the volunteers as a means to safeguard Home Rule and counterbalance the influence of the Ulster Volunteer Force within the North East amongst the British ruling class.

The establishment of the UVF gave nationalist Ireland the cover to establish a similar organisation without British interference. Despite his moderate politics, the IRB viewed MacNeill as the ideal candidate to head the volunteer force, largely on the basis of his known moderation and respectability. Bulmer Hobson, very interested by Eoin MacNeill's article, now arranged a meeting with the assistant editor of *An Claidheamh Soluis,* Michael O'Rahilly, and suggested that MacNeill should chair a meeting to establish the force. While the first meeting was held in Wynn's Hotel, Dublin on 11 November 1913, the inauguration of the Irish National Volunteers took place on 25 November in Dublin's Rotunda, the movement declaring its ambition to 'secure and maintain the rights and liberties common to all the people of Ireland'.[44] In America, the O'Donovan Rossas watched the developments in Ireland at a pace. Mary Jane eulogised the establishment of the Irish Volunteers, and it is evident that John Devoy kept her abreast of what the IRB intended to do with the nationalist force, in terms of endeavouring to infiltrate and use it as a vanguard for revolution in Ireland. Writing to Devoy she celebrated the establishment of the Volunteers but lamented how 'sad it is to think [O'Donovan Rossa] is not in a condition to realise what he always hoped for and believed sure to come and what is actually in the air at the present time, the return of the Irish people to the old doctrine of physical force!'[45]

The Volunteer movement, which was led by a provisional committee, grew rapidly throughout Ireland and by May 1914 its membership stood at 75,000 and was steadily growing. The movement now represented the greatest manifestation of Irish nationalism and was far too big an organisation for the Irish Parliamentary Party to ignore. The Volunteers, despite the fact that they professed to be organised in defence of Home Rule, manifested a strong challenge to the authority of the IPP and John Redmond was determined to bring the Volunteers under his influence or destroy it. Seeking control of the movement, Redmond demanded that the Volunteer Committee appoint twenty-five of his supporters to its leadership. This would consolidate the power of the IPP over the movement and not permit the emergence of a rival organisation. If the Provisional Committee refused to concede Redmond's demand, the IPP leader threatened to establish a rival militia backed by the powerful influence of the Irish Parliamentary Party. After intensive debate, the Provisional Committee was divided with the moderates, supported by Bulmer Hobson of the IRB, believing that it was better to accept Redmond's demand than to undermine the potential of the Volunteers. Unlike Hobson, however, other IRB members of the Provisional Committee were horrified, and now sought to exclude him from the revolutionary underground. Those who opposed Redmond's demand were Eamonn Ceannt, M. J. Judge, Con Colbert, John Fitzgibbon, Eamonn Martin, Patrick Pearse, Piaras Beaslai and Seán MacDiarmada. On 17 June 1914 they stated their opposition to Redmond's acquisition of the provisional committee as a 'violation of the general principles which up to the present have carried the Volunteer movement to success'.[46] Despite the hopes of nationalist Ireland, it was evident that split within the Volunteer Movement was imminent. Resultant from this Redmond would eventually force a split in the Volunteers upon the outbreak of the First World War when he called upon the Volunteers to enlist within the British Army. 170,000 Volunteers followed Redmond's appeal, and became known as the National Volunteers. A minority, 10,000, refused and retained the name Irish Volunteers.

As the Volunteers grew within Ireland and its leadership became increasingly fractured, in America, arrangements were made for the eventual death of O'Donovan Rossa. Central to this was John Devoy, who had met with Mary Jane in April 1914 and suggested that his body should be returned to Ireland for a burial. Devoy believed that O'Donovan Rossa could act as a catalyst for Irish Republicanism in Ireland, and in death could assist the Irish Republican Brotherhood. Devoy established a committee within Clan na Gael to bring the body of O'Donovan Rossa home when he died, if he received the permission of Mary Jane, who held that in death her husband 'had a chance to serve his country'.[47] Of complete importance to this initiative was Thomas James Clarke, whom Devoy intensely trusted. Clarke was the treasurer of the IRB Supreme Council and Devoy's right-hand-man in Ireland. Clarke and Devoy believed that the funeral of the old Fenian could be used to re-awaken the national spirit of the Irish people, who they feared were becoming more British than the British themselves. They had also hoped to show the strength of advanced nationalism within Ireland by providing a demonstration of the military discipline of the Irish Volunteers. O'Donovan Rossa, in one of his more sentient moments, was equally agreeable with the prospect of being buried in Ireland and saw that his death could be used for republican propaganda, and insisted to Devoy how his body was not to leave Ireland until Home Rule at the least 'if not absolute freedom from England',[48] believing his funeral could not only garner opposition to British Rule but could also inspire Irish republicanism to challenge the IPP as a viable alternative.

To Devoy's horror, however, the Irish Parliamentary Party, whom O'Donovan Rossa detested throughout his life, sought to control any future funeral arrangements. This was initially represented by the IPP attempting to work up a fund for his family's maintenance and organise his burial through two Clan na Gael members, Moriarity and Hynes, who had fallen out with Clarke. Meeting Mary Jane, Moriarity and Hynes had suggested that they would support the burial of O'Donovan Rossa in Ireland and had the money to facilitate the return of his body for repatriation when he died. What Mary Jane didn't know, however, was that that the two men were being funded by the Irish Parliamentary Party, through their electoral machine the United Irish League, meaning the IPP, rather than the IRB, could control the funeral. Horrified, Mary Jane withdrew her consent to allow Moriarity and Hynes take care of her husband's eventual funeral and meeting with Devoy, she gave him permission to bury her husband in Ireland. Devoy had convinced her of the importance of a symbolic funeral, drawing parallels to the Bellew MacManus funeral in Glasnevin Cemetery in 1861: 'holding our friends in Ireland would do the same with Rossa... [and] the matter should be in the hands of men who believed in Fenian principles'.[49]

Jeremiah O'Donovan Rossa died aged 84 in St Vincent's Hospital, Staten Island, on 29 June 1915. He was surrounded by his family, some staff nuns who prayed around his bed and the Hospital Chaplin, Father O'Neill, accompanied by a priest, Fr Farrell, who Rossa intimately knew from his Parish church, St Peter's. Holding his head as he died, Mary Jane wrote 'there was no struggle. There was pain. He simply stopped breathing and lay perfectly still with a large, conscious solemn gaze as if he saw grand visions of the future that satisfied his heart and soul'.[50] One of the nuns, Sister Susan, placed her own crucifix in his hands, and with the family's permission insisted he was to be buried with it. Embracing the nun, Mary Jane agreed and asked her to pray with the family, which she eagerly did. True to Sister Susan's wishes, her crucifix was buried with O'Donovan Rossa. His body was waked in the family home for three days at No. 194 Richmond Terrace, Staten Island and lamenting his passing, John Devoy, who had been the only non-family member to see his body, noted 'the face of the dead man bore no traces of suffering. His strong features were placid in death and with the exception that the cheeks were somewhat hollow, there was nothing to indicate that he had gone through an illness of several years'.[51] Finally removed from the family home, a Funeral Mass was said for him in St Peter's. Delivered by Monsignor Charles A. Cassidy, the Mass celebrated the life of O'Donovan Rossa and Cassidy delivered a touching sermon, noting how:

> It is not customary in our church to speak over the remains of the departed, but as every rule has been an exception, we feel that it would not be proper this morning to omit drawing a lesson from the life of this good, holy and patriotic Irishman. 'After life's fitful fever he sleeps well,' and those of you who are present this morning – most of you – even the Priests who are here on the altar, know the story of O'Donovan Rossa so well that it would be needless repetition for me to recall it to your lives today. But the two facts which stand out most prominently in his life were his love of God and his deep and abiding devotion to his country.[52]

After the Funeral Mass, O'Donovan Rossa was temporarily reposed at the nearby St Peter's Cemetery in anticipation of a potential return to Ireland. His remains were placed into a glass-lidded white-satin-lined copper case and had been placed into a solid mahogany coffin. The coffin was then placed into a further hardwood box for protection which was painted battleship-grey and furnished with a name plate and handles. In anticipation of his Funeral Mass and as a mark of respect to O'Donovan Rossa, Clan na Gael had organised a great procession to accompany the dead Fenian to St Peter's Cemetery. The procession, which was several miles long, included many men of prominence within Irish-America including Dr Thomas Addis Emmet, Supreme Court Judge John W. Goff, John Devoy, Jim Larkin, John Curtin and Luke Dillon. The New York City Mayor, John Purroy Mitchell, unable to attend the procession and Mass, was represented by Joseph Hartigan, while several religious orders sent further representatives including priests from the Bronx, New York City and Washington DC. The Clan had been eager to display the Irish Volunteers as part of the funeral procession and the cortege between the Rossa family home and St Peter's Church was led by a military detachment of the first regiment of Irish Volunteers. The Volunteers were followed by the Ancient Order of Hibernians, and a long line of honorary and official pallbearers, made up of O'Donovan Rossa's friends, family and supporters within advanced Irish-American republicanism, in what the Gaelic American described as: 'The most representative Irish crowd that has been seen in or near New York for more than thirty years.'[53]

The Clan were equally eager to have O'Donovan Rossa buried in Ireland, believing that his funeral could be a significant publicity coup for the republican movement and, upon his death, Devoy cabled Thomas James Clarke in Dublin, asking for advice as to what should be done. Clarke's response was characteristic of the man and telegraphing Devoy he simply said 'send his body home at once'.[54] For Clarke, a revolutionary in the mould of O'Donovan Rossa, the timing of Rossa's death was extraordinary considering the growth of the Volunteers in Ireland and the war in Europe. This was represented in a conversation which he had with his wife Kathleen, the niece of O'Donovan Rossa's former adversary John Daly, when he explained how 'if Rossa had planned to die at the most opportune time for serving his country, he could not have done better'.[55] On Devoy's initiative, Mary Jane sent Thomas Clarke £20 sterling to purchase a grave for O'Donovan Rossa in Glasnevin Cemetery, Dublin. Devoy had recommended Clarke as an honest man who could be relied upon by Mary Jane. On her behalf, Clarke had purchased a grave under the shadow of the Daniel O'Connell monument, beside republican icons James Stephens, John O'Leary and within walking distance of Ann Devlin. Ironically, the spot he had chosen was where O'Donovan Rossa had begun his tour of the cemetery in 1905, near to the Manchester Martyrs Memorial. Similarly, in

America, in anticipation of Mary Jane's arrival in Ireland, Clan na Gael had purchased Mary Jane and her daughter Eileen two tickets for the trans-Atlantic steamer the *St Louis* for 10 July 1915. It had been decided to place O'Donovan Rossa's body on the trans-Atlantic steamer the SS *St Paul* leaving New York on 17 July and Mary Jane had communicated with Clarke her hope that the press would not know about the removal until the body reached Ireland.[56] Thomas Clarke took absolute control of the O'Donovan Rossa funeral and represented the kind of man 'who believed in Fenian principles',[57] that the Clan had wanted. Having taken charge of the funeral proceedings, Clarke was faced by a controversy, however, which threatened to undermine the great potential of the funeral.

From London, *The Daily Telegraph* immediately sought to use the opportunity of O'Donovan Rossa's death as a means of justifying the War Effort and debunk Irish republicanism. To do so the newspaper published a false account of O'Donovan Rossa's last words, written by its New York correspondent, who claimed to be a friend of Rossa's, indicating that upon his deathbed he sought forgiveness for his past career and ultimately came to redeem himself to acceptance of British Rule in Ireland. Published in Britain, Ireland and America, it was noted that his dying wish was for the British people to know 'I have fought a good fight according to my views and long ago lost all hatred, let alone prejudice against the British government.'[58] Concluding the faux deathbed confession, *The Daily Telegraph* noted how Rossa had called upon Irishmen to join the British Army uniting with the English, Scottish and Welsh to 'fight Germany, the common enemy of civilisation'. The faux confession was eagerly seized upon by the IPP, who ludicrously claimed 'that Rossa was a devoted follower of John Redmond'.[59] This lie was added to by the IPP, who eagerly embraced it in their campaigning and John Dillon, the Deputy leader of the IPP, went so far as to comment, in the presence of Redmond at Thurles, that O'Donovan Rossa had praised the IPP leader as 'a man who had done much for Ireland', and in a reference to Home Rule he had hoped that the IPP should 'get fair play and a chance of settling the Irish question along your lines'.[60] This was all balderdash and was invented by the Deputy Leader. Similarly the Redmondite *Cork Weekly Examiner* ludicrously exclaimed of Rossa how:

> Though confined to his home in America owing to ill health for time past, he followed the work of the Irish Parliamentary Party with deep interest and was delighted when the ever careful members of that

Party under the able and brilliant leadership of Mr John E. Redmond, supported by his trustworthy lieutenants, Mr John Dillion and Mr Joseph Devlin, placed the home rule bill on the statute book... This object, for which a great deal has been sacrificed in the country, has thus been attained, and no Irishman derived greater honour from that fact than O'Donovan Rossa.[61]

When Mary Jane had learned of this deception she was furious and deciding 'to stem the false tide'[62] released a statement vindicating her deceased husband's career and condemned *The Daily Telegraph* for inaccurate journalism. Drawing back on his impassioned defence in 1865 Mary Jane announced how her husband was 'an Irishman since he was born, and I can testify that he was the same unconquerable Irishman, breathing the same unalterable desire for the absolute freedom of his country and its utter separation from England that he had breathed in the dock'.[63] Supported by the republican movement, Mary Jane's statement was distributed throughout Ireland and America in order to show the falsity of the claim that O'Donovan Rossa supported Home Rule and recruitment to the British Army. Examining the false allegations by comparison to O'Donovan Rossa's mental state, John Devoy poured scorn on the IPP and noted how he could not believe that O'Donovan Rossa who 'did not look at a newspaper for two years, did not know that the Home Rule Bill had been passed and then suspended, did not know that a great war was going on in Europe and would not have understood it if he was told', was considered to be following 'the work of the Irish Party with deep interest'. Debunking the faux deathbed confession, Devoy commented how 'the Party is surely in a bad way when an unconscious man has to be made speak for it in his last illness... The Irish people know that O'Donovan Rossa died as he had lived, an unrepentant Irish Rebel'.[64] Returning to Mary Jane, she remained firm in her denunciation of the *Daily Telegraph* and the IPP holding:

Rossa's whole heart and soul were wound around and around the idea and hope of his country's freedom, from earliest boyhood to his dying breath. If ever there was a pure, true, radiant soul of patriotism it was his, and I should be a credible witness, for I have often shared the penalty of his devotion and self-sacrifice. Rossa expected to live to be more than a hundred years old, and he believed he would see his country great, glorious and free, but I think on his last visit to Ireland in 1906 it was so borne in on him that the people were won over to the wrong track, from which it would take years and bitter experience to wean them, that his heart broke.[65]

This controversy over O'Donovan Rossa's deathbed confession left Clarke undaunted and when it was soon revealed to be a farce, caused him little concern, and he quickly set about organising an O'Donovan Rossa funeral committee. The committee was organised under the name of the Wolfe Tone Memorial Association and included a veritable who's who of Irish history, including Edward Daly, James Connolly, Patrick Pearse, Thomas MacDonagh and Major John MacBride, all of whom would tragically be executed following the Easter Rising in 1916. Other notable members of the funeral committee included Eamon de Valera, soon to become the dominant political voice of his generation, Cathal Brugha, Richard O'Carroll, Countess Markievicz, Arthur Griffith, Darrell Figgis, Kathleen Clarke, Seán McGarry and James Stritch. Clarke had chosen Thomas McDonagh to oversee the details of the funeral procession, which also included members of the GAA, the trade unions, the Irish Citizen Army and Redmond's National Volunteers. Interestingly, the funeral of O'Donovan Rossa would be the one and only time that the four organisations would parade together.

Mary Jane and Eileen O'Donovan Rossa arrived in Liverpool on 18 July 1915, where they were greeted by Tom Clarke's wife, Kathleen, accompanied by Seán McGarry and prominent members of the Liverpool Irish Volunteers. Making their way to Dublin, via Liverpool, the IRB purchased a room for them at the Gresham Hotel, on Dublin's fashionable O'Connell Street. Here, however, the O'Donovan Rossas were constantly shadowed by the police and their room was entered on several occasions when they had left, with the police searching for incriminating materials connecting them to the IRB. The body of O'Donovan Rossa arrived shortly afterwards and was escorted to Dublin's Pro-Cathedral on Marlboro Street on Tuesday 27 July where it was received by the Rev. Father Bowden who recited prayers for the dead with Mary Jane and her daughter Eileen. As organiser of the funeral, Thomas MacDonagh had arranged for a Requiem Mass at 11 a.m. on Wednesday 28 July at Dublin's Pro-Cathedral, Marlborough Street, celebrated by Fr J. P. Flanagan. It was attended by Mary Jane and her daughter Eileen, accompanied by Clarke. Despite the earlier opposition of the Catholic Church to his activities in Ireland during his youth, it was noted that in death he drew a large clerical attendance with representatives of the Dominicans, Benedictines, Carmelites and Capuchins, to name a few. From the Pro-Cathedral the Irish

Volunteers led the funeral procession toward Dublin's City Hall on Dame Street, where O'Donovan Rossa was to be held until his funeral on Sunday 1 August in Glasnevin Cemetery. The removal to City Hall was also viewed as an opportunity for the Irish people to pay their respects to the deceased Irishman as the coffin was placed on a catafalque with the upper portion of the casket removed to allow for viewing. In a militaristic show, his body was protected by a guard of honour led by Edward Daly, nephew of his former adversary John Daly. In a private service for the family and a small coterie of invited guests, the nationalist priest, Fr Michael O'Flanagan, delivered a fiery oration celebrating the life of O'Donovan Rossa:

> They loved the name of O'Donovan Rossa and they proposed to put his remains among the noblest of the uncrowned kings of Ireland because he typified to them a spirit of patriotism, the passion of patriotism and the virtue of patriotism. O'Donovan Rossa was great in his love of Ireland and even beyond his love of Ireland. There stood out still strong in his character his manly hatred of the oppressors of Ireland.

Condemning the allegations that he renounced his faith in republicanism, Flanagan condemned the British media, the Irish Parliamentary Party and constitutional politicians holding 'they will grasp at any straw when they tell you that O'Donovan Rossa, was false to the principles of his youth'.[66] When O'Flanagan had finished his oration, the doors of City Hall were thrown open, revealing a huge crowd queuing the length of Dame Street and South Great George's Street waiting to be admitted in order to see the old, unrepentant Fenian lying in state and to pay their respects.

The return of O'Donovan Rossa to Ireland increasingly set the scene for the forthcoming Easter Rising of 1916 and many figures involved with the Rising and its aftermath waxed lyrical about the life of the unrepentant Fenian. On behalf of the Trade Union Movement, James Connolly defined O'Donovan Rossa as an 'unconquerable fighter' for justice and a man committed to the defence of the underdog within society. Eulogising O'Donovan Rossa upon his burial in Glasnevin Cemetery, Connolly lamented his passing but celebrated his legacy, holding: 'the burial of the remains of O'Donovan Rossa in Irish soil, and the functions attendant thereon, must inevitably raise in the mind of every worker the question of his or her own mental attitude to the powers against which the departed hero was in revolt'.[67] Defining O'Donovan Rossa's life as one in contradiction to British rule in Ireland, he commented how the Trade Union Movement and the Irish Citizen Army were determined to establish an Irish Republic and upon the burial of O'Donovan Rossa it was the duty of the Irish nation to resist British rule and 'honour O'Donovan Rossa by right of our faith in the separate destiny of our country'. Similarly, Thomas MacDonagh, on behalf of the Irish Volunteers, produced a militant piece entitled 'The Irish Volunteers in 1915'. Again celebrating O'Donovan Rossa, he compared Seán MacDiarmada, who was in prison under the Defence of the Realm Act, to the deceased Irishman, and commended Irishmen such as MacDiarmada for their part in the broader republican movement. For MacDonagh, those who had subscribed to the Irish Volunteers represented 'the heir to Irish nationality, handed down from revolt to revolt since the alien plunderers came here seven hundred and fifty years ago. The Irish Volunteer has taken up in his generation the traditional policy of the Irish people, – abandoned for a few decades – the policy of physical force'.[68] Arthur Griffith, the founder of Sinn Féin, equally lamented his passage, celebrating his life as championing the cause of an independent Ireland, holding 'no man will watch the body of O'Donovan Rossa pass its tomb without remembering that the strength of an empire was baffled when it sought to subdue this man whose spirit was the free spirit of the Irish nation'.[69]

In a character study of the unrepentant Fenian, Patrick Pearse, himself a member of the Irish Republican Brotherhood, held that O'Donovan Rossa 'stood plainly for the Fenian ideal' who desired the establishment of an Irish Republic free from outside influence. Addressing his prison experiences in the 1860s, Pearse examined the treatment of the Fenian prisoners and noted that the British had a special hatred for O'Donovan Rossa resultant from what he represented. Pearse held 'they pursued him into his prison and tried to break his spirit by mean and petty cruelty. He stood up to them and fought them: he made their whole penal system odious and despicable in the eyes of Europe and America. So the English found Rossa in Prison a more terrible foe than Rossa at large.'[70] Supporting Connolly's earlier assertion that O'Donovan Rossa was unconquerable, Pearse lamented his passing but celebrated his life as one of unbridled resistance against foreign domination holding 'no man, no government, could either break or bend him'.[71] Patrick Pearse had been chosen by Clarke to deliver the graveside oration of Jeremiah O'Donovan Rossa at Glasnevin Cemetery. Clarke had been inspired by his speech writing capabilities and oratorical skills, believing that Pearse had the potential to be the vocal and youthful face of Irish republicanism. The choice of Patrick

Pearse to deliver the graveside oration, however, was a gamble by Clarke; Pearse was a novice within the IRB and had gravitated to republican politics after a flirtation with Home Rule and constitutional nationalism. There was also an older generation of men who would have been better suited to deliver the oration having known O'Donovan Rossa and devoted a life's work to the IRB. In choosing Pearse, however, Clarke had resisted the older more conservative tendency in the IRB and had sought to add vibrancy to the funeral proceedings. Meeting with an anxious Pearse, who knew that he was to deliver one of the most inspiring speeches of his career, Clarke explained how he wanted the oration to be 'as hot as hell', recommending he 'throw discretion to the winds'.[72]

Beginning at City Hall on 1 August 1915, the O'Donovan Rossa funeral procession, led by the James' Street Band, proceeded down Dame Street, onto George's Street and up towards Aungier Street at 2.15 p.m. Halfway up Aungier Street the procession made for nearby York Street, passing the Royal College of Surgeons and St Stephens Green. Proceeding down Kildare Street it joined the adjoining Nassau Street, marching past Grafton Street onto College Green and past Trinity College in the direction of O'Connell Street, and finally onwards toward Glasnevin Cemetery. Led by Thomas MacDonagh, the advance guard of the Dublin Brigade of the Irish Volunteers was followed by a contingent of the Irish Citizen Army, the Fianna, Cumann na mBan and the National Volunteers. On the morning of the funeral it had been arranged to have special trains arriving in Dublin so as to facilitate representation from throughout the country. With thousands lining the route of the funeral procession it was recalled how the procession was a fitting national tribute to the memory of O'Donovan Rossa. It was estimated that 200,000 people lined the streets of Dublin to pay their respects to Jeremiah O'Donovan Rossa. Such was the size of the assembled crowd that when the funeral cortège had arrived at the entrance of the cemetery, some contingents were still taking their place at the starting point of the funeral procession, and according to the *Freeman's Journal*, resultant from the size of the crowd, it took an hour and five minutes each to pass the main points on the route, while at Trinity College, O'Connell Street and the junction of the Rotunda Hall and Parnell Statue there was a tremendous congestion of spectators comparable to other areas.[73] Despite the heads of the procession arriving at the cemetery at 4.30 p.m., O'Donovan Rossa's remains did not arrive until 6.30 p.m., three hours later than expected by the Cemetery Committee. In a remarkable scene, the outside Finglas road was lined with spectators as for several hours beforehand crowds had been assembling at the cemetery in anticipation of viewing O'Donovan Rossa being finally laid to rest.

Upon entry, the Funeral Cortège was met by two lines of Irish Volunteers who had formed a line from the Mortuary Chapel to the cemetery gate. Following the line of Volunteers to the chapel, a brief Requiem Mass was said for O'Donovan Rossa by the reverend Daniel Byrne, the Cemetery Chaplain before the family accompanied O'Donovan Rossa to his grave, where Fr Michael O'Flanagan delivered a blessing. As O'Flanagan brought the religious ceremony to an end, Patrick Pearse, in the uniform of the Irish Volunteers, rose to deliver his graveside oration. Standing over the grave of Jeremiah O'Donovan Rossa, Pearse delivered a remarkable speech in which he not only eulogised the life of O'Donovan Rossa but reaffirmed O'Donovan Rossa's political beliefs, suggesting that the mantle of Irish republicanism, which had been held by older men such as O'Donovan Rossa, was passing to a younger generation. The implication of his speech was that this younger generation would rebel against British rule in Ireland and would 'pledge to Ireland our love and… pledge to English rule in Ireland our hate!' Capturing the attention of all the assembled crowd, Patrick Pearse finished his speech with what would become immortal words in Irish history:

> Our foes are strong and wise and wary: but strong and wise and wary as they are they cannot undo the miracles of God who ripens in the hearts of young men the seeds sown by the young men of a former generation. And the seeds sown by the young men of '65 and '67 are coming to their miraculous ripening today. Rulers and defenders of this realm had need to be wary if they would guard against such processes. Life springs from death; and from the graves of patriot men and women spring living nations. The defenders of this realm have worked well in the secret and the open. They think they have pacified Ireland. They think they have purchased half of use and intimidated the other half. They think they have foreseen everything, think they have provided against everything; but the fools, the fools, the fools! They have left us our Fenian dead, and while Ireland holds these graves, Ireland unfree shall never be at peace!

Followed by a volley of shots over the grave, led by Captain James O'Sullivan of the Irish Volunteers, Pearse's speech struck a chord with the assembled and symbolised the transition of republicanism from the older generation to the new. Having ramifications for Irish history, the speech was an ideological justification of the forthcoming Easter Rising in 1916 and the right of the Irish people to a republican self-government, a cause which O'Donovan Rossa had championed throughout his life. While O'Donovan Rossa did not live to see the Easter Rising, resultant from the graveside address of Patrick Pearse, his name will always be associated with the rebellion. On this, the occasion of the centenary of his burial at Glasnevin Cemetery, it is important to recognise the sacrifice, courage, disappointment and ultimate vindication of the name Jeremiah O'Donovan Rossa, an unrepentant Fenian to the last.

Appendix

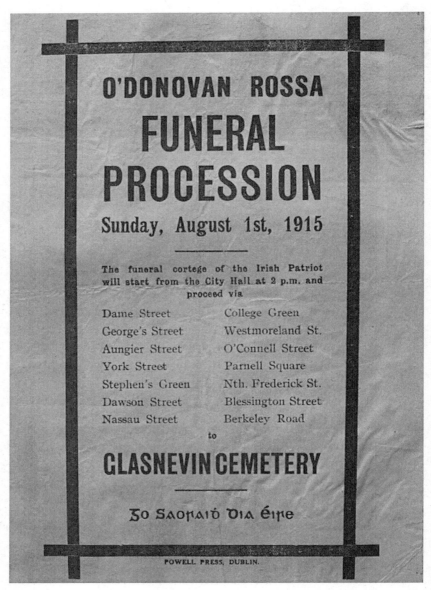

Poster announcing the funeral of O'Donovan Rossa, August 1915

The 'Graveside Pass' for the funeral of O'Donovan Rossa

Patrick Pearse's Graveside Oration, on the Occasion of the Funeral of Jeremiah O'Donovan Rossa, Glasnevin Cemetery, Dublin, 1 August 1915

It has seemed right, before we turn away from this place in which we have laid the mortal remains of O'Donovan Rossa, that one among us should, in the name of all, speak the praise of that valiant man, and endeavour to formulate the thought and the hope that are in us as we stand around his grave. And if there is anything that makes it fitting that I, rather than some other, rather than one of the grey-haired men who were young with him and shared in his labour and in his suffering, should speak here, it is perhaps that I may be taken as speaking on behalf of a new generation that has been re-baptised in the Fenian faith, and that has accepted the responsibility of carrying out the Fenian programme. I propose to you then that, here by the grave of this unrepentant Fenian, we renew our baptismal vows; that, here by the grave of this unconquered and unconquerable man, we ask of God, each one for himself, such unshakable purpose, such high and gallant courage, such unbreakable strength of soul as belonged to O'Donovan Rossa.

Deliberately here we avow ourselves, as he avowed himself in the dock, Irishmen of one allegiance only. We of the Irish Volunteers, and you others who are associated with us in to-day's task and duty, are bound together and must stand together henceforth in brotherly union for the achievement of the freedom of Ireland. And we know only one definition of freedom: it is Tone's definition, it is Mitchel's definition, it is Rossa's definition. Let no man blaspheme the cause that the dead generations of Ireland served by giving it any other name and definition than their name and their definition.

We stand at Rossa's grave not in sadness but rather in exaltation of spirit that it has been given to us to come thus into so close a communion with that brave and splendid Gael. Splendid and holy causes are served by men who are themselves splendid and holy. O'Donovan Rossa was splendid in the proud manhood of him, splendid in the heroic grace of him, splendid in the Gaelic strength and clarity and truth of him. And all that splendour and pride and strength was compatible with a humility and a simplicity of devotion to Ireland, to all that was olden and beautiful and Gaelic in Ireland, the holiness and simplicity of patriotism of a Michael O'Clery or of an Eoghan O'Growney. The clear true eyes of this man almost alone in his day visioned Ireland as we of to-day would surely have her: not free merely, but Gaelic as well; not Gaelic merely, but free as well.

In a closer spiritual communion with him now than ever before or perhaps ever again, in a spiritual communion with those of his day, living and dead, who suffered with him in English prisons, in communion of spirit too with our own dear comrades who suffer in English prisons to-day, and speaking on their behalf as well as our own, we pledge to Ireland our love, and we pledge to English rule in Ireland our hate.

This is a place of peace, sacred to the dead, where men should speak with all charity and with all restraint; but I hold it a Christian thing, as O'Donovan Rossa held it, to hate evil, to hate untruth, to hate oppression, and, hating them, to strive to overthrow them. Our foes are strong and wise and wary; but, strong and wise and wary as they are, they cannot undo the miracles of God who ripens in the hearts of young men the seeds sown by the young men of a former generation. And the seeds sown by the young men of '65 and '67 are coming to their miraculous ripening to-day. Rulers and Defenders of Realms had need to be wary if they would guard against such processes. Life springs from death; and from the graves of patriot men and women spring living nations. The Defenders of this Realm have worked well in secret and in the open. They think that they have pacified Ireland. They think that they have purchased half of us and intimidated the other half. They think that they have foreseen everything, think that they have provided against everything; but the fools, the fools, the fools! — they have left us our Fenian dead, and while Ireland holds these graves, Ireland unfree shall never be at peace

Why the Citizen Army Honours Rossa by James Connolly (1915)
Taken from the O'Donovan Rossa Souvenir Booklet (1915)

In honouring O'Donovan Rossa the workers of Ireland are doing more than merely paying homage to an unconquerable fighter. They are signifying their adhesion to the principle of which Rossa till his latest days was a living embodiment – the principle that the freedom of a people must in the last analysis rest in the hands of that people – that there is no outside force capable of enforcing slavery upon a people really resolved to be free, and valuing freedom more than life. We in Ireland have often forgotten that truth, indeed it may be even asserted that only an insignificant minority of the nation ever learned it. And yet, that truth once properly adopted as the creed of a nation would become the salvation of the nation.

For slavery is a thing of the soul, before it embodies itself in the material things of the world. I assert that before a nation can be reduced to slavery its soul must have been cowed, intimidated or corrupted by the oppressor. Only when so cowed, intimidated or corrupted does the soul of a nation cease to urge forward its body to resist the imposition of the shackles of slavery; only when the soul so surrenders does any part of the body consent to make truce with the foe of its national existence.

When the soul is conquered the articulate expression of the voice of the nation loses its defiant accent, and taking on the whining colour of compromise, begins to plead for the body. The unconquered soul asserts itself, and declares its sanctity to be more important than the interests of the body; the conquered soul ever pleads first that the body may be saved even if the soul is damned.

For generations this conflict between the sanctity of the soul and the interests of the body has been waged in Ireland. The soul of Ireland preached revolution, declared that no blood-letting could be as disastrous as a cowardly acceptance of the rule of the conqueror, nay, that the rule of the conqueror would necessarily entail more blood-letting than revolt against the rule. In fitful moments of spiritual exaltation Ireland accepted that idea, and such men as O'Donovan Rossa becoming possessed of it became thenceforth the living embodiment of that gospel. But such supreme moments passed for the multitude, and the nation as a nation sank again into its slavery, and its sole articulate expression to reach the ears of the world were couched in the fitful accents of the discontented, but spiritless slave – blatant in his discontent, spiritless in his acceptance of subjection as part of the changeless order of things.

The burial of the remains of O'Donovan Rossa in Irish soil, and the functions attendant thereon must inevitably raise in the mind of every worker the question of his or her own mental attitude to the powers against which the departed hero was in revolt. That involves the question whether those who accept that which Rossa rejected have any right to take part in honour paid to a man whose only title to honour lies in his continued rejection of that which they have accepted. It is a question each must answer for himself or herself. But it can neither be answered carelessly, nor evaded.

The Irish Citizen Army in its constitution pledges its members to fight for a Republican Freedom for Ireland. Its members are, therefore, of the number who believe that at the call of duty they may have to lay down their lives for Ireland, and have so trained themselves that at the worst the laying down of their lives shall constitute the starting point of another glorious tradition – a tradition that will keep alive the soul of the nation.

We are, therefore, present to honour O'Donovan Rossa by right of our faith in the separate destiny of our country, and our faith in the ability of the Irish workers to achieve that destiny.

O'Donovan Rossa: A Character Study by Patrick Pearse (1915)
Taken from the O'Donovan Rossa Souvenir Booklet (1915)

O'Donovan Rossa was not the greatest man of the Fenian generation, but he was its most typical man. He was the man that to the masses of his countrymen then and since stood most starkly and plainly for the Fenian idea. More lovable and understandable than the cold and enigmatic Stephens, better known than the shy and sensitive Kickham, more human than the scholarly and chivalrous O'Leary, more picturesque than the able and urbane Luby, older and more prominent than the man who, when the time comes to write his biography, will be recognised as the greatest of the Fenians—John Devoy— Rossa held a unique place in the hearts of Irish men and Irish women. They made songs about him, his very name passed into a proverb. To avow oneself a friend of O'Donovan Rossa meant in the days of our fathers to avow oneself a friend of Ireland; it meant more: it meant to avow oneself a 'mere' Irishman, an 'Irish enemy', an 'Irish savage', if you will, naked and unashamed. Rossa was not only 'extreme', but he represented the left wing of the 'extremists'. Not only would he have Ireland free, but he would have Ireland Gaelic.

And here we have the secret of Rossa's magic, of Rossa's power: he came out of the Gaelic tradition. He was of the Gael; he thought in a Gaelic way;

he spoke in Gaelic accents. He was the spiritual and intellectual descendant of ColmCille and of Seán an Díomais. With ColmCille he might have said, 'If I die it shall be from the love I bear the Gael'; with Shane O'Neill he held it debasing to 'twist his mouth with English'. To him the Gael and the Gaelic ways were splendid and holy, worthy of all homage and all service; for the English he had a hatred that was tinctured with contempt. He looked upon them as an inferior race, morally and intellectually; he despised their civilisation; he mocked at their institutions and made them look ridiculous.

And this again explains why the English hated him above all the Fenians. They hated him as they hated Shane O'Neill, and as they hated Parnell; but more. For the same 'crime' against English law as his associates he was sentenced to a more terrible penalty; and they pursued him into his prison and tried to break his spirit by mean and petty cruelty. He stood up to them and fought them: he made their whole penal system odious and despicable in the eyes of Europe and America. So the English found Rossa in prison a more terrible foe than Rossa at large; and they were glad at last when they had to let him go. Without any literary pretensions, his story of his prison life remains one of the sombre epics of the earthly inferno.

O'Donovan Rossa was not intellectually broad, but he had great intellectual intensity. His mind was like a hot flame. It seared and burned what was base and mean; it bored its way through falsehoods and conventions; it shot upwards, unerringly, to truth and principle. And this man had one of the toughest and most stubborn souls that have ever been. No man, no government, could either break or bend him. Literally he was incapable of compromise. He could not even parley with compromisers. Nay, he could not act, even for the furtherance of objects held in common, with those who did not hold and avow all his objects. It was characteristic of him that he refused to associate himself with the 'new departure' by which John Devoy threw the support of the Fenians into the land struggle behind Parnell and Davitt; even though the Fenians compromised nothing and even though their support were to mean (and did mean) the winning of the land war. Parnell and Davitt he distrusted; Home Rulers he always regarded as either foolish or dishonest. He knew only one way; and suspected all those who thought there might be two.

And while Rossa was thus unbending, unbending to the point of impracticability, there was no acerbity in his nature. He was full of a kindly Gaelic glee. The olden life of Munster, in which the seanchaidhe told tales in the firelight and songs were made at the autumn harvesting and at the winter spinning, was very dear to him. He saw that life crushed out, or nearly crushed out, in squalor and famine during '47 and '48; but it always lived in his heart. In English prisons and in American cities he remembered the humour and the lore of Carbery. He jested when he was before his judges; he jested when he was tortured by his jailors; sometimes he startled the silence of the prison corridors by laughing aloud and by singing Irish songs in his cell: they thought he was going mad, but he was only trying to keep himself sane.

I have heard from John Devoy the story of his first meeting with Rossa in prison. Rossa was being marched into the governor's office as Devoy was being marched out. In the gaunt man that passed him Devoy did not recognise at first the splendid Rossa he had known. Rossa stopped and said, 'John'. 'Who are you'? said Devoy: 'I don't know you'. 'I'm Rossa'. Then the warders came between them. Devoy has described another meeting with Rossa, and this time it was Rossa who did not know Devoy. One of the last issues of *The Gaelic American* that the British Government allowed to enter Ireland contained Devoy's account of a recent visit to Rossa in a hospital in Staten Island. It took a little time to make him realisewho it was that stood beside his bed. 'And are you John Devoy'? he said at last. During his long illness he constantly imagined that he was still in an English prison; and there was difficulty in preventing him from trying to make his escape through the window. I have not yet seen any account of his last hours; cabling of such things would imperil the Defence of the Realm.

Enough to know that the valiant soldier of Ireland is dead; that the unconquered spirit is free.

Notes

Introduction

1   *The Irish Times*, 30 June 1915.
2   Devoy, John, *Recollections of an Irish Rebel* (New York, 1929), p. 319.
3   Ibid.
4   Connolly, James, 'Why The Citizen Army Honours Rossa,' in *O'Donovan Rossa Funeral Souvenir Handbook* (Dublin, 1915), p. 6.
5   Griffith, Arthur, 'The Influence of Fenianism,' in *O'Donovan Rossa Funeral Souvenir Handbook* (Dublin, 1915), p.14.
6   Mrs Eileen O'Donovan Rossa McGowan to the Editor of *The Straits Times*, 8 March 1956 NLI Ms 10,974 (iii).
7   Pearse, Patrick, 'A Character Study,' in *O'Donovan Rossa Funeral Souvenir Handbook* (Dublin, 1915), p. 19.
8   Pearse, Patrick, 'Graveside Panegyric,' in *O'Donovan Rossa Funeral Souvenir Handbook* (Dublin, 1915), p. 2.
9   MacDonagh, Thomas, 'The Irish Volunteers in 1915,' in *O'Donovan Rossa Funeral Souvenir Handbook* (Dublin, 1915), p. 9.
10   Mrs Eileen O'Donovan Rossa McGowan to the Editor of *The Straits Times*, 8 March 1956 NLI Ms 10,974 (iii).
11   Ibid.

Chapter 1

1   O'Donovan Rossa, *Recollections* (Guilford, 2004), p. 10.
2   Ibid., pp., 31-32.
3   Rossa, Jeremiah O'Donovan, *Rossa Recollections 1838 to 1898 – Memoirs of an Irish Revolutionary* (Connecticut, 2004), p. 29.
4   Ibid., p. 64.
5   *The Illustrated London News,* 13 Feb. 1847
6   Quoted in Patrick Hickey, 'Mortality and Emigration in Six Parishes in the Union of Skibbereen, West Cork, 1846-47,' in Crowly, Smyth and Murphy (eds) *Atlas of the Great Irish Famine* (Cork, 2012), p.327.
7   *The Illustrated London News*, February 1847.
8   Rossa O'Donovan, Jeremiah, *Rossa's Recollections 1838–1898* (New York, 1898) p. 108.
9   O'Donovan Rossa, *Recollections* (Guildford, 2004), p. 109.
10   Ibid., p. 110.
11   Ibid., p. 122.
12   Ibid., p. 151.
13   Ibid., p. 142.

14   Ibid., p. 110.
15   Ibid.

Chapter Two

1   *The United Irishman*, 19 February 1887.
2   *The Nation*, 19 December 1857.
3   *The Brooklyn Eagle*, 7 June 1885.
4   Police memorandum to Sub Inspector Mason, 13 January 1858, Mayo Papers, NLI 11,187/1.
5   O'Donovan Rossa, *Recollections* (Guildford, 2004), pp. 190–1.
6   O'Donovan Rossa, *Irish Rebels in English Prisons* (Dingle, 1991), p. 22.
7   O'Donovan Rossa, *Recollections*, p. 201.
8   Devoy, John, *Recollections of an Irish Rebel* (New York, 1929), p.319.
9   O'Donovan Rossa, *Recollections*, p. 199.
10   Sub Inspector Mason, police memorandum, 28 August 1858, Mayo Papers, NLI 11,187/1.
11   *The Brooklyn Eagle*, 7 June 1885.
12   Sub Inspector Mason, police memorandum, 3 July 1858, Mayo Papers, NLI 11,187/1.
13   E. Hayes to Inspector General Irish Constabulary, 8 July 1858, Mayo Papers, NLI 11,187/1.
14   The 2nd statement of Robert Cusack, undated October 1858, 28 August 1858, Mayo Papers, NLI 11,187/1.
15   Sub Inspector Caulfield, police memorandum, 28 October 1858, Mayo Papers, NLI 11,187/1.
16   Sub Inspector Mason, police memorandum, 28 August 1858, Mayo Papers, NLI 11,187/1.
17   F. J. Davies memorandum to Dublin Castle, 4 September 1858, Mayo Papers, NLI 11,187/1.
18   Sub Inspector Caulfield, police memorandum, 24 September 1858, Mayo Papers, NLI 11,187/1.
19   Constable Hughes, police memorandum, 27 September 1858, Mayo Papers, NLI 11,187/1.
20   Sub Inspector Caulfield, police memorandum, 2 October 1858, Mayo Papers, NLI 11,187/1.
21   Sub Inspector Potter, police memorandum, 21 October 1858, Mayo Papers, NLI 11,187/1.
22   The 2nd statement of Robert Cusack, undated October 1858, 28 August 1858, Mayo Papers, NLI 11,187/1.
23   Sub Constable Monaghan, police memorandum, 1 November 1858, Mayo Papers, NLI 11,187/1.
24   George Fitzmaurice, 28 November 1858, Mayo Papers, NLI 11,187/1.
25   George Fitzmaurice, 26 November 1858, Mayo Papers, NLI 11,187/1.
26   Sub Inspector Caulfield, police memorandum, 29 September 1858, Mayo Papers, NLI 11,187/1.
27   Head Constable Brennan, police memorandum, 17 October 1858, Mayo Papers, NLI 11,187/1.
28   Sub Inspector Curling, police memorandum, 4 October 1858, Mayo Papers, NLI 11,187/1.
29   O'Donovan Rossa, *Irish Rebels in English Prisons* (Dingle, 1991), p. 31.
30   *The Freeman's Journal*, 4 December 1858.

31 F. J. Davies, memorandum 6 December 1858, Mayo Papers, NLI 11,187/1.
32 O'Donovan Rossa, Jeremiah, *Rossa's Recollections,* (Connecticut, 2004), p.215
33 O'Donovan Rossa, *Recollections*, p. 216 and see also George Fitzmaurice memorandum, 8 December 1858, Mayo Papers, NLI 11,187/1.
34 Sub Inspector Potter, police memorandum, 8 December 1858, Mayo Papers, NLI 11,187/1.
35 *The Freeman's Journal*, 11 December 1858.
36 Sub Inspector Caulfield, police memorandum, 8 December 1858, Mayo Papers, NLI 11,187/1.
37 O'Donovan Rossa, *Irish Rebels in English Prisons*, p. 24.
38 Ibid., p. 25.
39 Ibid., p. 25.
40 The deposition of Dan Sullivan given at Cork Jail, undated, Mayo Papers, NLI 11,187/1.
41 Ibid.
42 *The Belfast Newsletter*, 27 December 1858.
43 *The Daily News*, 27 December 1858.
44 *The Brooklyn Eagle*, 21 June 1885.
45 *The Brooklyn Eagle*, 21 June 1885.
46 George Fitzmaurice to Colonel Larcom, 9 February 1859, Mayo Papers, NLI 11,187/2.
47 Ibid.
48 Voluntary statement of Florence O'Sullivan, 9 December 1858, Mayo Papers, NLI 11,187/1.
49 *The Brooklyn Eagle*, 21 June 1885.
50 Ibid.
51 Ibid.
52 O'Donovan Rossa, *Recollections*, p.228.
53 O'Donovan Rossa, *Irish Rebels in English Prisons*, p. 40.
54 Devoy, John, *Recollections of an Irish Rebel* (New York, 1929), p. 321.
55 *The Brooklyn Eagle,* 28 June 1885.
56 Ibid.
57 O'Donovan Rossa, *Irish Rebels in English Prisons*, p. 41.
58 *The Brooklyn Eagle*, 21 June 1885.
59 O'Donovan Rossa, *Irish Rebels in English Prisons*, p. 40.
60 Ibid.
61 *The Brooklyn Eagle*, 21 June 1885.
62 O'Donovan Rossa, Jeremiah, *Rossa's Recollections* (Connecticut, 2004), p.365-33.

Chapter 3

1 O'Donovan Rossa, *Recollections* (Guildford, 2004), p. 321.
2 Ibid., p.323
3 Ibid., p.235
4 Ibid., p.238
5 *Reynolds Newspaper*, 10 November 1861.
6 Ibid.

7   Ibid.
8   *The Freeman's Journal*, 7 November 1861.
9   Ibid.
10 *The Nation*, 16 November 1861.
11 O'Donovan Rossa, *Recollections*, p. 241.
12 *The Skibbereen Eagle*, 25 October 1865.
13 O'Donovan Rossa, *Irish Rebels in English Prisons* (Dingle, 1991), p. 43.
14 Ibid.
15 *The Brooklyn Eagle*, 5 July 1885.
16 O'Donovan Rossa, *Recollections*, p. 378.
17 *The United Irishman*, 16 October 1886.
18 O'Donovan Rossa, *Recollections* (Guildford, 2004), p. 379
19 *The United Irishman*, 31 October 1896.
20 *The Brooklyn Eagle*, 5 July 1885.

Chapter 4

1   Denieffe, Joseph, *Recollections of the Irish Revolutionary Brotherhood* (New York, 1906), p. 82.
2   *The Brooklyn Eagle*, 12 July 1885.
3   Ó Broin, Leon, *Fenian Fever* (London, 1971), p. 4.
4   *The Irish People*
5   *The Irish People*, 9 January 1864.
6   Ibid., 3 December 1864.
7   Ibid., 28 November 1863.
8   Ibid.
9   *The Irish People*, 2 April 1864
10 Ibid., 24 September 1864.
11 Ibid., 2 April 1864.
12 Ibid., 22 October 1864.
13 *The Brooklyn Eagle*, 2 August 1885.
14 Ibid., 16 August 1885.
15 Ibid.
16 O'Donovan Rossa Cole, Margaret, *My Mother and Father were Irish* (New York, 1939), p. 26.
17 Devoy, John, *Recollections of an Irish Rebel* (New York, 1929), p. 113.
18 *The Freeman's Journal*, 4 December 1865.
19 *The Brooklyn Eagle,* 16 August 1885.
20 Ibid.
21 James Stephens to the Clonmel Bs, 8 September 1865, quoted in Sullivan, A.M., *New Ireland* (Philadelphia, 1878), p.350.
22 *The Brooklyn Eagle*, 16 August 1885.
23 Jeremiah O'Donovan Rossa to Mary Jane O'Donovan Rossa, 25 September 1865, Richmond Prison, CUA O'Donovan Rossa papers.
24 O'Donovan Rossa, *Irish Rebels in English Prisons* (Dingle, 1991), p. 53.
25 Ibid.

26 Wodehouse to Sir Thomas Larcom, 3 April 1866 NAI Fenian Papers A242.
27 John Devoy, *Recollections of an Irish Rebel* (New York, 1929), p. 113.
28 *The Irishman*, 28 October 1865 & *The Freeman's Journal*, 1 November 1865.
29 Ibid.
30 Ibid.
31 Novak, Rose, 'Keepers of Important Secrets' in *History Ireland* No.6 Volume 16.
32 Dr Cullen on Orangeism and Fenianism, *Daily Southern Cross*, 4 January 1866.
33 O'Donovan Rossa, Jeremiah, *Prison Life* (New York, 1874), p. 37.
34 *The Freeman's Journal*, October 20, 1865 & see also *The Liverpool Mercury*, 24 October 1865.
35 O'Donovan Rossa, *Irish Rebels in English Prisons* (Dingle, 1991), p. 54.
36 Ibid., p. 61.
37 Jeremiah O'Donovan Rossa to Mary Jane O'Donovan Rossa, undated, Kilmainham Gaol, CUA O'Donovan Rossa papers.
38 *The Belfast Newsletter*, 30 November 1865.
39 *The Freeman's Journal*, 4 December 1865.
40 Devoy, John, *Recollections of an Irish Rebel* (New York, 1929), p. 323.
41 Jeremiah O'Donovan Rossa to Mary Jane O'Donovan Rossa, undated, Kilmainham Gaol, CUA O'Donovan Rossa papers.
42 Ibid.
43 *The Belfast Newsletter*, 12 December 1865.
44 Ibid.
45 O'Donovan Rossa, *Irish Rebels in English Prisons* (Dingle, 1991), p. 65.
46 Ibid.
47 Ibid., p.71.
48 A. M.Sullivan, D. B. Sullivan & T. D. Sullivan, *Irish Speeches from the Dock* (New York, 1904), p. 165.
49 O'Donovan Rossa, *Irish Rebels in English Prisons* (Dingle, 1991), p. 76.
50 Ibid.
51 Ibid.
52 Ibid., p. 79.
53 Ibid.
54 A. M. Sullivan, D. B. Sullivan & T.D. Sullivan, *Irish Speeches from the Dock* (New York, 1904), p. 166.
55 O'Donovan Rossa to Mary Jane O'Donovan Rossa, Dec. 1865, Catholic University of America.

Chapter 5

1 Maconochie, Alexander, *Penal Discipline* (London, 1853), p. 1.
2 Jeremiah O'Donovan Rossa to Mary Jane Jeremiah O'Donovan Rossa, 1 December 1865 quoted in McConville, Sean, *Irish Political Prisoners* (New York, 2003), p. 124.
3 O'Donovan Rossa, *Irish Rebels in English Prisons* (Dingle, 1991), p. 82.
4 Ibid.
5 O'Luing, Sean, *Ó Donnabháin Rosa*, (), p. 258.

6   O'Donovan Rossa, *Irish Rebels in English Prisons* (Dingle, 1991), p. 85.
7   Ibid.
8   Ibid.
9   Ibid., p. 94.
10 Ibid.
11 O'Donovan Rossa, Jeremiah, *Prison Life* (New York, 1874), p. 99.
12 Ibid., p. 117.
13 Ibid.
14 O'Donovan Rossa, Jeremiah, *Prison Life*, p. 227.
15 O'Donovan Rossa, *Irish Rebels in English Prisons* (Dingle, 1991), p. 158.
16 Ibid.
17 O'Donovan Rossa, Jeremiah, *Prison Life,* p. 105.
18 Ibid., p. 117.
19 O'Donovan Rossa, *Irish Rebels in English Prisons*, p. 89–90.
20 O'Donovan Rossa, Jeremiah, *Prison Life* (New York, 1874), p. 106.
21 Ibid., p. 102.
22 Ibid, p. 110.
23 O'Donovan Rossa, Jeremiah, *Prison Life*, p. 121.
24 Ibid.
25 O'Donovan Rossa, Mary Jane, *Irish Lyrical Poems* (New York, 1867).
26 O'Donovan Rossa, Jeremiah, *Prison Life*, p. 126.
27 Ibid.
28 O'Donovan Rossa, Jeremiah, *Prison Life*, p. 137.
29 *Ibid,* p. 139.
30 Ibid.
31 O'Donovan Rossa, Jeremiah, *Prison Life*, p. 139.
32 O'Donovan Rossa, Jeremiah, *Prison Life*, p. 151.
33 O'Donovan Rossa, *Irish Rebels in English Prisons*, p. 122.
34 O'Donovan Rossa, Mary Jane, 'A Visit To My Husband In Prison, May 1866' (shortened version).
35 *The Irishman*, 16 March 1867.
36 O'Donovan Rossa, *Irish Rebels in English Prisons*, p. 127
37 Ibid.
38 *The Irishman*, 16 March 1867.

Chapter 6

1   TNA HO 45/9329/19461/104.
2   O'Luing, Sean, *Ó Donnabháin Rosa,* (), p. 287.
3   Diary of Mary Jane O'Donovan Rossa, NLI Ms 412.
4   Ibid.
5   *The Boston Pilot,* 3 October 1868.
6   *The Irish-American*, 6 June 1869.
7   *The United Irishman*, 30 July 1898.

8   O'Donovan Rossa, Jeremiah, *Prison Life* (New York, 1874), p. 329.

9   Ibid.,p. 268

10   Ibid., p. 269

11   O'Donovan Rossa, *Irish Rebels in English Prisons* (Dingle, 1991), p. 191.

12   Ibid.

13   Ibid., p.192.

14   Ibid.,p. 197.

15   Ibid. p.197

16   O'Donovan Rossa, *Irish Rebels in English Prisons*, p. 197.

17   O'Donovan Rossa, Jeremiah, *Prison Life*, p. 284.

18   Ibid.p. 291.

19   Ibid., p. 294

20   O'Donovan Rossa, *Irish Rebels in English Prisons*, p. 197.

21   Ibid.,p. 207.

22   Ibid.

23   Ibid., p. 207

24   Ibid.

25   Devoy, John, *Recollections of an Irish Rebel* (New York, 1929), p. 319

26   *The Irishman*, 13 November 1869.

27   O'Donovan Rossa, Jeremiah, *Prison Life* (New York, 1874), p. 319.

28   Ibid.

29   Ibid., p. 319.

30   Ibid., p. 320.

31   George Moore MP, Hansard, CIC, cols 1140-1; 3, March 1870.

32   *The Freeman's Journal*, 29 June 1870.

33   IRELAND (FENIANS): Commission on Treatment of Treason Felony Convicts in English Prisons (1870-1874) TNA HO 45/9330/19461A/62.

34   *The Freeman's Journal*, 6 July 1870.

35   The Devon Commission, p.16.

36   The Devon Commission, p.16.

37   *The Irish Times,* 28 November 1870.

38   Harry S. Mulleda, 22 December 1870.

Chapter 7

1   *The Milwaukee Sentinel,* 17 January 1871.

2   *The New York Times*, 'The Fenians Arrived', Wednesday 20 January 1871.

3   'Irish Political Prisoners,' *The Irish Citizen*, New York, For the week ending Saturday, 7 January 1871. p. 3.

4   *The New York Times*, 'The Fenians Arrived', Wednesday 20 January 1871.

5   O'Donovan Rossa, Jeremiah, *Irish Rebels in English Prisons* (Dingle, 1991) p.283.

6   Ibid. p. 280.

7   *The Daily Kansas Tribune*, 27 January 1871.

8   Ibid. p. 281.

9   *The Memphis Daily Appeal*, 27 January 1871.

10 A letter from the Cuba Five to the gentlemen of the several deputations for receiving Irish exiles in O'Brien William & Desmond Ryan (Eds) *Devoy's Post Bag* Vol. 1 (Dublin, 1948)p. 9

11 *The Daily Kansas Tribune,* 27 January 1871.

12 *The New York Herald*, 10 February 1871.

13 *The Memphis Daily Appeal*, 27 January 1871.

14 *The Cincinnati Enquirer*, 24 January 1871.

15 *The New York Herald*, 31 January 1871.

16 Ibid.

17 Among further exiles were Thomas Clarke Luby, John O'Leary, Richard O'Sullivan Burke and William Mackey.

18 *New York Herald*, 31 January 1871, quoted in William Darcy, *The Fenian Movement in the United States 1858–1886* (Washington, 1947) p. 371.

19 *The New York Times*, 23 February 1871.

20 *The New York Times*, 21 January 1871.

21 Letter from P. M. McGill to Jeremiah O'Donovan Rossa, 25 February 1871, Fenian Brotherhood collection Box 1 Folder 13 Item 19.

22 Ibid., p16.

23 Darcy, William, *The Fenian Movement in the United States 1858*–1886, p.327.

24 *United Irishman* circular, 18 February 1871 in *Devoy's Postbag* (Dublin, 1948), Vol.1, p. 32.

25 John Devoy to John Boyle O'Reilly, *The Boston Pilot,* 4 February 1871. p.5.

26 Charles Underwood O'Connell (Undated January – February 1871) the John Devoy papers (NLI Ms 18, 031 [3])

27 D.D. Mulcahy, New York, 8 February 1871 the John Devoy papers (NLI Ms 18, 031 [3]).

28 'Notes on organisation' John Devoy, 7 February 1871 the John Devoy papers (NLI Ms 18, 031 [3]).

29 Ibid.

30 Ibid.

31 'The Unity of the Irish Race in America', 8 February 1871 in O'Brien William & Desmond Ryan (Eds) *Devoy's Post Bag* Vol. 1 (Dublin, 1948)p 26.

32 *The Irish People,* 18 March 1871

33 Ibid.

34 'Union of Irish Nationalism,' *The Boston Pilot*, 25 February 1871. P.4.

35 'The Fenian Convention,' *The Boston Pilot*, 8 April 1871. P.1

36 Letter from William Halpin, to the directory of the Irish Confederation, 8 December 1871, John Devoy papers (Ms 18,031 [2])

37 The Central Office of the Irish Confederation, to the Clubs of the Irish Confederation, 9 February 1872. (John Devoy papers NLI Ms 18, 031[6])

38 Written by Patrick Boyle, Thomas O'Donnell and Hugh J. Leonard (John Devoy papers NLI Ms 18, 031[6]).

39 Constitution and by laws of the Irish Confederation, May 1872, Article 1 (John Devoy papers NLI Ms 18, 031[6]).

40 Ibid., Article 2.

41 *The United Irishman*, 21 August 1892.

42 O'Donovan Rossa, *Irish Rebels in English Prisons* (Dingle, 1991), p. 283.

43 Denis O'Donovan Rossa to Mary Jane O'Donovan Rossa, 5 July 1876 (O Luing Papers) NLI MS 26, 790.

44 O'Donovan Rossa, Margaret, *My Mother and Father were Irish* (New York, 1939), p. 57-8

45 O'Donovan Rossa, Margaret, *My Mother and Father were Irish* (New York, 1939), p. 54

46 O'Donovan Rossa, Margaret, *My Mother and Father were Irish* (New York, 1939), p. 54

47 Ibid.

48 O'Donovan Rossa, Margaret, *My Mother and Father were Irish* (New York, 1939), p. 34.

49 Ibid.

50 *The Irishman*, 6 January 1872.

51 *The New York Herald*, 1 November 1871

52 O'Donovan Rossa, *Irish Rebels in English Prisons* (Dingle, 1991), p. 284.

53 *The New York Standard*, 6 November 1871.

54 *The New York Daily Tribune*, 28 October 1871.

55 *The Globe*, 6 November 1871.

56 *The Nation*, 2 December 1871

57 Ibid.

58 Ibid.

59 Le Caron, Henri, *Twenty five years in the secret service – the recollections of a spy* (London, 1892) p. 115.

60 Ibid, p.116.

61 Kelly, M.J. *The Fenian Ideal and Irish Nationalism 1882-1916* (Woodbridge, 2006) p. 15.

62 *The Irish World*, 10 October 1874.

63 *The Irish World,* 4 December 1875.

64 The Skirmishing fund in O'Brien William & Desmond Ryan (Eds) *Devoy's post bag* Vol. 1 (Dublin, 1948) p. 141.

65 *The Irish World,* 4 December 1875.

66 *The Irish World*, 4 March 1876.

67 *The Irish World,* 4 December 1875.

68 According to Martha Crenshaw modernisation facilitated terrorism with sophisticated networks of transportation and communication offering mobility and the means of publicity for terrorism. Crenshaw, Martha, 'The Causes of Terrorism,' in *Comparative politics,* Vol.13 No.4(July, 1981) p. 381.

69 *The Irish World*, 28 August 1880 in Walther Laqueur, *The terrorism reader* (London, 1979) p. 113.

70 *The Irish World*, 11 March 1876.

71 *The Irish World*, 11 March 1876.

72 *The Irish World*, 11 March 1876.

73 B.K. Kennedy to Jeremiah O'Donovan Rossa, 16 June 1877 in O'Brien William & Desmond Ryan (Eds) *Devoy's post bag* Vol. 1 (Dublin, 1948) p. 255-6.

74 James Maxwell to Mary Jane O'Donovan Rossa, 22 March 1881 O'Donovan Rossa papers, NLI MS 10, 974 (iii).

75 Majendie, Colonel Vivian, 'Nitro-glycerine and dynamite,' in *The Fortnightly Review*, May 1883 (London, 1883) p. 644.

76 Brown, Terence, *Irish American Nationalism* (New York, 1966) p. 72

77 Cole, Sarah, 'Dynamite Violence and Literary Culture,' in *Modernism/Modernity*, Vol. 16 No. 2, p. 302.

78 *The Irish World*, 18 March 1876.

79 Stephens, James, *Fenianism: Past and present* [undated], The James Stephens papers NLI Ms 10, 492 [6]

80 Quoted in *The Special Commission Act, 1888 – Report of the proceedings before the commissioners appointed by the act,* Vol. IV (London, 1890) p. 189 and Davitt papers TCD, MS 9659d

81 James Stephens letter book 1876-1879, Davitt papers TCD MS 9659d/325.

82 John O'Leary to John Devoy, in O'Brien William & Desmond Ryan (Eds) *Devoy's post bag* Vol. 1 (Dublin, 1948) p. 142.

83 *The Irishman*, 27 March 1880.

84 Copy letter from Jeremiah O'Donovan Rossa, 9 March 1881 Fenian A Files Box 5 A663 NAI and TNA FO 5/7777

85 Tynan, Patrick, *The Irish National Invincibles and their times* (London, 1894) p. 20.

86 O'Donovan Rossa, Jeremiah, *Rossa's Recollections* (Connecticut, 2004) p. 147.

87 Crenshaw, Martha, 'the causes of terrorism,' in *Comparative politics* 13:4(July, 1981) p. 388.

88 O'Reilly, John Boyle, 'At Last!' in *The North American Review* vol. OIIVII (New York, 1866) p. 108.

89 Crenshaw, Martha, 'the causes of terrorism,' in *Comparative politics* 13:4(July, 1981) p. 387.

90 Crenshaw, Martha, 'The logic of Terrorism: Terrorist behaviour as a product of strategic choice,' in Walter Reich (ed), *Origins of Terrorism* (Cambridge, 1990) p. 11.

91 Ibid.

92 *The Irish World*, 16 April 1880.

93 Ibid, 4 December 1875.

94 Crenshaw, Martha, "The logic of Terrorism: Terrorist behaviour as a product of strategic choice,' in Walter Reich (ed), *Origins of Terrorism* (Cambridge, 1990) p. 10.

95 *The Irish World*, 16 April 1880.

96 *The San Francisco Chronicle* [Undated] in extracts from San Francisco journals respecting the proceedings of O'Donovan Rossa and other notorious Fenians, 22 May 1876, TNA MEPO 3.

97 Ibid, p. 18.

98 Le Caron, Henri, *Twenty five years in the British secret service – the recollections of a spy* (London, 1892) p.135.

99 John Devoy, 1 March 1876 in O'Brien William & Desmond Ryan (Eds) *Devoy's post bag* Vol. 1 (Dublin, 1948), p. 143.

100 John Devoy, 1 March 1876 in O'BrienWilliam & Desmond Ryan (Eds) *Devoy's post bag* Vol. 1 (Dublin, 1948), p. 143.

101 *The Irish Times*, 26 January 1878.

102 William Mackey Lomasney to John Devoy, 31 March 1881 in William O'Brienand Desmond Ryan (eds) *Devoy's postbag* Vol. II (Dublin, 1948), p. 58.

103 *The Irish World*, 4 March 1876.

104 John Devoy to James Reynolds, 21 June 1880, John Devoy Papers NLI Ms 18, 135 [2].

105 John Devoy, 1 March 1876 in O'Brien William & Desmond Ryan (Eds) *Devoy's post bag* Vol. 1 (Dublin, 1948) p. 143.

106 Dr. William Carroll to John Devoy, 29 March 1876, John Devoy Papers, Ms NLI 18,002 [2].

107 *The Irish World*, 25 March 1876.

108 *The Irish World*, 4 March 1876.

109 This money was invested in registered United States Bonds, and later converted into negotiable coupon bonds, without record, avoiding supervision by British intelligence assets. K.R.M Short, *The Dynamite War-Irish —American bombers in Victorian Britain* (Dublin, 1979) p44.

110 *The Irish world*, 21 April 1877 and Henri le Caron, *Twenty five years in the British secret service — the recollections of a spy* (London, 1892) p.p.135-136.

111 From John J Breslin, John Devoy, Thomas Clarke Luby and Thomas Francis Bourke 2 December 1877, John Devoy papers NLI Mss 18016 [6].

112 John Devoy to James Reynolds, 10 March 1878, John Devoy Papers NLI Ms 18, 135 [2].

113 Edward Archibald to the Earl Granville, 2 August 1881, TNA FO 5/1779 and *The New York Sun,* 31 July 1881.

114 Le Caron, Henri, *Twenty-five years in the British secret service — the recollections of a spy* (London, 1892) p.135.

115 *The Irish World,* 21 April 1877 and Henri Le Caron *Twenty-five years in the British secret service — the recollections of a spy* (London, 1892) p.p.136-137.

116 *The Special Commission Act, 1888 — Report of the proceedings before the commissioners appointed by the act,* Vol. IV (London, 1890) p. 292-293.

117 Golway, Terry, *Irish Rebel* (New York, 1995) p. 99.

118 John Devoy to James Reynolds, 10 March 1878, John Devoy papers NLI Ms 18, 135[2].

119 John Devoy to James Reynolds, 10 March 1878, John Devoy papers NLI Ms 18, 135[2].

120 John Devoy to James Reynolds, 10 March 1878, John Devoy papers NLI Ms 18, 135[2].

121 John Devoy to James Reynolds, 10 March 1878, in O'Brien William & Desmond Ryan (Eds) *Devoy's post bag* Vol. 1 (Dublin, 1948)p. 320.

122 John Devoy to James Reynolds, 26 march 1878, John Devoy papers NLI Ms 18,135[2].

123 Ibid.
124 John Devoy to James Reynolds, 26 march 1878, John Devoy papers NLI Ms 18,135[2].
125 Jeremiah O'Donovan Rossa to Thomas Francis Bourke, undated, in O'Brien William & Desmond Ryan (Eds) *Devoy's post bag* Vol. 1 (Dublin, 1948) p. 323.
126 Jeremiah O'Donovan Rossa to Thomas Francis Bourke, undated, in O'Brien William & Desmond Ryan (Eds) *Devoy's post bag* Vol. 1 (Dublin, 1948) p. 323.
127 Jeremiah O'Donovan Rossa to Thomas Francis Bourke, undated, in O'Brien William & Desmond Ryan (Eds) *Devoy's post bag* Vol. 1 (Dublin, 1948) p. 323.
128 John Devoy to James Reynolds, 28 March 1878, John Devoy Papers NLI Ms 18, 135 [2].
129 John Devoy to James Reynolds, 28 March 1878, John Devoy Papers NLI Ms 18, 135 [2].
130 John Devoy to James Reynolds, 28 March 1878, John Devoy Papers NLI Ms 18, 135 [2].
131 John Devoy to James Reynolds, 21 June 1878, John Devoy Papers NLI Ms 18, 135 [2].
132 Request to O'Donovan Rossa to resign the secretaryship of the national [skirmishing] fund, undated, [May 1878] Devoy papers NLI Ms 18016 [6] and O'Brien William & Desmond Ryan (Eds) *Devoy's post bag* Vol II p. 553.
133 *The Special Commission Act, 1888 − Report of the proceedings before the commissioners appointed by the act,* Vol. IV (London, 1890) p. 292.
134 *The Irish World,* 16 April 1881.
135 Townshend, Charles, *Political violence in Ireland* (Oxford, 1983) p. 123
136 Funchion, Michael Francis, *Chicago's Irish Nationalists, 1881-1890* (New York, 1976) p. 58.
137 Michael Davitt to Richard Pigott, 20 November 1878, *The Irishman,* 19 December 1879, TCD Davitt papers Ms 9360/669.
138 Devoy, John, *Land of Eire* (New York, 1882) p. 42
139 *Irish Freedom,* December 1914 Kilmainham Gaol and Museum 16 NW IK21 01.
140 O'Brien William & Desmond Ryan (Eds) *Devoy's post bag* Vol. 1 (Dublin, 1948) p. 370.
141 *The New York Herald,* 27 October 1878.
142 *The Dublin Weekly News,* Nov. 16 1878 TCD Davitt papers, Ms 9360/669, & *Irish Freedom,* January 1914.
143 O'Donovan, Rossa, Jeremiah, Irish Rebels in English prisons (Dingle, 1991) p. 291
144 Ibid. p. 219
145 O'Donovan Rossa, Jeremiah, *Rossa's Recollections* (Connecticut, 2004) p. 146.
146 Piggott, Richard, *Recollections of an Irish journalist* (Dublin, 1882) p. 383.
147 *The Irishman,* 7 December 1878 TCD Davitt papers, Ms 9360/669.
148 O'Donovan, Rossa, Jeremiah, *Irish Rebels in English prisons* (Dingle, 1991) p. 289.
149 O'Donovan, Rossa, Jeremiah, Irish Rebels in English prisons (Dingle, 1991) p. 291.

150 Jeremiah O'Donovan Rossa to anonymous, 15 March 1880 O'Brien William & Desmond Ryan (Eds) *Devoy's post bag* Vol. 1 (Dublin, 1948) p502.
151 William Archibald to the Earl Granville, 9 July 1880 Fenian A Files NAI A 630/631.
152 *The weekly Union,* Saturday 10 July 1880.
153 *The weekly Union,* Saturday 10 July 1880.
154 *The Weekly Union,* 10 July 1880 & *The Labour World,* 27 September 1890. There is no documentary evidence to substantiate McDermott's claim to having won the honour by an act of obvious bravery.
155 *The Weekly Union,* 10 July 1880 & *The Labour World,* 27 September 1890.
156 O'Donovan, Rossa, Jeremiah, *Irish Rebels in English prisons* (Dingle, 1991) p. 293.
157 O'Donovan Rossa, Margaret, My Mother and Father were Irish (New York, 1939), p. 24.
158 *The Labour World,* 11 October 1890.
159 *The United Irishman,* 11 February 1885.
160 *The Labour World,* 11 October 1890.
161 Devoy, John, *Recollections of an Irish Rebel* (New York, 1929), p. 329.
162 O'Donovan Rossa, Margaret, My Mother and Father were Irish (New York, 1939), p. 24.
163 *The New York Times,* 22 August 1881.
164 *The Irish Times,* 26 January 1878.

Chapter 8

1 O'Donovan Rossa, Jeremiah, *Irish Rebels in English Prisons* (Dingle, 1991) p. 291.
2 *The Birmingham Daily Post,* Saturday 15 January 1881, see also Police Orders, January 1881 TNA MEPO 3.
3 *The Bristol Mercury and Daily Post,* 15 January 1881 & see also Anon, *The Mysteries of Ireland* (London, 1883) p. 145.
4 *The Times,* Monday 17 January 1881.
5 A post mortem examination had found he was struck near the left eye, from which point the skull was fractured in several directions. The fractures were 'likely to have been caused by being struck very violently with some hard missile'. *The Times,* Thursday 20 January 1881.
6 Hansard Debates, 22 February 1883 (London, 1883) col. 621.
7 Edward Marshall, Chief Constable of Salford to Home Office, 17 January 1881. TNA HO 144/75/A1586F. By April 1881 the government had privately concluded beyond doubt that the Salford explosion was the work of O'Donovan Rossa's emissaries, Edward Archibald to the Earl of Granville, 6 April 1881 TNA FO 5/1777 & see also *The Nation,* 22 January 1881.
8 *The Irish Times,* 3 February 1881
9 *The Bristol Mercury and Daily Post,* 15 January 1881.
10 *The Manchester Times,* Monday 22 January 1881. The Home Office furthermore requested a stockpiling of ammunition stored at military barracks and the security afforded to such institutions. K or Bow Division London Metropolitan Police, return of barracks and places where arms and ammunition are stored and the protection afforded & see also Islington division and Whitechapel divisions, 28 January 1881, TNA MEPO 3.

11 Report of James Reynolds, Chairman of the Clan na Gael executive committee, at the Clan na Gael convention, 1881, Special Commission Act, 1888, *Reprint of the shorthand notes of the speeches, proceedings and evidence taken before the commissioners* (London, 1890) Vol. IV pp. 579-81.

12 William Mackey Lomasney to John Devoy, 26 January 1881 & 11 February 1881 in O'Brien William & Desmond Ryan (Eds) *Devoy's Post Bag* Vol. 2 (Dublin, 1948) pp. 33 &37.

13 Text of an untitled and unreferenced speech written by John Devoy, undated, in notes and drafts for John Devoy's recollections, NLI Ms 18, 014.

14 William Mackey Lomasney to John Devoy, 26 January 1881 & 11 February 1881 in O'Brien William & Desmond Ryan (Eds) *Devoy's Post Bag* Vol. 2 (Dublin, 1948) pp. 33 &37.

15 O'Connor had given Lomasney significant money for explosive experiments and his reconnaissance operations, Desmond Ryan Papers UCDA LA 10/K/23.

16 John O'Leary of the Supreme Council was horrified by such strategy, and in a highly cryptic letter to Devoy voiced his concerns over the possibility of reprisals against the Irish community in Britain should such a strategy be employed, 'purchase of said goods inadvisable for several reasons. First as far as I can gather from all of ye, next to no good for legitimate war, and may be highly injurious if worn on improper occasions. But all this not of much practical moment just now, as I was overruled about purchase, and besides I admit, to a certain limited extent [John O'Connor's] plea of expediency'. John O'Leary to John Devoy, January 1881, in O'Brien William & Desmond Ryan (Eds) *Devoy's Post Bag* Vol. II (Dublin, 1948) p. 34.

17 James Reynolds of the Clan allegedly had said Rossa's actions had 'only made a laughing stock of his countrymen,' and needed to be stopped, *The New York Sun*, 29 August 1882, Fenian A files box 5 NAI A736

18 Robert Clipperton to the Earl of Granville, 7 February 1881 Fenian A Files Box 5 NAI A648

19 William Mackey Lomasney [unsigned] to William Connolly, 20 April 1881 in O'Brien William & Desmond Ryan (Eds) *Devoy's Post Bag* Vol. II (Dublin, 1948) p. 68.

20 *Truth* 11 February 1881 Fenian A Files Box 5 NAI A652- 653.

21 *Truth* 11 February 1881 Fenian A Files Box 5 NAI A652- 653.

22 Intercepted letter from O'Donovan Rossa, 9 March 1881 TNA FO 5/777.

23 *The Annual Register: A Review of Public Events at Home and Abroad for the Year 1881* (London, 1882) p.13.

24 Gardiner, A.G., *The Life of Sir William Harcourt*, Vol. 1 (London, 1923) p. 426.

25 Ibid.

26 E. Thornton to the Earl of Granville, 5 April 1881 Fenian A Files Box 5 A663 NAI.

27 E. Thornton to the Earl of Granville, 5 April 1881, TNA FO 5/1777.

28 Clipperton to the Earl Granville 24 January 1881 Fenian A files A645 NAI TNA FO 5/ 1776.

29 Copy of a letter from Jeremiah O'Donovan Rossa, 2 March 1881 Fenian A Files Box 5 NAI A663.

30 Thomas Johnson to William Ewart Gladstone, 23 August 1881, TNA FO 5/1779.

31 E. Thornton to the Earl of Granville, 4 April 1881 TNA FO 5/1777.
32 R. Clipperton to the Earl Granville, 24 March 1881, TNA FO 5/1777.
33 Ibid.
34 Edward Thornton to the Earl Granville, 1 April 1881 TNA FO 5/1777.
35 Ibid.
36 Robert Clipperton to the Earl of Granville, 19 February 1881 Fenian A Files A654 NAI.
37 Ibid.
38 Ibid.
39 *The New York Mercury*, 17 April 1881.
40 Hansards debates third series Vol. CCLXXVII, the House of Commons, 17 March 1881 (London, 1881) Col. 1250.
41 *The Times*, 18 March 1881.
42 *The Times*, 18 March 1881 & see also Anon, *The Mysteries of Ireland* (London, 1883) p.148.
43 *Inspector of explosives annual report for the year 1881* [C-3262], H.C 1882.
44 *The Times*, 18 March 1881.
45 Anon, *The Mysteries of Ireland* (London, 1883) p. 148.
46 *The Times*, 18 March 1881.
47 *The Times*, 18 March 1881 & see also Anon, *The Mysteries of Ireland* (London, 1883) p. 148.
48 *The Annual Register: A Review of Public Events at Home and Abroad for the Year 1881* (London, 1882) p.19.
49 *The Times*, 18 March 1881, see also Detective Inspector A. Gernon to Edmund Henderson, Commissioner Metropolitan Police 21 January 1881 TNA MEPO 3.
50 Ibid.
51 Ibid.
52 *The Annual Register: A Review of Public Events at Home and Abroad for the Year 1881* (London, 1882) p.34
53 Ibid.
54 *The Pall Mall Gazette*, 6 May 1881.
55 *The Western Mail*, 7 May 1881. Barnaby Rudge was an idiotic character in Charles Dickens' historical novel *Barnaby Rudge: A tale of the riots of 'Eighty*.
56 Gardiner, A.G.., *The Life of Sir William Harcourt*, Vol. 1 (London, 1923) p. 430.
57 O'Donovan Rossa, *Irish Rebels in English Prisons* (Dingle, 1991) p. 297.
58 *Ibid,* p. 296
59 *The Boston Daily Advertiser*, 13 June 1881.
60 *The Annual Register: A Review of Public Events at Home and Abroad for the Year 1881* (London, 1882) p. 54
61 Ibid., p.56. Furthermore British inquiries had discovered on 16 June 1881 'a shipping order had been granted in the name of the "Phoenix manufacturing company" for ten barrels of cement to be conveyed to Liverpool, consigned to a John Lawson and that were shipped by the Bavaria.' Similar enquiries regarding the Malta indicated on 10 June 'a shipping order was applied for in the name of Charles Mills for ten barrels of cement to be conveyed to Liverpool, consigned to a Joseph Evens, and that these barrels were shipped,' aboard the *Malta*. British Consul Henderson (Boston) to the Earl Granville, 1 August 1881. TNA FO 5/ 1779.
62 Ibid., p. 54

63 The report of Dr James Campbell Brown, to Sir William Vernon Harcourt, Secretary of State for the Home Department, 4 July 1881 TNA HO 144/81/A5836 and see also Hansard debates, 25 July 1881 (London, 1881) col. 1751.

64 *Lloyds Weekly Newspaper,* 31 July 1881.

65 One of the clocks used was marked with the stamp of the Ansonia clock company, but on enquiries despite recognising the machinery, the company manager, concluding the machinery was improvised, informed the British Consul at New York, 'they have no means of discovering who purchased from them the movement in question,' Edward Archibald to the Earl Granville, 15 September 1881, TNA FO 5/ 1780.

66 *The Annual Register: a review of public events at home and abroad for the year 1881* (London, 1882) pp. 55–56 & Adolphus Liddell, Undersecretary of State for the Home Department to Lord Tenterden, Charles Abbott, Undersecretary at the Foreign Office Undersecretary of State for the Foreign Office, 16 August 1881, TNA FO 5/1779.

67 *The Aberdeen Weekly Journal,* 25 July 1881.

68 *The Pall Mall Gazette,* 25 July 1881.

69 Ibid.

70 Ibid.

71 How, F.D. & S.H. Jeyes, *The Life of Sir Howard Vincent* (London, 1912) p. 119

72 *The New York Herald,* 10 August 1881.

73 Hansards debates, 25 July 1881 (London, 1881) col. 1751.

74 *Lloyds Weekly Newspaper,* 31 July 1881.

75 Edwards to the Earl Granville, 2 August 1881, Fenian A Files NAI A689. Crowe was apparently arrested by the authorities although this story was later denied. Pierrepoint Edwards to the Earl Granville, 2 August 1881 TNA FO 5/1779 & *The New York Star,* 2 August 1881.

76 British diplomats in America would also come to believe that the clocks supplied for the smuggled bombs were crafted by a Denis O'Hara and had intended the bombs to be taken from Liverpool and placed aboard a British navel vessel at Plymouth, Victor Drummond to the Earl Granville, 8 August 1881, TNA FO 5/1779, see also Edward Archibald to the Earl Granville, 2 September 1881, TNA FO 5/ 1780.

77 *The New York Times,* 3 August 1881.

78 Legal advisor to O'Donovan Rossa and the United Irishmen of America. *The Saint Louis Globe-Democrat,* 30 July 1881.

79 Victor Drummond to the Earl Granville, 9 August 1881, TNA FO 5/1779.

80 *Lloyds Weekly Newspaper,* 31 July 1881.

81 *The Irish Times,* 6 August 1881.

82 Robert Clipperton to the Earl Granville, 19 August 1881, TNA FO 5/1779.

83 *The Saint Louis Globe-Democrat,* 30 July 1881.

84 *The New York Times,* 29 July 1881 & see also Professor Henry Wade Rogers, 'harbouring conspiracy', in *The North American review,* June 1884.

85 *The Daily Inter Ocean,* 26 July 1881.

86 Ibid.

87 *The Daily Evening Bulletin,* 2 August 1881.

88 Ibid.

89 O'Donovan Rossa, Jeremiah, *Irish Rebels in English Prisons* (Dingle, 1991) p. 292

90 *The Washington National Republican*, 29 July 1881.

91 James Russell Lowell to the Earl Granville, 1 August 1881, TNA FO 5/1779 and the Earl Granville to Consul Henderson 2 August 1881 TNA FO 5/1779.

92 *The New York Herald,* 10 August 1881.

93 Liverpool constabulary force, central police office to the Lord Mayor of Liverpool, 10 June 1881 TNA HO 144/81/A5836

94 Ibid.

95 James McGrath was the pseudonym of Robert Barton, of Derry, McKevitt had originally came from Warrenpoint Co. Down and was working as a dock labourer.

96 Liverpool constabulary force, central police office to the Lord Mayor of Liverpool, 10 June 1881 TNA HO 144/81/A5836

97 List of the more important outrages and attempts (chiefly of a political character) and suspicious cases of discoveries of explosives, which have engaged the attention of her majesties Inspectors of explosives. TNA PRO 30/60/12 & See also extracts from Special Fenian report book, 20 June 1881 TNA HO 144/81/A5836

98 Memorandum re report from Liverpool Constabulary Force re: Fenian outrages, extract from Special Fenian report book, 13 June 1881, p.4 NAI CSO RP 1881/23526.

99 Police Constable 884.

100 Police Constable 553.

101 Constable George McBurney (898) Constable Donald Sinclair (924) and Constable Edward Creighton (884) *The Times,* 11 June 1881.

102 Liverpool constabulary force, central police office to the Lord Mayor of Liverpool, 10 June 1881 TNA HO 144/81/A5836

103 *The Annual Register: A Review of Public Events at Home and Abroad for the Year 1881* (London, 1882) p.43 & see also Hansard debates, 11 June 1881, (London, 1881) col. 239

104 Memorandum re report from Liverpool Constabulary Force re: Fenian outrages, extract from Special Fenian report book, 13 June 1881, p.6 NAI CSO RP 1881/23526.

105 *The Times*, 13 June 1881.

106 *The Times,* 13 June 1881, see also Memorandum re report from Liverpool Constabulary Force re: Fenian outrages, extract from Special Fenian report book, 13 June 1881, p.6 NAI CSO RP 1881/23526.

107 Liverpool constabulary force, central police office to the Lord Mayor of Liverpool, 10 June 1881 TNA HO 144/81/A5836

108 The Lord Mayor of Liverpool to William Vernon Harcourt, 10 June 1881 TNA HO 144/81/A5836

109 Head Constable John Greig, to the Mayor of Liverpool, 10 June 1881, TNA HO 144/81/A5836.

110 Memorandum re report from Liverpool Constabulary Force re: Fenian outrages, extract from Special Fenian report book, 13 June 1881, p. 22 NAI CSO RP 1881/23526.

111 Memorandum re report from Liverpool Constabulary Force re: Fenian outrages, extract from Special Fenian report book, 13 June 1881, p. 22 NAI CSO RP 1881/23526 & TNA HO 144//81/A5836.

112 Head Constable John Greig, Liverpool Constabulary, extract from special Fenian report book, 20 June 1881 TNA HO 144/81/A5836.

113 Memorandum re report from Liverpool Constabulary Force re: Fenian outrages, extract from Special Fenian report book, 13 June 1881, p. 22 NAI CSO RP 1881/23526 & TNA HO 144//81/A5836.

114 Memorandum re report from Liverpool Constabulary Force re: Fenian outrages, extract from Special Fenian report book, 13 June 1881, p. 15 NAI CSO RP 1881/23526.

115 William Bower Forwood, Mayor of Liverpool, to Sir William Vernon Harcourt, Secretary of State for the Home Department, 15 June 1881, TNA HO 144/82/A5836.

116 Head Constable John Greig, Liverpool Constabulary, extract from special Fenian report book, 14 June 1881 TNA HO 144/81/A5836.

117 Alexander McCaul, Chief Constable Glasgow Constabulary, to Howard Vincent, 2 March 1881, GCA E4/2/19.

118 Alexander McCaul, Chief Constable Glasgow Constabulary, to Howard Vincent, 4 March 1881, GCA E4/2/19.

119 Telegram from Glasgow Chief Constable Alexander McCaul, to Head Constable John Greig, Liverpool Constabulary, extract from special Fenian report book, 15 June 1881 TNA HO 144/81/A5836 & see also Alexander McCaul to Howard Vincent, 22 April 1881 GCA E4/2/19.

120 William Bower Forwood, Mayor of Liverpool, to Sir William Vernon Harcourt, Secretary of State for the Home Department, 10 June 1881, TNA HO 144/81/A5836.

121 William Bower Forwood, Mayor of Liverpool, to Sir William Vernon Harcourt, Secretary of State for the Home Department, 14 June 1881, TNA HO 144/81/A5836.

122 Head Constable John Greig, Liverpool Constabulary, extract from special Fenian report book, 16 June 1881 TNA HO 144/81/A5836.

123 Ibid.,

124 *The Saint Louis Globe-Democrat*, 11 June 1881.

125 William Bower Forwood, Mayor of Liverpool, to Sir William Vernon Harcourt, Secretary of State for the Home Department, 16 June 1881, TNA HO 144/81/A5836.

126 Ibid.

127 William Bower Forwood, Mayor of Liverpool, to Sir William Vernon Harcourt, Secretary of State for the Home Department, 16 June 1881, TNA HO 144/81/A5836.

128 *Milwaukee Daily Sentinel*, 8 May 1882.

129 *St Louis Globe-Democrat,* 10 May 1882.

130 *The Galveston Daily News*, 12 May 1882.

131 *The North American*, 13 May 1882.

132 Ibid.

133 *The Aberdeen Weekly Journal*, 10 May 1882.

134 Quoted in Porter, Bernard, *The Origins of the Vigilant State* (London, 1987) p. 45.

135 See Major Nicholas Gosselin to Edward George Jenkinson, 9 November 1883 NAI CSB Papers 3/715/1.

136 Edward George Jenkinson, to Sir William Vernon Harcourt, Secretary of State for the Home Department, 4 September 1883, Ms Harcourt papers, Bodleian Library Oxford 103.

137 Henry Ponsonby to Sir William Vernon Harcourt, Secretary of State for the Home Department, 22 June 1882, Gardiner, A.G., *The Life of Sir William Harcourt*, Vol. 1 (London, 1923) p. 449.

138 *The Prevention of Crimes (Ireland) Bill.*
139 The Secretary of State for the Home Department, Sir William Vernon Harcourt to the Viceroy of Ireland, Earl Spencer, 20 May 1882, Ms Harcourt papers, Bodleian Library Oxford, 39.
140 Lord Northbrook to Earl Spencer, 7 May 1882 in Peter Gordon (ed.) *Red Earl: The Papers of the Fifth Earl Spencer 1835–1910* (Northampton, 1981) p. 193
141 Crenshaw, Martha, 'the causes of terrorism,' in *Comparative politics* 13:4 (July, 1981) pp. 384–5.
142 *The Irish World,* 27 May 1882.
143 Ibid., 10 June 1882.
144 Ibid.
145 Ibid., 10 June 1882.
146 Sir William Vernon Harcourt to Earl Spencer Irish Viceroy, 14 May 1882, Ms Harcourt papers, Bodleian Library Oxford 39.
147 *The Times,* 20 June 1882.
148 *The Irish World,* 27 May 1882 & 10 June 1882,
149 George Crump to the Earl Granville, 24 August 1882, Fenian A Files A742.
150 Ibid.
151 Ibid.
152 Robert Clipperton to the Earl of Granville, 15 February 1882, Fenian A Files A713.
153 Robert Clipperton to the Earl Granville, 9 May 1882, Fenian A Files A716, this was indeed correct that several of Rossa's emissary's in Britain were graduates of the dynamite school including John Francis Kearney, Thomas J. Mooney and William Lynch.
154 Pierrepoint Edwards to the Home Office and Foreign Office, 16 August 1882 Fenian A Files A730 and see also Robert Clipperton to the Earl Granville, 9 May 1882, Fenian A Files A716, Robert Clipperton to the Earl Granville, 3 April 1883, TNA FO 5/ 1861 & Pierrepoint Edwards to the Home Office and Foreign Office, 16 August 1882 Fenian A Files A730.
155 Alexander McCaul, Chief Constable Glasgow, to James Monro, Assistant Commissioner London Metropolitan Police, 27 April 1885, GCA E4/2/23.
156 Memorandum re report from Liverpool Constabulary Force re: Fenian outrages, extract from Special Fenian report book, 13 June 1881, p.6 NAI CSO RP 1881/23526.
157 Edward George Jenkinson, to Sir William Vernon Harcourt, Secretary of State for the Home Department, 14 April 1883 Ms Harcourt papers, Bodleian Library Oxford, 103.
158 O'Cathain, Sean, *Irish Republicanism in Scotland 1858-1916* (Dublin, 2007) p. 131
159 James N. Hart, Procurator Fiscal, to Alexander McCaul, Chief Constable Glasgow Constabulary, 1 December 1883. Alexander McCaul GCA E4/2/21
160 The examination of Sarah Douglas McLachlan in Couper, Charles Tennant, *Report of the trial of the dynamitards...* (Edinburgh, 1884) pp. 81-2.
161 *The Aberdeen Weekly Journal,* 22 January 1883.
162 *The Times,* 22 January 1882.
163 The examination of Thomas Butler in Couper, Charles Tennant, *Report of the trial of the dynamitards...* (Edinburgh, 1884) p. 29.
164 *The Aberdeen Weekly Journal,* 22 January 1883.
165 *The Birmingham Daily Post,* 22 January 1883.

166 The examination of Adam Barr, 23 May 1883 TNA ASSI 52/5.

167 *The Times,* 22 January 1882 & see also Majendie, Colonel Vivian, *Report to the right honourable secretary of state for the home department on the circumstances attending the three explosions which occurred in Glasgow on the night of Saturday, 20 January, and the morning of Sunday 21 January 1883* [C-3599], H.C. 1883 p.19. & See also the examination of Joseph Anderson, 23 May 1883, TNA ASSI 52/5.

168 *The Times,* 22 January 1882.

169 *The Glasgow Herald,* 22 January 1883.

170 *The Times,* 20 June 1882.

171 Five would be executed including Joseph Brady, Daniel Curley, Michael Fagan, Thomas Caffery and Timothy Kelly.

172 The Colonel would further note the blast 'very remarkably resembled in all its main features, one which occurred on the twentieth of January on the Possil canal bridge at Glasgow'. Majendie had made an interesting connection – the same skirmishing team were behind the London attacks. Colonel Majendie to Sir William Vernon Harcourt, Secretary of State for the Home Department, 19 March 1883 TNA HO 144/114/A25908, & see also ibid., 19 March 1883 TNA HO 144/81/A5836.

173 Colonel Vivian Majendie, to Sir William Vernon Harcourt, Secretary of State for the home Department, 19 March 1883, TNA HO 144/81/A5836.

174 The examination of Ebenezer Mears, in Couper, Charles Tennant, *Report of the trial of the dynamitard's...* (Edinburgh, 1884) p. 101.

175 *The Freeman's Journal,* 17 March 1883. Evens was an employee of Messer's Brake, Driver and Leaver manufacturing stationers.

176 *The Freeman's Journal,* 17 March 1883.

177 The *London Illustrated News,* 24 March 1883.

178 According to Sir Edward Walter Hamilton, Private Secretary to William Ewart Gladstone, Carey had suggested to Jenkinson that reprisal bombing raids would be a likelihood of his defection, and Hamilton, similar to Harcourt concluded the Whitehall explosion was an act of retaliation, holding 'it was probably one of those reprisals in London for which Carey prepared us.' Edward Walter Hamilton, 23 February 1883 & 18 March 1883 in Dudley Bahlman (Ed.) *The Diary of Sir Edward Walter Hamilton* (Oxford, 1972) pp. 402 & 409.

179 Sir William Vernon Harcourt, to the Earl Spencer, 16 March 1883 Ms Harcourt papers, Bodleian Library Oxford, 42.

180 Colonel Vivian Majendie to Sir William Vernon Harcourt, Secretary of State for the Home Department, 19 March 1883 TNA HO 144/81/A5836.

181 Majendie, Colonel Vivian, *Report to the right honourable secretary of state for the home department on the circumstances attending two explosions which occurred in London on the night of 15 March 1883, at the offices of the local government board in Whitehall and of the Times Newspaper in Play House yard respectively* [C-3611], H.C. 1883. p.1. See also Colonel Vivian Majendie, to Sir William Vernon Harcourt, Secretary of State for the Home Department, 19 March 1883, TNA HO 144/81/A5836.

182 *The Times,* 17 March 1883, & see also Colonel Vivian Majendie, to Sir William Vernon Harcourt, Secretary of State for the Home Department, 19 March 1883 TNA HO 144/81/A5836. Also see Majendie, Colonel Vivian, *Report to the right honourable secretary of state for*

the home department on the circumstances attending two explosions which occurred in London on the night of 15 March 1883, at the offices of the local government board in Whitehall and of the Times Newspaper in Play House yard respectively [C-3611], H.C. 1883 p. 5.

183 Sir William Vernon Harcourt, Secretary of State for the Home Department, to Earl Spencer, 16 March 1883, Ms Harcourt papers, Bodleian Library Oxford, 42.

184 *The Times*, 16 March 1883.

185 *The Cleveland Herald*, 17 March 1883

186 Ibid.

187 *The Irish Times*, 17 March 1883.

188 'Dynamite,' in *Afterwork*, (August, 1883) p. 143.

189 *The Washington National Republican*, 7 April 1883

190 *The New York Times*, 17 March 1883.

191 *The Citizen*, 22 December 1883 TNA HO 144/1537/1.

192 Consul Robert Clipperton to Earl Grenville, Secretary of State for the Foreign Office, 31 January 1884 TNA FO 5/1928.

193 *The Irish World*, 31 March 1883.

Chapter 9

1 Strictly private & confidential, William Henry Joyce memorandum, undated, Balfour Papers, NLI Ms 11, 119.

2 *The Weekly Union*, 10 July 1880 & *The Labour World*, 27 September 1890.

3 *The Labour World*, 27 September 1890.

4 *Reynolds Weekly Newspaper*, 10 March 1895 & see also Dr Mark Ryan, *Fenian Memories* (Dublin 1945) p. 127. According to Ryan, similar to the above extract 'Rossa was not a very good judge of human nature, and was sometimes rather easily imposed upon by designing people who professed strong nationalist sympathies.'

5 Interview with Matthew O'Brien, undated, TCD Davitt papers Mss 9441/ 3217/14.

6 TCD Davitt Papers Mss 9381/ 1161/4.

7 *The Irish Weekly Independent*, 9 June 1894.

8 Undated excerpt from *The Brooklyn Times*, TCD Davitt papers Ms 9381/ 1165.

9 *The Irish Weekly Independent*, 9 June 1894.

10 *The Irish World*, 25 August 1883.

11 Confidential Home Office Memorandum, regarding imprisoned dynamitards, undated, TNA PRO 30/60/12.

12 Confidential Home Office Memorandum, regarding imprisoned dynamitards, undated, TNA PRO 10/60/12 & Edward George Jenkinson to Sir William Vernon Harcourt, Secretary of State for the Home Department, 29 March 1883 Ms Harcourt papers, Bodleian Library Oxford, 103.

13 'The evidence of Constable William Porter' in Charles Tennant Couper, *Report of the trial of the dynamitard's...* (Edinburgh, 1884) p. 69.

14 James McDermott to Jeremiah O'Donovan Rossa, 3 April 1883 in *The New York Freeman's journal*, undated, 1894, TCD Davitt papers Ms 9381/ 1167.

15 The examination of Patrick Enright, 22 May 1883 TNA ASSI 52/5.

16 Edward George Jenkinson, the undersecretary for Police and Crime to Sir William Vernon Harcourt, Secretary of State for the Home Department, 29 March 1883, Ms Harcourt papers, Bodleian Library Oxford, 103.

17 See next Chapter on the Gallagher Cell & Edward George Jenkinson to Sir William Vernon Harcourt, 1 April 1883 Ms Harcourt papers, Bodleian Library Oxford 103.

18 Secret Home Office Memorandum, undated and unattributed, TNA PRO 30/60/12.

19 William Nott Bower, Liverpool head Constable to the Secretary of State for the Home Office, Sir William Vernon Harcourt, 29 March 1883 TNA 144/115/ A26302 & see also Edward George Jenkinson to Sir William Vernon Harcourt, 29 March 1883, Ms Harcourt papers, Bodleian Library Oxford, 103.

20 J.W.G. Dunsterville to Edward George Jenkinson, 4 April 1883, Ms Harcourt papers, Bodleian Library Oxford, 42.

21 The examination of Thomas Shannon, 23 May 1883 TNA ASSI 52/5. Deasy had told Shannon he was leaving soon for New York, indicating the explosion was imminent and he would make his escape to America free from arrest outside of British Jurisdiction.

22 Hamilton Cuffe, solicitor for Treasury Department, to Adolphus Liddell, Undersecretary for the Home Department, 15 August 1883, TNA HO 144/115/A26302C, & see also Hansard's debates third series Vol. CCLXXVII, the House of Commons 29 March 1883, (London, 1883) col. 994, & see also the examination of Detective Inspector George Marsh, in Couper, Charles Tennant, *Report of the trial of the dynamitards...* (Edinburgh, 1884) p. 95.

23 Edward George Jenkinson undersecretary for Police and Crime to Sir William Vernon Harcourt, Secretary of State for the Home Department, 31 March 1883, Ms Harcourt papers, Bodleian Library Oxford, 103.

24 Dr James Campbell Brown, to the Secretary of State for the Home Office, Sir William Vernon Harcourt, 29 March 1883, TNA 144/115/ A26302.

25 The examination of Dr James Campbell Brown, in Charles Tennant Couper, *Report of the trial of the dynamitard's...* (Edinburgh, 1884) p. 101.

26 Ibid.

27 Flanagan was undoubtedly in communication with other individuals concerned in the plot. In December 1882 had met Featherstone in the company of another Sutton Irishman, employed as a Labourer, named Sullivan. The examination of George Brown, 21 May 1883 TNA ASSI 52/5.

28 The Examination of Sergeant Samuel Wilkinson Canning, 23 May 1883 TNA ASSI 52/5

29 Ibid.

30 George Williams, Chief Superintendent, Liverpool Constabulary to Sir William Vernon Harcourt, Secretary of State for the Home Department, 9 April 1883, TNA 114/115/ A26302.

31 Confidential Home Office Memorandum, regarding imprisoned dynamitards, undated TNA PRO 30/60/12, & see also William Nott Bower, Liverpool Head Constable to the Secretary of State for the Home Office, Sir William Vernon Harcourt, Secretary of State for the Home Department, 31 March 1883, TNA HO 144/115/A26302.

32 'From private and reliable information, I, in the performance of my duty, arrested and took into custody on the 29th of March, about 6.30 pm in the borough of Cork, Timothy Featherstone, on a charge of being a member of an unlawful conspiracy. The object of

this conspiracy is to murder certain of her majesties subjects, and also to maliciously blow up and destroy public buildings in the United Kingdom. I subsequently arrested Timothy Carmody, and caused to be arrested Daniel O'Herlihy, both also on the charge of conspiracy to murder and to do malicious injury to property. The three are now in custody. I say that if they be remanded for a reasonable time, I have reasonable grounds to expect and believe that I will be able to produce material evidence to sustain the charges.' The statement of Robert Fitzwilliam Starkie, sub inspector of the Royal Irish Constabulary Cork, at the Cork trial of Timothy Featherstone and others, *The Irish World*, 12 April 1883 & see also secret Home Office memorandum, undated and unattributed, TNA PRO 30/60/12.

33   *The Times*, 14 April 1883, see also the examination of Robert Fitzwilliam Starkie, sub inspector of the Royal Irish Constabulary Cork, 19 May 1883, and the examination of David Vaughan, Head Constable Royal Irish Constabulary Cork, 19 May 1883, TNA ASSI 52/5 & Secret Home Office Memorandum, undated and unattributed, TNA PRO 30/30/12.

34   *The Times*, 4 April, 1883 and *The Aberdeen Weekly Journal*, 4 April 1883.

35   Ibid., 31 March 1883.

36   Ibid., 4 April 1883.

37   Ibid., 31 March 1883.

38   Sir William Vernon Harcourt, Secretary of State for the Home Department, to The Earl Spencer, 31 March 1883, Ms Harcourt papers, Bodleian Library Oxford, 103.

39   William Nott Bower, Liverpool Head Constable to the Secretary of State for the Home Office, Sir William Vernon Harcourt, Secretary of State for the Home Department, 31 March 1883, TNA HO 144/115/A26302.

40   *The Times*, 14 April 1883.

41   W. Marks, Prosecuting Solicitors Office, Liverpool to Hamilton Cuffe, solicitor for the treasury department, 15 August 1883 TNA HO 144/115/A26302C.

42   The examination of witness for the Cork and Liverpool dynamite plots, 19 May 1883, TNA ASSI 52/5.

43   Hamilton Cuffe, solicitor for Treasury Department, to Adolphus Liddell, Undersecretary for the Home Department, 13 August 1883, TNA HO 144/115/A26302C.

44   William Marks, prosecuting solicitor for Liverpool Corporation to Hamilton Cuffe, solicitor for Treasury Department, 15 August 1883 TNA HO 144/115/A26302C & see also Edward George Jenkinson, to Sir William Vernon Harcourt, Secretary of State for the Home Department, 11 August 1883, Ms Harcourt papers, Bodleian Library Oxford, 103.

45   Jim McDermott to Jeremiah O'Donovan Rossa, 3 April 1883 in *The Labour World*, 11 October 1890.

46   *The Irish World*, 25 August 1883.

47   Edward George Jenkinson to Sir William Vernon Harcourt, Secretary of State for the Home Department, 17 June 1883, Ms Harcourt papers, Bodleian Library Oxford, 103.

48   Edward George Jenkinson to Sir William Vernon Harcourt, Secretary of State for the Home Department, 10 June 1883, Ms Harcourt papers, Bodleian Library Oxford, 103.

49   Edward George Jenkinson to Sir William Vernon Harcourt, Secretary of State for the Home Department, 17 June 1883, Ms Harcourt papers, Bodleian Library Oxford, 103.

50   Campbell, Christy, *Fenian Fire* (London, 2002) p. 133.

51 *The Irish World*, 25 August 1883.

52 Jenkinson would later describe Gaynor as, 'a desperate character'. Edward George Jenkinson to Major Nicholas Gosselin, 26 November 1883, NAI CSB Papers 3/715/1.

53 Rossa would offer $3,000 for the capture of Red Jim McDermott 'dead or alive,' Robert Clipperton to the Earl Granville, 30 September 1884, TNA FO 5/1930

54 *Lloyds Weekly Newspaper*, 12 August 1883. Jim had been arrested by Head Constable Joseph Murphy, of the Royal Irish Constabulary, who had been tipped off by an anonymous telegraph. Hidden in his shirt collar was his letter of introduction to Henry Dalton signed by Timothy Featherstone. NAI CSB Papers Box 2.

55 *The Brooklyn Eagle,* 3 August 1883.

56 *The Irish World*, 25 August 1883.

57 Ibid.,7 September 1883.

58 Ibid.

59 Statement of Matthew O'Brien to Michael Davitt, Davitt papers TCD Ms 9441/3216.

60 *Old Bailey proceedings*, 11, 12, 13,14 June 1883, (London, 1883) 1883 p. 250, OBP t18830528–620.

61 Lynch had left America on the steamer *Spain*, on 9 March 1883, *The New York Times*, 20 April 1883.

62 *The Times*, 12 June 1883.

63 *The Times*, 7 April 1883 see also Davitt papers TCD MS Davitt papers 9365/ 735– 745a (745/1).

64 Borough of Birmingham, Draft report of the watch committee on the detection of Whitehead and others known as the dynamite conspirators TNA HO 144/116/A26493E.

65 *The Times*, 7 April 1883.

66 *Reynolds Weekly Newspaper,* 13 May 1883.

67 *The Illustrated Police News*, 14 April 1883.

68 Clarke had rented a Garret bedroom at 17 Nelson Square London from Charlotte Matilda Clare at the cost of 6 shillings a week. Clare recalled the portmanteau's in Clarke's room, days before his arrest and could place him with two others whom she could not identify. *Proceedings of the Central Criminal Court,* 11, 12, 13,14 June 1883, (London, 1883) 1883 p. 259, OBP t18830528–620.

69 *Proceedings of the Central Criminal Court*, 11, 12, 13,14 June 1883, (London, 1883) 1883 p. 273, OBP t18830528–620.

70 List of the more important outrages and attempts (chiefly of a political character) and suspicious cases of discoveries of explosives, which have engaged the attention of her majesties Inspectors of explosives. TNA PRO 30/60/12.

71 *St. Louis- Globe Democrat*, 6 April 1883.

72 Le Roux, Louis, *Tom Clarke and the Irish freedom movement* (Dublin, 1936) p. 31 & see also Regina V Thomas Gallagher, Alfred George Whitehead, Henry Hammond Wilson, William Ausburgh, John Curtin and Bernard Gallagher TNA CRIM 1/15/8.

73 Copy of a Home Office minute prepared by Adolphus Liddell, Undersecretary of State for the Home Department, to the Lord Chancellor, 24 May 1883 TNA HO 144/116/26493.

74 Anon, *The Mysteries of Ireland* (London, 1883), p.804.

75 *The Milwaukee Sentinel*, 29 February 1884.

76 John Daly to Jeremiah O'Donovan Rossa, 8 January 1883 CUA
77 *The Milwaukee Sentinel*, 12 January 1883.
78 Nicholas Gosselin to Henry Matthews, Secretary of State for the Home Department, 28 August 1891, TNA HO 144/193A/A6664B.
79 Edward George Jenkinson to the Earl Spencer, 12 April 1884, BL Althorp Papers Add 77033.
80 *The New York Times*, 15 February 1885
81 Ibid., 16 January 1885
82 *Birmingham Daily Post*, 4 February 1885.
83 *The Saint Louis Globe-Democrat*, 3 February 1885.
84 Ibid.
85 *The New York Times*, 3 February 1885
86 Ibid.
87 Ibid.
88 *The New York Herald*, quoted in *The Times*, 4 February 1885.
89 Ibid.
90 *The Brooklyn Eagle*, 3 February 1885.
91 *The Times*, 4 February 1885.
92 *The Birmingham Daily Post*, 3 February 1885.
93 *The Aberdeen Weekly Journal,* 4 February 1885.
94 *The Northern Echo*, 4 February 1885.
95 *The Saint Louis Globe-Democrat*, 3 February 1885.
96 *The Los Angeles Daily Times*, 3 February 1885.
97 *The British Medical Journal*, 7 February 1885.
98 *The Brooklyn Eagle*, 1 July 1885.
99 Ibid.
100 *The New York Times*, 2 July 1889.
101 *The United Irishman*, 22 May 1889.
102 Ibid.
103 Ibid.
104 Mary Jane O'Donovan Rossa to James Maxwell O'Donovan Rossa, 1 July 1889 in Seán O Luing, O Donnabhain Rosa, Vol. II, p. 175
105 Henry Labouchere, Hansard CCCXXX 12.XI. 1888.
106 O'Luing, Sean, *O'Donnabhain Rosa* (BAC 1979) p. 174
107 *The Brooklyn Daily Eagle*, 14 May 1889.
108 Ibid.
109 *Pittsburgh Dispatch*, 21 June 1889.
110 *The Brooklyn Daily Eagle*, 14 July 1889.
111 Mary Jane O'Donovan Rossa to Maxwell O'Donovan Rossa, 19 June 1889.
112 *Pittsburgh Dispatch*, 21 June 1889.
113 *The United Irishman*, 13 October, 1890.
114 O'Donovan Rossa to James G. Blaine, 13 January 1891 in Seán O Luing, O Donnabháin Rosa, Vol. II, pp 212-13.
115 *The Boston Pilot*, 4 February 1871,

116 O'Donovan Rossa, Margaret, *My Mother and Father were Irish* (New York, 1939), p. 53.

117 Seán O Luing, *O Donnabháin Rosa*, Vol. II, p. 220.

Chapter 10

1 *The United Irishman*, 25 November 1893.

2 O'Donovan Rossa, Margaret, *My Mother and Father were Irish* (New York, 1939), p. 97.

3 *The Freeman's Journal*, 28 May 1894

4 *The Sacred Heart Review*, 30 June 1894.

5 Ibid.

6 *The New Zealand Herald*, 28 July 1894

7 Ibid.

8 *The Freeman's Journal*, 28 May 1894

9 Ibid., 28 June 1894.

10 Ibid., 5 July 1894.

11 Ibid., 10 July 1894.

12 Ibid., 14 July 1894.

13 Ibid., 10 July 1894.

14 *The Tablet*, 21 July 1894.

15 *The Freeman's Journal*, 23 July 1894.

16 Ibid. 20 August 1894.

17 Ibid.

18 Ibid.

19 Ibid., 21 August 1894.

20 O'Donovan Rossa, Margaret, *My Mother and Father were Irish* (New York, 1939), p. 100.

21 *The Birmingham Daily Post*, 11 March 1895.

22 Ibid.

23 Ibid.

24 *The Western Mail*, 22 March 1895.

25 *The Freeman's Journal*, 8 May 1895.

26 *The Manchester Guardian*, 9 May 1895.

27 *The Aberdeen Weekly Journal*, 9 May 1895.

28 Ibid.

29 *The Pall Mall Gazette*, 9 May 1895.

30 *The Aberdeen Weekly Journal*, 9 May 1895

31 *The Belfast Newsletter,* 14 May 1895.

32 O'Lúing, Sean, *O'Donnabhain Rosa* (BAC 1979) p. 251

33 Ibid.

34 *The Brooklyn Eagle*, 24 June 1898.

35 Ibid., 25 June 1898.

Chapter 11

1 *The Brooklyn Daily Eagle*, 11 November 1904.

2 Ibid., 13 November, 1904.

3   Kelly, M. J. *The Fenian Ideal and Irish Nationalism 1882–1916* (Woodbridge, 2006), p. 15.

4   Griffith, Arthur, *The Resurrection of Hungary* (Dublin, 1918), p. 139.

5   Ibid.,p.161.

6   *The Southern Star,* 26 November 1904.

7   Ibid.

8   Ibid.

9   Ibid.

10 Ibid.

11 *The Southern Star,* 26 November 1904.

12 Ibid.

13 Ibid.

14 Ibid.

15 *The Irish Times*, 28 November 1904.

16 *The Southern Star*, 3 December 1904.

17 Ibid.

18 Ibid., 3 December 1904.

19 Ibid.

20 *The Irish Examiner,* 20 November 1905.

21 *The Freeman's Journal*, 20 November 1905.

22 *The Irish Independent*, 27 November 1905.

23 Ibid.

24 *The Cork Constitution*, 29 June 1906.

25 O'Donovan Rossa, Margaret, *My Mother and Father were Irish* (New York, 1939), pp. 154-5.

26 Ibid., p. 154.

27 *The United Irishman*, 28 July 1906.

28 *The Cork Constitution*, 29 June 1906.

29 *The Gaelic American*, 22 October 1910.

30 Mary Jane O'Donovan Rossa to John Devoy, 24 February 1913 in O'Brien and Ryan, *Devoy's Post Bag* (Dublin, 1948), p. 405.

31 Jeremiah O'Donovan Rossa to John Devoy, 24 February 1913 in O'Brien and Ryan, *Devoy's Post Bag* (Dublin, 1948), p. 405.

32 Devoy, John, *Recollections of an Irish Rebel* (New York, 1929), p.331.

33 Mary Jane O'Donovan Rossa to John Devoy, 17 March 1913 in O'Brien and Ryan, *Devoy's Post Bag* (Dublin, 1948), p. 405.

34 *The Gaelic American*, 25 October 1913.

35 Mary Jane O'Donovan Rossa to John Devoy, 3 October 1913 in O'Brien and Ryan, *Devoy's Post Bag* (Dublin, 1948), p. 415.

36 Mary Jane O'Donovan Rossa to John Devoy, 7 November 1913 in O'Brien and Ryan, *Devoy's Post Bag* (Dublin, 1948), p. 416.

37 Ibid.

38 Mary Jane O'Donovan Rossa to John Devoy, 30 November 1913 in O'Brien and Ryan, *Devoy's Post Bag* (Dublin, 1948), pp. 417-18.

39 The Ulster Solemn League and Covenant

40 *The Penny Illustrated Paper*, 22 March 1913.

41 *The Times*, 5 November 1913.

42 Ibid. 6 October 1913.

43 *McGee, Owe, The IRB from the Land League to Sinn Féin* (Dublin, 2005), p. 355.

44 'The North Began,' in *An Claidheamh Soluis,* 1 November 1913.

45 *The Irish Times*, 26 November 1913.

46 Mary Jane O'Donovan Rossa to John Devoy, 30 November 1913 in O'Brien and Ryan, *Devoy's Postbag* (Dublin, 1948), pp. 417-18.

47 Hobson, Bulmer, *A Short History of The Irish Volunteers* (Dublin, 1918), p. 128

48 *The Gaelic American*, September 1915.

49 John Mallon Dublin Metropolitan Police memorandum, 5 November 1878 NAI Fenian Files A550.

50 John Devoy to Patrick O'Mara, 28 June 1914 in O'Brien and Ryan, *Devoy's Post Bag* (Dublin, 1948), pp. 435-6.

51 *The Gaelic American*, September 1915.

52 Ibid.,10 July 1915.

53 Ibid.

54 Clarke, Kathleen, *Revolutionary Woman* (Dublin, 1991), p. 56.

55 Mary Jane O'Donovan Rossa to Thomas James Clarke, July 1915 in O'Brien and Ryan, *Devoy's Postbag* (Dublin, 1948), pp. 472.

56 Litton, Helen, *16 Lives:Edward Daly* (Dublin, 2013) p.129

57 Ibid.

58 John Devoy to Patrick O'Mara, 28 June 1914 in O'Brien and Ryan, *Devoy's Postbag* (Dublin, 1948), pp. 435-6.

59 *The Irish Independent,* 27 July 1915

60 *The Gaelic American* 21 August 1915

61 *Ibid,* 28 August 1915.

62 *The Cork Weekly Examiner* quoted in *The Gaelic American*, 28 August 1915.

63 *The Gaelic American*, 9 October 1915.

64 *The Irish Independent,* 27 July 1905.

65 *The Gaelic American*, 28 August 1915.

66 Ibid.,September 1915.

67 Connolly, James, 'Why the Citizen Army Honours Rossa.' *O'Donovan Rossa Souvenir Booklet,* July 1915

68 *The Kerryman,* 7 August 1915.

69 MacDonagh, Thomas, 'The Irish Volunteers in 1915', *O'Donovan Rossa Souvenir Booklet* (Dublin, 1915).

70 Pearse, Patrick, 'A Character Study', *O'Donovan Rossa Souvenir Booklet* (Dublin, 1915).

71 Connolly, James, 'Why the Citizen Army Honours Rossa', *O'Donovan Rossa Souvenir Booklet* (Dublin 1915).

72 Pearse, Patrick, 'A Character Study', *O'Donovan Rossa Souvenir booklet* (Dublin, 1915).

73 Clarke, Kathleen, *Revolutionary Woman* (Dublin, 1991), p. 56.

SELECT BIBLIOGRAPHY

Anon, *The Mysteries of Ireland* (London, 1883).

Anon, *The Annual Register: a review of public events at home and abroad for the year 1881* (London, 1882).

Campbell, Christy, *Fenian Fire* (London, 2002)

Clarke, Kathleen, *Revolutionary Woman* (Dublin, 1991).

Couper, Charles Tennant, *Report of the Trial of the Dynamitards* (Edinburgh, 1884)

Crowly, Smyth and Murphy (eds) *Atlas of the Great Irish Famine* (Cork, 2012)

Darcy, William. *The Fenian Movement in the United States 1858–1886* (Washington, 1947)

Denieffe, Joseph, *Recollections of the Irish Revolutionary Brotherhood* (New York, 1906)

Devoy, John, *Recollections of an Irish Rebel* (New York, 1929)

Devoy, John, *Land of Eire* (New York, 1882)

Funchion, Michael Francis, *Chicago's Irish Nationalists, 1881–1890* (New York, 1976)

O'Brien William & Desmond Ryan (eds) *Devoy's Post Bag* Vol. II (Dublin, 1948)

Old Bailey Proceedings, 11, 12, 13,14 June 1883 (London, 1883)

O'Donovan Rossa, Margaret, *My Mother and Father were Irish* (New York, 1939)

O'Donovan Rossa, Jeremiah, *Irish Rebels in English Prisons* (Dingle, 1991)

O'Donovan Rossa, Jeremiah, *Prison Life* (New York, 1874)

O'Donovan Rossa, Jeremiah, *Rossa's Recollections* (Connecticut, 2004)

Ó Broin, Leon, *Fenian Fever* (London, 1971)

Gardiner, A.G., *The Life of Sir William Harcourt*, Vol. 1 (London, 1923)

Golway, Terry, *Irish Rebel* (New York, 1995)

Government of the United Kingdom, *Reprint of the shorthand notes of the speeches, proceedings and evidence taken before the commissioners* (London, 1890)

Griffith, Arthur, 'The Influence of Fenianism', *O'Donovan Rossa Souvenir Booklet* (Dublin, 1915).

Griffith, Arthur, *The Resurrection of Hungary* (Dublin, 1918)

Hobson, Bulmer, *A Short History of The Irish Volunteers* (Dublin, 1918)

Kelly, M.J. *The Fenian Ideal and Irish Nationalism 1882–1916* (Woodbridge, 2006)

Kenna, Shane, *16Lives: Thomas MacDonagh* (Dublin, 2014)

Kenna, Shane, *War In The Shadows: The Irish-American Fenians Who Bombed Victorian Britain* (Dublin, 2013)

Le Caron, Henri *Twenty-Five Years in the British Secret Service – The Recollections of a Spy* (London, 1892)

MacDonagh, Thomas, 'The Irish Volunteers in 1915', *O'Donovan Rossa Souvenir Booklet* (Dublin, 1915).

McConville, Sean, *Irish Political Prisoners* (New York, 2003).

McGee, Owen, *The IRB from the Land League to Sinn Féin* (Dublin, 2005)

M. Sullivan, D. B. Sullivan & T. D. Sullivan, *Irish Speeches from the Dock* (New York, 1904)

Pearse, Patrick, 'A Character Study', *O'Donovan Rossa Souvenir Booklet* (Dublin, 1915).

Piggott, Richard, *Recollections of an Irish Journalist* (Dublin, 1882)

Porter, Bernard, *The Origins of the Vigilant State* (London, 1987)

Reich, Walter (ed.), *Origins of Terrorism* (Cambridge, 1990)

Seán O Luing, *O Donnabhain Rosa*, Vol. II

Short, K.R.M, *The Dynamite War: Irish-American Bombers in Victorian Britain* (Dublin, 1979)

Sullivan, A.M., *New Ireland* (Philadelphia, 1878)

Townshend, Charles, *Political Violence in Ireland* (Oxford, 1983)

INDEX